GETTING REAL ABOUT RACE

Second Edition

To my students, current and former, whose passion and curiosity continually inspire me. And to my coeditor, whose courage and determination continually humble me.

—Stephanie M. McClure

To my precious daughter and my amazing nephews—may you inherit a world that is a little kinder and understanding toward kids that look like you. To my students over the years who have fought the good fight and decided to do the hard work of understanding and fighting against inequality. And finally, to my coeditor, Steph, whose friendship continues to be generous and patient, and whose brilliance and passion inspire me every day.

—Cherise A. Harris

GETTING REAL ABOUT RACE

Second Edition

Editors

STEPHANIE M. McCLURE
Georgia College

CHERISE A. HARRIS
Connecticut College

Los Angeles | London | New Delhi
Singapore | Washington DC | Melbourne

FOR INFORMATION:

SAGE Publications, Inc.
2455 Teller Road
Thousand Oaks, California 91320
E-mail: order@sagepub.com

SAGE Publications Ltd.
1 Oliver's Yard
55 City Road
London EC1Y 1SP
United Kingdom

SAGE Publications India Pvt. Ltd.
B 1/I 1 Mohan Cooperative Industrial Area
Mathura Road, New Delhi 110 044
India

SAGE Publications Asia-Pacific Pte. Ltd.
3 Church Street
#10-04 Samsung Hub
Singapore 049763

Printed in the United States of America

Library of Congress Cataloging-in-Publication Data

Names: McClure, Stephanie M., editor. | Harris, Cherise A., 1976- editor.

Title: Getting real about race / editors: Stephanie M. McClure, Georgia College & State University; Cherise A. Harris, Connecticut College.

Description: Second edition. | Los Angeles : SAGE, 2018. | Includes bibliographical references.

Identifiers: LCCN 2017021394 | ISBN 9781506339306 (pbk. : alk. paper)

Subjects: LCSH: United States—Race relations. | Stereotypes (Social psychology)—United States. | Race.

Classification: LCC E184.A1 G43 2018 | DDC 305.800973—dc23
LC record available at https://lccn.loc.gov/2017021394

Acquisitions Editor: Jeff Lasser
Content Development Editor: Eve Oettinger
Editorial Assistant: Adeline Wilson
Production Editor: Jane Haenel
Copy Editor: Megan Granger
Typesetter: C&M Digitals (P) Ltd.
Proofreader: Theresa Kay
Cover Designer: Candice Harman
Marketing Manager: Kara Kindstrom

19 20 21 10 9 8 7 6 5 4 3

Contents

Preface   ix

Acknowledgments   xi

I. LAYING THE FOUNDATION   1

In this section, essay authors introduce key concepts and ideas regarding
race and racial inequality. These include how race is socially constructed
and how the construction process connects with questions of biology, history,
and power. The essays also provide students with information about how and
why we need to engage in meaningful, inclusive conversations about race in
contemporary American society.

**Essay 1: "But My Mother Says It's Rude to
Talk About Race!": How and Why We
Need to Discuss Race in the United States**   1

Cherise A. Harris and Stephanie M. McClure

**Essay 2: "Blacks Are Naturally Good Athletes":
The Myth of a Biological Basis for Race**   14

Daniel Buffington

**Essay 3: "Native American/Indian, Asian/Oriental,
Latino/Hispanic . . . Who Cares?": Language
and the Power of Self-Definition**   25

Bradley Koch

**Essay 4: "Is Discrimination Against Muslims Really
Racism?": The Racialization of Islamophobia**   35

Steve Garner and Saher Selod

II. DEBUNKING INDIVIDUAL ATTITUDES 45

The essays in this section consider widespread individual attitudes and beliefs about the current state of racial inequality in the United States, including beliefs about color blindness, meritocracy, and structures of opportunity. The authors compare these perceptions to social science research and information in psychology, sociology, history, and media studies. The information presented helps students consider the validity of these popular attitudes.

Essay 5: "If People Stopped Talking About Race, It Wouldn't Be a Problem Anymore": Silencing the Myth of a Color-Blind Society 45

Ted Thornhill

Essay 6: "Obama Says Blacks Should Just Work Harder; Isn't That Right?": The Myth of Meritocracy 60

Paula Ioanide

Essay 7: "If Only He Hadn't Worn the Hoodie . . .": Race, Selective Perception, and Stereotype Maintenance 72

Rashawn Ray

Essay 8: "My Family Had to Learn English When They Came, so Why Is Everything in Spanish for Them?": Race and the Spanish Language in the United States 85

Jennifer Domino Rudolph

Essay 9: "Asians Are Doing Great, so That Proves Race Really Doesn't Matter Anymore": The Model Minority Myth and the Sociological Reality 100

Min Zhou

Essay 10: "But Muslims Aren't Like Us!": Deconstructing Myths About Muslims in America 109

Jen'nan Ghazal Read

Essay 11: "But It's Honoring! It's Tradition!": The Persistence of Racialized Indian Mascots and Confederate Culture in Sports 118

Dana M. Williams

III. INSTITUTIONS, POLICIES, AND LEGACIES OF OPPRESSION 133

Following up on the history and attitudes discussed in the previous sections, these essays consider how misperceptions and beliefs about patterns of race and racial group differences manifest across social institutions. Some of the areas addressed include the family, education, the state and public policy, and the criminal justice system. In this section, the authors consider the impact of legal history, individual perceptions and beliefs, and media representations of racial dynamics.

FAMILY   133

Essay 12: "But What About the Children?": Understanding Contemporary Attitudes Toward Interracial Dating and Marriage   133

Nikki Khanna

Essay 13: "Black People Don't Value Marriage as Much as Others": Examining Structural Inequalities in Black Marriage Patterns   149

Dawne M. Mouzon

EDUCATION   160

Essay 14: "Well, That Culture Really Values Education": Culture Versus Structure in Educational Attainment   160

Hersheda Patel, Emily Meanwell, and Stephanie M. McClure

Essay 15: "They Don't Want to Be Integrated; They Even Have Their Own Greek Organizations": History, Institutional Context, and "Self-Segregation"   176

Stephanie M. McClure

Essay 16: "I Had a Friend Who Had Worse Scores Than Me and He Got Into a Better College": The Legal and Social Realities of the College Admissions Process   185

OiYan Poon

POLITICS, SOCIAL POLICY, AND THE STATE   203

Essay 17: "We Need to Take Care of 'Real Americans' First": Historical and Contemporary Definitions of Citizenship   203

Kara Cebulko

Essay 18: "If Black People Aren't Criminals, Then Why Are So Many of Them in Prison?": Confronting Racial Biases in Perceptions of Crime and Criminals   217

Sara Buck Doude

Essay 19: "What's the Point of 'Black Lives Matter' Protests?": Black Lives Matter as a Movement, Not a Moment   231

Keeanga-Yamahtta Taylor

**Essay 20: "If Only They Would Make Better Choices . . .":
Confronting Myths About Ethnoracial Health Disparities**   **252**

Dawne M. Mouzon

**Essay 21: "Now All the Good Jobs Go to Them!":
Affirmative Action in the Labor Market**   **271**

Wendy Leo Moore

IV. RACE IN EVERYDAY INTERACTIONS   **283**

This final selection of essays returns students to the level of the individual and considers some of the key questions they may have as they look to engage in further conversation about race. The topics addressed encourage the kind of meaningful dialogue that is necessary to help students think more carefully about how they engage others.

**Essay 22: "Why Do They Get to Use the N-Word
but I Can't?": Privilege, Power, and the
Politics of Language**   **283**

Geoff Harkness

**Essay 23: "It's Appreciation, Not Appropriation! I Don't
Know Why You're Offended!": Understanding
Exploitation and Cultural Appropriation**   **295**

Brittney Dennis

**Essay 24: "#BlackLivesMatter Is Racist; It Should
Be #AllLivesMatter!": #AllLivesMatter
as Post-Racial Rhetoric**   **305**

Mark Orbe

**Essay 25: "I'm Not Racist; Some of My Best Friends
Are . . .": Debunking the Friends Defense and
Revisiting Allyship in the Post-Obama Era**   **318**

Cherise A. Harris

About the Editors   **337**

Preface

Professors teaching introductory courses in race and ethnicity or "diversity" must not only communicate the long and complicated history, psychology, and sociology of these topics in just one semester but must also repeatedly respond to the myths and misperceptions of race that students bring with them into these courses. Some of these include the idea that race and racial classification systems are based on human biology or genetic variation; that systematic disenfranchisement by race ended with the culmination of the Civil War, the civil rights movement, or the election of the nation's first Black president; or that evidence for the persistence of racial discrimination is difficult to establish or does not exist. In teaching these topics semester after semester, it can become difficult for professors to summon the patience and empathy needed to engage students in early stages of critical awareness, particularly given how often we hear the same misperceptions. Furthermore, for instructors who may be wary of broaching these questions and discussing them in the classroom, a text that places the latest research at their fingertips can lead to essential learning in an area of society too often fraught with controversy and silence.

Drawing from our experience of teaching race for over 20 years, we believe professors will find it useful to have an engaging text that comprehensively and succinctly addresses the most common misconceptions about race held by students (and by many in the United States, in general). In this book, we have put together a collection of short essays that draw on the latest sociological research on these topics. It is a "one-stop-shopping" reader on the racial topics most often pondered by students and derived from their interests, questions, and concerns. Many scholars write on these topics in various places (e.g., journal articles, books, readers), but what is often lacking is a systematic deconstruction of specific, widely shared myths believed by students. Moreover, with other readers, the professor is left to pull out the key pieces of information in each reading, provide the additional supporting information to debunk a particular myth, and create consistency in a format that is understandable to students. The concise and topic-specific, short-essay format we use here aims to facilitate quicker movement from acknowledging misperceptions about race to examining and discussing the sociological evidence. Each of our contributors has also provided excellent follow-up discussion questions for in-class work and suggested out-of-class activities that can help students apply their new knowledge to their everyday lives.

What we saw as necessary, and what drove us to put this collection together, is the work of "translation." The information contained in these essays is available in many other places, and given our space constraints, we point to those outside sources at the end of each essay. What we saw happen in our own courses was that students often had difficulty connecting the primary text readings to the specific kinds of misinformation and misunderstanding they brought with them. We have tried to build a reader that speaks both languages—the language of the commonly held myths and the language of social science—so that the two are together in one book. Our contributors are those who have written books and articles on these topics or who have been "in the trenches" teaching these topics on a regular basis. As scholars who consistently cover these issues in the classroom and in their scholarship, they are well versed in the latest scholarly literature on controversial racial topics such as these.

The primary target audience for this text is lower-level or introductory race and ethnicity or diversity courses, especially those in the core or general education curriculum. Courses of this kind are taught every semester in colleges and universities across the country; class sizes are usually between 30 and 60 students. Other courses where this text might be useful include education courses, social psychology of race or racism courses, introduction to higher education courses, and ethnic studies courses.

Our hope is that this reader will make the work of translation less difficult for the many excellent instructors all across the country engaging these important topics in their classes every semester.

SUGGESTED ADDITIONAL RESOURCE

Fox, H. (2009). *"When race breaks out": Conversations about race and racism in college classrooms.* New York, NY: Peter Lang.

Acknowledgments

Putting together an edited volume is no small task and requires the assistance of many. As we were deciding on which topics would be covered, we sought the advice of treasured colleagues and friends who gave us the benefit of their many years of experience in the classroom. We would like to thank Nikki Khanna, Keisha Edwards Tassie, Michelle Petrie, Ronald J. O. Flores, Afshan Jafar, Michallene McDaniel, Kelly Manley, Victoria Bruce, Michael Ramirez, and E. M. "Woody" Beck for their input and support during the early stages of our project and for the advice and wisdom they offered along the way. We would also like to thank Jeff Lasser, Eve Oettinger, Adeline Wilson, and the rest of the team at SAGE who worked tirelessly to get this project off the ground and make our vision a reality.

Thanks go to the following reviewers for this second edition: Sofya Aptekar, University of Massachusetts Boston; Stacye A. Blount, Fayetteville State University; Jesus Jaime-Diaz, University of Arizona; and David Oberleitner, University of Bridgeport.

This project is the product of teaching these topics to thousands of students in race and ethnicity courses over many years. In that time, we have witnessed and moderated many challenging discussions—discussions that remind us just how much there is left to know in this area and how important it is that instructors continue to do this difficult work, while having the tools to do so. We thank all the students we have had over the years, as it is their questions and insights that fueled this anthology.

Finally, we would like to express our great appreciation and gratitude to the contributing authors for lending us their expertise and for writing essays that were better than we could have even hoped for when we first envisioned this project. We are honored and humbled to have you as colleagues and are beyond grateful for all you did to make this volume come to life.

"But My Mother Says It's Rude to Talk About Race!"

How and Why We Need to Discuss Race in the United States

Cherise A. Harris

Connecticut College

Stephanie M. McClure

Georgia College

In spite of our hesitance to talk about them, racial myths permeate our social world. They are frequently present in the mass media and public discourse, as well as in our everyday conversations with each other. Perhaps in your dorm rooms, dining halls, workplaces, or on social media, you have heard a variation on the following statements:

- We elected a Black president twice, which means racism doesn't exist anymore.
- We need to look out for "real Americans" first, not immigrants.
- Native American/Indian, Asian/Oriental, Latino/Hispanic—why does it matter what we call them?
- Asian Americans are doing very well. If other racial groups had their values, they would do well also.
- I know a minority who got worse scores than me and got into a better college!

- When people come here, they should learn the language.
- I don't know why people are so upset about team names like the Washington Redskins. It's really just a way of honoring Native American culture.

These kinds of statements reflect a great deal of the conventional wisdom around race. We define *conventional wisdom* as the received body of knowledge informally shared by a group or society that is often unstated, internally inconsistent, and resistant to change. This conventional wisdom is full of racial myths and misunderstandings. In this reader, we look at common racial myths that we and many sociology professors and race scholars have heard from students in race courses. In this essay, we will give you the tools necessary to use this reader and introduce some key ideas and questions to help you navigate discussions about race both inside and outside the classroom.

Early in our schooling, we learn a simplified history of America's founding that ignores the significant levels of racial conflict and inequality that have existed. For instance, it is often stated that America was founded on ideals of freedom and equality for all, an image that ignores the many groups who were excluded from that freedom and equality—namely, people of color. We also tend to think that racial or ethnic strife happened sometime *after* that idealized founding. However, as sociologist Joe Feagin (2013) notes in his book *The White Racial Frame: Centuries of Racial Framing and Counter-Framing*, "racial oppression was not added later on in the development of [U.S.] society, but was the foundation of the original colonial and U.S. social systems, and it remains as a foundation to the present day" (p. ix). Yet there is a tendency in American society to gloss over this history or in other ways minimize the import of race. We see this minimization in the present day when political pundits and others in the media characterize our society as *post-racial*, asserting that race no longer determines one's life chances, or determines them to a far lesser extent than it once did.

Indeed, since the election of President Barack Obama in 2008, we have heard more and more that we have moved beyond race, despite much evidence to the contrary. To be sure, the election of the nation's first Black president signaled a significant shift in the tenor of race relations in the United States, but not always for the positive. For this reason, you may see President Obama mentioned often in the essays in this volume, because his election was a watershed moment in American race relations. Yet his election has also been something of a miner's canary, signaling that perhaps we haven't come as far on the issue of race as we would like to think. Unique occurrences during his presidency, such as the "birtherism" movement, which many mark as the beginning of Donald Trump's political career, or his being called a liar by a congressman during a televised congressional address, suggest that we are far from post-racial. The reemergence of the Ku Klux Klan (KKK) in modern political discourse and the power of the white nationalist movement in the form of the "alt-right" in the United States (and abroad) reaffirm evidence that a "post-racial" diagnosis was premature.

The move toward post-racialism and an emphasis on color blindness are what Michael Omi and Howard Winant (1994) have referred to as *racial projects*. They are "simultaneously an interpretation, representation, or explanation of racial dynamics and an effort to reorganize and redistribute resources along particular racial lines" (p. 56). American history is replete with racial projects that have resulted in negative outcomes for people of color. The defining of Native Americans as *savages* that coincided with the violent removal of groups from their land; the current dehumanizing construct of Latinos (and Mexican Americans, specifically) as "illegal immigrants," thus prompting calls for stringent legislation and policy; and the branding of Black women as *welfare queens* undeserving of public assistance are all examples of racial projects and policies that have disenfranchised people of color. More recently, we have seen the racialization of Muslims as a racial project designed to mark Muslims as threatening (see Garner and Selod in this volume). As Ted Thornhill explains in greater detail in his essay, the post-racial/color-blind discourse also seems to be a racial project designed to convince Americans that the restrictive racial barriers of the past have fallen (particularly with the election of a Black president) and thus keep people from thinking or talking about the reality of race as it plays out in their day-to-day lives.

While empirical information about unequal outcomes in education, the criminal justice system, health, and the labor market clearly show all the ways many Americans' lives are still affected by race, in the context of a supposedly post-racial and meritocratic society, when people even mention race, they are often subject to silencing and even ridicule. You may have heard the statement, "Why can't people just stop talking about race? If they stopped talking about it, it would go away!" Perhaps you've even said it yourself. As difficult as it is to talk about, our ability to move toward greater social justice is severely limited by the silencing around race. Moreover, as Thornhill explains, "differences in skin color are not the problem; racism, racial discrimination, White racial privilege, and racial inequality are." Silence only begets further misunderstanding and inhibits progress.

To get the discussion started, let's talk about the role race plays in the college experience and why you might be hearing more about race than you have at other points in your life.

The Impact of the College Experience on Racial Thinking

As Stephanie McClure (one of the editors of this volume) points out in her essay on Black fraternities and sororities, the college experience has the potential to bring about a great deal of intellectual and personal growth and is an opportunity for students to obtain a degree and also learn more about who they are as individuals and who they would like to become (see also Astin, 1993; Pascarella & Terenzini, 2005). Sociologist Mary C. Waters (2013) writes that the college experience also often puts race in stark relief, where students find themselves thinking about race more than they did when they were younger:

> Sociologists and psychologists note that at the time people leave home and begin to live independently from their parents . . . they report a heightened

sense of racial and ethnic identity as they sort through how much of their beliefs and behaviors are idiosyncratic to their families and how much are shared with other people. It is not until one comes into close contact with many people who are different from oneself that individuals realize the ways in which their backgrounds may influence their individual personality. (p. 212; see also Aries, 2008; Tatum, 1997)

The effect of this experience may be even greater if the person has had very limited previous exposure to people of different races or ethnicities. Moreover, as Waters (2013) argues, prior to the college experience, many White students' relationship to their ethnicity is mostly symbolic, meaning that it is a voluntary relationship that is often enjoyable and expressed only intermittently (see also Gans, 1979). For instance, they may celebrate their distant Irish heritage on St. Patrick's Day, but otherwise rarely acknowledge it. Thus, their relationship to their race or ethnicity is fairly tenuous.

But "for all of the ways in which ethnicity [and race] does not matter for White Americans, it does matter for non-Whites" (Waters, 2013, p. 210). For students of color, and particularly those at predominantly White institutions (PWIs), race and ethnicity play a key role in their college experience. For example, in Elizabeth Aries's (2008, p. 36) study of race and class at an elite college, she found that race was something that almost every Black student in the study had thought about before arriving, while only half the White students in the study had (see also Tatum, 1997). In addition, many of the White students in her study seemed unaware of the privileges they possessed as a result of their race. One of those privileges is that college campuses are essentially built around White students' interests and needs; the food served in the dining halls, the membership and leadership of student organizations, the music played in dorm rooms and at campus parties, and even the course offerings at the college frequently center on the desires and interests of White students (see also Feagin & Sikes, 1995). In other words, the overall culture of the institution frequently reflects the things that Whites value. However, because Whiteness and White privilege is often made invisible (McIntosh, 2013), it is difficult for some White students to see.

Meanwhile, it is within this context that students of color must function. They may have grown up in cultures with different music, foods, and languages, for example, or have different life histories, experiences, and concerns that they find difficult to have validated in the context of a White-dominated institution. Thus, it is challenging for these students to enjoy the full college experience. As Beverly Daniel Tatum (1997) writes, they also frequently find themselves the target of racial prejudice, discrimination, and isolation on campus and in the classroom:

Whether it is the loneliness of being routinely overlooked as a lab partner in science courses, the irritation of being continually asked by curious classmates about Black hairstyles, the discomfort of being singled out by a professor to give the "Black perspective" in class discussion, the pain of racist graffiti scrawled on dormitory room doors, the insult of racist jokes circulated through campus e-mail, or the injury inflicted by racial epithets (and sometimes beer bottles) hurled from a passing car, Black students [and other students of color] on predominantly White campuses must cope with ongoing affronts to their racial identity. (p. 78; see also Feagin, 2013; Feagin & Sikes, 1994)

Recent events on college campuses bear out the nature of this hostility. For instance, in the past five years or so, a rash of "ghetto parties" have been held on college campuses, where attendees are encouraged to wear clothes with "urban" labels (FUBU, Rocawear, etc.), athletic jerseys, and gold teeth. Similarly, in 2012, a White fraternity at a prestigious university allegedly held an Asian-themed party, complete with conical hats, geisha outfits, and misspellings on the invitation designed to convey an Asian accent (Quan, 2013; see also Kingkade, 2013).

As a result of these hostilities, Black, Asian, Latino, Middle Eastern, and Native American students may find solace in hanging out with other students who belong to their racial or ethnic group. They may even join a racial or ethnic affinity group such as an Asian Student Union, a MeCHA group (Movimiento Estudiantil Chicano/a de Aztlán) representing Chicano students, or a Black Greek-letter organization (BGLO) as a way of feeling safe and valued while also feeling connected to the wider campus community. As McClure discusses, this process is known as *social integration* and is not only necessary for identity development but also plays a key role in successful college completion. Yet when White students enter a college campus and see racial affinity groups, they wonder why such things exist, because their race or ethnicity has never been very important in their lives. They may even feel a sense of being left out when they see students of color gathering together (Aries, 2008) or in organizations built around their interests. This is one of the many ways the college experience highlights the salience of race.

Race is also highlighted in college classrooms in a way that it often isn't in high school classrooms. For example, college is frequently the first time students are exposed to a history of the United States that analyzes race in a critical way. Historical accounts have long reflected an attempt "to sanitize this country's collective memories and to downplay or eliminate accurate understandings of our racist history" (Feagin, 2013, p. 17). For example, the story of contact between Native Americans and European settlers is often told (and represented in films such as Disney's *Pocahontas*) as two communities who struggled to respect each other's differences, rather than as a story of violent conflict and ultimate domination, colonization, and genocide on the part of White settlers. In another example, we are taught that true Black oppression ended with slavery or Jim Crow segregation, without looking at the legacy of systemic oppression and the destruction both of these systems left in their wake. In many cases, the college classroom is the first opportunity an individual has to seriously consider the true implications of race and the complicated and painful U.S. racial history. This can be a jarring and difficult experience.

Nonetheless, understanding the legacies of our racial history is a key emphasis of this book, for in understanding the history we can disprove many common racial myths and move toward greater social justice. For instance, Paula Ioanide disproves the commonly held myth that America is a meritocracy where anyone who works hard enough can get ahead. As Ioanide explains, Blacks and Whites with similar incomes, work histories, and family structures have "radically different relationships to wealth and inheritance," which is largely a function of Blacks' difficulty in accumulating wealth under restrictive social structures such as slavery and Jim Crow. Thus, "hard work" isn't enough to overcome disparities that began long ago. The history of Jim Crow is also connected to persistent educational segregation and inequality, as discussed by Patel, Meanwell, and McClure in this volume. Knowledge of these historical racial inequities in the American educational system are also necessary for understanding questions of affirmative action in higher education, as you'll read in the essay by OiYan Poon, and in the labor market, a topic analyzed by Wendy Leo Moore.

Legacies of oppression also affect individual attitudes and interpersonal interactions. For example, when Black men are perceived as inherently criminal, every Black man becomes a suspect, as Sara Buck Doude explains in her essay on bias in perceptions of crime and criminals. Stereotypical thinking and what social psychologists refer to as "ultimate attribution error" contribute to how hooded sweatshirts (also known as hoodies) are perceived very differently depending on the race of the wearer, a topic examined by Rashawn Ray. Legacies of racial oppression also live on in present-day attitudes toward interracial dating, as Nikki Khanna, author of *Biracial in America: Forming and Performing Racial Identity* (2011), discusses in her essay titled "'But What About the Children?': Understanding Contemporary Attitudes Toward Interracial Dating and Marriage." Here, she demonstrates how racist attitudes toward interracial dating are disguised as concern about the children of these unions and also reflect the country's long legacy of racial antipathy, particularly toward Blacks. In all these ways, race and legacies of racial struggles resonate decades and even centuries later.

When White students are first exposed to the history of White oppression, some feel guilty or ashamed that the racial group of which they are a part has been responsible for colonization, domination, and global hegemony. For instance, once White students learn of this history, they sometimes become anxious to present themselves as "one of the good ones." They may even say, "I'm not racist! Some of my best friends are [Black, Asian, Latino, Native American, etc.]." In reviewing the evidence from prominent sociologists such as Eduardo Bonilla-Silva and Joe Feagin, Cherise Harris (coeditor of this volume) points out that often when people claim to have friends of other racial or ethnic backgrounds, their "friendships" lack depth; they may not even know their "friend's" name, or the friendship disintegrates when the activity in which they have participated is over. They may also still harbor racist ideas despite their supposed friendship. While the friends defense is often an attempt by well-meaning Whites to present themselves as racial allies, as Harris points out, being an ally is a far more complicated process that, among other things, involves taking proactive steps to confront one's own racism and the racist views and actions of other Whites. Through clearer understanding of our racial history and the nature of our racial dynamics and interactions, we have a far better chance of moving toward a society with greater social justice. That is one of several goals of this book.

Our Job and Your Job

Given the United States' varied, complicated, and difficult racial history, it is no great surprise that race is a challenging sociological topic. This is the case for three important reasons: (1) A good deal of our information about race and ethnicity includes conventional (or folk) wisdom that is frequently incorrect; (2) much of that conventional wisdom has been handed down to us by agents of socialization (e.g., parents, extended family, peers, the church, and media) whose opinions tend to weigh heavily on us; and (3) there is an overall culture of silence around race that permeates the United States (see Tatum, 1997), thus prompting little critical analysis of that conventional wisdom. None of these should be underestimated in terms of their overall impact. For instance, it is problematic that conventional wisdom tends to reflect a sanitized racial history where our ugliest chapters are reimagined or deleted altogether (Feagin, 2013) yet repeated over and over again as truth in the media and in our everyday conversations. That the conventional wisdom is frequently repeated by our agents of socialization is problematic because our tendency is to uncritically accept what they say in their role as significant others to whom we are closest and who have taught us many other important and meaningful life lessons. It is from them that we get many important cues about race. For example, perhaps there were points in your life where a parent, teacher, or friend suggested it was rude to mention race, let alone discuss it as a serious topic. The cue you might have gotten then is to silence any discussion about race. At other times, perhaps you received messages that minimized or dismissed its significance. If you are a person of color, the cue you might have gotten is not to mention race or racism for fear that you would be accused of being "angry" or "playing the race card"; perhaps worse, you remain silent because you fear that no one will care about your experience. For all of the above reasons, both Whites and people of color remain silent on racial issues, and some are loathe to acknowledge its very existence. This is consistent with contemporary color-blind rhetoric, which leads to a dysfunctional national discourse on race.

The task of this volume is to open up critical discussions about racial topics and debunk many of the commonly held racial myths that college students often bring with them to race courses. Debunking involves unmasking and deconstructing some of our most commonly held notions and beliefs. As Peter Berger (1963) writes in *Invitation to Sociology,*

> The sociological frame of reference, with its built-in procedure of looking for levels of reality other than those given in the official interpretations of society, carries with it a logical imperative to unmask the pretensions and the propaganda by which [people] cloak their actions with each other. (p. 38)

A central premise of this reader is that debunking myths with accurate information and evidence can be an antidote to racism and racial prejudices. This is not an easy task, however. As Liz Grauerholz (2007), former editor of the journal *Teaching Sociology*, states, "All information that students learn is filtered through their prior understandings of the world and these preconceptions can present major barriers to gaining new knowledge about the social world" (p. 15).

To be clear, mere exposure to the information isn't sufficient. For good information to change attitudes, there must be a willingness to consider new information and an openness to change. For example, in *Asking the Right Questions: A Guide to Critical Thinking,* M. Neil Browne and Stuart M. Keeley (2001) explain,

> We bring lots of personal baggage to every decision we make—experiences, dreams, values, training, and cultural habits. If you are to grow, however, you need to recognize these feelings, and, as much as you are able, put them on the shelf for a bit. (p. 9)

Barriers to change exist for individuals in terms of their own ego and sense of identity, as well as their sense of the state of justice and fairness in the world. Indeed, we often perceive that we are being personally attacked when someone presents a position opposite to our own. The danger here is that

> being emotionally involved in an issue prior to any active thought about it [means] that you may fail to consider potential good reasons for other positions— reasons that might be sufficient to change your mind on the issue if you would only listen to them. (Browne & Keeley, 2001, p. 9)

Part of what you will need to do when considering the essays in this volume is engage your critical thinking skills. Critical thinking involves, among other things, identifying assumptions and value conflicts, evaluating evidence, assessing logic, identifying significant omitted information, coming up with alternative positions and ideas, and developing a reasonable conclusion (Browne & Keeley, 2001). It is through this process that many of our conventional notions about race are debunked.

Early in this volume, we debunk perhaps one of the most commonly held myths about race: that it is a biological entity that is fixed and unchangeable and that can even explain why, for instance, Blacks excel at particular sports. As Daniel Buffington explains, citing scientific evidence where genotype is concerned, human beings are 99.9% identical when looking at nucleotide pairs, one of the building blocks of DNA. Indeed, genetic research suggests great similarity across racial and ethnic groups. When looking at this and other scientific research, Buffington (like most social scientists) concludes that race is mostly a social construct, where "the assignment of social importance to physical features occurred through social relations—such as migration and conquest, competition for scarce resources, and political challenges against the state." This is a key claim of this volume: *Race is a social construct*. Because it is a social construct, the explanations for racial dynamics are located in the social as well. Thus, the overrepresentation of Blacks in certain sports, such as basketball, can be more directly attributed to social factors, such as more ample opportunity in those sports (e.g., access to basketball courts in neighborhoods and schools), coupled with limited opportunities in the occupational structure of the United States (e.g., limited employment opportunities, particularly for Blacks located in neighborhoods with underfunded and underresourced schools).

The essays in this volume similarly reflect critical perspectives on commonly held racial myths. As you read each essay, in addition to the questions raised by the author, consider the following questions: Where or from whom have you heard this myth? Do you believe it yourself? Why or why not? What evidence have you heard in support of this kind of conventional wisdom? How is the myth debunked by the author of the essay? What other information do you think would be useful for considering the questions raised in the essay, and where could you locate this information? Finally, ask yourself, why is this myth so often perpetuated? In other words, whose purposes are served by keeping this myth alive, and who is ultimately hurt by it? By considering these questions, you are deciding to make the effort to understand race in a critical fashion, as opposed to blindly accepting the multitude of racial myths that dominate American society.

Final Thoughts

The essays in this volume share several key assumptions:

1. History matters.

2. Context matters.

3. Dialogue matters.

As students of U.S. racial history and racial dynamics, you have the opportunity to change the nature of the dialogue around race. That requires a comprehensive understanding of the context in which we live (e.g., how race intersects with class, gender, and other axes of inequality) and also requires the courage, honesty, and good information needed to dispel conventional racial wisdom. Some of you may have been exposed to the information in this book already, and you may have done the work necessary to modify your ideas and beliefs to fit this reality. As such, it may be difficult to watch your classmates and peers encounter information about race for the first time and not become frustrated and angry. Our hope is that having in one place so much of the information needed to debunk some of the most common myths about race in the United States will be useful to you as you engage your classmates and peers in important conversation.

Cherise A. Harris is an associate professor of sociology at Connecticut College. She specializes in race, class, and gender, and teaches classes on the sociology of ethnic and race relations; the sociology of inequality; race, gender, and the mass media; and middle-class minorities. Her book, *The Cosby Cohort: Blessings and Burdens of Growing Up Black Middle Class*, was published in 2013. She is on the editorial board of *Teaching Sociology* and has published in other journals, such as *Sociological Spectrum* and *Journal of African American Studies*.

Stephanie M. McClure is a professor of sociology at Georgia College. She teaches classes on racial stratification, social theory, and the sociology of education. Her research interests are in the area of higher education, with a focus on college student persistence and retention across race, class, and gender, and a special emphasis on post-college student experiences that increase student social and academic integration. She has published in the *Journal of Higher Education*, *Symbolic Interaction*, and the *Journal of African American Studies*.

SUGGESTED ADDITIONAL RESOURCES

Berger, P. L. (1963). *Invitation to sociology: A humanistic perspective.* New York, NY: Anchor Books.

Browne, M. N., & Keeley, S. (2001). *Asking the right questions: A guide to critical thinking.* Upper Saddle River, NJ: Prentice Hall.

Feagin, J. R. (2010). *The white racial frame: Centuries of racial framing and counter-framing.* New York, NY: Routledge.

Kendi, I. X. (2016). *Stamped from the beginning: The definitive history of racist ideas in America.* New York, NY: Nation Books.

Omi, M., & Winant, H. (1994). *Racial formation in the U.S.: From the 1960s to the 1990s.* New York, NY: Routledge.

QUESTIONS FOR FURTHER DISCUSSION

1. Prior to beginning college, how often had you thought about your race? When you did think about it, which events or occurrences prompted it?

2. How would you characterize what you learned about America's racial and ethnic history? For example, what is the conventional wisdom you have heard surrounding Whites, Blacks, Latinos, Asians, Native Americans, and Middle Easterners?

3. As you begin this course, what are some of your questions surrounding race? If they are not covered in this book, write them down and bring them to class to discuss with your classmates. What can the essays in this book tell you about the answer(s) to your question(s)?

REACHING BEYOND THE COLOR LINE

Examining Your Attitudes Toward Race and Ethnicity: A Pretest and Posttest

Directions: At the beginning of the term, answer the questionnaire below. It is important to answer the questions as HONESTLY as possible, no matter how you think your answers may be perceived. After you have completed the course, look at your answers again to see if any have changed or if you think of these questions in a different way. What do you now know about race and ethnicity that you didn't know before?

1. When you were a child, did your parents talk about race? What messages about race did you receive from them? What messages did you receive from other relatives or agents of socialization (e.g., media, teachers, peers, religious figures)? What would you teach your children about race?

2. Do you think race is mostly about biology? Why or why not?

3. How do you define racism? Can anyone be racist?

4. Do you think Islamophobia should be considered a type of racism? Why or why not?

5. How have your views about race changed in the past 10 years? Have they changed at all since you began college? In what ways?

6. What comes to mind when you think of #blacklivesmatter?

7. Do you think it's time for people to stop talking about racism? Explain your answer.

8. Do you believe it is okay to make judgments about people based on how they dress, like whether they are wearing a hoodie, hijab, or turban? Can making judgments based on people's appearance ever be justified?

9. Consider our use of cultural items typically associated with groups of color, such as hip-hop music and Native American or (ostensibly) Asian symbols. Where is the line between respecting or celebrating these cultures and appropriating or exploiting them?

10. How do you explain the large numbers of Black men in prison? Is this the result of bad choices or something else?

11. Do some racial or ethnic groups value marriage more than others, or are there structural reasons that might account for any differences in marital rates?

12. Have we become more tolerant toward interracial relationships? Why or why not? Is the answer dependent on the racial or ethnic combination of the couple in question?

13. What do you think accounts for health disparities across different racial and ethnic groups?

14. Do Asian Americans value education more than other racial or ethnic groups? Is this a positive stereotype, or is it harmful to Asian Americans or other racial and ethnic groups in some way?

15. Why do you think people who come to this country don't immediately learn English?

16. American culture subscribes heavily to the idea that with hard work, anyone can succeed. Do you think this is true? What should we glean from the successes of people like Barack Obama or Oprah Winfrey? When figures like this promote meritocratic ideals, do you think that makes the American public cling harder to this notion? Why or why not?

17. Do you think that affirmative action is a good way to deal with racial or ethnic disparities in education or employment? Why or why not?

18. Consider the current debates over citizenship. Are our notions of citizenship based solely on documentation and paperwork? What other things might shape our understanding of who is and isn't a citizen or who should or shouldn't be a citizen?

19. Do you believe people are overly concerned with how we refer to racial or ethnic groups? Does it matter whether or not we use *African American* or *Black*, *Indian* or *Native American*, *Hispanic* or *Latino*?

20. Is it ever okay for non-Black groups to use the N-word? Why or why not?

21. Consider your campus community. Do students of different racial groups socialize with one another? Do you witness deep friendships across racial and ethnic lines? Why or why not?

22. Is it possible to be friends with someone of a different race and still be racist? Explain your answer.

23. What other questions would you add to this list?

REFERENCES

Aries, E. (2008). *Race and class matters at an elite college*. Philadelphia, PA: Temple University Press.

Astin, A. W. (1993). *What matters in college? Four critical years revisited*. San Francisco, CA: Jossey-Bass.

Berger, P. L. (1963). *Invitation to sociology: A humanistic perspective*. New York, NY: Anchor Books.

Browne, M. N., & Keeley, S. (2001). *Asking the right questions: A guide to critical thinking*. Upper Saddle River, NJ: Prentice Hall.

Feagin, J. R. (2013). *The white racial frame: Centuries of racial framing and counter-framing.* New York, NY: Routledge.

Feagin, J. R., & Sikes, M. P. (1994). *Living with racism: The Black middle-class experience.* Boston, MA: Beacon Press.

Feagin, J. R., & Sikes, M. P. (1995). How Black students cope with racism on White campuses. *Journal of Blacks in Higher Education, 8,* 91–97.

Gans, H. (1979). Symbolic ethnicity: The future of ethnic groups and cultures in America. *Ethnic and Racial Studies, 2,* 1–20.

Grauerholz, L. (2007, Fall). Getting past ideology for effective teaching. *Sociological Viewpoints, 23,* 15–28.

Kingkade, T. (2013, February 6). Duke University Kappa Sigma fraternity draws accusations of racism with "Asia Prime" party. *Huffington Post.* Retrieved from http://www.huffington post.com/2013/02/06/duke-kappa-sigma-party_n_2630598.html

McIntosh, P. (2013). White privilege: Unpacking the invisible knapsack. In M. L. Andersen & P. H. Collins (Eds.), *Race, class, & gender: An anthology* (8th ed., pp. 49–53). Belmont, CA: Cengage Learning.

Omi, M., & Winant, H. (1994). *Racial formation in the U.S.: From the 1960s to the 1990s.* New York, NY: Routledge.

Pascarella, E. T., & Terenzini, P. T. (2005). *How college affects students: A third decade of research* (Vol. 2). San Francisco, CA: Jossey-Bass.

Quan, K. (2013, February 7). Duke University fraternity suspended over Asian-themed "racist rager." *Time.* Retrieved from http://newsfeed.time.com/2013/02/07/duke-university-fraternity-suspended-over-asian-themed-racist-rager/

Tatum, B. D. (1997). *Why are all the Black kids sitting together in the cafeteria? And other conversations about race.* New York, NY: Basic Books.

Waters, M. C. (2013). Optional ethnicities: For Whites only? In M. L. Andersen & P. H. Collins (Eds.), *Race, class, & gender: An anthology* (pp. 209–217). Belmont, CA: Cengage Learning.

"Blacks Are Naturally Good Athletes"

The Myth of a Biological Basis for Race

Daniel Buffington

University of North Carolina–Wilmington

Journalist Jon Entine opened his 2001 book, *Taboo: Why Black Athletes Dominate Sports and Why We Are Afraid to Talk About It*, with the following scenario:

> Imagine an alien visitor chancing upon a basketball arena on a wintry night. It sees a curious sight: most of the faces of the extended tree trunks scampering around the court are black; the crowd, on the other hand, is almost all white. This alien would see much the same racial division at football games, boxing matches, and at track meets and running races around the world. Even in sports in which blacks are not a majority—baseball, soccer, rugby, cricket, even bob-sledding in some countries—blacks are represented in a greater number than their share in the population. (p. 3)

Entine goes on to argue that genes are the primary explanation for athletes of African descent being overrepresented in elite levels of sport. He is hardly alone in making this claim. On the eve of the 2012 Summer Olympics, former gold medalist sprinter Michael Johnson contended that slavery caused people of African descent to have a "superior athletic gene" (Beck, 2012) that manifested in success in the 100-meter sprint. In doing so, he joined the likes of Al Campanis and Jimmy "the Greek" Snyder, who have made similar comments. For Entine (and others coming from this perspective), skin color demarcates an unambiguous boundary between distinct populations and thus explains a pattern of human social behavior. That an alien visitor would do the same would be as surprising as it would be unlikely. Yet, to a human being, especially one socialized within American culture, the idea that

"Blacks are naturally good athletes" seems to make sense. That this myth exists to such a degree within our popular culture tells us a great deal about how the biophysical diversity of our species has been (mis)understood. For this reason, it serves as a useful starting point for debunking the biological basis for race.

In contemporary biology, the term *race* refers to a unit of taxonomy—like kingdom or phylum—and is used synonymously with *subspecies* to indicate two or more biologically distinct populations within a species. For example, zoologists divide tigers into nine subspecies, including the Bengal, Siberian, and Sumatran types. They do so on the basis of genotypic and phenotypic traits, although the amount of variation necessary to constitute subspecies separation is not agreed on and, therefore, is the subject of debate (Keita & Boyce, 2001). *Genotype* refers to the genetic makeup of an organism, including all genetic material inherited from one's parents or a portion of this material, such as chromosomes that code for eye color. *Phenotype* refers to the observable characteristics of an organism, such as body size, fingerprint pattern, or color of skin, hair, or feathers. While phenotype expresses an organism's genetic inheritance, it is also modified by environmental conditions, such as when exposure to sunlight darkens the color of human skin. Applying the biological meaning of race to humans suggests that our modern species, *Homo sapiens*, can be divided into a number of discrete, mutually exclusive subspecies based on phenotypic and genotypic differences, and that each subspecies will contain nearly uniform individuals who are more similar to each other than to members of other races.

If race strictly referred to a unit of taxonomy, it would be of no more than minor interest to sociologists. However, race has an even longer history of use outside biology. Although its origin is uncertain, the best evidence suggests the term entered the English language during the 16th century as a folk concept that referred to a breed of domesticated animals reproduced for specific behavioral or physical qualities (Smedley & Smedley, 2011). Over time, this meaning was applied to human beings such that race was used as a marker of social distinction, indicating membership in particular social groups. While physical appearance and ancestry played a crucial role in distinguishing between groups, so did behavior and social status. Indeed, as well-worn sayings such as "Blacks are naturally good athletes," "Asians are good at math," and "Whites can't dance" attest, in its more common, everyday usage, race was thought to influence a whole range of behaviors, from the athletic to the intellectual to the artistic. Even more, these different behavioral capacities were thought to naturally account for the unequal positions racial groups came to occupy in society.

A useful starting point, then, is to recognize at least two distinct uses and meanings of race. In the strictest biological sense, it refers to intraspecies variation measured by some unspecified amount of phenotypic and genotypic divergence, a meaning I will refer to as *biological race*. In contrast, the term *social race* will refer to its everyday use as a form of group identification, including how people identify themselves (self-identity) and how they are identified by others (social identity). This essay will focus on biological race and, in particular, whether or not the concept is useful for describing diversity within the human species.

Evidence for the Belief in a Biological Basis for Race

There is ample evidence that a significant portion of the general public believes there are biologically discrete human races. For example, a survey of Georgia residents found that 61.3% of respondents agreed with the statement that "genetics plays a primary role in determining an individual's race" (Condit, Parrott, Harris, Lynch, & Dubriwny, 2004, p. 260). Further evidence can be deduced from questionnaires that ask about racial differences in more limited ways. For example, a survey conducted in 2001 found that 74% of White men and 65% of White women believed that genetics contributed to differences in athleticism across racial groups (Sheldon, Jayaratne, & Petty, 2007). While support for genetic explanations of racial differences tends to be higher for Whites than other racial groups regarding athleticism, intelligence, the drive to succeed, and tendency toward violence, non-Whites (such as sprinter Michael Johnson) also express these views (Jayaratne et al., 2009). Open-ended questions show that beliefs about racial differences involve a complex mixture of biological, cultural, environmental, and personal explanations (Buffington & Fraley, 2011; Condit et al., 2004; Morning, 2011), with biology playing a particularly important role. Longitudinal evidence, however, suggests that these beliefs may be fading. In the 2010 version of the General Social Survey, only 10.3% of all respondents agreed that Blacks had lower socioeconomic status due to an "inborn disability," compared with 26% in 1977, the first year this question was asked. However, it is unclear whether this decline is due to an actual change in attitudes or increasing social stigma attached to such responses (Bonilla-Silva, 2010). Indeed, responses to surveys and interviews should be interpreted as a conservative estimate of the belief in a biological basis for race, given the well-documented tendency for respondents to supply socially desirable answers.

It is clear, then, that a significant portion of the general public—including some minority-group members—believe, to some degree, in the idea of biologically distinct human races. Yet a number of scientists who specifically study human biodiversity (biologists, geneticists, and physical anthropologists) have questioned biological race's ability to accurately capture the type of variation found in the human species. To understand this doubt, we must return to the definition. Recall that race implies several things of note: that the human species can be divided into a number of distinct groupings on the basis of genotypic and phenotypic differences; that these groupings are mutually exclusive (a person can fall into one, and only one, of these groupings); and that these subpopulations contain individuals who are only minimally different from one another. It is important, therefore, to examine the degree of genotypic and phenotypic diversity within the human species.

Reviewing the Evidence: Variation Within the Human Species

Considering genotype, humans are remarkably similar. On average, human beings are 99.9% identical in terms of nucleotide pairs (one of the building blocks of DNA), far more than many other species (Barbujani & Colonna, 2010). The vast majority of the remaining 0.1% variation (ranging from 80%–95%, depending on the specific markers examined and samples used) is found within any local population—meaning two nonrelated individuals from the same population will, on average, be only slightly more genetically similar to each other than two unrelated individuals from different continents. Furthermore, only a small portion of all alleles in the human genome are "private"—that is, found in only one region—and none of these are found with great frequency in the region where they occur (Rosenberg et al., 2002). This tremendous genetic similarity augments archeological evidence regarding the recentness of our species, suggesting there has not been much time for subspecies separation.

How is this minimal amount of diversity distributed across human populations? Most of this genetic variation is *clinal* (Barbujani & Colonna, 2010; Cavilla-Sforza & Cavilla-Sforza, 1995; Rosenberg et al., 2005); that is, it varies gradually over geographic space in correspondence to transitions in environmental conditions. Not surprisingly, phenotypic traits that are significantly impacted by climate also display this type of continuous variation (Relethford, 2009). The classic example is skin color, a trait that has been central to a number of racial classification systems, especially in the United States. Of course, there are human populations with relatively dark skin and those with relatively light skin. However, when we arrange all human beings from dark to light, we find gradual variation—that is, innumerous shades between the light and dark extremes. These differences correspond strongly to environmental conditions, such that darker skin is found most frequently in the tropics, where sunlight is particularly intense, and lighter-colored skin is found nearer the poles (see Figure 2.1). Clinal variation leads to a general axiom: Populations differ by distance, such that the farther apart any two populations are in geographic space, the more genetically different they will be. Importantly, gradual variation poses a serious problem to attempts to divide humanity into separate units. Although individuals and groups will have distinctive traits in such a system, there are no obvious and clearly demarcated boundaries, meaning divisions will *always* be arbitrary and subjective, and the result of decisions made by human beings.

That small portion of biodiversity that is not clinal is mostly the result of barriers—geographic boundaries such as mountain ranges, deserts, large bodies of water, and narrow isthmuses—that made reproduction between adjacent populations very difficult (Barbujani & Colonna, 2010; Cavilla-Sforza, 2000; Cavilla-Sforza & Cavilla-Sforza, 1995). As such, because the Mediterranean Sea is less difficult to cross than the Sahara desert, North Africans are more genetically similar to Southern Europeans than they are to sub-Saharan Africans, despite these regions being of similar distance from each other. Social barriers—such as social preferences for mating with members of one's own social group—are also significant. Therefore, many of these differences in biodiversity appear at the borders between sociolinguistic groups (Cavilla-Sforza, 2000) or between groups that have strong social rules against intimate relationships, such as the castes in India (Barbujani & Colonna, 2010).

Using multiple genetic markers simultaneously, researchers can examine these discontinuities and even classify an individual's geographic origins accurately

Figure 2.1 Worldwide Distribution of Skin Color Variation

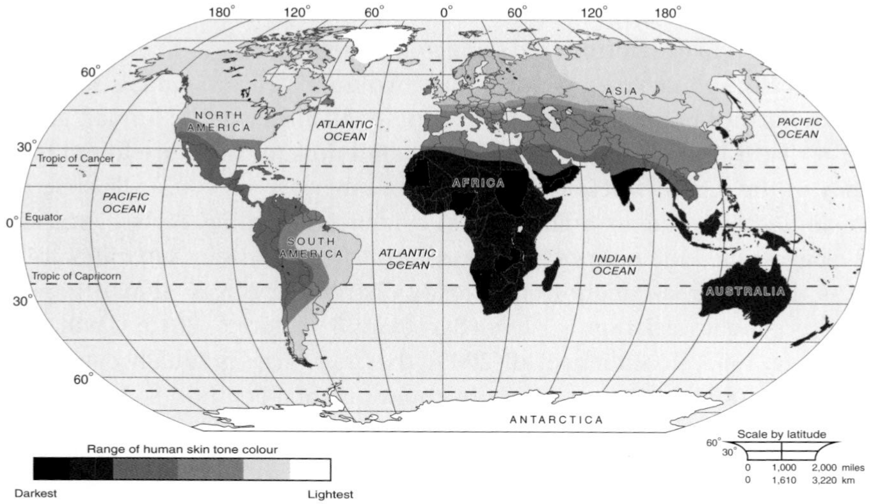

Source: Worldwide distribution of skin color variation [Map]. In *Encyclopedia Britannica*. Retrieved from https://www .britannica.com/topic/race-human

(Bamshad, Wooding, Salisbury, & Stephens, 2004; Rosenberg et al., 2002), at least for those populations whose grandparents came from a single point of origin. Similarly, phenotypes that are minimally impacted by environmental conditions, such as skull size and shape, display a form of geographic clustering that allows researchers to accurately classify individuals using multiple measurements (Ousely, Jantz, & Freid, 2009; Relethford, 2009). However, the genetic similarities produced using this method are inconsistent and vary based on the markers examined, the sample distribution, and method of analysis (Barbujani & Colonna, 2010). Furthermore, the groupings suggested by this method of clustering stray quite far from the general understanding of biological races as large, continent-wide distinctions (Long, Li, & Healy, 2009).

For example, using multiple measurements of the skull, physical anthropologists can distinguish between the crania of American Whites and American Blacks with a very high degree of accuracy. However, this same technique can also distinguish with a similar level of accuracy between populations commonly thought to belong to the same racial group, such as Central and South Africans, northern and southern Native Americans, and northern and southern Japanese (Ousely et al., 2009; also see Relethford, 2009). Perhaps most surprising, the skulls of White males born in the mid-1800s and White males born in the mid-1900s display a similar amount of difference. Therefore, if the ability to group individuals on the basis of crania were taken as evidence of the existence of racial groups, there would be thousands of them and they would correspond very imperfectly with the social race categories we use in our everyday lives.

What About Forensics and Medical Research on Biological Race?

At this point, some might argue that forensic anthropologists can determine the racial identity of unidentified skeletal remains at a better than random rate and that medical researchers use race to predict susceptibility to certain diseases. Forensicists in the United States are able to do so, in part, because the major population groups they deal with come from vastly different areas of the globe. Since differences in physical traits (i.e., phenotype) increase with geographical distance, accurate classification is possible using multiple measurements (Ousely et al., 2009). Still, identification only becomes accurate when compared against the known demographic composition of the location in which the remains are found (Konigsberg, Algee-Hewitt, & Steadman, 2009). This means that a set of bones found in rural Iowa and identified as White would be classified as Easter Island Polynesian if found in the much more diverse location of Hawaii. If found in Gary, Indiana—the city with the highest proportion of Blacks in the United States—the same skeleton would be reported as Black.

Medical researchers are interested in race as a proxy for ancestry, and they are interested in ancestry as a way of predicting the likelihood of an individual's possessing a genetic abnormality that can lead to illness. For example, individuals with ancestors from regions where malaria was frequent (including West Africa, India, the Middle East, and southern Europe) are more likely to be carriers of the sickle-cell trait and therefore develop medical complications. Most studies of the relationship between race and disease rely on self-reported ancestry, which is problematic because the kinship systems used to trace ancestry are culturally (that is to say, socially) constructed. For example, the United States tends to practice a system of hypodescent (more commonly known as the one-drop rule), in which children of European–African sexual relations are socially designated as Black despite their mixed ancestry (Davis, 1991). This means that asking a descendant of one of these relationships his or her self-reported racial identity may provide only a partial understanding of the actual genetic ancestry. Still, medical researchers persist in using self-identity because it provides a rough (if imprecise) approximation of ancestry that is cheaper and less time-consuming than the more accurate methods of detailed genealogical research or analysis of a person's entire genetic makeup (Bamshad et al., 2004; Collins, 2004). Clearly, then, neither forensicists nor medical researchers have discovered something about race that was missed by other researchers.

The Sociological Perspective on Race

Given this, many students are curious as to why sociologists continue to use the word *race* and specific racial group designations such as White, Black, and Native American as if these correspond to distinct entities. To argue that race is not biological is not the same thing as saying it does not exist. As already indicated, there is a "social" meaning of race distinct from its use in biology, and it is this meaning to which sociologists most frequently refer. Race in this sense refers to a type of social identification in which certain physical features have been assigned social significance. Importantly, this definition incorporates, rather than discounts, biological variation. As we have seen, human beings do differ in terms of physical traits, and these visible differences became the primary criteria for placing individuals into racial categories. However, this classification process only took place once humans came to believe that physical features were salient markers of differences. Although different theoretical perspectives within sociology disagree about the exact mechanisms, all concur that the assignment of social importance to physical features occurred through social relations—such as migration and conquest, competition for scarce resources, and political challenges against the state—that brought different populations into sustained contact with each other. It was only once social importance had been assigned to physical differences that people began to act on them, treating members of their perceived racial in-group different from members of their perceived racial out-group. The result has been the formation of more-or-less coherent social groups that differ in ways that matter a great deal to sociologists: in terms of identity, cultural practices, access to important societal resources, and treatment by the larger society. It is for this reason that sociologists continue to study and use the term *race*.

Explaining Differences in Athletic Participation and Performance

Understanding the actual distribution of human biodiversity casts doubt on perspectives that rely on biological race as the primary explanation for behavioral differences, such as elite athletic performance. Conversely, recognizing that racial groups form through social interactions opens up the examination of a whole range of social forces. Considering athletic participation, it should be noted that Blacks are overrepresented in only a handful of sports[1]; therefore, a key question becomes, why only these sports? Sociological explanations call attention to two social features shared by members of the Black category: the occupational structure of society and the opportunity structure within sport itself. The former emphasizes that as a subordinate group, Blacks face limited employment prospects in many occupational fields. Conversely, the institution of sports was among the first to integrate and has subsequently offered a number of high-profile opportunities. These twin forces (ample opportunities in sports coupled with limited opportunities in other occupational fields) funnel a significant number of Blacks into elite sports participation (Coakley, 2009; Edwards, 1973). The opportunity structure within sports channels these participants into particular sports. A relative lack of material resources means that Black participation rates are highest in sports for which facilities, training, and competition are available in widely accessible social institutions such as schools (Coakley, 2009; Phillips, 1993). Conversely, sports in which most training occurs in private clubs or through lessons (such as golf, tennis, and swimming) are the sports in which Black participation rates are low.

This is not to say that biology has no impact on an individual's ability to perform a particular activity. Both rules and tactical strategies mean that sports often favor particular phenotypes, such as height in volleyball and basketball. All other things being equal, a relatively tall individual will be at a distinct advantage in these endeavors. Because certain populations are taller on average than others, some groups would appear to have an advantage. However, because of the tremendous amount of diversity within any population, many members of relatively tall groups will not be tall at all. In addition, because of the high degree of shared genes across populations, many members of other groups—including those that are relatively short—will be quite tall. Finally, it must be remembered that phenotypes are malleable due to environmental factors (such as nutrition) and are acted on in social situations shaped by cultural preferences. The Dutch, the group with the tallest average height in the world, have contributed very few elite basketball players, because of this sport's lack of popularity. To the degree that individuals succeed because of the contribution of a particular genotype or phenotype, this would be because of their individual genetic inheritance, not biological features they share in common with members of their racial group.

Conclusion

By way of conclusion, reconsider how well biological race captures variation within the human species. As stated above, the clinal distribution of most of the variance within the human population makes the creation of distinct groupings difficult. Using sophisticated computer modeling focused on that small portion of human variation that is not clinal does allow for a reasonable classification scheme; however, the corresponding categories are inconsistent and reveal thousands of biological divisions. Further, racial categories are not mutually exclusive, so a person cannot fall into one, and only one, classification. While the use of multiple genetic markers allows for a highly accurate classification of individuals, even these techniques fail to accurately classify everyone in their samples. Some individuals, and even entire groups, could be classified into multiple categories. If this is the case with samples whose recent ancestors all come from the same self-identified group, this suggests classification would be even more difficult for that significant and growing portion of the human populace that lives in multicultural societies where diverse ancestry is common. At best, biological race very crudely corresponds to diversity within the human species, misrepresenting this variation far more often than it enhances our understanding of it.

It is for this reason that sociologists have instead conceived of race as a social construction—that is, a way of assigning meaning to the social world. In the case of race, minor and primarily gradual biophysical differences between individuals and groups have become understood in everyday social interactions as deeply meaningful markers of boundaries between social groups. It is the actions based on this assigned meaning, not the biophysical differences, that account for most of the differential outcomes among racial categories, including differences in sports participation. As such, biological race within the human species is most accurately described as a myth.

Daniel Buffington is an associate professor in the Department of Sociology and Criminology at the University of North Carolina–Wilmington. He is the coauthor of "Racetalk and Sport: The Color Consciousness of Contemporary Discourse on Basketball," published in *Sociological Inquiry* in 2011. He researches in the area of race, sport, and culture.

NOTE

1. Black participation rates exceeded their proportion of the overall U.S. population for only 8 of 38 NCAA-level sports during the 2009–2010 season, including men's and women's basketball, men's and women's indoor and outdoor track, football, and women's bowling (Irick & National Collegiate Athletics Association, 2011). A similar pattern emerges when examining professional and Olympic-level competition (Phillips, 1993).

SUGGESTED ADDITIONAL RESOURCES

Antrosio, J. (2012). *Part 1, biological anthropology: Human nature, race, evolution* [Web log comment]. Retrieved from http://www.livinganthropologically.com/anthropology/human-nature-race-evolution-biological-anthropology

Edgar, H., & Hunley, K. (Eds.). (2009). Race reconciled: How biological anthropologists view human variation [Special issue]. *American Journal of Physical Anthropology, 139*(1).

Herbes-Sommers, C. (Writer & Director). (2003). Episode 1: The difference between us [Television series episode]. In L. Adelman (Producer), *Race: The power of an illusion.* San Francisco: California Newsreel.

Smedley, A., & Smedley, B. D. (2011). *Race in North America: Origin and evolution of a worldview* (4th ed.). Boulder, CO: Westview Press.

QUESTIONS FOR FURTHER DISCUSSION

1. What is clinal variation, and why does it cast doubt on attempts to categorize humans into discrete racial groups?

2. Compare and contrast the biological and sociological explanations for different outcomes between racial groups, such as elite athletic participation.

3. If races are not biologically distinct groups, how do sociologists explain their existence in society? What factors does the author suggest contribute to the formation of racial groups? Can you think of others?

REACHING BEYOND THE COLOR LINE

1. Examine the map in Figure 2.1. Do members of the same racial group share the same skin tone? Do members of different racial groups have distinct skin tones not shared by members of other racial groups? What are the implications of this activity for the biological basis of race?

2. Take the "race test" designed by Guido Barbujani in collaboration with Todd Disotell. In it, you will be asked to sort 44 people from around the world based on physical resemblance (http://www.guidobarbujani.it/images/Take_the_race_test_files/pr-930-file_it-Racetest1EN.pdf). What do the results tell you about the social construction of racial categories?

REFERENCES

Bamshad, M., Wooding, S., Salisbury, B. A., & Stephens, J. C. (2004). Deconstructing the relationship between genetics and race. *Nature Reviews Genetics, 5,* 598–608.

Barbujani, G., & Colonna, V. (2010). Human genome diversity: Frequently asked questions. *Trends in Genetics, 26*(7), 285–295.

Beck, S. (2012, June 30). Survival of the fastest: Why descendants of slaves will take the medals in the London 2012 sprint finals. *DailyMail.com.* Retrieved from http://www.dailymail.co.uk/news/article-2167064/London-2012-Olympics-Michael-Johnson-descendants-slaves-medals-sprint-finals.html#ixzz2q9LySGTZ

Bonilla-Silva, E. (2010). *Racism without racists: Color-blind racism and the persistence of racial inequality in the United States* (3rd ed.). Lanham, MD: Rowan & Littlefield.

Buffington, D. T., & Fraley, T. (2011). Racetalk and sport: The color consciousness of contemporary discourse on basketball. *Sociological Inquiry, 81*(5), 333–352.

Cavilla-Sforza, L. L. (2000). *Genes, peoples, and languages.* New York, NY: North Point Press.

Cavilla-Sforza, L. L., & Cavilla-Sforza, F. (1995). *The great human diasporas.* Reading, MA: Addison-Wesley.

Coakley, J. (2009). *Sports in society: Issues and controversies* (10th ed.). New York, NY: McGraw-Hill.

Collins, F. (2004). What we do and don't know about "race," "ethnicity," genetics and health at the dawn of the genome era. *Nature Genetics Supplement, 36*(11), S13–S15.

Condit, C. M., Parrott, R. L., Harris, T. M., Lynch, J., & Dubriwny, T. (2004). The role of "genetics" in popular understanding of race in the United States. *Public Understanding of Science, 13,* 249–272.

Davis, F. J. (1991). *Who is Black? One nation's definition.* University Park: Pennsylvania State University Press.

Edwards, H. (1973). *Sociology of sport.* Homewood, IL: Dorsey Press.

Entine, J. (2001). *Taboo: Why Black athletes dominate sports and why we are afraid to talk about it.* New York, NY: Public Affairs.

Irick, E., & National Collegiate Athletics Association. (2011). *NCAA race and gender demographics 1995–2011* [Data file]. Retrieved from http://web1.ncaa.org/rgdSearch/exec/main

Jayaratne, T. E., Gelman, S., Feldbaum, M., Sheldon, J. P., Petty, E. M., & Kardia, S. L. (2009). The perennial debate: Nature, nurture, or choice? Black and White Americans' explanations for individual differences. *Review of General Psychology, 13*(1), 24–33.

Keita, S. O., & Boyce, A. J. (2001). Race: Confusion about zoological and social taxonomies, and their places in science. *American Journal of Human Biology, 13,* 569–575.

Konigsberg, L. W., Algee-Hewitt, B. F., & Steadman, D. W. (2009). Estimation and evidence in forensic anthropology: Sex and race. *American Journal of Physical Anthropology, 139*(1), 77–90.

Long, J. C., Li, J., & Healy, M. E. (2009). Human DNA sequences: More variation and less race. *American Journal of Physical Anthropology, 139*(1), 23–34.

Morning, A. (2011). *The nature of race: How scientists think and teach about human difference.* Berkeley: University of California Press.

Ousely, S., Jantz, R., & Freid, D. (2009). Understanding race and human variation: Why forensic anthropologists are good at identifying race. *American Journal of Physical Anthropology, 139*(1), 68–76.

Phillips, J. C. (1993). *Sociology of sport.* Boston, MA: Allyn & Bacon.

Relethford, J. H. (2009). Race and global patterns of phenotypic variation. *American Journal of Physical Anthropology, 139*(1), 16–22.

Rosenberg, N. A., Mahajan, S., Ramachandran, S., Zhao, C., Pritchard, J. K., & Feldman, M. W. (2005). Clines, clusters, and the effect of study design on the inference of human populations structure. *PLoS Genetics, 1*(6), e70.

Rosenberg, N. A., Pritchard, J. K., Weber, J. L., Cann, H. M., Kidd, K. K., & Zhivotovsky, L. A. (2002). Genetic structure of human populations. *Science, 298,* 2381–2385.

Sheldon, J. P., Jayaratne, T. E., & Petty, E. M. (2007). White Americans' genetic explanations for a perceived race difference in athleticism: The relation to prejudice toward stereotyping Blacks. *Athletic Insight: The Online Journal of Sport Psychology, 9*(3), 31–56.

Smedley, A., & Smedley, B. D. (2011). *Race in North America: Origin and evolution of a worldview* (4th ed.). Boulder, CO: Westview Press.

"Native American/ Indian, Asian/Oriental, Latino/Hispanic . . . Who Cares?"

Language and the Power of Self-Definition

Bradley Koch

Georgia College

S tudents are often intimidated when it comes to discussing race in a public setting such as a classroom. Discussions of race appear to them like minefields, wrought with unseen danger, with the potential to maim and disfigure. Because of what seems like the vagaries of usage, many students assume that they should avoid certain words simply out of a sense of political correctness. To be "politically correct" is to avoid offense and the semblance of injury or ill intent. The problem with both the practice of political correctness and the framing of this issue in terms of political correctness is that it ignores the structural nature of racism and the subtleties of unrecognized individual racism.

One place where we see the notion of political correctness muddying the waters is with the avoidance of racial terms that are not racist at all. As a hypercorrection, people often avoid terms such as *Mexican*, *Jew*, *Puerto Rican*, and even *Black*, assuming that the terms are negative. There is a great irony here, however, because when we extend a politically correct prohibition to words that are not in and of themselves socially or psychologically damaging, such as *Mexican*, *Jew*, or *Puerto Rican*, we unintentionally stigmatize the identities of those who should otherwise proudly embrace them. In these ways, language and terminology are important and carry social meanings that merit attention.

Race and the Importance of Language

When most students think of racism, they imagine overt individual racism. They think of a White man in a robe burning a cross or a storeowner who refuses to serve Black customers. The good news is that the civil rights movement has been largely successful in reducing this kind of racism. However, there has been less success in convincing people that racism also exists in the invisible patterns of our social behavior and in the often unconscious biases that are difficult to recognize.

Sociologists recognize that people create and transmit meaning through language. Because of that, words can have great power. The meaning and intent behind the use of racial pejoratives, such as the N-word, is to denigrate a racial group—and in the case of the N-word, that has been the intent of the word since its coining (Asim, 2007; see also Harkness in this volume). It is not, however, only about pejoratives. Many terms that are not inherently offensive and are not leveled intentionally as a way to demean and dehumanize nonetheless perpetuate differences in the historical and lingering advantages, power, and privilege between different racial and ethnic groups. Sociologically, the greater concern is the inequality. We are worried about how the biases inherent in language reinforce unequal outcomes by race. The way we all write, talk, and ultimately think about who we are—and who "they" are—influences these outcomes.

One way to think about the importance of language is to engage the language of identity as reflected in the question: "What are you?" It is hard to imagine a less couth question, and yet it strikes at the heart of two issues: What is one's identity, and who gets to decide? There is tremendous power embedded in the process of definition. Historically, colonization has left some telling scars. As world powers began dominating other peoples, they regularly imposed their own labels on them. Take, for example, the original human inhabitants of the Americas. We continue to call many of these peoples *Indians* after Christopher Columbus's lifelong and mistaken belief that he had made it to India. Despite its inaccuracy, the term has stuck. As time has passed and overt imperial domination has largely waned (replaced by a system of global capitalism), many racial and ethnic groups have attempted to shed historically subjugating *exonyms,* or terms for a group created by an outside dominant group, for *endonyms,* or terms for a group created by the group members themselves.

Latino, for example, is an endonym, the name that those to whom the term refers use for themselves. *Hispanic* (literally "Spanish-speaking"), on the other hand, is an exonym, a name outsiders impose on those to whom the term refers. After all, one's language is not a designation that would help those who already know they speak the same language. Interestingly, Pew Research from 2012 indicates that most Hispanics/Latinos (51%) surveyed preferred their family's country of origin as a descriptor of their ethnicity, meaning they preferred not to use panethnic terms such as *Hispanic* or *Latino* and instead identified as Mexican, Cuban, or Dominican, for example. Only about one quarter (24%) said they used *Hispanic* or *Latino* most often to describe their identity (Taylor, Lopez, Martínez, & Velasco, 2012). Regarding the terms *Hispanic* and *Latino,* most (51%) had no preference for either term, but when a preference was indicated, *Hispanic* was preferred over *Latino* (33% vs. 14%, respectively). This shows some preference for exonyms, perhaps because they tend to have been present in the culture longer than some endonyms and also tend to be terms (historically) used on government documents.

Oriental—literally meaning "of the east"—is an exonym, too. It begs the question, east of what? *Oriental* only makes sense from the perspective of those in the West. The perspective and ascription of the terms matter. In fact, one way to make sense of racial or ethnic categories is as ascribed statuses. Ascribed statuses are social positions that others impose on individuals irrespective of the individual's wishes (Linton, 1936). All exonyms are ascribed statuses. Inasmuch as there is widespread cultural acceptance of the term, exonyms carry with them a reminder of the social and political power that the subjugating group wields over the oppressed group. In these terms, it is not difficult to see why groups would be anxious to shed their exonyms and replace them with endonyms. First, such substitutions challenge the historically oppressive social relationships between groups, and second, the individual-level sense of agency that comes from self-definition can increase self-esteem and reduce anxiety (Cahill, 1986).

Changes in Racial Language

As a way to orient yourself to this social process, it is useful to think about how racial terminology has shifted over time as the concepts of race and ethnicity have shifted. One great new tool with which to see this is Google Ngrams. The Ngram tool draws from Google's growing collection of digitized books (Michel et al., 2011). By searching a word or series of words, Ngram will chart the frequency of those words as they show up in books over time. It is not a perfect tool in that it restricts analysis to content that elites have created for themselves, it cannot differentiate between critical and noncritical usages, and it cannot control for any other independent factors, making Ngrams of limited use for rigorous scholarship. They can, nonetheless, point to larger historical trends in usage in ways that can be informative.

I begin by comparing the terms *American Indian* and *Native American* (Figure 3.1).[1] I use *American Indian* instead of just *Indian* to avoid any confusion with Asian Indians. (Years below in curly brackets {} represent the first recorded use of the term and come from Harper [2001].)

While both terms are relatively scarce until the early 1900s, *Native American* {1956}, which had been the less frequent term, overtakes *American Indian* {1553?} around 1992, signaling a significant victory for Native Americans in their ability to self-define. While the term is still of European origin, it at least is not a coinage of an unapologetic conqueror.

The tough thing, of course, with *Asian* {late 1300s} and *Oriental* {1701} is that they can just as easily refer to inanimate objects (e.g., rugs) as they can human beings. Still, *Asian American* is slowly replacing *Oriental* (see Figure 3.2). Interestingly, though, more than three quarters (76%) of Asian Americans do not often describe themselves with the terms *Asian* or *Asian American*; instead, most (62%) prefer to use their

Figure 3.1   *American Indian* Versus *Native American* Ngram

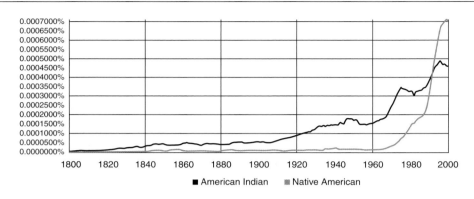

country of origin to define themselves (e.g., Chinese; Pew Research Center, 2012). In fact, the ability of the dominant group (e.g., Whites) to impose a term such as *Asian* on a set of heterogeneous ethnic groups obscures diversity and thus further reifies the power of the dominant group.

Use of both *Latino* {1946} and the corresponding *Hispanic* {c. 1972} spike in the 1970s and 1980s (see Figure 3.3). What most of us assume is a neologism is often the older of the two terms. *Latino,* for example, is older than *Hispanic*, and increasingly, many academics and progressives view *Latina* and *Latino* as more appropriate. As with Asian Americans, people of these ethnicities are questioning the use of many of these terms, though, and even the very existence of an all-encompassing ethnicity. As stated above, most prefer national labels (e.g., Mexican) to either *Hispanic* or *Latino*, and more than two thirds (69%) believe that the latter two terms represent multiple cultures (Taylor et al., 2012). Adding a further level of complexity, many use the term *Latin@* or *Latinx* (see Delgado, 2010) as not to normalize the masculine and devalue the feminine.

Figure 3.2   *Asian American* Versus *Oriental* Ngram

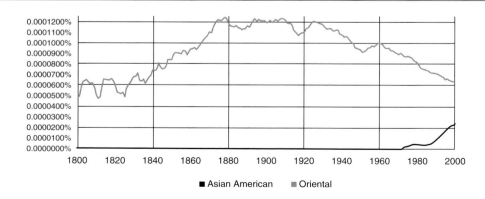

Figure 3.3 *Latino/a* Versus *Hispanic* Ngram

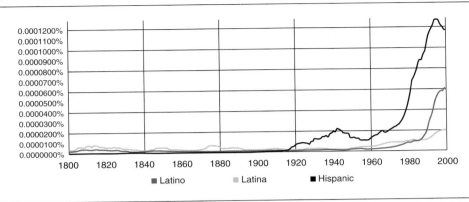

I do not show all the Ngrams for the terms related to the *Black* racial category here, but they still deserve our attention, as they are important in and of themselves and illustrative of the other terms we have addressed above. (Notably, it is nearly impossible to compare *Black* {1620s} to these other terms, because it has several definitions pertaining to the color that are unrelated to race.)

When we look at Ngrams comparing terms used for Black Americans, three things are apparent. First, use of both the N-word {1786} and *Negro* {1550s} peak during the Civil War and at the tail end of the civil rights movement; however, *Negro* has until recently dwarfed all other terms, even though it is out of date and considered offensive by some (Figure 3.4). Certainly, the deliberate use of outdated terms is one way to signal intentional insult. Imagine a White speaker emphatically using *Negro* when we could assume he is aware of the alternative and generally accepted terms such as *Black*. Though older speakers may have been socialized to use now-bygone terms, even the most aged of speakers are likely today to be aware of such changes in convention, and breaks with convention carry symbolic power. Second,

Figure 3.4 N-Word Ngram

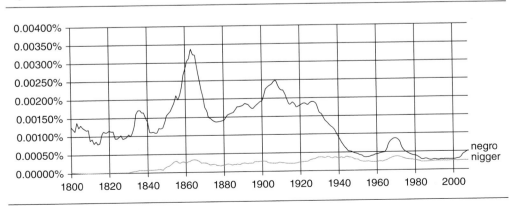

use of the N-word has remained surprisingly high from the mid-1800s on. Finally, *African American* {1969} developed only quite recently, while *Afro American* {1853} has always been rare (Figure 3.5).

Students often are not aware that most generally consider *Colored people* {1610s} an offensive term and prefer *people of color* {?}. Admittedly, it is an odd distinction. Unlike other terms that are preferred over alternatives because they are endonyms (e.g., *Native American* vs. *Indian*), there does not seem to be an obvious reason to favor *of color* over *Colored* aside from convention. It may be that *Colored* serves as a reminder for much of the language and hatred of the segregated South, but its semblance to *of color* makes the distinction confusing for some. The related Ngrams are below (Figures 3.6 and 3.7).

Colored starts to fall out of favor around 1970, and *of color* replaces it beginning around 1988 to 1989. Initially, though, *of color* declined with *Colored*. It was only later that it gained acceptance and became a replacement. While *of color* solves some problems when trying to reference those who are not White (as if whiteness were the

Figure 3.5 *African American* Versus *Afro American* Ngram

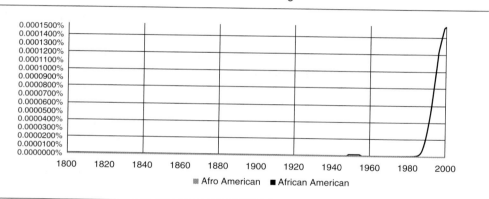

Figure 3.6 *Person of Color* Versus *Colored Person* Ngram

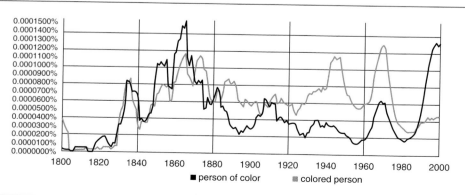

Figure 3.7 *People of Color* Versus *Colored People* Ngram

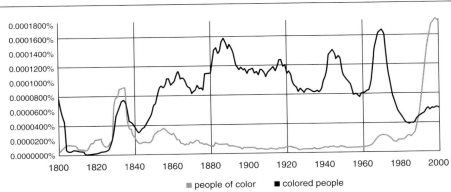

absence of color), it is relatively imprecise. I encourage students to say and write *Black* when they mean Black. If they mean "those who are not White," *non-White* is sometimes permissible. (This distinction is related to the common practice in quantitative sociological analysis of dichotomizing race to Black/non-Black or White/non-White because of limitations of many datasets or for ease of interpretation.) Even this, however, is problematic, as it normalizes Whiteness while othering all other identities. Whenever possible, specificity is preferred.

The confusion over these terms is not isolated to people of color. Students are equally confused about how to refer to Whites. Many will use the term *Caucasian* {1807}. It has a ring of intellectualism, so students will use it to appear more erudite. The term, however, comes from a misunderstanding about race that began in 1795 when the German anthropologist Johann Blumenbach (1865) theorized that the ancestral homeland of White Europeans was in the Caucasus Mountain region of what is today the border between Russia and Georgia. While scientists discredited the theory long ago, use of the term has persisted. *White* {c. 1600} is a better term.

Language as a Form of "Othering"

Many of us who are instructors worry about what some of our less-than-tactful students might say in classroom discussions about contentious issues such as those that sociology is wont to address, but we often worry about the wrong kind of tactlessness. Fears about egregious and inappropriate use of the N-word are largely hollow. What should be of far greater concern is language that is much more subtle and, thus, much more dangerous. It is usually something along the lines of, "Professor, why are *they* [meaning Blacks] so much more likely to be poor?" Because students are not accustomed to openly discussing topics such as race that are largely taboo in American culture, they do not think critically about the vocabulary they employ. Too often, it becomes "we" versus "they." Students rarely do this in an intentionally malicious manner, however. As in the example above, it is often an honest attempt at understanding or benevolence (albeit condescending); however, the employment of this kind of language can be alienating to the "theys" in the class and is an insidious route by which racism is reified. Along with we/they–us/them dichotomies, students are often prone to phrases such as "you people" or "*the* Blacks." The inclusion of pronouns or articles has the unintended effect of distancing the speaker from the subject, further exacerbating racism.

Talking About Talking About Race

It is one thing to read and think about these racial terms and quite another to take the understanding and apply it in one's life. Most people loathe confrontation, especially with people whom they love and respect. It often happens that a friend or family member will unwittingly say something quite hateful or ignorant, and regularly, classmates—and at times even faculty—will speak in ways that may give one pause. While sociologists are trained to spot these instances, they are often much less obvious to others. As I half-jokingly tell my students, any sentence that begins, "I'm not a racist, but . . ." (or less frequently, "Not to sound like a racist, but . . .") almost invariably is followed by a blatantly racist statement. If we were quick enough, we might try to catch these folks after the *but* and ask if what they are about to say in any way is in conflict with what they just said. In effect, it would be wonderful to be able to kindly make salient people's cognitive dissonance. Alas, even the most motivated among us rarely do this. More often than not, we avoid the confrontation altogether, typically hoping that the conversation will change topic as quickly as possible. In many ways, this is an abdication of our civic duty to confront such ignorance. It is all too easy to rationalize such interactions, arguing that we do better in the long run to model appropriate speaking and thinking instead of risking the wholesale dismissal of our ideas and expertise. It takes both confidence and a soft touch to deal with this topic.

I, along with my fellow authors and the editors of this volume, hope that if you began with any reticence toward learning about race and the problems that come along with it, you are a bit more confident about the topic now. Even if this is the case, though, you likely still have some reservations about how to discuss such topics with others, particularly family, friends, and other loved ones who use outmoded language and hold damaging beliefs. Here are two important tips. First, it is important to be prepared for others to be dismissive. Do not take it personally. Dismissiveness is a reaction prompted by misunderstanding and unrecognized privilege. Open, respectful dialogue is the only way to overcome that misunderstanding. Second, even when one follows the above advice, not every battle needs to be fought. As much as you might lament it, you cannot change the world in a day, and you are not even likely to rearrange a person's thinking and speaking in an afternoon. Be selective in your critiques, and keep your goals long and broad.

Conclusion

Racial and ethnic dynamics change over time, which means the language used to refer to the dynamics changes over time. The meanings inherent to the terminology around race and ethnicity are about power and dominance. By fighting to replace ascribed exonyms with endonyms, groups have correspondingly challenged the structural oppression the terms themselves have reflected. By contextualizing public discussions about the proper use of language when identifying racial and ethnic groups, we help recognize and, ultimately, critically engage the historical legacy of colonialism and racism and discard the misguided belief that it is all a matter of being politically correct.

New understanding often leads to more questions than answers. If you have reached the end of this essay and are unsatisfied by the absence of simple, straightforward answers, I hope you recognize, first, that you are not alone and, second, that the confusing language around race and ethnicity is a symptom of both the messy and lamentable history of the topic and the complexity of social interaction. It is only by engaging in this topic that we can move together toward a more equitable future.

Bradley Koch is an associate professor of sociology at Georgia College. He teaches Introduction to Sociology, Research Methods, Social Problems, Society and the Individual, and the Senior Seminar. His research interests include religion, music, and teaching and learning. Brad blogs at http://socingoutloud.com/.

NOTE

1. I use the 1800 to 2008 corpus of terms with a smoothing of 3 years for all Ngrams below.

SUGGESTED ADDITIONAL RESOURCES

Google. (2013). Google Books Ngram viewer. Retrieved from http://books.google.com/ngrams

Pew Research Center. (2012). The rise of Asian Americans. *Pew Research Center: Social & Demographic Trends*. Retrieved from http://www.pewsocialtrends.org/asianamericans

Taylor, P., Lopez, M. H., Martínez, J. H., & Velasco, G. (2012). When labels don't fit: Hispanics and their views of identity. *Pew Research Center: Hispanic Trends*. Retrieved from http://www.pewhispanic.org/2012/04/04/when-labels-dont-fit-hispanics-and-their-views-of-identity

QUESTIONS FOR FURTHER DISCUSSION

1. What fears do you have about using or hearing inappropriate language regarding race? What prior experiences do you have with these issues? How does this illustrate the complex and "messy" nature of race and identity that the author discusses in this essay?

2. Can you identify currently acceptable racial or ethnic terms not mentioned in the essay that you believe still reflect historic and ongoing oppression?

REACHING BEYOND THE COLOR LINE

1. Make your own Ngrams. Choose a race or ethnicity with different labels (e.g., *African American* and *Negro* [or *negro*]), and go to the Ngram website to investigate the changes in the use of these terms over time.

2. In small groups, role-play a situation in which someone uses inappropriate or outdated racial terminology. Stage a mock intervention in which group members attempt to correct the lone member's thinking and speech.

3. Interview older members of your own family about their ethnic and racial identities. What terms do they use? What terms do they prefer? How have the terms that others have used for them changed over their lifetime?

4. Ask people in the course of everyday interactions what terms they prefer. Devise other ways to determine what terms your peers use and prefer.

REFERENCES

Asim, J. (2007). *The N word: Who can say it, who shouldn't, and why*. New York, NY: Houghton Mifflin.

Blumenbach, J. (1865). *The anthropological treatises of Johann Friedrich Blumenbach* [1775–1833]. London, UK: Anthropological Society.

Cahill, S. E. (1986). Language practices and self definition: The case of gender identity acquisition. *Sociological Quarterly, 27*(3), 295–311.

Delgado, D. (2010). Middle-class Latin@ identity: Building a theoretical and conceptual framework. *Sociology Compass, 4*(11), 947–964.

Harper, D. (2001). *Online etymology dictionary*. Retrieved June 27, 2012, from http://www.etymonline.com

Linton, R. (1936). *The study of man: An introduction*. New York, NY: Appleton-Century-Crofts.

Michel, J.-B., Shen, Y. K., Aiden, A. P., Veres, A., Gray, M. K., the Google Books Team, Pickett, J. P. . . . Aiden, E. L. (2011). Quantitative analysis of culture using millions of digitized books. *Science, 331*(6014), 176–182.

Pew Research Center. (2012). The rise of Asian Americans. *Pew Research Center: Social & Demographic Trends*. Retrieved from http://www.pewsocialtrends.org/asianamericans

Taylor, P., Lopez, M. H., Martínez, J. H., & Velasco, G. (2012). When labels don't fit: Hispanics and their views of identity. *Pew Research Center: Hispanic Trends*. Retrieved from http://www.pewhispanic.org/2012/04/04/when-labels-dont-fit-hispanics-and-their-views-of-identity

"Is Discrimination Against Muslims Really Racism?"

The Racialization of Islamophobia

Steve Garner

Birmingham City University, United Kingdom

Saher Selod

Simmons College

Muslims in Europe and the United States are increasingly facing discrimination and prejudice from the state and their fellow citizens. In France, the association of terrorism with Islam has led the state to enact a policy that prohibits Muslim women from covering their faces in public. The French prime minister at the time, Manuel Valls, stated French universities should ban Muslim women from wearing the hijab (Chrisafis, 2016). "Flying while Muslim" is an expression that has been coined to describe the discriminatory treatment many Muslims have experienced at airports or on airplanes. For example, passengers who speak Arabic or wear the hijab have been removed from flights because of the fear it incites in their fellow passengers or flight attendants. A Muslim student was kicked off of a Southwest Airlines flight for speaking Arabic (Westcott, 2016), and a Muslim family, where the mother was wearing a hijab, was escorted off a United Airlines plane after they asked for assistance with a booster seat for their child. Additionally, mosques are increasingly being vandalized (American Civil Liberties Union, 2017). In January 2017, two mosques in Texas were burned to the ground (Garcia, 2017). In August 2016,

Adapted from Steve Garner and Saher Selod, 2015, "'Is Discrimination Against Muslims Really Racism?': The Racial Formation of Islamophobia," *Critical Sociology* 41(1), 9–19. Used with permission of SAGE Publications, Ltd.

in a suburb of Portland, Maine, Iraqi residents of an apartment complex found scattered around the complex typed notes that read, "All Muslims are Terrorists should be Killed [sic]" (Doyle, 2017). Muslims in the United States and Europe fear for their civil liberties and safety because of growing anti-Muslim sentiments, and indeed in the years since 9/11, anti-Muslim sentiments in the United States and Europe have increased.

According to statistics from the Federal Bureau of Investigations (FBI, 2001), hate crimes against Muslims grew from 28 to 481 incidents, a 1,600% increase, in 2001 alone. While this number decreased the following year, anti-Muslim sentiments steadily grew in the decade after 9/11. According to the FBI, in 2015, hate crimes toward Muslims increased by 67% from the previous year. These crimes differed from hate crimes against other religious groups because they were more likely to target individuals rather than property (Kishi, 2016). The anti-Muslim rhetoric that characterized the 2016 Republican presidential campaign, coupled with terrorist attacks in Europe and the United States, has only added to an increase in prejudice and discrimination against Muslim Americans. For example, while campaigning, President Donald Trump proposed banning Muslims from entering the United States, creating a registry for Muslims living in the United States, and requiring Muslims in the United States to wear identification cards. In the month after Trump won the presidential election, the Southern Poverty Law Center documented 112 anti-Muslim hate crimes (Hatewatch Staff, 2016).

Religion and race have historically been treated as separate identities; however, this chapter seeks to uncover the ways religion has increasingly acquired racial meaning for Muslims in a post-9/11 society. *Islamophobia*, an unfounded fear of Islam, is a term that conveys these negative experiences. These statistics reflect this intersection of race and religion as a result of stereotypes that plague the religious identity of Muslims worldwide. These experiences can best be understood as the process of racialization, similar to the process applied to Jews in Nazi Germany. We argue *Islamophobia* must incorporate in its definition an understanding of racism and racialization to place these experiences within a larger context of the social construction of race.

Racism/Racialization/Islamophobia

If we are going to argue that Islamophobia is a form of racism and that racialization is a valid way to interrogate the experiences of a faith-based social group, we need to supply working definitions of *racism, racialization,* and *Islamophobia*. These definitions cannot and should not attempt to capture a phenomenon in a one-size-fits-all fashion, because forms of racism are by their nature dynamic and specific to historical, cultural, geographic, and political contexts. As Sajid (2005) notes regarding the long historical evolution of Islamophobia, "It may be more apt to speak of 'Islamophobias' rather than of a single phenomenon. Each version of Islamophobia has its own features as well as similarities with, and borrowings from, other versions" (p. 2). Thus, a definition of racism, as Klug (2012) notes, should be based on the notion of Wittgenstein's "family resemblances"; that is, the various forms share principal traits, but each form may have slightly different lesser characteristics. The core of racism then comprises three elements (see Garner, 2010):

1. **A set of ideas** [*ideology*] in which the human race is divisible into distinct "races," each with specific natural characteristics derived from culture, physical appearance, or both.

2. **A historical power relationship** in which, over time, groups are *racialized*—that is, treated as if specific characteristics were natural and innate to each member of the group.

3. **Forms of discrimination** flowing from these [*practices*], ranging on a spectrum from denial of access to material resources on one end to genocide on the other.

The forms of racism experienced by people in 21st-century Europe and North America have quite different contexts from each other, as well as a large body of shared terrain. Yet these are not the same geographical and political spaces as they were in the early 19th century, for example, when the institution of slavery was legal in both Europe and the United States. That ideas and practices of racism evolve, temporally and spatially, like any other social relationship ought to be an uncontroversial premise. More difficult in this chain of logic linking religion to racism is the way "race" is conceptualized. The above definition of racism is based on an understanding of race as not being exclusively derived from phenotypes. One logic, "religion cannot be raced," runs as follows:

1. Religious groups are not defined by what has been commonly perceived as *natural* distinctions of people into groups determined by what they look like. Despite ambivalence about the hierarchies, the body-centered understanding of "race" is essential.

2. All the major world faiths include a variety of people drawn from all these "racial" groups, and Islam is no exception.

3. Racism is focused on one or more distinct racialized groups.

4. Therefore, if (1), (2), and (3) are accurate, how can Islamophobia be a form of racism?

Using this logic makes it difficult to analyze Muslim experiences with racism. As such, our response is an alternative logic—religion *can* be raced, based on the following social facts:

1. "Race" has historically been derived from both physical *and* cultural characteristics. The long 19th-century canon of body-fixated race theory is an anomaly in a longer history that evidences various combinations of culture and phenotype being used to define racial characteristics. In other words, world history indicates that race has been defined by cultural and physical characteristics, where we define Islam as not only a religion but a culture.

2. On the basis of these definitions, groups thus racialized are assigned to a hierarchy, with White Europeans at the top and other groups in their wake. The process of racialization entails ascribing sets of characteristics viewed as inherent to members of a group because of their physical or cultural traits. These traits are not limited to skin tone or pigmentation but include myriad attributes, among them cultural traits such as language, clothing, and religious practices. The characteristics thus emerge as "racial" as an outcome of the process.

3. Muslims have historically been one of these groups that experience racism, as have other faith-based groups, most obviously Jews. Their racialization is accomplished not only by reference to religion but other aspects of culture such as physical appearance (including, but not limited to, dress).

4. Muslims can be racialized, and the ways this occurs can be understood as constituting Islamophobia.

5. Islamophobia is therefore a specific form of racism targeting Muslims, and racialization is a concept that helps capture this process across time and place.

Scholars have shown how people map Muslim-ness on to individuals by using a combination of ideas about culture and appearance (Carr & Haynes, 2013; Garner & Selod, 2014; Mac an Ghaill & Haywood, 2014; Moosavi, 2014). If the markers of Islam (e.g., hijab, jilbaab, a Muslim name, nation of origin) are absent, "passing" as a non-Muslim is possible.

Deploying the "religion can be raced" logic means we can employ *Islamophobia* as a set of ideas and practices that amalgamate all Muslims into one group and treat the characteristics associated with Muslims as if they are innate (e.g., violence, misogyny, political allegiance or disloyalty, incompatibility with Western values; see also Read in this volume). If this is the case, then it is useful to use the concept of racialization to study this phenomenon in practice. In any case, "race" is never finished, never stable, never precisely defined or definable. If it were, there would already be a consensus on its meaning. The main problem with *Islamophobia* as a term is its linguistic base. Using the suffix *-phobia* introduces the idea of irrational fears, which is not necessarily a bad thing to have in proximity to racism (Rustin, 1991). However, the use of this suffix also often denotes a mental disorder, moving us further toward the individual and the psychological and further from the social, the collective, the structural, or the systemic. Our argument relies on ideas and practices being inherently social and shared, rather than deviant psychological responses.

Racialization

The history of the concept of "racialization" stretches back into the 19th century (Barot & Bird, 2001), but its recent resurgence in the social sciences can be traced to the late 1970s and early 1980s. Different understandings of racialization can be identified in the works of Fanon (1963), where it is a synonym of *dehumanization,* and Banton (1977), who describes the process of Europeans' ascribing characteristics to the people they encountered during colonization. While European scholars have been at the forefront of advancing the concept of racialization (Murji & Solomos, 2005), some efforts have also been made in the United States. Omi and Winant (2014) define *racialization* as "the extension of racial meaning to a previously racially unclassified relationship, social practice, or group" (p. 111). While their definition is important and a major contribution to expanding scholarship on race, it is still tied to phenotypes, thus limiting an analysis of cultural attributes that also racialize individuals. For instance, they state, "We provide a concept of racialization to emphasize how the phenomic, the corporeal dimensions of human bodies, acquires meaning in social life" (p. 109). This characterization prevents an analysis of how other attributes, such as clothing, language, and religious signifiers, can also racialize individuals. It also ignores how racially classified groups experience newer forms of racism that are different from past forms.

Therefore, while racialization has never been the object of consensus, the overwhelming area of agreement appears to be that racialization is something the powerful do to the less powerful. Wolfe's (2002) concise statement summarizes this argument, where he says that racialization "is an exercise of power in its own right, as opposed to a commentary that enables or facilitates a prior exercise of power" (p. 52). There is a lot to be said for thinking of racialization in this way, with the state, the media, and other authorities as key agents in the process, but we are sure that racialization can also be used as an act of resistance, as well as a demonstration of power (see also Koch in this volume). For example, Miles and Brown (2003) assert that racialization is a "two-way process" (p. 102) whereby groups can racialize themselves as a political strategy for organizing around an identity. An example of this would be the Black power movement, whose activities included countering and refuting a number of negative ideas about Blacks. Additionally, racialization is being used to understand mass incarceration in the United States as an extension of macro systems resulting in the economic, political, and social disenfranchisement of communities of color (Brewer & Heitzeg, 2008). Racialization can also be seen in the policing of perceived undocumented immigrants, where the word *immigrant* seems to almost exclusively denote a person of Mexican descent (see Cebulko in this volume).

So what does racialization actually do? It (1) draws a line around all the members of the group, (2) instigates a feeling of "we-ness," and (3) ascribes particular cultural and social characteristics that may or may not ring true. In this way, ostensibly White groups such as Jews (Brodkin, 1998), Gypsy-Travelers (Bancroft, 2005), and eastern European migrants (Fox, Morosanu, & Szilassy, 2012) can be racialized in the United States and Europe; the British can be said to have racialized the Irish in colonial times (Garner, 2003, 2010); and more important, heterogeneous groups such as asylum seekers and Muslims can be racialized, as well. This is not due to their all looking vaguely the same but, rather, to the essentializing gaze. As Chao (2015) states, "It is hence not Islam, the 'religious origin,' but the perpetrators' projections about what Islam is, that constitutes the discrimination" (p. 58). In other words, those who produce, absorb, and reproduce representations of asylum seekers, and Muslims, can transform the clearly culturally and phenotypically dissimilar individuals who fall into this bureaucratic category (asylum seeker), or are simply devotees of the same religion (Muslims), into a homogeneous bloc. This is the basis of the racialization of Muslims (the process) and of Islamophobia (the snapshot of outcomes of this process).

Rethinking Race: The Transatlantic Racialization of Muslims

Using racialization as a key analytical concept allows us to make sense of the fact that regardless of physical appearance, country of origin, and economic situation, Muslims are homogenized and degraded by Islamophobic discourse and practices in their everyday lives. They are seen solely as Muslims. This relates dress to visible physical markers, thus transforming their bodies into racialized Others: Muslims. Paradoxically, this is illustrated in the experiences of White converts to Islam, who see their Whiteness questioned and downgraded as a consequence of their new belonging to the Muslim faith.

Du Bois' (1903/1994) widely used concept of double consciousness has famously underpinned a whole stream of work on African Americans' experiences in the United States. However, its basic premise, which is that minority groups learn to read themselves through the eyes and mindsets of the majority population and regulate their behavior accordingly in specific contexts, is also more widely applicable. If anything emerges from the work here, it is that all over the West, Muslims are deploying brands of "double consciousness" to manage the risks of discrimination, confrontation, and abuse.

It is our hope that we can begin a conversation on the dire need to create or revise language that will enable a discussion of newer forms of racism. Racisms are fluid, changing in form across time and place. At this point and time, we cannot conceptualize the Muslim experience as existing wholly outside of a racial paradigm. Until Muslims are viewed as fully human and treated as such, we must continue to document their experiences with racism.

Steve Garner is professor of Critical Race Studies and head of Criminology and Sociology at Birmingham City University, United Kingdom. He has published widely on racisms and their intersections with class and nation. His latest book is *A Moral Economy of Whiteness* (Routledge).

Saher Selod is an assistant professor of sociology at Simmons College. Her research focuses on race, religion, and gender. More specifically, she examines how Muslim Americans are racialized through hypersurveillance. She teaches courses on social inequalities, research methods, Islamophobia, race theory, and mass media and popular culture. Professor Selod has also published articles in journals such as *Sociology Compass* and *Critical Sociology*.

SUGGESTED ADDITIONAL RESOURCES

Alsutany, E. (2012). *Arabs and Muslims in the media: Race and representation after 9/11.* New York: New York University Press.

Bail, C. (2015). *Terrified: How anti-Muslim fringe organizations became mainstream.* Princeton, NJ: Princeton University Press.

Bayoumi, M. (2015). *This Muslim American life: Dispatches from the war on terror.* New York: New York University Press.

Cainkar, L. (2009). *Homeland insecurity: The Arab and Muslim American experience after 9/11.* Baltimore, MD: Russell Sage Foundation.

Chao, E. (2015). The-truth-about-Islam.com: Ordinary theories of racism and cyber Islamophobia. *Critical Sociology, 41*(1), 57–75.

QUESTIONS FOR FURTHER DISCUSSION

1. What are some of the stereotypes that have come to define Muslims? What impact do you think these stereotypes have on Muslims' daily lives?

2. How does rhetoric in the media influence what you know about Muslims? What have you heard about Muslims from politicians recently?

3. What does it mean to be an American? Who is able to claim an American identity, and who is not? How does being a Muslim impact one's American identity?

REACHING BEYOND THE COLOR LINE

1. Go to the Internet and do a search of the term *Muslim* in Google's news section. Read carefully through five different articles and write down descriptions of the language used to describe Muslims in each article. After reading these articles, what did you learn about Muslims? Are Muslims represented as average Americans? Did you feel there was bias in the articles? Did they focus on one particular issue surrounding Muslims? How did the news sources differ from one another?

2. Some policies have impacted Muslims living in the United States and in Europe. In France, the government passed a ban on Muslim women's covering their faces in public, known as the burqa ban. In the United States, the National Security Entry-Exit Registration System (NSEERS) was instituted from 2002 to 2011, requiring Muslim noncitizen men over the age of 16 to register with the government, where they were fingerprinted, interrogated, and photographed. Do some research on these two policies and write up a brief paragraph about how they can result in the state targeting Muslims unfairly.

REFERENCES

American Civil Liberties Union. (2017). Nationwide anti-mosque activity. Retrieved February 8, 2017, from https://www.aclu.org/map/nationwide-anti-mosque-activity

Bancroft, A. (2005). *Roma and Gypsy-Travellers in Europe: Modernity, race, space, and exclusion.* Aldershot, Hants: Ashgate.

Banton, M. (1977). *The idea of race*. London: Tavistock.

Barot, R., & Bird, J. (2001). Racialization: The genealogy and critique of a concept. *Ethnic and Racial Studies, 24*(4), 601–618.

Brewer, R. M., & Heitzeg, N. A. (2008). The racialization of crime and punishment: Criminal justice, color-blind racism, and the political economy of the prison industrial complex. *American Behavioral Scientist, 51*(5), 625–644.

Brodkin, K. (1998). *How did Jews become White folks and what does that say about race in America?* (2nd ed.). New Brunswick, NJ: Rutgers University Press.

Carr, J., & Haynes, A. (2013). A clash of racializations: The policing of "race" and of anti-Muslim racism in Ireland. *Critical Sociology, 41*(1), 21–40.

Chao, E. (2015). The-truth-about-Islam.com: Ordinary theories of racism and cyber Islamophobia. *Critical Sociology, 41*(1), 57–75.

Chrisafis, A. (2016, April 14). French PM calls for ban on Islamic headscarves at universities. *The Guardian*. Retrieved from https://www.theguardian.com/world/2016/apr/13/french-pm-ban-islamic-headscarves-universities-manuel-valls

Doyle, M. (2017, January 3). Investigation of anti-Muslim hate crime in Westbrook ends with no answers. *Portland Press Herald*. Retrieved February 8, 2017, from http://www.pressherald.com/2017/01/03/caring-police-calm-fears-after-unsettling-hate-crime-in-westbrook/

Du Bois, W. E. B. (1994). *The souls of black folk* (Unabridged ed.). New York: Dover. (Original work published 1903)

Fanon, F. (1963). *The wretched of the earth* (C. Farrington, Trans.). New York: Grove Weidenfeld.

Federal Bureau of Investigations. (2001). *Hate crime statistics, 2001*. Retrieved February 8, 2017, from http://www.fbi.gov/about-us/cjis/ucr/hate-crime/2001/hatecrime01.pdf/view?searchterm=hate%20crime%202001

Fox, J. E., Morosanu, L., & Szilassy, E. (2012). The racialization of the new European migration to the UK. *Sociology, 46*(4), 680–695.

Garcia, J. (2017, January 30). Texas mosque fire "too close to home." *USA Today*. Retrieved from http://www.usatoday.com/story/news/nation-now/2017/01/29/texas-mosque-fire-too-close-home/97230972/

Garner, S. (2003). *Racism in the Irish experience*. London: Pluto Press.

Garner, S. (2010). *Racisms: An introduction*. Los Angeles, CA: SAGE.

Garner, S., & Selod, S. (2014). The racialization of Muslims: Empirical studies of Islamophobia. *Critical Sociology, 41*(1), 9–19.

Hatewatch Staff. (2016, December 16). *Update: 1,094 bias-related incidents in the month following the election*. Montgomery, AL: Southern Poverty Law Center. Retrieved January 4, 2017, from https://www.splcenter.org/hatewatch/2016/12/16/update-1094-bias-related-incidents-month-following-election

Kishi, K. (2016, November 21). Anti-Muslim assaults reach 9/11-era levels, FBI data show. *Pew Research Center: Factank*. Retrieved February 8, 2017, from http://www.pewresearch.org/fact-tank/2016/11/21/anti-muslim-assaults-reach-911-era-levels-fbi-data-show/#

Klug, B. (2012). Islamophobia: A concept comes of age. *Ethnicities, 12*(5), 665–681.

Mac an Ghaill, M., & Haywood, C. (2014). British-born Pakistani and Bangladeshi young men: Exploring unstable concepts of Muslim, Islamophobia and racialization. *Critical Sociology, 41*(1), 97–114.

Miles, R. H., & Brown, M. (2003). *Racism* (2nd ed.). London: Taylor & Francis.

Moosavi, L. (2014). The racialization of Muslim converts in Britain and their experiences of Islamophobia. *Critical Sociology, 41*(1), 41–56.

Murji, K., & Solomos, J. (2005). Introduction: Racialization in theory and practice. In K. Murji & J. Solomos (Eds.), *Racialization: Studies in theory and practice* (pp. 1–12). Oxford, UK: Oxford University Press.

Omi, M., & Winant, H. (2014). *Racial formation in the United States* (3rd ed.). London: Routledge.

Rustin, M. (1991). *The good society and the inner world: Psychoanalysis, politics and culture.* London: Verso Books.

Sajid, A. (2005). *Islamophobia: A new word for an old fear.* Paper presented at the OSCE Conference on Anti-Semitism and on Other Forms of Intolerance, Cordoba, June 8–9, 2005. Retrieved from http://www.osce.org/cio/15618

Westcott, L. (2016, April 19). Muslim student kicked off Southwest Airlines flight for speaking Arabic. *Newsweek.* Retrieved from http://www.newsweek.com/muslim-student-southwest-airlines-arabic-449598

Wolfe, P. (2002). Race and racialisation: Some thoughts. *Postcolonial Studies, 5*(1), 51–62.

PART II

"If People Stopped Talking About Race, It Wouldn't Be a Problem Anymore"

Silencing the Myth of a Color-Blind Society

Ted Thornhill

Florida Gulf Coast University

Most White Americans firmly believe that race no longer matters and that in the United States anybody can get ahead if they work hard enough (Bonilla-Silva, 2018; Gallagher, 2012). This is one of the hallmarks of the color-blind perspective. In sociological terms, *color blindness* actually has two meanings—one prescriptive, the other descriptive. The former suggests that it is both possible and preferable to think and act toward others without acknowledging skin color. The latter, sometimes called post-racialism, refers to the belief that race no longer determines individuals' life chances in contemporary U.S. society (Gallagher, 2012). Most Whites have internalized both of these meanings, allowing them to rest secure in the racial status quo, comforted by their post-racial delusion. Charles Gallagher (2012) explains it the following way,

> The rosy picture that colorblindness presumes about race relations and the satisfying sense that one is part of a period in American history that is morally superior to the racist days of the past is, quite simply, a less stressful and more pleasurable social place for whites to inhabit. (p. 93)

For most White Americans, it is those who would notice race and invoke it publicly (e.g., in policy discussions, classrooms, courtrooms, or the media) who are the real obstacles to a racially harmonious, color-blind society. This sentiment is frequently expressed in statements such as, "If people stopped talking about race, it wouldn't be a problem anymore." Yet differences in skin color are not the problem; White racism, racial discrimination, White privilege, and racial inequality are.

Color Blindness: Whites' Delusion

National surveys show that the vast majority of Whites believe that the United States is a color-blind or post-racial society. A 2015 *New York Times*/CBS News poll found that 55% of Whites believe that Whites and Blacks have "about an equal chance of getting ahead in today's society" (7% actually believe that Blacks have a competitive advantage). A similar poll found that 74% of Whites believe that the Blacks living in their community "have as good a chance as Whites" in finding employment for which they are qualified (Gallup, 2014). Whites were even more confident that Blacks received equal treatment in the areas of education (80%) and housing (85%). This helps explain why fully two-thirds of Whites (66%) believe that those "who can't get ahead in this country are mostly responsible for their own condition" (Pew Research Center, 2014). It also helps explain why nearly three-quarters of Whites (73%) *disagree* that "every possible effort to improve the position of Blacks and other minorities" should be made "even if it means giving them preferential treatment" (Pew Research Center, 2012). That most Whites oppose race-conscious policies as a means of redressing historical racial oppression is understandable, if not morally defensible, once we also consider that only 43% of Whites agree that racism is a "big problem" (DiJulio, Norton, Jackson, & Brodie, 2015). A significant number of these Whites agree that racism is a "big problem" precisely because they see themselves as a victim of it. Indeed, findings from the *2015 American Values Survey* reveal a stunning 50% of Whites now believe that "discrimination against Whites has become as big a problem today as discrimination against Blacks and other minorities" (Public Religion Research Institute, 2015). Yes, you read that correctly. Roughly every other White American now believes that Whites not only experience racism and racial discrimination, but that it is occurring on a scale comparable to that experienced by Blacks and other Americans of color.

   In-depth interviews and focus groups with Whites further reflect this pattern. These studies show that most Whites strongly believe Americans of color have an "equal opportunity" to succeed and as such they should stop dwelling on race, "playing the race card," and engaging in "self-defeating" behaviors (see, for example, Bonilla-Silva, 2018; DiTomaso, Parks-Yancy, & Post, 2003; Gallagher, 2012). As with the survey data, qualitative studies also reveal Whites' belief that the pendulum of racial preference has swung so far in the opposite direction that Americans of color are now the beneficiaries of "reverse discrimination" or "reverse racism" against Whites (Bonilla-Silva, 2018; DiTomaso et al., 2003; see also Moore in this volume). This sentiment is captured in the following quote by one White interviewee: "I think we find it sometimes going in the other direction. We bend over backwards for the minorities and the person that suffers is the White person" (DiTomaso et al., 2003, p. 195). This is indeed a delusion.

Two additional locations where color-blind claims are commonly found are the comments sections of online news reports and Facebook or blog postings. Even a cursory scanning of comments to articles or posts that address topics such as affirmative action, immigration, police killing of unarmed black men and women, and the lack of racial diversity in the Oscars reveal a color-blind ideology. Although there is not a reliable way to discern the racial identity of these individuals, except for profile pictures and self-reports within the body of the text, the tenor of their comments suggests most are White. Consider the following example.

In January 2012, a coalition of nonprofit organizations in Duluth, Minnesota, launched the Un-Fair Campaign, which was designed to promote awareness and initiate a conversation about White racial privilege and racism through the medium of roadside billboards. These billboards were intentionally provocative, with phrases such as "It's hard to see racism when you're White" written in bold letters on the faces of White women and men. The billboards sparked considerable controversy, locally and nationally. Opponents of the Un-Fair Campaign created a Facebook group in an effort to communicate their frustrations. Consider the following representative comment posted on the "STOP Racist Unfair Campaign" (2012) Facebook group wall:

> Racism is Racism no matter how you slice it, and this ad campaign is RACIST! We all see color, how we react to all the colors we see in the world is up to each individual!! I was always taught to treat others as I would like to be treated, last time I looked an individual's color was not factored into what I was taught!!!!!! I will not apologize for being White and I would not ask anyone of color to apologize either!!!

This post is indicative of the problem with color blindness; it assumes that we already inhabit a society where racial equality prevails. When White privilege and White racism are implicated as real barriers to racial equality, the tendency is for White Americans to summarily dismiss the well-established body of readily available evidence and respond with hollow claims of racism, particularly against Whites. Unfortunately, this practice is all too common. As mentioned earlier, broaching the topics of racial disparities between Whites and Americans of color in areas such as wealth, education, jobs, health care, and treatment by the criminal justice system is often cited as evidence of racism against Whites.

By now you may be wondering whether Americans of color advocate color blindness, too. Some do, though not to the same extent as Whites. Sociologist Eduardo Bonilla-Silva (2018) explains this phenomenon in the following way:

> An ideology is not dominant because it affects all actors in a social system in the *same* way and to the *same* degree. Instead, an ideology is dominant if *most* members (dominant and subordinate) of a social system must accommodate their views vis-à-vis that ideology. (p. 161; emphasis in original)

In other words, since the ideology of color blindness is hegemonic, some people of color will be persuaded by its claims.

So what's wrong with color blindness? It just means that you want to see people as human beings, not colors, right? Not exactly. The color-blind narrative omits crucial facts about how we arrived at the current racial reality in the first place. To begin with, the process of racialization is ignored. Racialization involves "creat[ing] difference where previously no phenotypical or biological difference existed" (Desmond & Emirbayer, 2010, p. 9). Europeans used certain physical features, most notably skin color, to classify non-Europeans as distinct "races," brand them as genetically and culturally inferior, and justify various forms of oppression against them, such as genocide, slavery, theft, and apartheid (Feagin, 2013, 2014). What are now considered distinct racial groups (e.g., Black, White, Asian, Native American) are actually social constructions originating from Europeans' desire to dominate those perceived as "other." Race is not a biological reality that, with focused effort, can be ignored and rendered inconsequential, as the color-blind perspective suggests (see also Buffington in this volume). Instead, it is a social construct, contingent on history, politics, geography, and *time*.

In reality, color blindness is a powerful example of what sociologists Michael Omi and Howard Winant (1994) have called a "racial project," which they define as "*simultaneously an interpretation, representation, or explanation of racial dynamics, and an effort to reorganize and redistribute resources along particular racial lines*" (p. 56; emphasis in original). As such, racial conflict of the past did not simply evaporate with the passage of the landmark civil rights legislation of the mid-20th century; it merely adapted to a different period. The overarching goal of the civil rights movement was to abolish the overt, state-sanctioned apartheid system that severely limited the life chances of Blacks, and other Americans of color, throughout the United States, particularly in the Southern states. Civil rights activists also demanded that Americans of color be accorded the same rights, privileges, and opportunities as Whites based on their common humanity and citizenship. The first goal was accomplished; the second goal has been only partially fulfilled.

Explaining Color-Blind Ideology

During the civil rights movement, activists often invoked the idea of a color-blind society—a sentiment embodied most strongly by Dr. Martin Luther King Jr.'s (1963) "I Have a Dream" speech, in which he envisioned a day where individuals "[would] not be judged by the color of their skin but by the content of their character." This phrase has since been co-opted by political conservatives to proselytize a rendering of post–civil rights America that is inconsistent with reality. These individuals, and an increasing number of liberals, too, are steadfast in their mission to eliminate the very laws, programs, and policies meant to ensure that Americans of color would be fully incorporated into American society, unencumbered by the effects of historical White supremacy and its contemporary manifestations (Brown et al., 2003; Wise, 2010).

Civil rights legislation has not eliminated the need for programs such as affirmative action that help offset the continued effects of state-sanctioned racial injustices of the past and contemporary forms of racism in the present.

While the civil rights movement did not eliminate racial inequality, it did initiate a reshaping of the discourse around race. One positive benefit of this restructuring is that the use of explicitly racist language has been eliminated from most public forums. The exception to this appears to be the Internet, where some individuals use social media and the anonymity of online chat rooms and forums, blogs, and e-mail to use racial epithets, promote racial stereotypes, and advocate White supremacy (Daniels, 2009; Steinfeldt et al., 2010). However, in most public forums, the discursive space around the topic of race is now dominated by the ideology of color blindness.

Color blindness is buttressed by several key assumptions. First, within the color-blind racial project, racism is conflated with racial prejudice. This fails to recognize that racism is a structural phenomenon that is "variable" and often takes on a different character in different historical periods (Bonilla-Silva, 1996, p. 470). When coupled with the sacrosanct color-blind imperative of "no race talk," it becomes impossible to address post–civil rights era racism and racial discrimination, which in the present is more often subtle, institutional, and at times even unintentional. The color-blind perspective demands a permanent gag order against opponents of racial injustice and White supremacy (Guinier & Torres, 2002). And in the flawed logic of color blindness, merely suggesting that White racial privilege and White racism are real barriers to racial equality often results in the label of "racial rabble-rouser" for violating the color-blind imperative (see also Harris and McClure in this volume). This is problematic for several reasons, the most important of which is the fact that there are many institutional practices that produce negative and disparate outcomes by race, often without any overt racial animus or intent on the part of individual Whites. Under color-blind rhetoric, none of these issues can be addressed.

Consider the seemingly benign practice of many organizations' giving preference in hiring to the family members and friends of current employees. On the surface, this practice appears entirely nonracial. However, most Americans of color were barred from employment in nearly all historically White organizations through the better part of the 20th century. When coupled with the high level of racially endogamous marriages and peer groups among Whites, it is more likely than not that the family members and friends of White employees will be White. Color-blind rhetoric to the contrary, advocating for the dismantling of these types of racially unequal arrangements does not make one a racist, nor does a willingness to critically examine contemporary social issues (e.g., the police killing of 12-year-old Tamir Rice in Cleveland, Ohio, or the lead-contaminated drinking water in Flint, Michigan) from a race-conscious perspective.

Another key assumption of color blindness is that the civil rights movement was largely successful in dismantling all significant barriers to upward social mobility for Americans of color (i.e., contemporary racial discrimination is minimal). Here, the claim is regularly made that *Brown v. Board of Education* (1954), along with the landmark civil rights legislation of the 1960s, all but eliminated racial discrimination in education, housing, voting, and the labor market. As such, advocates of color blindness believe that racial discrimination in these areas occurs only on rare or infrequent occasions because the practice is illegal. Martin Luther King Jr. succinctly addressed this White fallacy in his final book, *Where Do We Go From Here: Chaos or Community* (1968), where he wrote: "The recording of the law in itself is treated as the reality of the reform" (p. 5). A half century since King penned these words, many Whites remain disposed to this position. However, it does not hold water, as there are federal and state laws and local ordinances that prohibit all sorts of other behaviors (e.g., murder, theft, pollution, speeding, tax evasion, breach of contract, driving under the influence of drugs and alcohol). Yet no one would claim that since we have laws and ordinances prohibiting these acts that they are not violated every day in the United States. Similarly, despite legal prohibitions against racial discrimination in areas such as housing, education, and employment, these laws are also violated every day in the United States. In 2016 alone, there were 32,309 employment-based racial discrimination complaints filed with the Equal Employment Opportunity Commission (EEOC). These complaints account for only a fraction of the actual number of violations, as most cases of racial discrimination in employment are likely to go unreported because most individuals are unaware that they have been victimized (Bendick, Jackson, & Reinoso, 1994). The claim that the modern civil rights movement eliminated racial discrimination or reduced it to the point of social insignificance is entirely inconsistent with the evidence.

The color-blind racial project is in essence the 21st-century equivalent of the ideology of White supremacy that prevailed in the United States prior to the achievements of the modern civil rights era. While the logic and presentation of these two belief systems are quite different, the effect remains the same: a racially unequal society where Whites are afforded greater life chances than Americans of color. This was the stated goal during the period when the ideology of White supremacy was dominant, but in the post–civil rights era, the ideology of color blindness guarantees the same result.

It is important to note that the racially unequal status quo that is in large measure perpetuated by the ideology of color blindness is not only harmful to people of color; it adversely affects Whites, too. While a considerable body of research and writing has documented the numerous material and psychological benefits of White racial privilege (e.g., Jensen, 2005; Lipsitz, 1998; McIntosh, 2013), there are also costs associated with these unearned advantages. White racial privilege that is today buttressed by color-blind thinking can have the effect of enveloping its beneficiaries in "a bubble of unreality" that prevents an accurate understanding of "the way the world really works" (Wise, 2008, p. 155). Wise further states that it can also produce emotional and psychological costs that result from benefiting unjustly from racial advantages that harm other human beings. This is particularly the case in an American society that pretends it is *the* archetype of meritocracy in the world.

There are also more tangible costs associated with White racial advantage. As Brown et al. (2003) claim,

White Americans may win better jobs, better housing in better neighborhoods, a better shot at a high-quality education for their children. But they must also pay, and pay handsomely, for the prisons, police, mopping-up health care services, and other reactive measures predictably required by the maintenance of drastically unequal social conditions. (p. 249)

In his memoir, *White Like Me: Reflections on Race From a Privileged Son,* antiracist author Tim Wise (2008) asserts, "Racism and white privilege are dangerous to us, even as they pay dividends—sort of like a precious gem that turns out to be toxic if held too close" (p. 148). In essence, there are manifold ways the ideology of color blindness can have indirect negative effects for Whites. Yet the fact remains that people of color are inarguably those most adversely and directly affected by a society that has permitted the chimera of color blindness to become the popular understanding of race in America—that is, an understanding that race no longer matters. In the next section, I provide evidence that shows the color-blind perspective is, in a word, wrong.

Race Still Matters: The Case of Education and the Labor Market

A concise review of the many ways in which, and social locations where, race continues to shape individuals' life chances would require a book-length treatment. However, a thorough repudiation of the myth of a color-blind society does not require such an exhaustive approach. Highlighting the falsity of this perspective requires only sufficient evidence that racism and racial discrimination remain durable and regular features of American society. Research has shown that racial inequities continue to exist in areas such as education, the labor market, housing, politics, health and health care access, the criminal justice system, exposure to industrial toxins, retail experiences, and media depictions, to name but a few (see, for example, Feagin, 2014; Feagin & McKinney, 2003; Feagin & Sikes, 1994). In this section, I show how race affects Americans' experiences in the areas of education and the labor market. I focus on these two social areas because they are institutions with which nearly all Americans must interact fairly regularly throughout their lives and because the law explicitly prohibits racial discrimination in both of them.

Race Matters in Education

Americans view education as the principal means of upward social mobility, a central pillar of the "American dream." In our "meritocratic" society, high academic achievement is supposed to grease the wheels of mobility and propel one toward occupational and financial success throughout life. This process tends to work marvelously for the average White student. Unfortunately, for many students of color, it operates in a wholly different manner due in large part to the poor quality of their schools.

In the United States, most children and adolescents attend schools based on where they live. However, the ghettoization of Blacks, Latinos, and Asians in cities and the forced relocation of indigenous peoples to reservations across the United States have ensured that children of color do not receive equal schooling, both prior to *Brown v. Board of Education* (because separate is *not* equal) and up to the present day (because separate is *still not* equal). Yet because color-blind rhetoric prevails in public discourse, we pretend that Americans who find their children's schools unsatisfactory always have the option of moving to another location with better schools; whether they decide to do so is entirely an individual decision. These types of statements ignore the overwhelming body of evidence showing that racially segregated urban ghettos were intentionally created by Whites through practices such as redlining, blockbusting and panic selling, threats and violence, and restrictive covenants. Today, racial residential segregation is maintained and expanded (either contiguously or noncontiguously) through such illegal practices as racially discriminatory lending and racial steering on the part of real estate agents, as well as freedom of choice [read: White flight] (Lewis, Emerson, & Klineberg, 2011; Massey & Denton, 1993; Zubrinsky Charles, 2003). Where one lives matters for a variety of reasons, including the availability of jobs, exposure to pollution (water, air, soil, noise), violent victimization, the availability of fresh fruits and vegetables, and most especially, the quality of schools that one's children will attend (McKoy & Vincent, 2008).

Due to the legacy of forced racial residential segregation, students of color, particularly Blacks and Latinos, are more likely than White students to attend inferior racially segregated schools, for example, with less qualified teachers and limited gifted, honors, and advanced placement classes (Kozol, 1991, 2005). This is partially due to social class differences by race. Yet the social class advantage held by Whites is itself a product of White racism, both past and present (Feagin, 2013). Even when students of color, especially Blacks, attend diverse schools, they are still more likely than White students to be "tracked low," independent of their abilities and aspirations and their parents' preferences (Diamond, 2006; Tyson, 2011). That is, they are disproportionately placed in developmental courses, dropout prevention, and vocational programs.

Students of color also routinely experience explicit and implicit racism on the part of some White teachers and students, which creates a significant disruption in their learning (see, for example, Kailin, 1999, and Kohli, 2008). Examples of implicit racism include teachers and administrators subscribing to negative racial stereotypes about Black students' having poor moral character and disliking academic pursuits. More overt forms of racism would include racially coded or not-so-veiled comments such as, "Come on, Calvin (who is Black), you should know the answer to this question about slavery" or "Kim (who is Chinese American), how did your grandparents feel about the internment of Japanese Americans during World War II?" These types of statements and questions may come from teachers, administrators, or students. And at the intersection of both explicit and implicit racial bias lies the well-documented lower expectations of many White teachers for Black and Latino students relative to White students (Landsman, 2004; Roscigno & Ainsworth-Darnell, 1999).

At this point, some may argue that students of color could overcome these barriers to academic excellence through hard work. Indeed, some of them do. However, pointing to examples of "motivated minorities" who attend poor schools, graduate at the top of their respective classes, and earn scholarships to prestigious colleges and universities as evidence of what is possible is disingenuous. The "homeless to Harvard" and "jail to Yale" stories that appear in the popular media at seemingly regular intervals are extremely rare exceptions and, by definition, are far outside the norm. Further, given the differences in the educational experiences of White students and students of color, it would be unrealistic to expect both groups to have comparable educational outcomes even if they worked equally hard, to say nothing of the social class advantages of White students. This begs the question: Why should a herculean effort be required of students of color to compensate for all the educational inequities they experience? This doesn't comport with the widespread perception of education as "the great equalizer," or the claim of a color-blind society where race no longer has material consequences.

Race Matters in the Labor Market

Regarding the labor market, in terms of income, the U.S. Department of Labor (2016) reports Blacks and Latinos consistently earn less than their White and Asian counterparts across all major occupational groups (e.g., management, professional, service, and sales). The median income among Latinos (of any race) in 2015 was $17,443 compared with $35,707 among non-Hispanic Whites. This already sizable difference increased by an additional $1,692 since 2011. Blacks fared only marginally better than Latinos, earning a median income of only $20,380 in 2015. Since 2011, the already significant income gap between Blacks and non-Hispanic Whites grew by an additional $1,600. During the same year, Asian Americans earned a median income of $34,502, about $1,205 below that of Whites. While this is a positive sign given the magnitude of the Black–White and Latino–White income gaps, this seeming parity masks the great variation in income that exists among Asian ethnic groups. For example, the median incomes of Japanese, Filipino, and Hmong Americans in 2015 were $43,286, $31,970, and $14,808, respectively (U.S. Census Bureau, 2015). Moreover, members of those Asian ethnic groups with both higher and lower median incomes still pay a "race tax," as evidence reveals that they must be better educated and more experienced than their White counterparts to realize similar pay and promotion opportunities (Chou & Feagin, 2014; Woo, 2000). Unfortunately, Asian Americans' burden of having to be more qualified than their White colleagues to realize equal treatment in the workplace is widely ignored due to the invidious "model minority" myth (see Zhou in this volume).

From education to the labor market, research has shown that even among vocational school graduates—that is, those for whom marketable skills are of the utmost importance—the stigma of non-White skin color presents itself as a significant barrier to gainful employment. An important study by Deirdre Royster (2003) documented this phenomenon by following two groups—one Black and one White, similar in all relevant respects (i.e., motivation, grades, skill level, etc.)—of recent male graduates of a vocational school in Baltimore, Maryland, to assess their labor market experiences. She found that they had greatly disparate rates of success in the blue-collar labor market. The White graduates found more lucrative jobs in the areas in which they were trained and did so relatively quickly. The Black graduates did not have the extensive networks of the White graduates due to historical racial discrimination in the blue-collar labor market and the exclusionary policies of most craft unions. Royster also found that Blacks' ability to develop these types of materially valuable social networks is stymied, in part, by the fallacious belief among White employers that Whites are routinely facing "reverse discrimination" and that they are "underdogs" in the labor market. Therefore, White employers find it necessary to look out for fellow Whites struggling to find employment in what they perceive to be a political climate overly concerned with issues of diversity and affirmative action. Royster concludes that

> because older White men actively recruit and assist younger White men—even those who are not family members, to the virtual exclusion of young Black men—patterns that unfairly advantaged White men during the pre-civil rights era continue to do so now. (p. 177)

Conclusion

White Americans and Americans of color have significantly different opportunities in nearly every sphere of life. Color blindness supports this racially unequal status quo, and most Whites, and some people of color, buy into this ideology. So how do we resolve this dilemma? Is there a viable alternative to color blindness? Thankfully, there is. Rather than a color-blind society, we need to strive for a society that is both racism-free and racially equal. This first requires that we become race or color conscious. Antiracist writer Tim Wise (2010) has suggested "illuminated individualism" as a way toward racial equity. Here, we must first acknowledge that individual identities matter; we are not simply raceless, generic Americans. Next, we need to realize that we have different lived experiences and be reflexive about how race has shaped those experiences. Last, it is imperative that we remain cognizant of the influence of historical and contemporary racism on the life chances of people of color in the United States. In essence, we need to adopt both a sociological and historical perspective. Without doing so, we can never hope to achieve a society where race does not determine individuals' life chances. We *can* move forward together as Americans of all hues, but only after sincerely and completely addressing America's racist past, committing to address racism in the present, and resolving to confront racism in the future when, not if, it rears it unsightly head.

Ted Thornhill received his PhD in sociology from the University of Massachusetts–Amherst and is currently an assistant professor of sociology at Florida Gulf Coast University. He teaches courses on racial stratification and crime and inequality. His research and writing examines how color-blind ideology and institutional policies and practices promote racial inequality, particularly in K–12 and higher education, the labor market, and the criminal "justice" system. He is the author of "Racial Salience and the Consequences of Making White People Uncomfortable: Intra-Racial Discrimination, Racial Screening, and the Maintenance of White Supremacy," published in *Sociology Compass* in 2015.

SUGGESTED ADDITIONAL RESOURCES

Bonilla-Silva, E. (2018). *Racism without racists: Color-blind racism and the persistence of racial inequality in America* (5th ed.). Lanham, MD: Rowman & Littlefield.

Brown, M. K., Carnoy, M., Currie, E., Duster, T., Oppenheimer, D. B., Shultz, M. M., & Wellman, D. (2003). *Whitewashing race: The myth of a color-blind society.* Berkeley: University of California Press.

Feagin, J. R. (2014). *Racist America: Roots, current realities, and future reparations* (3rd ed.). New York, NY: Routledge.

Wise, T. (2010). *Color-blind: The rise of post-racial politics and the retreat from racial equity.* San Francisco, CA: City Lights Books.

Websites

Racism Review: http://www.racismreview.com

"Racism Review is intended to provide a credible and reliable source of information for journalists, students and members of the general public who are seeking solid evidence-based research and analysis of 'race,' racism, ethnicity, and immigration issues, especially as they undergird and shape U.S. society within a global setting. We also provide substantive research and analysis on local, national, and global resistance to racial and ethnic oppression, including the many types of antiracist activism."

Tim Wise: http://www.timwise.org

This is the personal website of antiracist activist and author Tim Wise. Many of his essays are posted here, as well as interviews, speeches, and his speaking schedule.

The White Privilege Conference: http://www.whiteprivilegeconference.com

This is the website of the annual White Privilege Conference. This organization is dedicated to "examin[ing] challenging concepts of privilege and oppression and offers solutions and team building strategies to work toward a more equitable world." They also state that the conference is not "designed to attack, degrade or beat up on white folks" but rather to promote "a philosophy of 'understanding, respecting and connecting.'"

Audio/Visual

Race: The Power of an Illusion (2003): This is a three-part PBS documentary. The executive producer Larry Adelman writes, "Our hope is that this series can help us all navigate through our myths and misconceptions, and scrutinize some of the assumptions we take for granted. In that sense, the real subject of the film is not so much race but the viewer, or more precisely, the notions about race we all hold."

Colorblind: The Rise of Post-Racial Politics and the Retreat from Racial Equity (2011): "In this powerful lecture, anti-racist activist and author Tim Wise discusses the pitfalls of 'colorblind-ness' in the Obama era and argues for deeper color-consciousness in both public and private practice. Wise argues that we can only begin to move toward authentic social and economic equity by acknowledging the diverse identities that have shaped our perceptions and the role that race continues to play in the maintenance of disparities between whites and people of color in the United States today."

White Like Me: Race, Racism, & White Privilege in America (2013): "*White Like Me*, based on the work of acclaimed anti-racist educator and author Tim Wise, explores race and racism in the U.S. through the lens of whiteness and white privilege. In a stunning reassessment of the American ideal of meritocracy and claims that we've entered a post-racial society, Wise offers a fascinating look back at the race-based white entitlement programs that built the American middle class, and argues that our failure as a society to come to terms with this legacy of white privilege continues to perpetuate racial inequality and race-driven political resentments today."

QUESTIONS FOR FURTHER DISCUSSION

1. Having learned about the problems with the color-blind perspective, do you still find that you are sympathetic to its claims? Why or why not?

2. Do you think a truly post-racial America is possible? Why or why not? If so, what do you think some of the preconditions might be for this to become a reality?

3. Why do you think some Americans of color endorse color blindness, whereas other Americans of color strongly resist such claims?

REACHING BEYOND THE COLOR LINE

1. If you are a White student, consider sharing with your White family members and friends how the color-blind perspective actually harms both White Americans and Americans of color. Would this be difficult to do? Why or why not? What steps might you take to become more comfortable talking about race and racial inequality?

2. If you are a student of color, think about how the color-blind perspective has shaped your understanding about race in both your own life and the larger society. How has the ideology of color blindness played a role in how you interpret social issues?

3. If you have family members and friends of different races, make the decision to regularly talk with them about how race continues to be relevant.

REFERENCES

Bendick, M., Jr., Jackson, C. W., & Reinoso, V. A. (1994). Measuring employment discrimination through controlled experiments. *Review of Black Political Economy, 23*(1), 25–48.

Bonilla-Silva, E. (1996). Rethinking racism: Toward a structural interpretation. *American Sociological Review, 62*(3), 465–480.

Bonilla-Silva, E. (2018). *Racism without racists: Color-blind racism and the persistence of racial inequality in America* (5th ed.). Lanham, MD: Rowman & Littlefield.

Brown, M. K., Carnoy, M., Currie, E., Duster, T., Oppenheimer, D. B., Shultz, M. M., & Wellman, D. (2003). *Whitewashing race: The myth of a color-blind society.* Berkeley: University of California Press.

Brown v. Board of Education, 347 U.S. (1954).

Chou, R. S., & Feagin, J. R. (2014). *The myth of the model minority: Asian Americans facing racism* (2nd ed.). Boulder, CO: Paradigm.

Daniels, J. (2009). *Cyber racism: White supremacy online and the new attack on civil rights.* Lanham, MD: Rowman & Littlefield.

Desmond, M., & Emirbayer, M. (2010). *Racial domination, racial progress: The sociology of race in America.* New York, NY: McGraw-Hill.

Diamond, J. B. (2006). Still separate and unequal: Examining race, opportunity, and school achievement in "integrated" suburbs. *Journal of Negro Education, 75*(3), 495–505.

DiJulio, B., Norton, M., Jackson, S., & Brodie, M. (2015, November). *Kaiser Family Foundation/ CNN: Survey of Americans on race.* Menlo Park, CA: Kaiser Family Foundation. Retrieved on May 6, 2016, from http://files.kff.org/attachment/report-survey-of-americans-on-race

DiTomaso, N., Parks-Yancy, R., & Post, C. (2003). White views of civil rights: Color blindness and equal opportunity. In A. W. Doane & E. Bonilla-Silva (Eds.), *White out: The continuing significance of racism* (pp. 189–198). New York, NY: Routledge.

Feagin, J. R. (2013). *The White racial frame: Centuries of racial framing and counter-framing* (2nd ed.). New York, NY: Routledge.

Feagin, J. R. (2014). *Racist America: Roots, current realities, and future reparations* (3rd ed.). New York, NY: Routledge.

Feagin, J. R., & McKinney, K. D. (2003). *The many costs of racism.* Lanham, MD: Rowman & Littlefield.

Feagin, J. R., & Sikes, M. P. (1994). *Living with racism: The Black middle class experience.* Boston, MA: Beacon Press.

Gallagher, C. A. (2012). Color-blind privilege: The social and political functions of erasing the color line in post race America. In C. A. Gallagher (Ed.), *Rethinking the color line: Readings in race and ethnicity* (pp. 92–100). New York, NY: McGraw-Hill.

Gallup. (2014, December 12). *Gallup review: Black and white differences in views on race.* Retrieved on May 24, 2016, from http://www.gallup.com/poll/180107/gallup-review-black-white-differences-views-race.aspx

Guinier, L., & Torres, G. (2002). *The miner's canary: Enlisting race, resisting power, and transforming democracy.* Cambridge, MA: Harvard University Press.

Jensen, R. (2005). *The heart of Whiteness: Confronting race, racism, and White privilege.* San Francisco, CA: City Light Books.

Kailin, J. (1999). How White teachers perceive the problem of racism in their schools: A case study in "liberal" Lakeview. *Teachers College Record, 100*(4), 724–750.

King, M. L., Jr. (1963). I have a dream. In J. M. Washington (Ed.), *A testament of hope: The essential writings and speeches of Martin Luther King, Jr.* (pp. 217–220). New York, NY: HarperOne.

King, M. L., Jr. (1968). *Where do we go from here: Chaos or community?* Boston, MA: Beacon Press.

Kohli, R. (2008). Breaking the cycle of racism in the classroom: Critical race reflections from future teachers of color. *Teacher Education Quarterly, 35*(4), 177–188.

Kozol, J. (1991). *Savage inequalities: Children in America's schools.* New York, NY: Harper-Perennial.

Kozol, J. (2005). *The shame of the nation: The restoration of apartheid schooling in America.* New York, NY: Three Rivers Press.

Landsman, J. (2004). Confronting the racism of low expectation. *Educational Leadership, 62*(3), 28–32.

Lewis, V. A., Emerson, M. O., & Klineberg, S. L. (2011). Who we'll live with: Neighborhood racial composition preferences of Whites, Blacks, and Latinos. *Social Forces, 89*(4), 1385–1407.

Lipsitz, G. (1998). *The possessive investment in Whiteness: How White people profit from identity politics.* Philadelphia, PA: Temple University Press.

Massey, D. S., & Denton, N. A. (1993). *American apartheid: Segregation and the making of the underclass.* Cambridge, MA: Harvard University Press.

McIntosh, P. (2013). White privilege: Unpacking the invisible knapsack. In M. L. Anderson & P. Hill Collins (Eds.), *Race, class, and gender: An anthology* (8th ed., pp. 49–53). Belmont, CA: Wadsworth/Cengage Learning.

McKoy, D. L., & Vincent, J. M. (2008). Housing and education: The inextricable link. In J. H. Carr & N. K. Kutty (Eds.), *Segregation: The rising costs for America* (pp. 125–150). New York, NY: Routledge.

New York Times & CBS News. (2015, July 23). New York Times/CBS News poll on race relations in the U.S. *New York Times.* Retrieved May 6, 2016, from http://www.nytimes.com/interactive/2015/07/23/us/document-new-york-timescbs-news-poll-on-race-relations-in-the-us.html

Omi, M., & Winant, H. (1994). *Racial formation in the United States: From the 1960s to the 1990s.* New York, NY: Routledge.

Pew Research Center. (2012, June 4). *Trends in American values: 1987–2012: Partisan polarization surges in Bush, Obama years.* Washington, DC: Author.

Pew Research Center. (2014). *Pew Research Center poll: 2014 political typology/polarization survey, January 2014* [dataset]. Cornell University, Ithaca, NY: Roper Center for Public Opinion Research.

Public Religion Research Institute. (2015, November 17). *Anxiety, nostalgia, and mistrust: Findings from the 2015 American Values Survey.* Washington, DC: Robert P. Jones, Daniel Cox, Betsy Cooper, and Rachel Lienesch.

Roscigno, V. J., & Ainsworth-Darnell, J. W. (1999). Race, cultural capital, and educational resources: Persistent inequalities and achievement returns. *Sociology of Education, 72*(3), 158–178.

Royster, D. A. (2003). *Race and the invisible hand: How White networks exclude Black men from blue-collar jobs.* Berkeley: University of California Press.

Steinfeldt, J. A., Foltz, B. D., Kaladow, J. K., Carlson, T. N., Pagano, L.A., Jr., Benton, E., & Steinfeldt, M. C. (2010). Racism in the electronic age: Role of online forums in expressing racial attitudes about American Indians. *Cultural Diversity and Ethnic Minority Psychology, 16*(3), 362–371.

STOP Racist Unfair Campaign. (2012). Facebook group page. Retrieved July 12, 2012, from http://www.facebook.com/groups/stopunfaircampaign

Tyson, K. (2011). *Integration interrupted: Tracking, Black students, and acting White after Brown.* New York, NY: Oxford University Press.

U.S. Census Bureau. (2015). *American Community Survey 1-year estimates, 2015, detailed tables.* Generated by Ted Thornhill using American FactFinder. Retrieved April 9, 2017, from factfinder.census.gov

U.S. Department of Labor. (2016). *Labor force characteristics by race and ethnicity, 2015* (Report No. 1062). Washington, DC: U.S. Bureau of Labor Statistics.

U.S. Equal Employment Opportunity Commission. (2016). *Race-based charges, FY 1997–FY 2016.* Retrieved April 9, 2017, from https://www.eeoc.gov/eeoc/statistics/enforcement/race.cfm

Wise, T. (2008). *White like me: Reflections on race from a privileged son.* Brooklyn, NY: Soft Skull Press.

Wise, T. (2010). *Color-blind: The rise of post-racial politics and the retreat from racial equity.* San Francisco, CA: City Lights Books.

Woo, D. (2000). *Glass ceilings and Asian Americans: The new face of workplace barriers.* Walnut Creek, CA: AltaMira Press.

Zubrinsky Charles, C. (2003). The dynamics of racial residential segregation. *Annual Review of Sociology, 29*, 167–207.

"Obama Says Blacks Should Just Work Harder; Isn't That Right?"

The Myth of Meritocracy

Paula Ioanide

Ithaca College

Often, when we hear Black politicians and celebrities promote the American ideals of hard work, merit, and individualism, our tendency is to cast them as authorities on "the Black experience" and racial realities in the United States, and thus we give their comments greater weight. Political leaders such as Barack Obama, for example, encourage Americans to believe that all dreams are achievable in U.S. society if a person works hard enough, irrespective of one's race, class, or gender identity. In his November 6, 2012, reelection speech, President Obama claimed that

> we can keep the promise of our founders, the idea that if you're willing to work hard, it doesn't matter who you are or where you come from or what you look like or who you love. It doesn't matter whether you're black or white or Hispanic or Asian or Native American or young or old or rich or poor, able, disabled, gay or straight, you can make it here in America if you're willing to try.

Celebrities such as talk-show host Oprah Winfrey and rapper Jay-Z echo popular beliefs in meritocracy, along with the idea that U.S. society now has a structure of equal access and opportunity. Their rags-to-riches stories tend to make people believe that anyone willing to pursue his or her goals has a fair chance in the United States. While most people concede that poor people, people of color, and women continue to face some obstacles in U.S. society, the dominant belief is that they generally have a fair chance to achieve their goals. The perception is that if Jay-Z, Beyoncé, Will Smith, Oprah Winfrey, and President Obama managed to do so, other people of color and women should also be able to succeed. Under this logic, those who fail to achieve their dreams presumably have only themselves to blame.

Indeed, throughout his 8-year term, President Obama often advocated the values of hard work and personal responsibility. Similarly, First Lady Michelle Obama encouraged children to do well in school, obtain a college degree, and establish themselves in professional careers to secure the stability and status afforded by wealth and income. The Obamas uphold values that are central to popular American narratives and culture. The narrative of hard work and perseverance mirrors stories of immigrants who came to Ellis Island penniless and managed to reach the "American dream." Whether that "American dream" involves owning a home, obtaining a well-paying job that provides for one's family, or the ability to acquire other symbols of wealth and success, many Americans believe that individuals who take the "personal responsibility" to obtain success are likely to reach their goals. What's more, people often assume that a person's success is a direct reflection of how hard that person worked to earn it.

Like all good narratives, there is some truth to such notions of meritocracy, hard work, and opportunity. Certainly, people who put little or no effort into pursuing their goals in education, work, business, or creative projects rarely reach their objectives. Personal experiences of overcoming obstacles to achieve particular aspirations similarly give legitimacy to the idea that hard work produces good results that are well deserved. The accomplishments of individuals such as President Obama and the changing conditions of U.S. society cannot be discounted given that only one or two generations ago, the possibility of a Black person being elected president seemed inconceivable. Indeed, due to their agency and perseverance, a growing number of Black people have pursued new opportunities in education and employment that only a few decades ago were primarily reserved for Whites. Such perseverance has led to some measurable gains in Black people's class mobility (Lacy, 2007; Oliver & Shapiro, 1995).

When considering U.S. institutional structures and systems, however, the dominant belief that people are rewarded primarily on the basis of merit and that we live in a society of equal opportunity turns out to be much more myth than fact. An extensive body of sociological facts and empirical evidence shows that a person's life chances and opportunities in the United States—by which I mean people's ability to access and obtain homeownership, sustainable employment, good education, effective health care, and quality transportation—continue to be significantly shaped by a person's racial identity.

To be sure, a person's gender, class, sexual orientation, nationality, citizenship, religion, and other markers of identity intersect with a person's racial identity to further complicate the ways a person's life chances and opportunities are determined. But the relationship between race and life chances in the United States deserves particular scrutiny. As George Lipsitz (2011) argues, "More than four decades after the civil rights activism of the 1960s, and nearly one hundred and fifty years after the abolition of slavery, race remains the most important single variable determining opportunities and life chances in the United States" (p. 15).

This seems like a radical claim to make given that some people argue that institutional, policy-based forms of racial exclusion and discrimination have largely been eliminated in today's society. To understand why this claim is unfounded and why life chances and opportunities are still severely skewed along racial lines, we must understand the historical connection between race and wealth in the United States. Specifically, we must consider how the wealth and inheritances of White Americans today originate directly from unfair gains and unjust advantages made possible by past racial discrimination.

Race and Wealth in the United States

Wealth and inheritance play a critical role in an American's life chances. Sociologist Thomas Shapiro (2004) demonstrates that inheritance is more important than college degrees, number of children in the family, marital status, full-time employment, or household composition in giving a person opportunities to succeed economically in U.S. society (Lipsitz, 2011). This is because wealth and inheritance allow people to get a head start in accessing opportunities that subsequently yield the potential to build more wealth. People use wealth and inheritance to pay for private schools and college, to buy homes in well-to-do neighborhoods, and to start small businesses. All these things require work and perseverance, but the initial capital required to start such initiatives makes it so that the hard work of people who already have wealth is much more likely to yield economic rewards than the hard work of people who must use their entire income simply to manage bills and expenses.

Black and White people with similar incomes, work histories, and family structures have radically different relationships to wealth and inheritance. For example, "on the average, whites inherit $102,167 more than blacks" (Lipsitz, 2011, p. 4). Because they tend to inherit significantly less money from their parents and grandparents, Blacks, Latinos, Native Americans, and other people of color are more likely to be asset poor. This means that they don't have savings to fall back on in the event a family member loses a job, experiences the onset of an illness or disability, or has to stop working to take care of children. According to Lipsitz (2011), "only 26 percent of white children grow up in asset-poor households, but 52 percent of blacks and 54 percent of Latinos grow up in these economically fragile households" (p. 4).

Why are White Americans today much more likely to inherit wealth than Blacks, Latinos, Native Americans, and other people of color? The answer to this question has much less to do with White Americans' good work ethic than with policies and practices that purposefully and exclusively gave Whites opportunities to gain wealth in the past. Indeed, for most of U.S. history, racially discriminatory policies and practices did not simply produce disadvantages for Blacks, Latinos, Asian Americans, and Native Americans; they also produced calculable advantages for Whites. For example, 46 million Americans today can trace the origins of their family wealth to the 1862 Homestead Act, a federal policy that gave farmland (typically of 160 acres) west of the Mississippi River to those who applied. Because the Homestead Act had restrictions that were expressly designed to exclude Black people, this land was overwhelmingly allocated to Whites, essentially producing intergenerational wealth advantages for millions of White Americans (Lipsitz, 2006). Such exclusive opportunities for White wealth accumulation were also facilitated by federal and state policies that dispossessed and forcibly removed Native Americans onto reservations west of the Mississippi, allowing White settlers to overtake and develop land in the northeast (Rogin, 1991).

White Americans today can also trace the origins of their wealth and inheritance to the trillions of dollars accumulated through the appreciation of home values that were secured through federally insured loans granted between 1932 and 1968. As part of Franklin D. Roosevelt's New Deal policies, Federal Housing Administration (FHA) mortgage loans enabled working-class people who previously would not have been able to afford to buy homes the benefits of wealth accumulation through homeownership. Once again, however, this opportunity was granted almost exclusively to Whites. As Lipsitz (2006) shows, "98 percent of FHA loans made during that era went to whites via the openly racist categories utilized in the agency's official manuals for appraisers" (p. 107). Because of the racially discriminatory practices in mortgage lending and real estate agencies, the American dream of owning a home, and the capital accumulated through the gradual increase in property values, means that White people were much more likely to reap the benefits of their hard work than were people of color. As a cornerstone of racial inequality, residential segregation and the differential effects of homeownership mean that middle-class Whites have between "3 and 5 times as much wealth as equally achieving blacks" (Lipsitz, 2011, p. 3).

Housing policies and practices were not the only mechanism through which Whites were given unearned economic advantages. New Deal policies such as the 1935 Social Security Act, the Wagner Act, and the 1944 GI Bill of Rights were central to White working-class people's ability to climb the economic ladder (Roediger, 2005; see also Brown, 1988; Lipsitz, 2001; Williams, 2003). Although these policies were technically "race-neutral" and did not explicitly exclude people of color, their application in the larger context of racial inequality meant that they disproportionately granted taxpayer-subsidized advantages to White men. For example, the GI Bill offered some benefits to Black veterans and historically Black colleges, but the disqualification of Black men from military service as a consequence of segregated schools and poor health meant that they were underrepresented among GI Bill beneficiaries. As Linda Faye Williams (2003) notes, "In 1950, the first census year after World War II ended, of 15,386,000 veterans eligible for GI benefits, 920,000 or 6 percent, were African Americans, although they accounted for 10 percent of the adult male population" (p. 113).

It may seem that once overtly discriminatory and exclusionary policies were eliminated as a result of the racial justice struggles of the 1950s through the 1970s, the significance of race, wealth, and opportunity would diminish. But because assets transferred to subsequent generations tend to compound in value, the significance of White wealth advantages obtained as a result of past injustices actually becomes greater in the present. A 2010 study showed that "the wealth gap between Blacks and

Whites quadrupled between 1984 and 2007" (Lipsitz, 2011, p. 4). The baby boom generation is estimated to inherit between $7 trillion and $9 trillion between 1990 and 2020. Lipsitz (2011) writes that virtually all this money is

> rooted in profits made by whites from overtly discriminatory housing markets before 1968. Adult white wage earners routinely inherit money *from* parents, while adult non-white wage earners routinely send out money *to* their parents to compensate for the low wages and lack of assets they [the parents] possess because of racial discrimination. (pp. 3–4)

The racial wealth gap is also exacerbated by contemporary policies that are seemingly race-neutral or "color-blind." Reducing taxation on inheritance and capital gains, as well as granting deductions to local property taxes, adds value to wealth created through past discrimination in lending and housing policies (Lipsitz, 2006). Moreover, subprime mortgage lending practices that are technically color-blind have been applied in race-specific ways and have produced disproportionate losses in wealth for people of color, particularly for Black and Latino people (Rugh & Massey, 2010). Subprime loans purportedly have higher interest rates and less favorable repayment terms to make up for some home buyers' higher credit risk. Yet studies have found that even when people of color have income and debt characteristics similar to those of White applicants, they are disproportionately sold subprime loans (Lipsitz, 2011). A United for a Fair Economy report titled "State of the Dream 2008: Foreclosed" found that people of color were more than three times more likely to be sold subprime loans. Based on federal data, the study estimated that high-cost loans account for 55% of loans to Black people but only 17% of loans to Whites. Because of such racially discriminatory lending practices, people of color were disproportionately dispossessed of their wealth as the housing market began to collapse in 2007. The report estimated that people of color are expected to lose between $164 billion and $213 billion as a result of the subprime mortgage crisis. This represents the greatest theft of wealth in modern U.S. history. Although Whites also suffered economically as a result of the crisis, had subprime loans been distributed equitably, losses for White people would be 44.5% higher and losses for people of color would be about 24% lower (Rivera, Cotto-Escalera, Desai, Huezo, & Muhammad, 2008, p. vii). Numerous other studies, scholarly books, and policy evaluations also show that the shift to color-blind policies has not resulted in greater racial equality when it comes to wealth distribution (Bonilla-Silva, 2001, 2006; Feagin, 2000; Massey, 2007; Massey & Denton, 1993; Williams, 2003).

Economic capital is not the only unearned advantage Whites possess; social capital also facilitates White people's access to job opportunities. Social scientists have shown that personal contacts are the single most important advantage in obtaining employment. Moreover, most jobs in the United States are not listed in classified advertisements or conducted through publicly advertised searches (Lipsitz, 2006). Because White people dominate supervisory, hiring, and decision-making roles in most companies and institutions, White people often offer jobs to insiders in their social networks, creating a hidden advantage that is difficult to quantify or contest. In addition, institutional hiring practices consistently show patterns of racial discrimination against people of color and foreigners. Even when supervisors do not explicitly intend to produce such racially skewed outcomes, their unconscious racial bias against applicants who have non-White names, foreign accents, or appearances produce discriminatory effects (Bertrand & Mullainathan, 2004; Dovidio & Gaertner, 2000; Rooth, 2010; Ziegert & Hanges, 2005).

Although I have focused on the economic advantages White Americans obtain as a result of past and contemporary forms of discrimination, race is also enormously significant in determining other factors critical to obtaining well-being. The opportunity to attain a good education, adequate health care, and physical safety are similarly shaped by the convergences between race and place. People of color systematically experience disproportionate vulnerability to environmental hazards, police violence, longer sentences and punishment in the criminal justice system, and health effects such as asthma and lead poisoning in their neighborhoods, while White Americans are protected from these vulnerabilities due to privileges afforded by their skin color and suburban locales (Lipsitz, 2006, 2011; Massey & Denton, 1993).

Persistent Myths About Race and Wealth

Despite a growing body of evidence that race continues to be the single most significant factor in determining life chances and opportunities, the myths of meritocracy, hard work, personal responsibility, and equal opportunity continue to trump these facts. Indeed, even when presented with mountains of empirical evidence that White Americans' advantages are overwhelmingly rooted in past and present discriminatory practices, many people continue to believe that Whites tend to be at the top of the socioeconomic ladder as a result of merit and hard work (Ioanide, 2015). Today, common explanations for Black and Latino poverty rarely acknowledge the effects of past and present discrimination on the basis of race, citizenship, and ethnicity; instead, the low socioeconomic status of Black and Latino people tends to be attributed to "cultural pathologies" that purportedly encourage low aspirations for educational attainment, poor work ethic, family and sexual nonnormativity (e.g., single-parent households or teenage pregnancy), and "welfare dependence." Such racist myths were gratuitously reinforced during Donald Trump's 2016 presidential campaign, when he claimed that

> the U.S. has become a dumping ground for everybody else's problems. When Mexico sends its people, they're not sending their best. They're sending people that have lots of problems, and they're bringing those problems with us. They're bringing drugs. They're bringing crime. They're rapists. And some, I assume, are good people. (McRady, 2015)

Similar race-baiting strategies were used during the 2012 presidential campaign when Republican candidates Rick Santorum, Newt Gingrich, and Mitt Romney made numerous remarks that equated Black people with dependency, laziness, and unwillingness to work. Mitt Romney extended this notion of "welfare dependency" to President Obama's entire voter base. At a private fundraiser in Florida, Romney claimed that 47% of Americans would vote for Obama because they are "dependent upon government," consider themselves "victims," and don't take "personal responsibility and care for their lives." Consciously or unconsciously, Romney implied a connection between "welfare dependence" and the "browning/blackening" of America under the leadership of a Black president. In other words, voting for Obama was understood as a process of adopting a work ethic historically associated with Black people because of oft-repeated and unfounded racist ideologies.

What do we do when copious amounts of facts and evidence fail to make a difference in changing people's dominant beliefs and perceptions about people of color? And why do people hold on to largely unfounded myths even when extensive evidence is presented to challenge and unravel these myths? Such denials, disavowals, and displacements suggest that people's investments in the myths of meritocracy and hard work are not simply based on ignorance or lack of sound information. That is, people may hold on to false beliefs despite being exposed to evidence-based "correctives" because these mythologies provide a sense of ideological, psychological, and identity-based coherence.

For White people, holding on to these beliefs despite the extensive evidence of ongoing systemic racism often has to do with avoiding the guilt, pain, and moral questions raised by a violent history that continues to grant them unearned advantages and privileges. A White person may be avidly committed to stopping discrimination on the basis of race or ethnicity, but he or she still inherits some aspect of privilege and advantage by virtue of being White. Even poor White Americans who face significant economic obstacles are at the very least granted the privilege of not being constantly subject to discrimination on the basis of skin color.

When White Americans do accept the overwhelming evidence of White advantages and privileges yielded by a long legacy of racism, the worldviews, ideologies, and belief systems through which White people are encouraged to understand themselves tend to crumble. If I believe that I got to the top of my class solely on the basis of my individual hard work, I may feel justified in considering myself superior to those who are lower than me in rank. If instead I consider all the unearned and unjust advantages I inherited by virtue of my race, my hard work has to be reconsidered in the context of these unjust advantages and disadvantages. By extension, I likely have to confront ethical questions about my role and responsibility in a system that gives me advantages through the exclusion, exploitation, and dispossession of people of color.

For people of color, investments in the myths of meritocracy and hard work are often rooted in something quite different. For the past 40 years, politicians, pundits, and media representations have blamed and demonized poor Native, Black, and Latino people for high poverty rates, school dropouts, teenage pregnancies, criminality, and "welfare dependence" (Kim, 2000; Lee, 1999; Reeves, 1994; Springer, 2005). As a result, some people of color invest in notions of hard work, merit, and personal responsibility to dissociate themselves from these negative stereotypes, particularly from the stigmatization of dependence. Indeed, because the "Black urban underclass," "illegal immigrants," and "welfare dependents" are so stigmatized, people of color are constantly compelled to prove their exceptionality from these imposed perceptions.

For Asian Americans, who tend to be stereotyped as "the model minority," investments in the myth of meritocracy and hard work may be rooted in the desire to preserve a status that is relatively valorized in comparison with other groups of color. This often functions to socially divide groups who share experiences of racial discrimination and exclusion, emphasizing differences over similarities that could produce generative political alliances.

At times, people of color who obtain middle- and upper-class status through education, entrepreneurship, or employment also adopt the rhetoric of blaming poor people of color for their class status and begin advocating the myth of meritocracy and hard work. They offer their own experiences of success as "proof" of other people's unwillingness to pursue opportunities. While there may be some truth to this correlation, such views often minimize the number of systemic obstacles poor people of color would have to overcome to reach economic ascendance *as a group*. In other words, the U.S. racial order has conceded class mobility for a small number of people of color. But if it were to allow the economic ascent of a *majority* of people of color, it would have to radically alter its wealth, opportunity, and social structure. White people would have to relinquish their long-term dominance in the domains of property and business ownership, employment, education, and political office and share these resources and opportunities with people of color.

Middle- and upper-class people of color may also advocate notions of meritocracy and hard work to obtain or preserve higher positions of power. Such positions, particularly if they are situated in predominantly White institutions, often require that people of color adopt the values, rhetoric, and practices of those institutions. For example, it is not likely that people such as former Secretary of State Condoleezza Rice or Justice Clarence Thomas would have gained entry into such high governmental and judicial positions had they made public critiques of institutional racism in the United States.

When people of color advocate, defend, and invest in notions of hard work, personal responsibility, and equal opportunity without also revealing the ongoing significance of racial discrimination and inequality, the myth of meritocracy is reinforced. Television shows such as *Scandal, Black-ish, Ugly Betty,* and *Fresh Off the Boat* present media representations of dignity, resilience, humor, and self-empowerment common in many families of color in the United States. Yet because these qualities are often depicted without also offering critiques of institutional racism, people of color who defend a pull-yourself-up-by-your-own-bootstraps ideology reinforce the myth of meritocracy in the post–civil rights era (Dyson, 2005; Gray, 1995; Hunt, 2005; Jhally & Lewis, 2005; McKnight, 2014; Warner, 2015). In other words, while these shows are groundbreaking in humanizing people of color to predominantly White audiences, they do little to bring systemic aspects of racial discrimination into full view.

There is nothing inevitable about a White person's complying with a system that continues to stratify advantages on the basis of racially unjust practices and policies. It is also not inevitable that a person of color will elect to fight such a system, though people of color have often spearheaded social justice movements that have collectively benefited the U.S. social fabric. Lipsitz (2006) reminds us that

> we do not choose our color, but we do choose our commitments. We do not choose our parents, but we do choose our politics. Yet we do not make these decisions in a vacuum; they occur within a social structure that gives value to Whiteness and offers rewards for racism. (p. viii)

Those who find justice irresistible and White supremacy intolerable always have the option to collectively organize to transform their society toward what W. E. B. Du Bois (1998) called "abolition democracy" (see also Taylor in this volume). Abolition democracy does not mean opening up U.S. structures of opportunity so people of color can simply compete better while leaving a radically hierarchal system intact. Instead, abolition democracy refers to democratization processes that undo the inherent hierarchies in wealth and opportunity this country has built along racial lines. It means changing the very structure of our socioeconomic system so its conditions are increasingly conducive to communal health, safety, healing, and ethical integrity.

Paula Ioanide is an associate professor of comparative race and ethnicity studies in the Center for the Study of Culture, Race, and Ethnicity at Ithaca College in New York. Her research focuses on the injustices of mass incarceration, militarized policing, immigrant exclusion and detention, neoliberal impoverishment, and warfare. Dr. Ioanide teaches courses about prisons, race and sexual politics, and social movements.

SUGGESTED ADDITIONAL RESOURCES

Bonilla-Silva, E. (2006). *Racism without racists: Color-blind racism and the persistence of racial inequality in the United States* (2nd ed.). Lanham, MD: Rowman & Littlefield.

Dyson, M. E. (2005). *Is Bill Cosby right? Or has the Black middle class lost its mind?* New York, NY: Basic Civitas Books.

Jhally, S., & Lewis, J. (2005). White responses: The emergence of "enlightened" racism. In D. M. Hunt (Ed.), *Channeling Blackness: Studies on television and race in America* (pp. 74–88). New York, NY: Oxford University Press.

Lee, R. G. (1999). *Orientals: Asian Americans in popular culture.* Philadelphia, PA: Temple University Press.

Lipsitz, G. (2006). *The possessive investment in Whiteness: How White people profit from identity politics* (Rev. and expanded ed.). Philadelphia, PA: Temple University Press.

Roediger, D. (2005). *Working toward Whiteness: How America's immigrants became White; The strange journey from Ellis Island to the suburbs.* New York, NY: Basic Books.

Shapiro, T. (2004). *The hidden cost of being African American: How wealth perpetuates inequality.* New York, NY: Oxford University Press.

Williams, L. F. (2003). *The constraint of race: Legacies of White skin privilege in America.* University Park: Pennsylvania State University Press.

QUESTIONS FOR FURTHER DISCUSSION

1. What role does the author believe hard work and personal responsibility play in life chances and outcomes? How invested are you in the idea of hard work and personal responsibility? How do these ideas affect the ways you act in school, at work, or in your family?

2. Does the evidence of racial discrimination and the root causes of wealth inequalities change your perception of "hard work" and the ways it is rewarded, or do you find yourself dismissing this evidence, needing further evidence? If so, why?

3. What are the differences between White students' investments in meritocracy and the investments of students of color? Based on this essay, what do you believe accounts for these differences?

REACHING BEYOND THE COLOR LINE

1. Take some time to discuss family expectations and self-imposed expectations regarding achievement, success, educational attainment, and hopes for future employment. Are these expectations expressed differently by students of color and by White students? Why do you think these differences exist?

2. In a multiracial group, discuss whether White students and families acknowledge privileges and advantages on the basis of race. Also discuss the extent to which families and students of color expect to be faced with the obstacles and challenges of racial discrimination in college and beyond. What is the root of these different narratives and explanations?

REFERENCES

Bertrand, M., & Mullainathan, S. (2004). Are Emily and Greg more employable than Lakisha and Jamal? A field experiment on labor market discrimination. *American Economic Review, 94,* 991–1013.

Bonilla-Silva, E. (2001). *White supremacy and racism in the post–civil rights era.* Boulder, CO: L. Rienner.

Bonilla-Silva, E. (2006). *Racism without racists: Color-blind racism and the persistence of racial inequality in the United States* (2nd ed.). Lanham, MD: Rowman & Littlefield.

Brown, M. K. (1988). *Remaking the welfare state: Retrenchment and social policy in America and Europe.* Philadelphia, PA: Temple University Press.

Dovidio, J., & Gaertner, S. (2000). Aversive racism and selection decisions: 1989 and 1999. *Psychological Science, 11,* 315–319.

Du Bois, W. E. B. (1998). *Black reconstruction in America, 1860–1880*. New York, NY: Free Press.

Dyson, M. E. (2005). *Is Bill Cosby right? Or has the Black middle class lost its mind?* New York, NY: Basic Civitas Books.

Feagin, J. R. (2000). *Racist America: Roots, current realities, and future reparations*. New York, NY: Routledge.

Gray, H. (1995). *Watching race: Television and the struggle for "Blackness."* Minneapolis: University of Minnesota Press.

Hunt, D. M. (Ed.). (2005). *Channeling Blackness: Studies on television and race in America*. New York, NY: Oxford University Press.

Ioanide, P. (2015). *The emotional politics of racism: How feelings trump facts in an era of colorblindness*. Palo Alto, CA: Stanford University Press.

Jhally, S., & Lewis, J. (2005). White responses: The emergence of "enlightened" racism. In D. M. Hunt (Ed.), *Channeling Blackness: Studies on television and race in America* (pp. 74–88). New York, NY: Oxford University Press.

Kim, C. J. (2000). *Bitter fruit: The politics of Black-Korean conflict in New York City*. New Haven, CT: Yale University Press.

Lacy, K. R. (2007). *Blue-chip Black: Race, class, and status in the new Black middle class*. Berkeley, CA: University of California Press.

Lee, R. G. (1999). *Orientals: Asian Americans in popular culture*. Philadelphia, PA: Temple University Press.

Lipsitz, G. (2001). *American studies in a moment of danger*. Minneapolis: University of Minnesota Press.

Lipsitz, G. (2006). *The possessive investment in Whiteness: How White people profit from identity politics* (Rev. and expanded ed.). Philadelphia, PA: Temple University Press.

Lipsitz, G. (2011). *How racism takes place*. Philadelphia, PA: Temple University Press.

Massey, D. S. (2007). *Categorically unequal: The American stratification system*. New York, NY: Russell Sage Foundation.

Massey, D. S., & Denton, N. (1993). *American apartheid: Segregation and the making of the underclass*. Cambridge, MA: Harvard University Press.

McKnight, U. (2014). The fantastic Olivia Pope: The construction of a Black feminist subject. *Souls: A Critical Journal of Black Politics, 16*(3–4), 183–197.

McRady, R. (2015, July 1). Donald Trump gets his own piñata in Mexico after racist comments. *US Weekly*. Retrieved from http://www.usmagazine.com/celebrity-news/news/donald-trump-pinata-mexico-racist-comments-pics-201517

Oliver, M., & Shapiro, T. M. (1995). *Black wealth/White wealth: A new perspective on racial inequality*. New York, NY: Routledge.

Reeves, J. (1994). *Cracked coverage: Television news, the anti-cocaine crusade, and the Reagan legacy*. Durham, NC: Duke University Press.

Rivera, A., Cotto-Escalera, B., Desai, A., Huezo, J., & Muhammad, D. (2008). *State of the dream 2008: Foreclosed*. Boston, MA: United for a Fair Economy. Retrieved from http://www.faireconomy.org/dream

Roediger, D. (2005). *Working toward Whiteness: How America's immigrants became White; The strange journey from Ellis Island to the suburbs*. New York, NY: Basic Books.

Rogin, M. P. (1991). *Fathers and children: Andrew Jackson and the subjugation of the American Indian*. New Brunswick, NJ: Transaction.

Rooth, D. (2010). Automatic associations and discrimination in hiring: Real world evidence. *Labour Economics, 17*, 523–534.

Rugh, J., & Massey, D. (2010). Racial segregation and the American foreclosure crisis. *American Sociological Review, 75*(5), 629–651.

Shapiro, T. (2004). *The hidden cost of being African American: How wealth perpetuates inequality.* New York, NY: Oxford University Press.

Springer, K. (2005). *Living for the revolution: Black feminist organizations, 1968–1980.* Durham, NC: Duke University Press.

Warner, K. J. (2015). The racial logic of *Grey's Anatomy*: Shonda Rhimes and her "post-civil rights, post-feminist" series. *Television & New Media, 16*(7), 631–647.

Williams, L. F. (2003). *The constraint of race: Legacies of White skin privilege in America.* University Park: Pennsylvania State University Press.

Ziegert, J., & Hanges, P. (2005). Employment discrimination: The role of implicit attitudes, motivation, and a climate for racial bias. *Journal of Applied Psychology, 90,* 553–562.

"If Only He Hadn't Worn the Hoodie . . . "

Race, Selective Perception, and Stereotype Maintenance

Rashawn Ray

University of Maryland

On February 26, 2012, in Sanford, Florida, during halftime of the television airing of the National Basketball Association's all-star game, 17-year-old Trayvon Martin (who was on the phone with a friend) was walking back from a local convenience store to his father's girlfriend's apartment with a bag of Skittles and a bottled iced tea. There was a light rain in the air and Martin had on a jacket with a hood, commonly called a "hoodie." George Zimmerman, who was the self-appointed neighborhood watchperson, thought Martin looked suspicious and began following him. Zimmerman then called 911 and reported that a police officer should be sent to the apartment complex because he saw a suspicious man walking around. When he reached a 911 operator, Zimmerman was specifically instructed to stop following Martin and wait for police to arrive. Minutes later, an altercation ensued between Zimmerman and Martin, leaving Zimmerman bruised and bloodied and Martin shot dead.

Zimmerman, who had a gun permit and had been previously arrested for assaulting a police officer, was arrested for questioning and later released under Florida's Stand Your Ground law. The law allows individuals to defend themselves by using deadly force if they feel their lives are in danger (Cheng & Hoekstra, 2012). Zimmerman claimed he felt his life was in danger and he had no choice but to shoot Martin. Martin's body was initially labeled a "John Doe" and not identified until the following day, when his father filed a police report. Calling this incident a national tragedy, President Barack Obama stated, "When I think about this boy, I think about my own kids. . . . If I had a son, he'd look like Trayvon."

Following the shooting death of Martin, a national uproar with racial undertones ensued that ultimately led to Zimmerman's being charged with second-degree murder. Zimmerman, who is perceived by some as phenotypically White, has a White father and Peruvian mother and identifies as Hispanic. Martin's mother and father are Black. Some in the media claimed that if Martin had not been wearing the hoodie, he would not have looked suspicious. Among them was Fox News host Geraldo Rivera (2012), who stated:

> I am urging the parents of Black and Latino youngsters particularly not to let their children go out wearing hoodies. I think the hoodie is as much responsible for Trayvon Martin's death as George Zimmerman was. . . . Trayvon Martin, God bless him, an innocent kid, a wonderful kid, a box of Skittles in his hands. He didn't deserve to die. But I bet you money, if he didn't have that hoodie on, that nutty neighborhood watch guy wouldn't have responded in that violent and aggressive way.

Rivera's statement proved controversial in its effort to remove blame from Zimmerman and transfer it to Martin for choosing to wear a hoodie in drizzly weather.

As the case reached a level of national conversation, many argued that Zimmerman had targeted Martin solely because he was Black. This argument asserts that there is something unique about being a Black male that results in their being perceived as suspicious, untrustworthy, and dangerous. Zimmerman refuted the claim that he had targeted Martin because of his race but did report that a series of break-ins had occurred in the complex and the perpetrators were believed to be Black males. As Benjamin Crump, lawyer for the Martin family, claimed in a September 29, 2012, interview with the *Orlando Sentinel*, race was "the elephant in the room" (Boedeker, 2012). A *Washington Post*–ABC poll taken in April of 2012 ultimately supported his statement, as it found that 80% of Blacks believed that Martin's killing was unjustified, compared with about 40% of Whites (Cohen, 2013). Concepts from the social psychology of race can help us better understand these kinds of significant racial differences in perceptions and attitudes.

The Social Psychology of Racial Stereotyping

Prominent sociologists Michael Omi and Howard Winant (1994) note that we often use physical attributes, including articles of clothing such as a hoodie, as mental shorthand for racial scripts. However, it is important to note that our racial cues are not limited to a hoodie or other articles of clothing. We use physical attributes such as skin tone, facial features, and hairstyles to make racial assumptions. Accordingly, the social psychological processes described here relate to other forms of stereotypical thinking, such as assuming that anyone who looks Mexican is "illegal," that all Asians are good at math, that most Arab Americans are terrorists, or that all Native Americans are alcoholics. These are *stereotypes*, or oversimplified sets of beliefs about members of a particular group.

Negative attributes are often placed on Black men who wear hoodies, because of their race and gender. In this context, the negative attribute in question is anticipated crime, which leads to these group members being perceived as suspicious and dangerous to others. These attributes are not simply impromptu. Rather, they stem from intergroup attitudes that are formulated via broader sociohistorical contexts. In other words, the hoodie combined with Blackness and maleness triggers certain stereotypes based on preexisting "knowledge" about group members. Knowledge, in this context, does not refer to education, facts, or reality. Instead, it refers to the conventional wisdom that individuals use to make sense of personal interactions (see also Harris and McClure in this volume). I address this point more directly below.

Thomas F. Pettigrew's (1979) research suggests that individuals who perceive Black men with hoodies as a threat commit the *ultimate attribution error*. Ultimate attribution error asserts that undesirable characteristics exhibited by out-group members (i.e., Blacks and other people of color) are more likely to be perceived by those in the in-group (i.e., Whites) as innate and a part of one's personality. In other words, negative behaviors are perceived to be biological or rooted in the culture of the group (see Buffington; Patel, Meanwell, & McClure; and Zhou in this volume for further discussion). On the other hand, positive characteristics (e.g., being a law-abiding citizen) are attributed to factors external to the individual, such as education. In addition, out-group members who are perceived positively are viewed as exceptions to the norm of "bad" behavior from their group.

Pettigrew (1998) highlights that attribution error occurs because of limited information about a particular group. As more information is obtained about out-group members, individuals are less likely to exhibit prejudiced attitudes, because they come to view out-group members as more heterogeneous instead of more homogenous. As I will show later, the type and quality of information is key for changing prejudiced attitudes. Stereotypes about certain groups largely stem from public discourses. Public discourses can be conceptualized as mainstream narratives that become assumed facts about a particular group or how society operates. For example, during his 1976 presidential campaign, Ronald Reagan stated the following allegations about a woman on Chicago's South Side:

> She has eighty names, thirty addresses, twelve Social Security cards and is collecting veteran's benefits on four non-existing deceased husbands. And she is collecting Social Security on her cards. She's got Medicaid, getting food stamps, and she is collecting welfare under each of her names. Her tax-free cash income is over $150,000.

Although the woman associated with this infamous overexaggeration was convicted of less than $10,000 in fraud, this statement led to Black women's being stereotypically associated with the infamous "welfare queen," much more than White women (Gilliam, 1999). Discourses transform language beyond the boundaries of words and sentences to make a real impact on policies and also on how individuals interact with each other.

Media play a dominant role in formulating stereotypical discourses, in part because there is a limited amount of interaction across racial and social class divides. U.S. neighborhoods and schools are just as segregated today as they were in the 1950s (Dixon, 2006). Therefore, social media, television, movies, and music are dominant forms of public discourse that often portray people of color in stereotypical ways. For example, some movies suggest that the sexual predator a woman should be afraid of is a male stranger walking down a dark street, possibly wearing a hoodie, when research shows that women are more likely to be raped by someone they know (Armstrong, Hamilton, & Sweeney, 2006). News media, in particular, can play a critical role in this perception. Communication scholars Robert Entman and Andrew Rojecki (2000) found that Black suspects and criminals are more likely to be featured on the news than White suspects and criminals. With limited interpersonal interactions across racial divides, these images lead to stereotypical thinking that all Black men are dangerous and threatening. For example, though more Whites commit violent crime, respondents estimated that Blacks commit 40% more violent crime than they actually do (see Entman & Rojecki, 2000).

Hogg (2000) highlights the importance of *subjective uncertainty,* which asserts that when there is minimal understanding about how someone should be categorized (e.g., individuals with hoodies or Black males), individuals express a "state of subjective uncertainty" where they infer stereotypes and, in turn, exhibit some form of discrimination against the person in question (Hogg, 2003). When individuals are categorized largely by group membership (under conditions of subjective uncertainty that are largely due to limited interpersonal interaction), others evaluate and interact with them based on the scripts perceived to be associated with that group.

Similarly, individuals engage in *selective perception* by seeing only the types of behaviors that confirm their stereotypes and not those that refute them. In other words, even when individuals encounter a man in a hoodie or a Black man walking down the street and nothing happens (or they have a positive interaction), the combination of selective perception (i.e., seeing only what we want to see), subjective uncertainty (i.e., categorizing people inaccurately due to limited information about other groups), and ultimate attribution error (i.e., believing that undesirable characteristics are an innate part of out-group members, such as "all Black men with hoodies are dangerous") means that positive interactions mostly lead to in-group members' ignoring that example or perceiving it as an "exception to the rule." This process is an attempt to avoid cognitive dissonance and maintain stereotypical thinking.

Aligning one's beliefs to avoid disharmony or inconsistency (Festinger & Kelly, 1951), or cognitive dissonance, can lead to irrational behavior. For example, individuals who hold prejudiced attitudes about Blacks being criminal may have a normal, satisfying, and uneventful social interaction with a Black man in a parking lot but not include this positive interaction in their knowledge base to evaluate the next Black man they encounter in a parking lot. Instead, their resolution of the cognitive dissonance will tell them to be afraid just as before. Another example is a person who interacts with a Latino person and finds out that person was born in the United States. Instead of thinking that the next Latino encountered could also be a U.S. citizen, the person continues to assume Latinos are "illegal" immigrants, failing to take the previous experience into account.

Taken together, all these processes are connected to arguments about why Martin was followed by Zimmerman. Below, I dissect the arguments about whether Martin was followed because of a hoodie or his Blackness.

If He Hadn't Been Wearing a Hoodie . . .

To investigate the role the hoodie actually played in the Zimmerman case, we must examine a series of underlying assumptions and claims. The first claim is that a hoodie, and thus anyone wearing one, is suspicious. In other words, there is something about a hoodie that makes someone threatening. One approach to test this claim is to look at other social contexts where individuals wear hoodies to see if those individuals are perceived as suspicious or innocuous. One person who wears a hoodie frequently is Facebook founder and CEO Mark Zuckerberg. Zuckerberg wears hoodies during casual encounters and even professional business meetings; however, he is not perceived as suspicious. Instead, as Benjamin Nugent's May 2012 CNN article states, "The hooded sweatshirt [is] a symbol of his independent-mindedness, his youth, his authenticity, his loyalty to the culture of Silicon Valley." At worst, Zuckerberg is regarded as "immature," but definitely not suspicious.

Another example is New England Patriots head football coach Bill Belichick, who can be seen in a hoodie on the sideline of every game. He is never regarded as suspicious or less than a coach because he wears a hoodie. In fact, he is evaluated only by his team's success and not his clothing or the behavior of fans who may have on a hoodie and engage in violent or illegal behavior.

In addition to celebrities such as Zuckerberg and Belichick, college students often walk around campuses with hoodies representing their university or favorite team. When it rains, snows, or is simply cold, individuals in public spaces wear hoodies to protect themselves from the weather. These groups of people are generally not regarded as suspicious or threatening, unless there is another attribution placed on them that implies danger. We also know that Zimmerman, who was 28 at the time of the incident, thought Martin was older. As he said during his arraignment: "I did not know how old he was. I thought he was a little bit younger than I am, and I did not know if he was armed or not." Zimmerman's own statement implies that there was at least one additional attribute, besides the hoodie, that led to Martin's looking suspicious. Even Rivera's statement about hoodies draws on another attribute: race. He specifically references "Black and Latino youngsters" and excludes White and Asian youth from his statement about who should and should not wear hoodies. While Asians have their own stereotypes, such as being unassimilable, passive, and unable to lead, Blacks and Latinos are more likely to be stereotyped as criminal than Whites and Asians.

Collectively, the hoodie argument simply does not hold. Individuals wear hoodies regularly and are not followed or perceived as threatening. Instead, placing the focus on the hoodie not only moves the blame to Martin for wearing the hoodie, but it also allows individuals to avoid admitting their own racial prejudices.

Maybe It's Because Trayvon Was Black. . . .

Given the previous discussion of racial stereotyping, a second claim that must be examined in looking at the role of the hoodie in the Zimmerman case is that perhaps the hoodie wasn't really the major factor in Martin's being followed; perhaps Zimmerman targeted Martin because he was a Black male. Given that Blackness is at the center of this argument, one appropriate way to explore this perspective is to determine whether Black men not wearing hoodies are considered suspicious. Below, I provide examples where Black men are perceived as suspicious in various social contexts.

New York City (NYC) is notorious for its stop-and-frisk program (Center for Constitutional Rights, 2012; see also Doude in this volume). In 2011, NYC police officers performed nearly 700,000 stops. Blacks represented more than one half of these stops, compared with one third for Latinos and less than one tenth for Whites. More than one half of all stops involved frisks. Of the nearly 140,000 times force was used, Blacks represented roughly 55%. Obviously, we would assume from these statistics that the overwhelming majority of individuals who were stopped, frisked, and exposed to force were engaged in criminal activity. However, this is not the case. Only 2% of the nearly 700,000 stops resulted in the discovery of contraband (Center for Constitutional Rights, 2012). This means that more than 9 out of 10 Black and Latino men stopped by the police were innocent and engaging in no wrongdoing.

Despite the very low number of individuals who are actually engaging in illegal activity during a stop-and-frisk, and the fact that in 2013 the stop-and-frisk program was ruled unconstitutional under the Fourth Amendment and the Equal Protection Clause of the Fourteenth Amendment, the perception is that Black and Latino men are dangerous. In fact, former NYC mayor Bloomberg in a WOR-NY radio interview on June 28, 2013, stated, "I think, we disproportionately stop Whites too much and minorities too little." As a result, some Black and Latino men have a difficult time engaging in activities that every U.S. citizen is granted the right to do—walking down a street, breathing fresh air, or catching a cab. In the early 2000s, former mayor Rudolph Giuliani of New York introduced a sting operation to confirm the discrimination Black men encounter when trying to catch a cab. Giuliani set up undercover operations to fine taxi drivers for passing Black riders. One may initially think, *Why is this an issue?* Well, cab drivers and Black men have a long, contentious history where cab drivers have been suspected of skipping Black men as potential passengers because they fear they will be robbed. The sting operation implemented by Mayor Giuliani stemmed from a lawsuit by actor Danny Glover (most known for his role in the *Lethal Weapon* films) after he claimed that at least five taxicabs passed him, his daughter, and her roommate. Then the taxicab that did stop refused to allow Glover to sit in the front seat.

Some may still say if Glover and other Black men had on hoodies, it is understandable that the cabs passed them up; they looked suspicious. But what if the Black men were wearing business suits? On the 2008 presidential campaign trail,

President Barack Obama was continuously asked if he identified as Black. His response was a colloquial, "The last time I tried to catch a cab in New York City. . . . " His statement implies that he has difficulty catching a cab because he is a Black male. President Obama is not the only notable Black man to make this claim. Dr. Cornel West, formerly of Harvard and Princeton Universities, wrote in the preface of his acclaimed book *Race Matters* (1994) that when he was going to finish his deal with the publisher, he was late for the meeting because he could not catch a cab while wearing a suit. He mentions that 10 cabs passed by him. Below, I detail a few more examples of Black men in different social contexts who did not have on a hoodie but were considered suspicious, threatening, or dangerous.

In 2009, Dr. Henry Louis Gates, Harvard University W. E. B. Du Bois Professor of African American Studies, returned from a research trip in China to find his front door jammed shut. He and the driver of his car proceeded to force it open. A neighbor called 911 to report a breaking and entering in progress. After police arrived, events ensued that ultimately led to the arrest of Gates in his own home. This incident culminated in what is now known as the "Beer Summit," where President Obama invited Dr. Gates and the arresting officer to the White House for a beer to discuss the incident and race relations more broadly.

In another example, in Murfreesboro, Tennessee, in 2012, police officers were in pursuit of what was described as a young Asian male. Officers came upon Joseph Sushak, a Nigerian-born, 58-year-old graduate student, who was about to change the oil of his truck in his driveway. Upon seeing Sushak, the police officers started asking him a series of questions about his whereabouts. Within a matter of seconds, Sushak was beaten, handcuffed, and facedown on his own property. He suffered injuries and had to go to the emergency room. Sushak claimed he had been a victim of police brutality, but the case against the police was ultimately dismissed.

Finally, on December 31, 2008, at 2 a.m., Robbie Tolan, a Black minor league baseball player, was driving home with his cousin from a night on the town celebrating the New Year. As they pulled into Tolan's driveway, a police car pulled up, asked the men what they were doing there, and made them lie facedown on the ground. At this time, Tolan's parents came out of the house, trying to determine what was going on, and began explaining to the officers that their son lived there. One of the officers aggressively approached Tolan's mother. Tolan proceeded to get off the ground to protect his mother and was shot. Tolan's house was in a predominately White, upper-middle-class neighborhood in Houston, Texas. The officer who shot Tolan was brought up on charges but ultimately acquitted.

Given these examples, it becomes clear that it was not the hoodie that made Trayvon Martin look suspicious. Similar to these men, it was his Blackness and maleness. As mentioned above, Black men are not the only ones who are victimized by stereotypical thinking. There are numerous incidents of Latino men being arrested, held in prison for months, or even killed for suspicion of "illegal" immigration (Golash-Boza, 2012). Furthermore, Asian Americans are victimized for posing an economic threat to some American workers. The tragic death of Chinese American Vincent Chin in 1982 highlights the most visceral type of stereotypical thinking. Chin was viciously murdered by

White autoworkers in Detroit, Michigan, after being misidentified as Japanese at a time when Detroit was laying off its auto workers as a result of Japanese automakers' dominance in the market.

Since 9/11, Arab Americans have been profiled and discriminated against in airports and other public venues. In 2013, Atif Irfan and his wife, Sobia Ijaz, along with six relatives, were trying to decide where to sit on an Air Tran flight from Washington, DC, to Orlando, Florida, for a religious conference. Another passenger overheard this conversation, and before the family knew it, they were being escorted off the plane by security. Air Tran then removed all passengers to sweep the plane and rescreen all baggage. After hours of questioning, during which the children were unable to eat, the FBI released the family, stating it was simply a misunderstanding. Air Tran refused to rebook the family on another flight (instead giving them a refund), thus forcing the family to book a flight on another airline for double the cost. All the family members except one were born in the United States, and Irfan is a lawyer from Detroit, Michigan. In these ways, many people of color find themselves the targets of racism and discrimination due to a variety of different attribution errors. As the Irfan and Ijaz case shows, there are many costs to individuals who are victimized this way, including financial ones. Yet the costs may be far greater than this. In the next section, I use the role of criminalization in Black men's lives as a case study for how people of color are affected by these patterns.

Black Male Criminalization and Its Effects

Criminalization is the inability to separate a person from criminality based on the person's group identity. In this case, Black male criminalization is the inability to separate Black males from criminals (Muhammad, 2010). These stereotypes are evident when women clutch their purses when they see a Black man, or when Whites scurry to the other side of the street or out of the purview of an approaching Black man (Feagin, 1991). Criminalization is something that is all too common for Blacks. Black mothers responded to Martin's death with statements such as, "That could have been my son." Black men commonly made statements such as, "That could have been me." Following the Zimmerman verdict, in fact, President Obama stated, "Trayvon Martin could have been me, 35 years ago." In the case of Martin, his life ended tragically before his 18th birthday. However, even Black men who are not killed still suffer psychologically, educationally, economically, and physically from criminalization.

Psychologically, Black men have to deal with the effects of criminality and come to terms with the fact that socioeconomic status (as highlighted by the experiences of President Obama and Drs. West and Gates) does not protect them from being perceived as suspicious and threatening. As a result, they have worse mental health outcomes than do similar Whites (Jackson, 1997). Educationally, Ferguson (2000) shows that Black boys in grade school are perceived by teachers as troublemakers, reprimanded more severely for the same behaviors as White students, and more likely to be suspended, thus impacting their educational outcomes. Economically, Pager (2007) shows a staggering trend. Comparing the job prospects of Black and White men (some with a criminal record and some without), she found that not only were White men without a criminal record hired more often than Black men, but White men *with* a criminal record were hired more often than Black men *without* a criminal record. Physically, Black men's health suffers. My research on the effects of the racial composition of neighborhoods on physical activity finds that Black men in predominately White neighborhoods are significantly less likely to be physically active than Black men in predominately Black neighborhoods. Black men in predominantly White neighborhoods are less likely to exercise because of their experiences with and fear of criminalization and the psychological processes with which they must engage when they leave their homes.

The question remains: What do we do about racial stereotyping? Research suggests that there are various ways to decrease stereotyping. Most of these ways involve some social interaction with people of different racial groups. For instance, *contact theory* asserts that when a sizable proportion of a minority group is present, there are increased opportunities for contact between majority and minority group members. Gordon W. Allport (1954) argues that the effects of contact on prejudice depend on the *quality of contact*: (1) Is the contact voluntary or involuntary? (2) When majority and minority group members come in contact, are they of equal status? (3) Does the contact occur in competitive or collaborative environments? Contact that is voluntary, equal, and collaborative should lead to less prejudicial attitudes. Along these lines, the *type of contact* also matters. Friendships among majority and minority group members decrease prejudice, while acquaintanceships moderately decrease prejudice. Repetitive, positive, informal contact (i.e., in a dorm or classroom of students) at times decreases prejudice, while the more rigorous conditions required for equal-status contact are usually effective but rarely met.

Significantly, Jackman and Crane (1986) find that the effect of contact on reducing prejudicial attitudes varies by socioeconomic status. Specifically, Whites' negative attitudes toward Blacks become relatively obsolete when they have higher-status Black friends. Unfortunately, as Jackman and Crane note, rarely do higher-status Blacks interact with lower-status Whites in meaningful ways. Additionally, having Black friends and acquaintances hardly affects Whites' attitudes about race-based policies. As a result, the researchers conclude that the *diversity of contacts* is more important than the intimacy of contacts, because diversity contributes to changing stereotypes of the entire group compared with just changing stereotypes of a particular individual. This distinction is important considering that Lawrence Bobo's (2012) research finds that Whites' positive interactions with Latinos and Asians alter their perceptions of the entire race, while positive interactions with Blacks alter their perceptions of only that individual (see Bobo & Hutchings, 1996). This finding further illuminates ultimate attribution error.

In sum, this research suggests that the quality, type, and diversity of contact across racial divides can facilitate meaningful conversations and knowledge exchanges about race relations. If contact facilitates more accurate knowledge about the lives of people of color, it will ultimately help Whites reassess their own group, form effective social networks with people of color, and perhaps decrease their prejudices and tendency to stereotype.

Conclusion

Ultimately, George Zimmerman was found not guilty of second-degree murder and manslaughter, despite evidence that suggested he followed (or "profiled") Trayvon Martin. In the court of public opinion, however, Americans are still clearly conflicted. Zimmerman received an outpouring of financial support from individuals wanting to help with his defense. On the other hand, hundreds of thousands have marched or shown solidarity with the Martin family by wearing hoodies on specified days. The hoodie has been transformed into a symbol of protest even though it had very little to do with why Trayvon Martin was killed. The hoodie was simply a scapegoat for those trying to reconcile (their racial) cognitive dissonance. Most Black men, similar to most White men, are not criminals or untrustworthy; they are law-abiding citizens. Individuals must recognize significant and meaningful nonverbal cues and symbols, instead of ubiquitously categorizing Black men as dangerous. These changes in individuals' perceptions could contribute to reducing the criminalization of Black men and the stereotyping of all marginalized groups.

Rashawn Ray is an associate professor of sociology at the University of Maryland, College Park. He received a PhD in sociology from Indiana University in 2010. Ray's research interests are social psychology, race and ethnic relations, and race–class–gender. His work addresses three key areas: the determinants and consequences of social class identification, men's treatment of women, and how racial stratification structures social life. Ray is the editor of *Race and Ethnic Relations in the 21st Century: History, Theory, Institutions, and Policy*. His work has appeared in *Ethnic and Racial Studies, American Behavioral Scientist, Journal of Contemporary Ethnography, Journal of Higher Education,* and *Journal of African American Studies*.

SUGGESTED ADDITIONAL RESOURCES

Berger, R., & Free, M. (2016, September 28). Policing, profiling, and crime. *WISE GUYS: An Online Magazine*. Retrieved from https://wiseguys2015.com/2016/09/28/policing-profiling-and-crime/

Correll, J., Park, B., Judd, C. M., & Wittenbrink, B. (2002). The police officer's dilemma: Using ethnicity to disambiguate potentially threatening individuals. *Journal of Personality and Social Psychology, 83*(6), 1314–1329.

Katznelson, I. (2006). *When affirmative action was White: An untold history of racial inequality in twentieth-century America.* New York, NY: W. W. Norton.

Mazzocco, P. J., Brock, T. C., Brock, G. J., Olson, K. R., & Banaji, M. R. (2006). The cost of being Black: White Americans' perceptions and the question of reparations. *Du Bois Review, 3,* 261–297.

Ray, R. (Ed.). (2010). *Race and ethnic relations in the 21st century: History, theory, institutions, and policy.* San Diego, CA: Cognella.

Websites

Center for Constitutional Rights: http://stopandfrisk.org

Harvard's Implicit Association Tests: https://implicit.harvard.edu/implicit/demo

Audio/Visual

Peters, W. (Writer & Director), & Cobb, C. (Writer). (1985, March 26). A class divided [Television series episode]. In J. McFadden (Producer), *Frontline.* Boston, MA: Public Broadcasting System.

QUESTIONS FOR FURTHER DISCUSSION

1. What, if any, conversations have you had about the Zimmerman case? Have they included people whose background and racial group membership are different from your own? Why or why not?

2. Based on this review, do you think conflict is inevitable when distinct groups interact? Why or why not?

3. Given the author's discussion of contact, how do we encourage meaningful, equitable social interactions across racial groups?

4. How do we encourage candid conversations across racial groups about how race/ethnicity, racism, discrimination, and White privilege impact people's lives?

REACHING BEYOND THE COLOR LINE

1. Consider examples from your own life and how stereotypical thinking might have shaped your perceptions. What could you do differently in the future, when faced with similar situations?

2. Watch these two scenes from the movie *Crash* and reflect on the social interactions.

   a. "Hey, Osama, I'm an American citizen!"

      i. What is the conflict and source of conflict?

      ii. Does the gun store owner engage in subjective uncertainty?

b. "I want the locks changed in the morning. Your amigo is going to sell our keys to one of his homies!"

    i. Is the wife prejudiced, or are her attitudes justified? Is she trying to be color blind?

    ii. Did the wife perform ultimate attribution error?

    iii. What did this robbery do to the stereotypical thinking about Blacks/ Latinos/Asians/Whites?

REFERENCES

Allport, G. W. (1954). *The nature of prejudice.* New York, NY: Doubleday.

Armstrong, E., Hamilton, L., & Sweeney, B. (2006). Sexual assault on campus: A multilevel explanation of party rape. *Social Problems, 53,* 483–499.

Bobo, L. D. (2012). The *real* record on racial attitudes. In P. V. Marsden (Ed.), *Social trends in American life: Findings from the General Social Survey since 1972* (pp. 38–83). Princeton, NJ: University Press.

Bobo, L. D., & Hutchings, V. L. (1996). Perceptions of racial group competition: Extending Blumer's theory of group position to a multiracial social context. *American Sociological Review, 61,* 951–972.

Boedeker, H. (2012, September 29). Trayvon Martin: Attorney calls race 'the elephant in the room.' *Orlando Sentinel.* Retrieved from http://articles.orlandosentinel.com/2012-09-29/ entertainment/os-trayvon-martin-benjamin-crump-20120929_1_trayvon-martin-martin-george-zimmerman-benjamin-crump

Center for Constitutional Rights. (2012). *2011 data reveals record number of stop-and-frisks with no change in racial disparities* [Press release]. Retrieved from https://ccrjustice.org/ home/press-center/press-releases/2011-data-reveals-record-number-stop-and-frisks-no-change-racial

Cheng, C., & Hoekstra, M. (2012). *Does strengthening self-defense law deter crime or escalate violence? Evidence from castle doctrine* (NBER Working Paper No. 18134). Retrieved from http://www.nber.org/papers/w18134

Cohen, J. (2013, July 22). Zimmerman verdict: 86 percent of African Americans disapprove. *Washington Post.* Retrieved from https://www.washingtonpost.com/news/post-politics/ wp/2013/07/22/zimmerman-verdict-86-percent-of-african-americans-disapprove/?utm_ term=.a6ba07459cc7

Dixon, J. C. (2006). The ties that bind and those that don't: Toward reconciling group threat and contact theories of prejudice. *Social Forces, 84,* 2179–2204.

Entman, R. M., & Rojecki, A. (2000). *The Black image in the White mind: Media and race in America.* Chicago, IL: University of Chicago Press.

Feagin, J. R. (1991). The continuing significance of race: Antiblack discrimination in public places. *American Sociological Review, 56*(1), 101–116.

Ferguson, A. A. (2000). *Black boys: Public schools in the making of Black masculinity.* Ann Arbor: University of Michigan Press.

Festinger, L., & Kelly, H. H. (1951). *Changing attitudes through social contact.* Ann Arbor, MI: Lithoprinted.

Gilliam, F. D., Jr. (1999). The "welfare queen experiment": How viewers react to images of African-American mothers on welfare. *Nieman Reports, 53*(2). Cambridge, MA: Nieman Foundation for Journalism at Harvard University.

Golash-Boza, T. M. (2012). *Immigration nation.* St. Paul, MN: Paradigm.

Hogg, M. A. (2000). Subjective uncertainty reduction through self-categorization: A motivational theory of social identity processes. *European Review of Social Psychology, 11,* 223–255.

Hogg, M. A. (2003). Intergroup relations. In J. DeLamater (Ed.), *Handbook of social psychology* (pp. 479–502). New York, NY: Kluwer Academic/Plenum.

Jackman, M. R., & Crane, M. (1986). "Some of my best friends are Black . . . ": Interracial friendship and Whites' racial attitudes. *Public Opinion Quarterly, 50,* 459–486.

Jackson, P. B. (1997). Role occupancy and minority mental health. *Journal of Health and Social Behavior, 38,* 237–255.

Muhammad, K. G. (2010). *The condemnation of Blackness: Ideas about race and crime in the making of modern urban America.* Cambridge, MA: Harvard University Press.

Nugent, B. (2012, May 17). Zuckerberg's hoodie is savvy, not snotty. *CNN.* Retrieved from http://www.cnn.com/2012/05/16/opinion/nugent-facebook-zuckerberg/

Omi, M., & Winant, H. (1994). *Racial formation in the United States: From the 1960s to the 1990s* (2nd ed.). New York, NY: Routledge.

Pager, D. (2007). *Market: Race, crime, and finding work in an era of mass incarceration.* Chicago, IL: University of Chicago Press.

Pettigrew, T. F. (1979). The ultimate attribution error: Extending Allport's cognitive analysis of prejudice. *Personality and Social Psychology Bulletin, 5,* 461–476.

Pettigrew, T. F. (1998). Intergroup contact theory. *Annual Review of Psychology, 49,* 65–85.

Rivera, G. (2012, March 23). I am urging the parents of Black and Latino youngsters . . . *Fox & Friends.* New York, NY: Fox Broadcasting.

West, C. (1994). *Race matters.* New York, NY: Vintage Books.

"My Family Had to Learn English When They Came, so Why Is Everything in Spanish for Them?"

Race and the Spanish Language in the United States

Jennifer Domino Rudolph

Connecticut College

We are lo que hablamos.

—Bill Santiago (2008)

I n a café on Michigan Avenue, Chicago's high-end shopping district, I, a White U.S. American woman, sat speaking Spanish with a group of Latin Americans and Spaniards when a White, U.S. American man approached our group and, looking directly at me, stated: "You should not speak that language. It devalues you." By contrast, in a recent conversation with the son of a Mexican immigrant woman whose English language skills are limited, he said that his mother has described her inability to speak English at a high level of proficiency as being similar to "wearing handcuffs." These two experiences highlight ideologies and conventional wisdom around bilingualism, especially Spanish bilingualism, in the United States. Language ability and use are inextricably linked to race and racialization in the United States; simply put, we understand and construct language based on the perceived race and social position of the person speaking. Spanish has a very particular history connected with colonization and racial formation in the United States. Despite the fact that Spanish has been present in what is now the United States for hundreds of years, deep resentment of

Spanish and Spanish speakers as parasitic and unwilling to truly "be American" persists to this day in everyday conversations, media, politics, and the legal system. At the core of this belief is a strong anti-immigrant presumption that immigrants from Latin America, especially Mexico, refuse to assimilate and follow previous immigrant groups assumed to have joined the U.S. "melting pot" by learning English immediately and not relying on services in their native language.

A further examination of the two above experiences reveals some of the tensions around Spanish and misconceptions of Spanish speakers. First, in that café on Michigan Avenue, though addressing our entire group, why did that man look specifically at a fellow White U.S. American when speaking? Perhaps it was because he felt he needed to warn me not to relinquish any of the privileges of Whiteness I might lose by speaking Spanish? Also likely is that he felt my Latin American and Spanish friends were a lost cause and would resist learning English because he did not recognize them as "American," though one member of the group was of Mexican descent but born in the United States and others were naturalized citizens or residents of the United States. With regard to the Mexican immigrant woman who likened not speaking English at a near native level to "wearing handcuffs," she understands the importance of English in the United States but lacks the resources (e.g., access to adult education programs) to learn it. Moreover, at best she knows that she lacks access to the resources that come with English proficiency, and at worst she understands the connection between the criminalization of (undocumented) immigration and the Spanish language. Thus, this essay examines and debunks the following misconceptions about Latina/os[1] and Spanish: (1) that Latina/os refuse to learn English, (2) that Latina/os are perpetually foreign and wish to live apart from dominant/White society by speaking Spanish, and (3) that Spanish is a foreign language, spoken only by poor, undocumented immigrants.

Spanish Speakers in the United States

The greatest myth attributed to Spanish in the United States is that it is spoken only by a population of undocumented and poor immigrants from Latin America. This population is much more complicated in terms of its ethnoracial and class profile. In fact, the United States is home to the world's fifth-largest Spanish-speaking population (Escobar & Potowski, 2015, p. 1). According to a study by the Pew Hispanic Center, not all Spanish speakers identify as Hispanic/Latina/o. According to this 2011 study, of the roughly 52 million persons of Hispanic descent over age 5 in the United States, 34.8 million (74%) speak Spanish. These data do not include about 11 million undocumented Latin American residents in the United States, nor do they include 2.8 million non-Latina/os who report speaking Spanish at home, according to U.S. Census and Pew Hispanic Center data (González-Barrera & López, 2013). Thus, all told, 48.6 million Spanish speakers reside in the United States (Escobar & Potowski, 2015, p. 1). This population includes all economic classes, from economic migrants in search of manual labor positions to what have been termed "brain drain" migrants, or educated middle- and upper-class Latin Americans and Spaniards who come to study in the United States and decide to stay or who come as trained professionals to practice in the more economically favorable U.S. labor market. The 2.8 million non-Latina/os who report speaking Spanish in their homes may speak Spanish as a result of privilege tied to education, employment, or travel/residence in a Spanish-speaking country. In the remainder of this essay, I will explore the complexities of this population with regard to the three aforementioned myths to complicate and challenge the conventional wisdom around Spanish and its speakers.

How Spanish Is Understood by Whites

As noted in my experience at the café and with the Mexican immigrant who likened limited English skills to wearing handcuffs, we see manifestations of these three beliefs about Latina/os and Spanish in daily conversations, but also in media and politics. Examinations of a few recent media and political events reveal the saturation of Latina/o Spanish speakers as "un-American" and threats to the United States. In fact, media workers themselves receive criticism for speaking in Spanish in public speeches or for pronouncing words in Spanish using the sound system of Spanish on English-language newscasts. During her May 22, 2016, commencement address to the School of Communications at California State University, Fullerton, Univisión anchor María Elena Salinas delivered part of her speech in Spanish. Though Salinas spoke in Spanish for only 25 seconds, some in the crowd answered her with boos and screams of "Get off the stage!" and she was called "trash." This also ignited a heated Internet dialogue in support of and opposing Salinas (Svrluga, 2016). Similarly, Phoenix NBC News 12 anchor Vanessa Ruíz came under fire with some viewers in September 2015 for pronouncing Spanish words as they would be pronounced in the Spanish language—particularly, rolling her *Rs*—during her English-language newscasts (Santos & Hauser, 2015).

This policing of Spanish and English also extends to public figures and politicians, especially with regard to U.S. nationalism. The most salient example of this is Donald Trump's presidential campaign rhetoric, which included lambasting Mexicans and Spanish speakers as a means to marshal support from White U.S. Americans through White supremacist nationalist discourse. During the second Republican presidential debate, Trump stated, "We have a country, where, to assimilate, you have to speak English. This is a country where we speak English, not Spanish" (Marks, 2015). Again, Internet chatter emerged on both sides of this issue. Such remarks helped cement his position as the Republican candidate in the 2016 presidential election. The media and Internet debates mentioned here illustrate the strong connections among language, race, and nationalism. It is important to note that when applied to White U.S. American Spanish-language learners, these dynamics do not apply—a topic to which I will return in a later section. Nevertheless, these same debates occlude the reality of Latina/os' use, attitudes toward, and perceptions of Spanish and English.

What Latina/os Really Think About Spanish and English

Actual data on language use and attitudes/beliefs among Latina/os shows a similar pattern of linguistic assimilation as that found in other ethnic and racial groups, including European immigrants—namely, near to total loss of the family's heritage language by the third generation. In April 2012, the Pew Hispanic Center published an extensive study titled "When Labels Don't Fit: Hispanics and Their Views of Identity" (Taylor, López, Martínez, & Velasco, 2012). The survey and report include a section dedicated to language use and attitudes among Latina/os that challenges the beliefs that Latina/os don't want to learn English and wish to live apart from dominant White society by speaking Spanish. When asked if they felt that adult Hispanic immigrants to the United States need to learn English to succeed, 87% responded yes while 11% responded no (Taylor et al., 2012, p. 23). When asked if it is important for future generations of Hispanics living in the United States to speak Spanish, 95% of informants said it was very or somewhat important, whereas 4% of respondents said it was "not too important" or "not important at all" (p. 23). Strong evidence of the shift from Spanish to English dominance emerges in the generational data on speaking and reading ability in English. While 61% of all Hispanics surveyed said that they speak English well and 60% reported reading English well, 96% of third-generation and higher informants said that they speak English well and 94% said that they read English well (p. 24). An even more striking generational pattern emerges with regard to reporting of primary language spoken. Of all Hispanics surveyed, 38% reported being Spanish-dominant, 38% reported being bilingual, and 24% reported being English-dominant. By the third generation and higher, 1% reported being Spanish-dominant, 29% reported being bilingual, and 69% reported being English-dominant (p. 26). Given that these data parallel generational linguistic assimilation of European immigrant groups, where do dominant beliefs about Latina/os' linguistic use and attitudes come from?

Where Dominant Beliefs Come From

There's a joke in Spanish that roughly translates as follows:

What do you call a person who speaks three languages? Trilingual.

What do you call a person who speaks two languages? Bilingual.

What do you call a person who speaks one language? American.

This joke appears in a textbook that I use in my Spanish grammar and composition courses for both second-language learners and students who grew up in bilingual homes. The different reactions of the two groups illustrate how distinct experiences of race and language connect to nationalism and U.S. American identities. My bilingual students, for the most part, laugh and are glad that this joke calls out how English-language-centric the United States is. My second-language learners are often very uneasy with that same joke, either remaining silent or questioning the truth behind it. I definitely sense that these students feel threatened by this portrayal of U.S. Americans as provincial and even xenophobic. They want to believe that their country is egalitarian and welcoming to all and are disturbed by suggestions to the contrary. Also, most students have not given any real thought to the role of language in their lives, especially its connection to privilege and race, so they read this joke as an attack on "America."

There are many reasons for this, but first and foremost, the English language—specifically White middle-class English—has been inscribed into the history of the United States as a core component of U.S. nationalism, metaphorically used as the binding agent that supposedly brings U.S. Americans together. Media, politics, and the education system are three chief places where this ideology is indoctrinated as linked to U.S. citizenship and nationalism. As Rosina Lippi-Green (2011) argues in *English With an Accent*, in media and popular culture, accented English is used to inscribe characteristics such as trustworthiness and diligence or the lack thereof in different ethnic groups, and accented English is marked as "un-American." Additionally, political debates and the structure of the educational system since the formation of the United States have focused on the need to control language use and impart English-language instruction. In the 19th century, when significant German communities populated Pennsylvania and Wisconsin, congressmen worried about the spread of German language and culture and its potential to displace English and Anglo-American culture in these states.

This belief that the English language ties together U.S. Americans also racializes and marks the Spanish language and its speakers as "un-American." Two concepts—"Spanish as a racialized marker" and "mock Spanish"—help us systematically understand the relationship between race and language in the United States. In the documentary *Latinos Beyond Reel* (Picker & Sun, 2013), Isabel Molina-Guzmán has identified Spanish as a "racialized marker." This means that White Americans use the Spanish language and accents associated with Spanish as a means to identify who is Latina/o and thus who should not gain full access to the rights and privileges of U.S. citizenship. It is not enough to simply place Spanish and its speakers outside of U.S. national belonging. White American linguistic culture also subordinates Spanish and its speakers to English and its speakers via what has been called "mock Spanish." Jane Hill (2007) defines this as both the pronunciation of words in Spanish with a heavy U.S. English accent and the invention of grammatically incorrect "Spanish" words by putting vowels on the ends of English words—for example, "no problemo" and "el cheapo." According to Hill, mock Spanish functions both to deem Spanish as an illegitimate form of communication in the United States and to present a nonserious, joking persona among White Americans.

Joe Feagin's (2010), Eduardo Bonilla-Silva's (2003), and Leo Chávez's (2008) work on race, Whiteness, Latina/o identity, and structural inequality is useful in unpacking and understanding the meanings and ideologies behind mock Spanish and Spanish as a racialized marker. In *The White Racial Frame*, Feagin (2010) documents the ways

Whiteness is embedded in the historical, political, economic, and linguistic formation of the United States and has ensured the perpetuation of structural inequality in terms of poverty, residential segregation, and educational outcomes, among others. Similarly, in *Racism Without Racists,* Bonilla-Silva (2003) argues that White Americans currently articulate racism and White supremacy in ways that attempt to distance these acts from the individuals committing them and instead attribute them to perceived cultural deficiencies of people of color or structures they believe to be out of their control. Finally, Chávez (2008) uses the phrase "the Latino threat" to express the widely held perception that Latina/os (1) want to reclaim the U.S. Southwest as part of Mexico, (2) refuse to learn English so as not to assimilate into the United States, and (3) intend to gain power through massive reproduction and population growth. Taken together, Feagin, Bonilla-Silva, and Chávez's work unpacks the histories and structures that have led to the conventional wisdom about Spanish and its speakers in the United States. These same historical measures continue today in the form of legislation at the federal and state levels, as well as formation of national groups promoting the connection between the English language and U.S. nationalism—namely, English-only and U.S. English (Golash-Boza, 2015).

The Legal Education and Labor Market Consequences of the Racialization of Spanish

Both the English-only and U.S. English movements seek to grant English a status that would cement its connection to U.S. American national identity. The English-only movement traces back to 1981 and the proposal of an amendment to the Constitution. If it had passed, this amendment would have severely limited the use of languages other than English in state and federal government business and function. Though this law did not pass, its proponents continue to propose it annually (Escobar & Potowski, 2015, p. 190). In the 1990s, English-only proponents changed strategies, renaming their movement Official English, thus focusing solely on a federal law, as opposed to a law at both the state and federal levels (Crawford, 2008). Though this law did not pass, at this writing, 31 states have passed laws that declare English to be the official state language (www.us-english.org). Several states have also passed legislation targeting bilingual education and use of languages other than English. Under the guise of language, this legislation promotes a White supremacist agenda, tied primarily to hostility toward immigrants. Examples of this type of legislation include (1) Proposition 227, passed in California in 1998, which prohibited educational instruction in languages other than English; (2) Propositions 106 and 203, passed in Arizona in 2000, which named English as the official state language and eliminated bilingual education programs in state schools; and (3) English for the Children of Massachusetts, also known as Question 2, proposed in 2002 to limit bilingual education (Escobar & Potowski, 2015, pp. 192–193). Though these legislative measures do not specifically target Spanish and Latin American immigrants, sociolinguists such as Alim, Rickford, and Ball (2016), Escobar and Potowski (2015), and Zentella (2008) argue that the true motive behind them is a concern over the increasing presence of people of Latin American descent in the United States.

In contrast, the U.S. English movement, founded in 1983, represents a somewhat less stringent but more strategic attitude toward language use and legislation. Its proponents do not advocate for English as the official language of the United States but do argue that learning English is essential for immigrants' success, thus also supporting the study of other languages in the United States for purposes of business and diplomacy (Escobar & Potowski, 2015, p. 190). This signals an important distinction related to race and language. The idea of studying language for reasons of business and diplomacy separates languages from the cultures and power differentials that surround them as it emphasizes U.S. political and economic dominance. One significant outcome is that it makes a difference who speaks and studies a language, particularly Spanish in the United States.

Frances R. Aparicio's (1998) work on differential bilingualism is useful here. In her interviews with university students who were White American second-language learners or bilingual/heritage learners, Aparicio found that while studying Spanish is considered an important way to enhance career goals and marketability in the labor force for many White American language learners, the conventional wisdom with regard to bilingual or heritage Spanish speakers is that their home Spanish is deficient in some way and is not valued in the job market. This is the case even though bilingual/heritage speakers often speak a more fluent, if sometimes informal, variety of Spanish. Aparicio also found that most White American students had never considered the imperative around English in the United States in their own family's loss of language shortly after immigrating to the United States, further exemplifying the "unmarked" linguistic and cultural dominance of English, similar to the unmarked nature of Whiteness. A most striking example of differential bilingualism emerged when Hillary Rodham Clinton announced her vice presidential running mate, Tim Kaine, on July 22, 2016. A media firestorm ensued when CNN pundit and Donald Trump supporter Scottie Nell Hughes criticized Kaine for a bilingual speech he gave in Miami. Shortly before the start of the Democratic National Convention, she told Wolf Blitzer,

> What Mr. Trump did, he spoke in a language all Americans can understand—that language is English. I didn't have to get a translator for anything that was going on at the [Republican National Convention]. I'm hoping I'm not going to have to start brushing up on my *Dora the Explorer* to understand some of the speeches given this week. (Golgowski, 2016)

Hughes was branded a hypocrite when it was revealed that her own children study Spanish. Despite her efforts to apologize, pointing out that her own children study Spanish and that she is not against Spanish, the damage was done.

In addition to the legislation and uneven valorization of Spanish speakers mentioned above, anti-Spanish policies have emerged in the public education system, as well. One of the chief mandates of schooling is to educate children in citizenship and nationalism. It is in schools where children often first encounter information about their country's history, laws, and social structure—all told from the point of view of those in power. In the United States, part of this indoctrination comes in the form of language and English instruction. For example, in 1906, the Nationality Act required that all immigrants learn English, and subsequently, in 1919, Congress decreed that all schools, both public and private, must teach only in English—a dictate that was not reversed until the intervention of civil rights activists in the 1960s (Escobar & Potowski, 2015, p. 224). As we have already seen in states such as California, Arizona, and Massachusetts, interventions persist to limit bilingual education and ethnic studies programs, largely targeting Spanish and Latina/o Americans. Indeed, as Fuller (2013) argues, the two dominant ideologies around language instruction and education in the United States are that (1) "monolingualism is the right and natural state for a particular political region" and (2) "if individuals do speak two languages, they should keep them strictly separate" (p. 134). Despite the fact that research shows bilingual programs that maintain Spanish for bilingual children yield more successful educational outcomes (Lynch, 2013), most bilingual programs in the United States are what are called transitional bilingual programs, the goal of which is to teach children English as quickly as possible and do nothing to retain the home language. The relatively few dual immersion programs in the United States—a model that seeks to balance native speakers of English with speakers of another language, with curriculum and instruction in both languages—show successful educational outcomes for all students. These schools tend to be located in areas where Whites have committed to investing in their children's bilingualism to give them an advantage in the labor market, a further example of how resources related to bilingualism cater to White privilege (Perea, 1998; Potowski, 2007).

Cases of linguistic discrimination and uneven valorization abound in the labor market. It is important to begin by noting that 59% of Latina/os work in manual labor or nonspecialized industries, a context that in and of itself is overly susceptible to discriminatory labor practices and lack of protections such as labor unions (Brown & Patten, 2013; Motel & Patten, 2013). For example, many companies have official policies limiting or prohibiting languages other than English and frequently reprimand their employees for speaking Spanish during breaks but expect these same employees to use Spanish with Spanish-speaking clients, often advertising services in Spanish to attract business. These same bilingual employees often receive neither extra compensation nor training in interpretation (Alarcón & Heyman, 2013; Heller, 2010; MacGregor-Mendoza, 2009). Worse still, despite the fact that it is illegal to discriminate against workers who don't speak English or who speak English with an accent, as per the Civil Rights Act of 1964, in lawsuits filed by employees on the grounds of linguistic discrimination, judges often side with employers, thus perpetuating and further entrenching systemic inequality linked to language (Gutiérrez & Amengual, 2013; MacGregor-Mendoza, 2009).

The history, legislation, and labor issues described here work together to sustain a White supremacist social system. The evidence amply demonstrates that linguistic discrimination is an outcome of the history and development of racialized social systems from the formation of the United States to the present moment. Simply put, speaking a language other than English or speaking English with an accent renders Latina/os as un-American in the eyes of dominant society. Faced with this knowledge, how then do Latina/os respond and how does this shape their identity formation within the United States?

Spanish Language and Latina/o Identity

Comedian Bill Santiago has built a career on interrogating the complexities of Latina/os' language identity. His stand-up routines and his book, *Pardon My Spanglish ¡Porque Because!* (2008), use humor to unpack how code-switching between English and Spanish, also referred to as "Spanglish," impacts the daily lives of Latina/os. In a skit about baseball, Santiago jokes that it is sometimes unclear if a baseball broadcast is in English or in Spanish when announcers say things like, "Alex Rodríguez says *adios* to *la pelota*." Santiago's humor and performance style capture the tensions that Latina/os often negotiate with regard to the connection between language and identity. In addition to the social and institutional structures of dominant society mentioned above, within Latina/o communities, there is much debate as to whether an individual is "Latina/o enough" if he or she doesn't speak Spanish, or mixes Spanish and English.

To understand these dynamics, Gloria Anzaldúa's (1987) construct of "linguistic terrorism" is extremely useful. *Linguistic terrorism* refers to the ways individuals and groups use language to maintain social hierarchies based on race, class, and gender. The following two examples illustrate how linguistic terrorism operates in Latina/os' lived experiences. First, when I was in high school, I talked to friends at a women's Catholic high school in a south suburb of Chicago who explained to me that there were two tables in the cafeteria where the school's significant Mexican American population sat—one for girls who spoke Spanish and one for girls who did not. The Latina authenticity of those who did not speak Spanish was constantly called into question, and the two groups rarely mixed. In a different instance and many years later, a Mexican American student at the college where I currently teach tearfully recalled her study-abroad experience in Mexico, where one of her Mexican instructors graded her work more harshly in terms of Spanish grammar and style than the work of the White American students in the class, explaining to my student that her Spanish should be better if she wants to claim Mexican identity.

It is very true that "we are *lo que hablamos* [we are what we speak]." Others inside and outside of our families and communities use the language we speak and the way we speak it to categorize us and to grant or deny us access to belonging, social institutions, and capital. Spanish in the United States is a perfect example of how race and class status shape our identities, as the White middle- and upper-class Americans who study it in large numbers to gain an edge in the labor market are valorized while Latina/os who grow up speaking Spanish in their homes are considered foreign and "un-American." As with other parts of our master identities, such as race, class, and gender, language works to uphold our place in the social hierarchies we inhabit.

The question that follows is, what can we do about it? Ana Celia Zentella's concept of "anthropolitical linguistics" serves as an entry into language and social justice. According to Zentella, it "involves not only unmasking the hidden, it is also doing something about it" (quoted in Figueroa, 2015). As individuals, we can consciously choose not to criticize and judge others based on how they speak and we can reject media, political, and institutional messages that claim (1) Latina/os refuse to learn English, (2) Latina/os are perpetually foreign and wish to live apart from dominant/ White society by speaking Spanish, and (3) that Spanish is a foreign language spoken only by poor, undocumented immigrants.

Jennifer Domino Rudolph is an associate professor of Hispanic Studies at Connecticut College, specializing in US Latino/a identity formation as it intersects with race, class, and gender/sexuality. She teaches courses on Latino/a identities, popular culture, and Latino Chicago. Her book, *Embodying Latino Masculinities, Producing Masculatinidad*, was published in 2012. She has also published in *Aztlán* and *CENTRO Journal*.

NOTE

1. I use the term *Latina/o* throughout. The term *Latinx* is emerging to avoid the gender binary of previous terms. While I respect the reasoning behind that term, I believe that *Latina/o* is a more familiar term to a general audience at present.

SUGGESTED ADDITIONAL RESOURCES

Aparicio, F. R. (1998). Whose Spanish, whose language, whose power? Testifying to differential bilingualism. *Indiana Journal of Hispanic Literatures, 12*, 5–25.

Chávez, L. (2008). *The Latino threat: Constructing immigrants, citizens, and the nation.* Stanford, CA: Stanford University Press.

Escobar, A. M., & Potowski, K. (2015). *El Español de los Estados Unidos.* Cambridge, UK: Cambridge University Press.

Fuller, J. (2013). *Spanish speakers in the USA.* Buffalo, NY: Multilingual Matters.

Lippi-Green, R. (2011). *English with an accent: Language, ideology and discrimination in the United States.* New York, NY: Routledge.

Santiago, B. (2008). *Pardon my Spanglish ¡porque because!* Philadelphia, PA: Quirk Books.

Websites

Pew Hispanic Center: http://www.pewhispanic.org

The Pew Hispanic Center keeps up-to-date statistical data on the Latina/o population in the United States, including language use and attitudes.

Language Policy Web Site & Emporium: http://www.languagepolicy.net

This website provides information on language policy and planning in the United States.

Institute for Language and Education Policy: http://elladvocates.org

> The Institute for Language and Education Policy is an advocacy group for the preservation of heritage languages in the United States.

American Association of Teachers of Spanish and Portuguese: http://www.aatsp.org

> The American Association of Teachers of Spanish and Portuguese provides information and tools related to the teaching of Spanish, including data on the significance and state of Spanish in the U.S. education system.

Modern Language Association: https://www.mla.org/Resources

> The Modern Language Association provides data and information on the study of languages in the United States.

Audio/Visual

Jarmel, M., & Schneider, K. (2009). *Speaking in tongues.* United States: Patchwork Films. (Film documents the tensions and lived experiences of bilingual children among the tensions and antibilingual sentiment in the United States.)

Picker, M., & Sun, C. F. (Directors). (2013). *Latinos beyond reel: Challenging media stereotypes.* United States: Media Education Foundation. (Film documents the history of Latina/o stereotyping in the media. Significant attention is paid to representations of language.)

QUESTIONS FOR FURTHER DISCUSSION

1. Some linguists and educators have compared African American Vernacular English/Black English and the Spanish spoken by Latina/os born in the United States, in that both are considered by many native speakers to be "nonprestige dialects." As such, some argue that the main goal of educating Latina/os and Black American children should be to teach them the prestige dialects of Spanish and English. Given what you now know about language, race, and power, do you agree with this goal?

2. In some bilingual households, parents insist that their children speak only English or only Spanish, never mixing the two languages. Their concern is that their children will not learn either language completely or proficiently. How do the two goals of language in the education system identified by Fuller in the discussion of language and education apply here? To what degree do you think parents have internalized ideologies of monolingualism and linguistic purity?

3. In the Tim Kaine controversy mentioned in this essay, in addition to Scottie Nell Hughes's criticism that he spoke Spanish and not "all Americans" understand it, others have criticized the Spanish he learned in Honduras as "butchered" and accuse him of "pandering to Latina/os," arguing that he does not have the "right" to speak Spanish. What is your position with regard to this debate? Is it possible to say that people do or do not have the right to speak a language?

4. Thinking about the concept of anthropolitical linguistics, which entails not only "unmasking the hidden" but also "doing something about it," what is one thing you can do in your life to address hierarchies related to race and language?

REACHING BEYOND THE COLOR LINE

Linguistic Autobiography

The goal of this exercise is to apply what you have read to your own experiences with language and race. Please read the following prompts and answer all that apply to you:

1. If you identify as a Black American, describe your identity in terms of class and gender. Has there been a time when others criticized the way you or your friends and family speak English? If so, describe where you were, who criticized you in terms of ethnic/racial identity, and the context of the situation. Was it someone you know well? Why do you think the person did that? How did you react/feel when it happened? Do you or others in your community change the way you speak when you are outside of your home/community? If so, why do you think that is? What does how you speak have to do with your identity in terms of race, class, and gender? How much do you know about your African ancestry? Given that Black Americans are in the United States as a result of enslavement and have limited ties to their African ancestry, would you like to speak the language of your ancestors? If you don't know what language your ancestors spoke, do you wish that you did? Do you feel a connection to your ancestral language(s)? Why or why not? Do you ever feel like the language(s) or way(s) you speak cause conflict in your identity? Do you ever use language to mark your identity or to evoke pride in who you are?

2. If you identify as White, briefly describe your social class and gender identity. Can you think of times when others criticized you or members of your family/ community for the way you speak English? Why do you think the person did that? Can you think of a time when the way you spoke English helped you succeed? What does how you speak have to do with your identity in terms of race, class, and gender? Do/did you study a language other than English in grammar school, high school, or college? If so, what language(s)? Why did you pick that/those languages? Do you know much about your ancestry? If so, do you speak the language(s) of your ancestry? If so, where and how often do you speak that/those language(s)? If not, would you like to speak that/those language(s)? Do you feel a connection to your ancestral languages? Why or why not? Do you ever feel like the language(s) or way(s) you speak cause conflict in your identity? Do you ever use language to mark your identity or to evoke pride in who you are?

3. If you identify as Latina/o, describe your identity in terms of race/ethnicity, class, and gender. Do you speak Spanish or an indigenous language? Do the language(s) you speak have equal social power/privilege in the United States? Do you change

the way you speak when you are outside your home/community? How? When? Why? Do some members of your family criticize the way you speak? If so, why do you think they do that? Does anyone in your family directly or indirectly encourage you to speak a certain language or speak your language in a certain way? If so, please provide an example. Why do you think they do/did that? Do you ever feel like the language(s) or way(s) you speak cause conflict in your identity? Do you ever use language to mark your identity or to evoke pride in who you are? Do you think Latina/os should speak Spanish?

4. If you identify as mixed race, describe your identity in terms of race/ethnicity, class, and gender. What language(s) do you speak? Do the language(s) associated with your racial/ethnic identities have equal social power/privilege in the United States? Do you change the way you speak when you are with the different racial groups you identify with? How? When? Why? Do some members of your family criticize the way you speak? If so, why do you think they do that? Does anyone in your family directly or indirectly encourage you to speak a certain language or speak your language in a certain way? If so, please provide an example. Why do you think they do/did that? Do you ever feel like the language(s) or way(s) you speak cause conflict in your identity? Do you ever use language to mark your identity or to evoke pride in who you are?

5. If you identify as an immigrant, describe your identity in terms of race/ethnicity, class, and gender. What are the circumstances of your immigration? What is the political relationship between your country of origin and the United States? What language(s) do you speak? Do the language(s) associated with your racial/ethnic identities have equal social power/privilege in the United States? Do you feel safe speaking the language of your country of origin in the United States? Do you change the way you speak when you are with the different racial groups you identify with? How? When? Why? Do some members of your family criticize the way you speak? If so, why do you think they do that? Does anyone in your family directly or indirectly encourage you to speak a certain language or speak your language in a certain way? If so, please provide an example. Why do you think they do/did that? Do you ever feel like the language(s) or way(s) you speak cause conflict in your identity? Do you ever use language to mark your identity or to evoke pride in who you are?

6. If none of the above prompts accurately describes how you identify, describe how you identify in terms of race, ethnicity, class, and gender. What language(s) do you speak? Do the language(s) associated with your racial/ethnic identities have equal social power/privilege in the United States? Do you change the way you speak when you are with the different racial, ethnic, class, and gender groups? How? When? Why? Do some members of your family criticize the way you speak? If so, why do you think they do that? Does anyone in your family directly or indirectly encourage you to speak a certain language or speak your language in a certain way? If so, please provide an example. Why do you think they do/did that? Do you ever feel like the language(s) or way(s) you speak cause conflict in your identity? Do you ever use language to mark your identity or to evoke pride in who you are?

REFERENCES

Alarcón, A., & Heyman, J. M. (2013). Bilingual call centers at the US-Mexican border: Location and linguistic markers of exploitability. *Language in Society, 42*(1), 1–21.

Alim, H. S., Rickford, J. R., & Ball, A. F. (2016). *Raciolinguistics: How language shapes our ideas about race.* Cambridge, MA: Oxford University Press.

Anzaldúa, G. (1987). *Borderlands la frontera: The new mestiza.* San Francisco, CA: Aunt Lute.

Aparicio, F. R. (1998). Whose Spanish, whose language, whose power? Testifying to differential bilingualism. *Indiana Journal of Hispanic Literatures, 12,* 5–25.

Bonilla-Silva, E. (2003). *Racism without racists: Color-blind racism and the persistence of racial inequality in the United States.* Lanham, MD: Rowman & Littlefield.

Brown, A., & Patten, E. (2013, June 19). *Hispanic origin profiles.* Washington, DC: Pew Hispanic Center.

Chávez, L. (2008). *The Latino threat: Constructing immigrants, citizens, and the nation.* Stanford, CA: Stanford University Press.

Crawford, J. (2008). *Frequently asked questions about official English.* Portland, OR: Institute for Language and Education Policy. Retrieved from http://www.diversitylearningk12.com/articles/Crawford_Official_English_FAQ.pdf

Escobar, A. M., & Potowski, K. (2015). *El Español de los Estados Unidos.* Cambridge, UK: Cambridge University Press.

Feagin, J. (2010). *The White racial frame: Centuries of racial framing and counter-framing.* New York, NY: Routledge.

Figueroa, Y. (2015, January 14). Ana Celia Zentella on anthropolitical linguistics, Tato Laviera, and the power of Nuyorican poetry. CUNY Puerto Rican Studies Center. Retrieved from https://centropr.hunter.cuny.edu/centrovoices/arts-culture/ana-celia-zentella-anthropolitical-linguistics-tato-laviera-and-power

Fuller, J. (2013). *Spanish speakers in the USA.* Buffalo, NY: Multilingual Matters.

Golash-Boza, T. (2015). *Deported: Immigrant policing, disposable labor and global capitalism.* New York: New York University Press.

Golgowski, N. (2016, July 24). CNN pundit ignites fury after criticizing Tim Kaine's use of Spanish. *Huffington Post: Latino Voices.* Retrieved from http://www.huffingtonpost.com/entry/pundit-slams-tim-kaines-spanish_us_5794cacce4b01180b52f4c6a?

González-Barrera, A., & López, M. H. (2013, August 13). *Spanish is the most spoken non-English language in U.S. homes, even among non-Hispanics.* Washington, DC: Pew Hispanic Center.

Gutiérrez, M. E., & Amengual, M. (2013). *Attitudes and judgements towards accented speech: The influence of ethnicity and language experience.* Paper presented at the 24th Conference on Spanish in Contact with Other Languages, University of Texas-Pan American, McAllen, TX, March 6–9, 2013.

Heller, M. (2010). The commodification of language. *Annual Review of Anthropology, 39,* 101–114.

Hill, J. (2007). Mock Spanish: A site for the endexical reproduction of racism in American English. In J. Healey, & E. O'Brien (Eds.), *Race, ethnicity and gender* (pp. 270–285). Los Angeles, CA: Pine Forge Press.

Lippi-Green, R. (2011). *English with an accent: Language, ideology and discrimination in the United States.* New York, NY: Routledge.

Lynch, A. (2013). Observaciones sobre comunidad y (dis)continuidad en el estudio sociolingüístico del Español en Estados Unidos. In D. Dumitrescu & G. Piña-Rosales (Eds.), *¿E pluribus unum?: Enfoques multidisciplinarios* (pp. 67–83). New York, NY: ANLE.

MacGregor-Mendoza, P. (2009). *Legally bilingual: How linguistics has, hasn't and can shape the legal interpretation of bilingualism.* [manuscript, 18 pp.] New Mexico State University at Las Cruces.

Marks, M. (2015, September 18). Bonehead quote of the week: Donald Trump wants you to stop speaking Spanish. *San Antonio Dispatch.* Retrieved from http://www.sacurrent.com/Blogs/archives/2015/09/18/bonehead-quote-of-the-week-donald-trump-wants-you-to-stop-speaking-spanish

Motel, S., & Patten, E. (2013, February 15). *Statistical portrait of Hispanics in the United States, 2011.* Washington, DC: Pew Hispanic Center.

Perea, J. (1998). Death by English. In R. Delgado & J. Stephanic (Eds.), *The Latino/a condition* (pp. 583–595). New York: New York University Press.

Picker, M., & Sun, C. F. (Directors). (2013). *Latinos beyond reel: Challenging media stereotypes.* United States: Media Education Foundation.

Potowski, K. (2007). *Language and identity in a dual immersion school.* Clevedon, UK: Multilingual Matters.

Santiago, B. (2008). *Pardon my Spanglish ¡Porque because!* Philadelphia, PA: Quirk Books.

Santos, F., & Hauser, C. (2015, September 4). Arizona news anchor is drawn into debate on her accent and the use of Spanish. *New York Times.* Retrieved from http://www.nytimes.com/2015/09/04/us/latina-arizona-news-anchor-vanessa-ruiz-spanish-pronunciation.html?_r=0

Svrluga, S. (2016, May 24). 'Get off the stage!' Crowd yells at commencement speaker after she uses Spanish, mentions Trump. *Washington Post.* Retrieved from https://www.washingtonpost.com/news/grade-point/wp/2016/05/24/commencement-speaker-gets-booed-after-speaking-briefly-in-spanish-and-criticizing-trump/

Taylor, P., López, M. H., Martínez, J. H., & Velasco, G. (2012, April 4). *When labels don't fit: Hispanics and their views of identity.* Washington, DC: Pew Hispanic Center.

Zentella, A. C. (2008). Preface. In M. Niño-Murcia & J. Rothman (Eds.), *Bilingualism and linguistic identity* (pp. 3–9). Amsterdam: John Benjamins.

"Asians Are Doing Great, so That Proves Race Really Doesn't Matter Anymore"

The Model Minority Myth and the Sociological Reality

Min Zhou

University of California, Los Angeles

> *I never asked to be white. I am not literally white. That is, I do not have white skin or white ancestors. I have yellow skin and yellow ancestors, hundreds of generations of them. But like so many other Asian Americans of the second generation, I find myself now the bearer of a strange new status: white, by acclamation. Thus it is that I have been described as an "honorary white," by other whites, and as a "banana" by other Asians . . . to the extent that I have moved away from the periphery and toward the center of American life, I have become white inside.*

> —Eric Liu (1999, p. 34)

The "model minority" image of Asian Americans appeared in the mid-1960s, at the peak of the civil rights movement and the ethnic consciousness movements, but *before* the rising waves of immigration and refugee influx from Asia. Two articles in 1966—"Success Story, Japanese-American Style" by William Petersen in the *New York Times Magazine,* and "Success of One Minority Group in U.S." by the *US News and World Report* staff—marked a significant departure from how Asian immigrants and their descendants had been traditionally depicted in the media. Both articles extolled Japanese and Chinese Americans for their persistence in

Adapted and updated from Zhou, M. Are Asians becoming White? (2004). *Contexts, 3*(1), 29–37. Used with the permission of the American Sociological Association.

overcoming extreme hardships and discrimination to achieve success, unmatched even by U.S.-born Whites, with "their own almost totally unaided effort" and "no help from anyone else."

Since then, Asian Americans have been celebrated as a "model minority" for their "superior" cultures that encourage a strong work ethic, a respect for elders, and a reverence for family. More important, they have been celebrated for their high rates of educational, occupational, and income attainment and low high school dropout rates, as well as low rates of teen pregnancy and incarceration. They are declared to be on their way to becoming "White." These expectations are a burden and the predictions surely premature given the "foreigner" image Americans still have of Asians. In classrooms, as well as in society at large, the apparent success story of Asian Americans is often used to justify that race is no longer a determining factor in American life. This essay speaks to the actual existing realities of the diverse range of communities encompassed by the panethnic "Asian American" label and also considers the power and role of the model minority myth in the overall discourse of race and equality.

Issues of Terminology and Classification

Asian Americans have occupied an in-between status in America's racial hierarchy. They are often distinguished from other underrepresented racial groups, such as Blacks and Latinos, and are classified with Whites for equal opportunity programs. Although Asian Americans as a group have attained levels of education, occupation, and income equated with or even surpassing those of Whites,[1] and although many have moved near to or even married Whites, they still remain culturally distinct and suspect in society.

At issue is how to define Asian American and White. The term *Asian American* was coined by the late historian and activist Yuji Ichioka during the ethnic consciousness movements of the late 1960s. To adopt this identity is to reject the Western-imposed label of *Oriental*. Today, "Asian American" is an umbrella category that includes both U.S. citizens and immigrants whose ancestors came from Asia east of Pakistan. Although widely used in public discussions, most Asian-origin Americans are ambivalent about this label, reflecting the difficulty of being American and still keeping some ethnic identity: Is one, for example, Asian American or Japanese American?

Similarly, "White" is an arbitrary label having more to do with privilege than biology. In the United States, groups initially considered non-White such as Irish and Jews have attained White membership by acquiring status and wealth. It is hardly surprising, then, that people of color would aspire to become "White" as a mark of and a tool for material success. However, becoming White can mean distancing oneself from people of color or selling out one's ethnicity. Panethnic identities—Asian American, African American, Latino—are one way the politically vocal in any group try to stem defections; these collective identities may restrain aspirations for individual mobility.

Varieties of Asian Americans

Privately, few Americans of Asian ancestry would spontaneously identify themselves as Asian, and fewer still as Asian American. They instead link their identities to specific countries of origin, such as Chinese, Japanese, Korean, Filipino, Indian, Vietnamese, and so on. In a study of Vietnamese youth in San Diego, for example, I found that 53% identified themselves as Vietnamese, 32% as Vietnamese American, and only 14% as Asian American, and that nearly 60% of these youth considered their chosen identity as very important to them (Zhou, 2001).

Some Americans of Asian origin have family histories in the United States longer than many Americans of eastern or southern European origins. However, they became numerous only after 1970, rising from 1.4 million to 17.3 million (including multiracials), or nearly 5.6% of the total U.S. population, in 2010. Before 1970, the Asian-origin population was largely made up of Japanese, Chinese, and Filipinos. Now Americans of Chinese, Filipino, and Indian origin are the largest subgroups (at 3.8 million, 3.4 million, and 3.2 million, respectively), followed by Vietnamese (1.7 million), Koreans (1.7 million), and Japanese (1.3 million). Some 20 other national-origin groups such as Cambodians, Pakistanis, Lao, Thai, Indonesians, and Bangladeshis were officially counted in government statistics only after 1980, and together amounted to more than 2.2 million in 2010.

The exponential growth of the Asian-origin population in the span of 40 years is primarily due to the accelerated immigration subsequent to the Hart–Celler Act of 1965, which ended the national origins quota system, and the historic resettlement of Southeast Asian refugees after the Vietnam War. Currently, about 60% of the Asian-origin population are foreign-born (the first generation), another 30% are U.S. born of foreign-born parentage (the second generation), and just about 10% are born to U.S.-born parents (the third generation and beyond). The only exception to this pattern is Japanese Americans who have a fourth generation and many U.S.-born elderly.

Unlike earlier immigrants from Asia or Europe at the turn of the 20th century, who were mostly low-skilled laborers looking for work, new immigrants from Asia have more varied backgrounds and come for many reasons, such as to join their families, to invest their money in the U.S. economy, to fulfill the demand for highly skilled labor, or to escape war, political or religious persecution, and economic hardship. For example, Chinese, Taiwanese, Indian, and Filipino Americans tend to be overrepresented among scientists, engineers, physicians, and other skilled professionals, but less educated, low-skilled workers are more common among Vietnamese, Cambodian, Laotian, and Hmong Americans, most of whom entered the United States as refugees. While middle-class immigrants are able to start their American lives with high-paying professional careers and comfortable suburban living, low-skilled immigrants and refugees often have to endure low-paying menial jobs and live in inner-city ghettos. Asian Americans tend to settle in large metropolitan areas and concentrate in the West. California is home to about a third of all Asian Americans. But recently, other states such as Texas, Minnesota, and Wisconsin, which historically received few Asian immigrants, have become destinations for Asian American settlement. Traditional ethnic enclaves such as Chinatown, Little Tokyo, Manilatown, Koreatown, Little Phnom Penh, and Thaitown persist or have emerged in gateway cities, helping new arrivals cope with cultural and language difficulties in their initial stage of resettlement. However, affluent and highly skilled immigrants tend to bypass inner-city enclaves and settle in suburbs upon arrival, belying the stereotype of the "unacculturated" immigrant. Today, more than half of the Asian-origin population is spreading out in suburbs surrounding traditional gateway cities, as well as in new urban centers of Asian settlement across the country.

Differences in national origins, timing of immigration, affluence, and settlement patterns profoundly affect the formation of a panethnic identity. Recent arrivals are less likely than those born or raised in the United States to identify as Asian American. They are also so busy settling in that they have little time to think about being Asian or Asian American, or for that matter, White. Their diverse origins evoke drastic differences in languages and dialects, religions, foodways, and customs. Many nationalities also brought to America their histories of conflict (such as the Japanese colonization of Korea and Taiwan, Japanese attacks on China, and the Chinese invasion of Vietnam). Immigrants who are predominantly middle-class professionals, such as the Taiwanese and Indians, or predominantly small-business owners, such as Koreans, share few of the same concerns and priorities as those who are predominantly uneducated, low-skilled refugees, such as Cambodians and Hmong.

Finally, Asian-origin people living in San Francisco or Los Angeles, among many other Asians and self-conscious Asian Americans, develop sharper ethnic sensitivity than those living in, say, Latino-dominant Miami or White-dominant Minneapolis. A politician might get away with calling Asians "Oriental" in Miami but get into big trouble in San Francisco. All these differences can create obstacles to fostering a cohesive pan-Asian solidarity. As sociologist Yen Le Espiritu shows in her research, pan-Asianism is primarily a political ideology of U.S.-born, American-educated, and middle-class Asians rather than of Asian immigrants, who are conscious of their national origins and overburdened with their daily struggles for survival.

Underneath the Model Minority: "White" or "Other"

The model minority has become a new stereotype imposed on Americans of Asian ancestry since the 1960s. On the surface, Asian Americans seem to be on their way to becoming White, just like the offspring of earlier European immigrants. But the model minority image implicitly casts Asian Americans as different from Whites. By placing Asian Americans above Whites, the model minority image also sets them apart from other Americans, White or non-White, in the public mind.

One consequence of this new form of stereotyping is to buttress the myth that the United States is devoid of racism and accords equal opportunity to all, and that those who lag behind do so because of their own poor choices and inferior culture (see also Patel, Meanwell, & McClure in this volume). Celebrating this model minority can help thwart other racial minorities' demands for social justice by pitting groups of color against each other. It can also pit Asian Americans against Whites.

Let me point to two less obvious effects. The model minority stereotype holds Asian Americans to higher standards, distinguishing them from average Americans. "What's wrong with being a model minority?" asked a Black student in a class I taught on race. "I'd rather be in the model minority than in the downtrodden minority that nobody respects." Whether people are in a model minority or a downtrodden minority, they are judged by standards *different* from average Americans. Also, the model minority stereotype places particular expectations on members of the group so labeled, channeling them to specific avenues of success, such as science and engineering, which in turn unintentionally reinforces barriers for Asian Americans in pursuing careers outside these designated fields. Falling into this trap, a Chinese immigrant father might be upset if his son told him that he had decided to change his major from engineering to English. Disregarding his son's passion and talent for creative writing, the father would rationalize his concern by saying, "You have a 90% chance of getting a decent job with an engineering degree, but what chance would you have of earning income as a writer?" This rationale reflects more than simple parental concern over career choices typical of middle-class families; it constitutes the self-fulfilling prophecy of a stereotype.

In the end, the celebration of Asian Americans as a model minority is based on the judgment that many Asian Americans perform at levels above the American average, which sets them apart not only from other people of color but also from Whites. The truth of the matter is that the larger-than-average size of the middle and upper-middle class in some Asian-origin groups, such as the Chinese, Indians, and Koreans, paves a much smoother path for the immigrants and their offspring to regain their middle-class status in the new homeland. The financial resources that immigrants brought with them to this country also help build viable ethnic economies and institutions, such as private after-school programs, for the less fortunate group members to move ahead in society at a much faster pace than they would if they did not have access to these ethnic resources.

"It's Not So Much Being White as Being American"

In everyday reality, most Asian Americans seem to accept that "White" is mainstream, average, and "normal," and look to Whites as their frame of reference for attaining higher social positions. Similarly, researchers often use non-Hispanic Whites as the standard against which other groups are compared, even though there is great diversity among Whites, too. Like most other immigrants to the United States, many Asian immigrants tend to believe in the American dream and measure their achievements materially. As a Chinese immigrant said to me in an interview, "I hope to accomplish nothing but three things: to own a home, to be my own boss, and to send my children to the Ivy League." Those with sufficient education, job skills, and money manage to move into White middle-class suburban neighborhoods immediately upon arrival, while others work intensively to accumulate enough savings to move their families up and out of inner-city ethnic enclaves. Consequently, many children of Asian ancestry have lived their entire childhood in White communities, made friends with mostly White peers, and grown up speaking only English. In fact, Asian Americans are the most acculturated non-European group in the United States. By the second generation, most have lost fluency in their parents' native languages. Sociologist David Lopez (1996) finds that in Los Angeles, more than three quarters of second-generation Asian Americans (as opposed to about one quarter of second-generation Mexicans) speak only English at home. Asian Americans also intermarry extensively with Whites and with members of other minority groups. Sociologists Jennifer Lee and Frank Bean (2010) find that more than one quarter of married Asian Americans have a partner of a different racial background, and 87% of intermarried Asians marry Whites; they also find that 12% of all Asian Americans claim a multiracial background, compared with 2% of Whites and 4% of Blacks.

Even though U.S.-born or U.S.-raised Asian Americans are relatively acculturated and often intermarry with Whites, they may be more ambivalent about becoming White than their immigrant parents. Many only cynically agree that "White" is synonymous with "American." A Vietnamese high school student in New Orleans told me in an interview, "An American is White. You often hear people say, hey, so-and-so is dating an 'American.' You know she's dating a White boy. If he were Black, then people would say he's Black." But while they recognize Whites as a frame of reference, some reject the idea of becoming White themselves. "It's not so much being White as being American," commented a Korean American student in my class on the new second generation. This aversion to becoming White is particularly common among the well-educated and privileged second-generation college student who have taken ethnic studies courses, or among Asian American community activists. However, most of the second generation continues to strive for the privileged status associated with Whiteness, just like their parents. For example, most U.S.-born or U.S.-raised Chinese American youth end up studying engineering, medicine, and law at college, believing that these areas of study will guarantee well-paying jobs and middle-class living and enhance social contact with Whites.

Second-generation Asian Americans are also more conscious of the disadvantages associated with being non-White than their parents, who as immigrants tend to be optimistic about overcoming the disadvantages. As a Chinese American woman points out from her own experience,

> The truth is, no matter how American you think you are or try to be, if you have almond-shaped eyes, straight black hair, and a yellow complexion, you are a foreigner by default. . . . You can certainly be as good as or even better than Whites, but you will never become accepted as White.

This remark echoes a common frustration among second-generation Asian Americans who detest being treated as immigrants or foreigners. Their experience suggests that Whitening has more to do with the beliefs of White America than with the actual situation of Asian Americans. Speaking perfect English, effortlessly adopting mainstream cultural values, and even marrying members of the dominant group may help reduce this "otherness" at the individual level, but they have little effect on the group as a whole. New stereotypes can emerge and "un-Whiten" Asian Americans anytime and anywhere, no matter how "successful" and "assimilated" they have become.

The stereotype of the "honorary White" or model minority goes hand in hand with that of the "forever foreigner." In the 21st century, globalization and U.S.–Asia relations, combined with continually high rates of immigration, affect how Asian Americans are perceived in American society. Many historical stereotypes, such as the "yellow peril" and "Chinese menace," have found their way into contemporary American life, as revealed in such highly publicized incidents as the murder of Vincent Chin, a Chinese American mistaken for Japanese and beaten to death by a disgruntled Michigan auto worker in the 1980s; the trial of Wen Ho Lee, a nuclear scientist suspected of spying for the Chinese government in the mid-1990s (eventually proven innocent); and the 2001 Abercrombie & Fitch T-shirts with cartoon characters that depicted Asians in stereotypically negative ways—slanted eyes, thick glasses, and heavy Asian accents. Asian-looking Americans are still in an ambivalent position as neither White nor Black, and neither "American" nor "Asian." Ironically, the ambivalent, conditional nature of White acceptance of Asian Americans prompts them to organize panethnically to fight back—which consequently heightens their racial distinctiveness. So becoming White or not is beside the point. Asian Americans still have to constantly prove they are truly loyal Americans, especially in times when U.S.–Asia relations are in the spotlight.

Min Zhou is a professor of sociology and Asian American studies and Walter and Shirley Wang Endowed Chair in U.S.–China relations and communications at UCLA. Her main research interests include international migration, ethnic and racial relations, immigrant entrepreneurship, education and the new second generation, Asia and Asian America, and urban sociology. She is the author of *Chinatown: The Socioeconomic Potential of an Urban Enclave, Contemporary Chinese America: Immigration, Ethnicity, and Community Transformation,* and *The Accidental Sociologist in Asian American Studies,* and coauthor of *Growing Up American: How Vietnamese Children Adapt to Life in the United States* and *The Asian American Achievement Paradox.*

NOTE

1. The 2010 U.S. census shows that 49.3% of Asian Americans age 25 and over had at least a college degree (20% had an advanced graduate degree), compared with 31% of non-Hispanic Whites. Also, 48% of Asian Americans age 16 and over held a professional occupation, compared with 40% of non-Hispanic Whites. Finally, the median family income for Asian American families was $78,152, compared with $69,531 for non-Hispanic White families.

SUGGESTED ADDITIONAL RESOURCES

Lee, J., & Zhou, M. (2015). *The Asian American achievement paradox.* New York, NY: Russell Sage Foundation Press.

Lee, W. H. (2002). *My country versus me: The first-hand account by the Los Alamos scientist who was falsely accused of being a spy.* New York, NY: Hyperion Books.

Maira, S. M. (2009). *Missing: Youth, citizenship, and empire after 9/11.* Durham, NC: Duke University Press.

Park, L. (2007). A letter to my sister. In M. Zhou & J. V. Gatewood (Eds.), *Contemporary Asian America: A multidisciplinary reader* (2nd ed., pp. 425–430). New York: New York University Press.

Tuan, M. (1999). *Forever foreign or honorary White? The Asian ethnic experience today.* New Brunswick, NJ: Rutgers University Press.

Audio/Visual

Choy, C., & Tajima-Pena, R. (Directors). (1987). *Who killed Vincent Chin* [Documentary]. United States: Film News Now Foundation.

Lin, J. (Director), & Asato, J. (Producer). (2002). *Better luck tomorrow* [Motion picture]. United States: Paramount.

Nakamura, R. A. (Director). (1996). *Looking like the enemy* [Documentary]. United States: Japanese American National Museum.

Park, R. (Director). (2007). *Never perfect* [Documentary]. United States: Single Drop Films.

Sakya, S., Young, D., & Yu, K. (Directors). (2003). *Searching for Asian America* [Television documentary]. Public Broadcasting Service. United States: Center for Asian American Media (CAAM), KVIE.

Wong, C. (Director). (2010). *Whatever it takes* [Documentary]. United States: PBS Indies.

QUESTIONS FOR FURTHER DISCUSSION

1. What are the origins of the model minority stereotype? How does this compare with previous depictions of Asian Americans as "yellow peril"? What, if anything, is significant about the evolution of these stereotypes over time? What, in your opinion, has prompted these changes in the model minority myth? Is it still used with the same political agenda in mind?

2. To what extent—if any—does the model minority myth factor into contemporary debates about Asian American identity? Can you think of any ways the media continue to perpetuate this stereotype? What negative effects does it continue to perpetuate for contemporary Asian Americans?

3. What are some stereotypical representations of Asian Americans on prime-time television? What are some of the positive or neutral representations of Asian Americans that you've seen? How do the representations of Asian Americans compare to those of other racial groups? Why do you think there are discrepancies?

4. What do you think are the key mechanisms for stereotyping Asian Americans in American society? How would Asian Americans and the society as a whole act to counter the negative effects of stereotyping?

REACHING BEYOND THE COLOR LINE

1. Consider the blog post at the link provided below:

   "Asian Americans respond to Pew: We're not your model minority," by Julianne Hing, http://colorlines.com/archives/2012/06/pew_asian_american_study.html

   How does the controversy Hing describes connect to the issues raised in this essay? What does it add to your understanding of how and why the model minority myth is problematic?

2. Using the data provided by the American Community Survey FactFinder tool (http://factfinder2.census.gov/faces/nav/jsf/pages/searchresults.xhtml?refresh=t), locate the racial composition data on your home county and compare it to the United States overall. How do they compare? What does this tell you about the in-group variation hidden by the label "Asian American"? Why is this important?

REFERENCES

Lee, J., & Bean, F. (2010). *The diversity paradox: Immigration and the color line in twenty-first century America.* New York, NY: Russell Sage Foundation.

Liu, E. (1999). *The accidental Asian: Notes of a native speaker.* New York, NY: Vintage.

Lopez, D. E. (1996). Language: Diversity and assimilation. In R. Waldinger (Ed.), *Ethnic Los Angeles* (pp. 139–159). New York, NY: Russell Sage Foundation.

Petersen, W. (1966, January 9). Success story, Japanese-American style. *New York Times Magazine,* p. 180.

Success of one minority group in U.S. (1966, December 26). *US News and World Report.*

Zhou, M. (2001). Straddling different worlds: The acculturation of Vietnamese refugee children in San Diego. In R. G. Rumbaut & A. Portes (Eds.), *Ethnicities: Coming of age in immigrant America* (pp. 187–227). Berkeley, CA, & New York, NY: University of California Press & Russell Sage Foundation.

Zhou, M. (2004). Are Asian Americans becoming White? *Contexts, 3*(1), 29–37.

"But Muslims Aren't Like Us!"

Deconstructing Myths About Muslims in America

Jen'nan Ghazal Read

Duke University

Nearly two decades after the terrorist attacks on U.S. soil catapulted Muslims into the American spotlight, concerns and fears over their presence and assimilation remain at an all-time high. The comments made by President Donald Trump during his election campaign—that all Muslims should be barred from entering the United States—followed by his executive order barring entry of individuals coming from seven Muslim-majority countries deemed a threat to national security represent a more worrying trend captured in nationwide polls. In 2010, a Pew Research Poll of 1,003 Americans found that 38% of Americans have an unfavorable view of Islam, 35% believe Islam is more likely than other religions to encourage violence, and 51% objected to a mosque being built near the site of the World Trade Center. All this despite the fact that 55% admit they know very little about Islam (Pew Research Center, 2010). And yet Americans rank Muslims second only to atheists as a group that doesn't share their vision of American society (Edgell, Gerteis, & Hartmann, 2006).

These fears have had consequences. In 2001, the U.S. Department of Justice recorded a 1,600% increase in anti-Muslim hate crimes from the prior year, and these numbers rose 10% between 2005 and 2006. The Council on American-Islamic Relations (CAIR, 2013) processed 2,647 civil rights complaints in 2006, a 25% increase from the prior year and a 600% increase since 2000. The largest category involved complaints against U.S. government agencies (37%). Since these years, Islamophobia has decreased somewhat, but data still indicate that the sentiment remains. In 2012, the Federal Bureau of

Adapted and updated from Read, J. G. Muslims in America. (2008). *Contexts*, 7(4), 39–43. Used with the permission of the American Sociological Association.

Investigation's (FBI) Uniform Crime Report recorded that of the 1,166 hate crimes motivated by religious bias, nearly 13% were anti-Islamic. Moreover, a 2013 report from CAIR titled "Legislating Fear: Islamophobia and Its Impact in the United States" documents the existence of at least 37 groups whose primary purpose is to promote prejudice against or hatred of Islam and Muslims and an additional 32 groups who regularly participate in this kind of activity. The report also finds that from 2011 to 2012 there were 51 recorded anti-mosque acts, further indicating the presence of anti-Muslim sentiment.

Clearly, many Americans are convinced Muslim Americans pose some kind of threat to American society and that they aren't like other Americans.

Two widespread assumptions fuel these fears. First is the assumption that there's only one kind of Islam and one kind of Muslim, both characterized by violence and antidemocratic tendencies. Second is that being a Muslim is the most salient identity for Muslim Americans when it comes to their political attitudes and behaviors, that it trumps their social class position, national origin, racial or ethnic group membership, and gender—or worse, that it trumps their commitment to a secular democracy.

Research on Muslim Americans themselves supports neither of these assumptions. Interviews with 3,627 Muslim Americans in 2001 and 2004 by the Georgetown University Muslims in the American Public Square (MAPS) project and Pew Research Center data collected in 2007 and 2011 all show that Muslim Americans are diverse, well integrated, and largely mainstream in their attitudes, values, and behaviors. They are also well aware of and deeply affected by the degree of anti-Muslim sentiment that exists today. A majority (53%) report that it has become more difficult to be a Muslim in the United States since the September 11 terrorist attacks, and most (55%) believe that the government singles out Muslims for increased surveillance and monitoring (Pew Research Center, 2011). Arab Muslims have felt especially vulnerable, in part because the 9/11 acts were carried out by Arabs and because the subsequent U.S. war on terror focused on Iraq as much as Afghanistan. Arab Muslims have also had a long history dealing with anti-Arab stereotypes in the West, many of which continue to be used by anti-Muslim organizations to amplify their Islamophobic messages (Bail, 2012; Shaheen, 2009).

However, the data do not support the common belief that Muslims allow religion to dictate their behaviors and participation in American society. In fact, the data show that being a Muslim is less important for participating in American political and civic life than how Muslim you are, how much money you make, whether you're an African American Muslim or an Arab American Muslim, and whether you're a man or a woman.

The notion that Muslims privilege their Muslim identity over their other interests and affiliations has been projected onto the group rather than emerged from the beliefs and practices of the group itself. It's what sociologists call a *social construction*, and it's one that has implications for how these Americans are included in the national dialogue.

Some Basic Demographics

Let's start with who Muslim Americans really are. Pew Research Center (2011) demographers estimate that there are roughly 2.75 million Muslims of all ages living in the

United States. Within that number is a great deal of variation in the social and demographic characteristics of the community.

Muslim Americans are the most ethnically diverse Muslim population in the world, originating from more than 80 countries on four continents. Sixty-three percent are first-generation immigrants to the United States, with 45% having arrived since 1990 (Pew Research Center, 2011). A little over a third (37%) were born in the United States. While the population largely consists of immigrants, it is important to note that 81% of Muslim Americans are U.S. citizens, including the 70% born abroad. About 4 in 10 first-generation, Muslim American immigrants are from the Middle East or North Africa, while a little over a quarter come from South Asian nations such as Pakistan (14%), Bangladesh (5%), and India (3%). Others are from sub-Saharan Africa (11%), various countries in Europe (7%), Iran (5%), or other countries (9%). Also reflecting the diversity of the Muslim American population is that among the roughly 1 in 5 whose parents were born in the United States, 59% are Black and mainly converts. In fact, there is a great deal of racial diversity among Muslim Americans, with 30% identifying as White, 23% as Black, 21% as Asian, 6% as Latino, and 19% as mixed race or other (Pew Research Center, 2011).

Muslim Americans also tend to be highly educated, politically conscious, and fluent in English, all of which reflects the restrictive immigration policies that limit who gains admission into the United States. On average, in fact, Muslim Americans share similar socioeconomic characteristics with the general U.S. population: 26% have a bachelor's degree or higher (compared with 28% of the general population), 22% live in households with incomes of $75,000 per year or more (versus 28% in the general population), and both 59% of the Muslim American population and the general public are employed either full-time or part-time. Nevertheless, some Muslims do live in poverty and have poor English-language skills and few resources to improve their situations.

One of the most important and overlooked facts about Muslim Americans is that they are not uniformly religious and devout. Some are religiously devout, some are religiously moderate, and some are nonpracticing and secular, basically Muslim in name only, similar to a good proportion of U.S. Christians and Jews. Some attend a mosque on a weekly basis and pray every day, and others don't engage in either practice. Even among the more religiously devout, there is a sharp distinction between being a good Muslim and being an Islamic extremist (see also Pew Research Center, 2007, 2011).

None of this should be surprising. Many Muslim Americans emigrated from countries in the Middle East (now targeted in the war on terror) to practice—or not practice—their religion and politics more freely in the United States. And their religion is diverse. There is no monolithic Islam that all Muslims adhere to. Just as Christianity has many different theologies, denominations, and sects, so does Islam. And just like Christianity, these theologies, denominations, and sects are often in conflict and disagreement over how to interpret and practice the faith tradition. This diversity mimics other ethnic and immigrant groups in the United States.

Evidence from the Pew Research Center (2011) demonstrates that Muslim Americans are also more politically integrated than the common stereotypes imply.

Consider some common indicators of political involvement, such as party affiliation, voter registration, and civic engagement. Compared with the general public, Muslim Americans are just slightly less likely to be registered to vote, reflecting the immigrant composition and voter eligibility of this group (66% compared with 79% of the general population). But they are as likely to have worked with others to fix neighborhood or community problems as the general population (33% vs. 38%, respectively). And like other racial and ethnic minority groups, they are also more likely to affiliate with the Democratic Party (70% compared with 48% of the general population).

All these data demonstrate that, contrary to fears that Muslim Americans compose a monolithic minority ill-suited to participation in American democracy, Muslim Americans are actually highly diverse and already politically integrated.

Attitudes, Values, and Variation

Muslim Americans, by and large, tend to be more conservative on social issues while being more liberal on foreign policy matters. For example, Muslim Americans are somewhat more conservative on the issue of homosexuality than the general public, where 39% of U.S. Muslims believe that homosexuality should be accepted by society versus 58% of the general public (Pew Center Research, 2011). They are also slightly more conservative than the general public when it comes to abortion: 48% believe it should be illegal in all or most cases, compared with 43% of the general population (Pew Research Center, 2008). In addition, Muslim Americans are more likely than the general public to believe that the federal government should do more to protect morality in society (59% vs. 37%, respectively; Pew Research Center, 2007).

In contrast to their more conservative views on American social policy, American Muslims are more liberal than the general public with regard to foreign policy, especially pertaining to the Middle East. In 2007, for example, the general public was nearly four times as likely to say the war in Iraq was the "right decision" and twice as likely to provide the same response to the war in Afghanistan (61% compared with 35% of Muslim Americans).

In short, these numbers tell us that Muslim Americans lean to the right on social issues but to the left on foreign policy. But these generalizations don't tell the whole story; in particular, these averages don't demonstrate the diversity that exists within the Muslim population by racial and ethnic group membership, national origin, socioeconomic status, degree of religiosity, or nativity and citizenship status.

Consider, for example, Muslim Americans' levels of satisfaction and feelings of inclusion (or exclusion) in American society—major building blocks of a liberal democracy. In examining how these perceptions vary by racial and ethnic group membership within the group, we see that African American Muslims express more dissatisfaction and feel more excluded from American society than Arab or South Asian Muslims (Project MAPS, 2004). They're more likely to feel the United States is fighting a war against Islam, to believe Americans are intolerant of Islam and Muslims, and to have experienced discrimination in the past year (whether racial, religious, or both is unclear). South Asians feel the least marginalized, and Arab Muslims fall in between. These racial and ethnic differences reflect a host of factors, including the immigrant composition and higher socioeconomic status of the South Asian and Arab populations and the long-standing racialized and marginalized position of African Americans. Indeed, many (though not all) African Americans converted to Islam seeking a form of religious inclusion they felt lacking in the largely White Judeo-Christian traditions.

Incidentally, most African American Muslims adhere to mainstream Islam (Sunni or Shi'a), similar to South Asian and Arab Muslim populations. They should not be confused with the Nation of Islam, a group that became popular during the civil rights era by providing a cultural identity that separated Black Americans from mainstream Christianity. Indigenous Muslims have historically distanced themselves from the Nation of Islam to establish organizations that focus more on cultural and religious (rather than racial) oppression.

Before we can determine whether religion is the driving force behind all Muslims' political opinions and behaviors—whether Islam, as is popularly assumed, trumps Muslim Americans' other commitments and relationships to nationality, ethnicity, race, and even democracy—let's step back and place Muslim Americans in a broader historical context of religion and American politics.

When Religion Matters, and Doesn't

Muslim Americans aren't the first religious or ethnic group considered a threat to America's religious and cultural unity. At the turn of the 20th century, Jewish and Italian immigrants were vilified in the mainstream as racially inferior to other Americans. Of course today, those same fears have been projected onto Hispanic, Asian, and Middle Eastern immigrants. The Muslim American case shares with these other immigrant experiences the fact that with a religion different from the mainstream comes the fear that it will dilute, possibly even sabotage, America's thriving religious landscape.

Yes, thriving. By all accounts, the United States is considerably more religious than any of its economically developed Western counterparts. In 2013, 92% of Americans said they believed in God or a universal spirit, 78% claimed affiliation with a specific religious denomination, and 59% reported membership in a church or synagogue (Gallup, 2013). The vast majority of American adults identify themselves as Christian (41% Protestant and 24% Catholic), with Judaism claiming the second-largest group of adherents (2%), giving America a decidedly Judeo-Christian face (Gallup, 2013). There are an infinite number of denominations within these broad categories, ranging from the ultraconservative to the ultraliberal. And there is extensive diversity among individuals in their levels of religiosity within any given denomination, again ranging from those who are devout, practicing believers to those who are secular and nonpracticing.

This diversity has sparked extensive debates among academics, policymakers, and pundits over whether American politics is characterized by "culture wars," best summarized as the belief that Americans are polarized into two camps, one conservative and one liberal, on moral and ethical issues such as abortion and gay rights. Nowhere was the debate played out more vividly than the arena of religion and politics, where religiously based mobilization efforts by the Christian Right helped defeat liberal-leaning candidates and secure President Bush's reelection in 2004. In the 2008 and 2012 elections, these efforts were not as successful at the presidential level, but gains occurred on the state and local levels. So when does religion matter for politics and when doesn't it?

Here we come back to the Muslim American case. Like Muslim Americans, Americans generally have multiple, competing identities that shape their political attitudes and behaviors. For example, in 2008, 92% of Americans believed in God or a universal spirit, but only 14% cited their religious beliefs as the main influence on their political thinking (Pew Research Center, 2008). In other words, just because most Americans are religiously affiliated doesn't mean most Americans base their politics on religion. To put it somewhat differently, the same factors that influence other Americans' attitudes and behaviors influence Muslim Americans' attitudes and behaviors. Those who are more educated, have higher incomes, have higher levels of group consciousness, and feel more marginalized from mainstream society are more politically active than those without these characteristics. Similar to other Americans, these are individuals who feel they have more at stake in political outcomes and thus are more motivated to try to influence such outcomes.

Muslims, on average, look like other Americans on social and domestic policies because, on average, they share the same social standing as other Americans, and on average, they are about as religious as other Americans. Both Christian Americans and Muslim Americans are quite religious, with 69% of U.S. Muslims saying religion is very important in their lives, compared with 70% of Christians (Pew Research Center, 2011). In addition, a sizable proportion of Muslims attend services once a week or more, which is also on par with Christians (47% and 45%, respectively).

Again, these numbers tell only part of the story. What's missing is that religion's relationship to politics is multidimensional. In more complex analyses, it has become clear that the more personal dimensions of religious identity—or being a devout Muslim who prays every day—have little influence on political attitudes or behaviors, which runs counter to stereotypes that link Islamic devotion to political fanaticism.

In contrast, the more organized dimensions of Muslim identity—namely, frequent mosque attendance—provide a collective identity that stimulates political activity. This is similar to what we know about the role of the church and synagogue for U.S. Christians and Jews. Congregations provide a collective environment that heightens group consciousness and awareness of issues that need to be addressed through political mobilization. Thus, it is somewhat ironic that one of the staunchest defenders of the war on terror—the Christian Right—may be overlooking a potential ally in the culture wars—devout Muslim Americans.

An Exceptional Experience

In many ways, these findings track closely with what we know about the religion–politics connection among other U.S. ethnic and religious groups, be they Evangelical Christians or African Americans. They also suggest that the Muslim experience may be less distinct than popular beliefs imply. In fact, Muslim Americans share much in common with earlier immigrant groups who were considered inassimilable even though they held mainstream American values (think Italian, Irish, and Polish immigrants).

At the same time, though, we can't deny that the Muslim American experience, particularly since 9/11, has been "exceptional" in a country marked by a declining salience of religious boundaries and increasing acceptance of religious difference. Muslim Americans have largely been excluded from this ecumenical trend. If we're going to face our nation's challenges in a truly democratic way, we need to move past the fear that Muslim Americans are un-American so we can bring them into the national dialogue.

Jen'nan Ghazal Read is an associate professor in the Sociology Department and Global Health Institute at Duke University. She is a Carnegie scholar studying the economic, political, and cultural integration of Muslim Americans and Arab Americans.

SUGGESTED ADDITIONAL RESOURCES

Abu-Lughod, L. (2002). Ethics forum: September 11 and ethnographic responsibility. Do Muslim women really need saving? Anthropological reflections on cultural relativism and its others. *American Anthropologist, 104*(3), 783–790.

Bail, C. A. (2012). The fringe effect: Civil society organizations and the evolution of media discourse about Islam. *American Sociological Review, 77*, 855–879.

Bakalian, A., & Bozorgmehr, M. (2009). *Backlash 9/11: Middle Eastern and Muslim Americans respond.* Berkeley: University of California Press. (One of the most comprehensive assessments of the experiences of Middle Eastern Americans in the aftermath of 9/11)

Foner, N. (2005). *In a new land: A comparative view of immigration.* New York: New York University Press. (A thorough historical, comparative account of immigration in the United States)

Gerstle, G., & Mollenkopf, J. (Eds.). (2001). *E pluribus unum? Contemporary and historical perspectives on immigrant political incorporation.* New York, NY: Russell Sage Foundation. (This edited volume places contemporary immigration politics in historical and comparative context.)

Jelen, T. J. (2006). Religion and politics in the United States: Persistence, limitations, and the prophetic voice. *Social Compass, 53*, 329–343. (A useful overview of the U.S. religion–politics connection situated in comparison to other Western, industrialized nations)

Kalkan, K. O., Layman, G. C., & Uslaner, E. M. (2009). "Bands of others"? Attitudes toward Muslims in contemporary American society. *Journal of Politics, 71*(3), 1–16.

Tarlo, E. (2010). *Visibly Muslim: Fashion, politics, faith.* New York, NY: Bloomsbury Academic.

Audio/Visual

Jam Productions. (2007). *The aftermath: American-Muslims after September 11th* [Documentary]. Retrieved from https://www.youtube.com/watch?v=pKMoz--mFtw

Spurlock, M. (2005). Muslims and America [Television series episode]. *30 Days*. New York, NY: FX Network.

QUESTIONS FOR FURTHER DISCUSSION

1. What are the most common misconceptions about Muslims in America? Where do these come from? How do the data presented debunk these misconceptions?

2. What is the role of religious beliefs in shaping your own political values and ideas? What misconceptions do others have of you based on your own religious or nonreligious identity?

REACHING BEYOND THE COLOR LINE

1. Given the variation discussed in this essay, take the opportunity over the next 2 weeks to attend religious services in a tradition that is new to you. Compare your observations and interactions with your previous ideas and write a brief reflection that connects these observations to the topics discussed in this essay.

2. Access the most recent Pew report on Muslim Americans at the Pew Research Center website (http://www.pewresearch.org). What changes does it show as compared with the 2007 survey? What other questions would you like to explore from this data? Write up a brief summary of the findings that are most intriguing to you.

3. Listen to the story of Sam Slaven and Yousef Radeef in *This American Life* Episode 340, titled "The Devil in Me, Act 1: And So We Meet Again" (https://www.thisamericanlife.org/radio-archives/episode/340/the-devil-in-me). What can you learn from Sam and Yousef's story, in terms of your own college experiences and activities?

REFERENCES

Bail, C. A. (2012). The fringe effect: Civil society organizations and the evolution of media discourse about Islam. *American Sociological Review, 77*, 855–879.

Council on American-Islamic Relations. (2013). *Legislating fear: Islamophobia and its impact in the United States.* Retrieved from http://www.cair.com/islamophobia/legislating-fear-2013-report.html

Edgell, P., Gerteis, J., & Hartmann, D. (2006). Atheists as "other": Moral boundaries and cultural membership in American society. *American Sociological Review, 71*, 211–234.

Gallup. (2013). *Religion: What is your religious preference?* Retrieved from http://www.gallup.com/poll/1690/Religion.aspx

Pew Research Center. (2007). *Muslim Americans: Middle class and mostly mainstream.* Retrieved from http://pewresearch.org/files/old-assets/pdf/muslim-americans.pdf

Pew Research Center. (2008). U.S. religious landscape survey: Religious beliefs and practices. *Pew Research Center: Religion & Public Life.* Retrieved from http://www.pewforum .org/2008/06/01/u-s-religious-landscape-survey-religious-beliefs-and-practices/

Pew Research Center. (2010). Public remains conflicted over Islam. *Pew Research Center: Religion & Public Life.* Retrieved from http://www.pewforum.org/2010/08/24/public-remains-conflicted-over-islam/

Pew Research Center. (2011). Muslim Americans: No signs of growth in alienation or support for extremism. *Pew Research Center: Religion & Public Life.* Retrieved from http://www .pewforum.org/2011/08/30/muslim-americans-no-signs-of-growth-in-alienation-or-support-for-extremism/

Project MAPS. (2004). *Muslims in the American Public Square: Shifting political winds & fallout from 9/11, Afghanistan, and Iraq* [News release]. Retrieved from www.aclu.org/files/fbimappingfoia/20111110/ACLURM001733.pdf

Shaheen, J. (2009). *Reel bad Arabs: How Hollywood vilifies a people.* Northampton, MA: Olive Branch Press.

Uniform Crime Report. (2012). *2012 hate crime statistics.* Federal Bureau of Investigation. Retrieved from http://www.fbi.gov/about-us/cjis/ucr/hate-crime/2012

"But It's Honoring! It's Tradition!"

The Persistence of Racialized Indian Mascots and Confederate Culture in Sports

Dana M. Williams

California State University, Chico

According to the defenders of Native American mascots and team names, these monikers are meant to honor and show respect for Native American culture. All sorts of "positive" stereotypes are used to support this claim: Native people are said to be brave, noble, and fierce warriors. Thus, these nicknames are said to compliment Native American peoples. Additionally, advocates argue that this practice is a way to remember Native Americans' important place in U.S. history; why else use these names and this imagery if they are not part of a "noble" past? Finally, some argue that there are other racial and ethnic mascots in the sports world, such as the Notre Dame Fighting Irish and the Minnesota Vikings, so what's the big deal with using Native American mascots and team names?

Native American mascots and team names are remarkably common in the United States. While there are only a handful of White ethnic team names, hundreds of high school, college, and professional teams reference Native Americans. This phenomenon is also unique because these teams are not typically owned by Native Americans, nor are they composed of Native American athletes, nor are the teams or schools usually located in areas with large Native American populations (with only a few exceptions). The most common nicknames include Braves, Chiefs, Indians (by far the most popular), Redmen, Savages, and Warriors, as well as numerous specific nations, such as Apaches, Hurons, Mohawks, and Seminoles. For most of the history of this practice, few Americans have complained about these team names.

However, sports are not as apolitical as people typically assume. They are often a battleground for struggles over important societal symbols, including those related to race. For example, in 2005, the National Collegiate Athletic Association (NCAA) declared that 18 American universities had "hostile or abusive" Native American team names and determined that it was the NCAA's ethical obligation to prevent those teams from performing in conference playoff games. In the resulting uproar, numerous schools—including Newberry College, Arkansas State University, and Indiana University of Pennsylvania—changed their mascots and team names, others sought (and sometimes received) support from local Native American tribes, and some sued the NCAA.

The most controversial team name in professional sports is the Washington Redskins. Some Native Americans consider the term *redskin* to be as offensive as many Blacks consider the N-word and thus write the word as "r******n." Many Native Americans consider the term to be racist, and scholars have argued about whether the name also refers to the bloody red pulp from the top of someone's head, called a scalp, that White settlers collected from dead Indians for government-paid "scalp bounties" (see Goddard, 2005; Holmes, 2014). The White owner of the Washington football team (itself worth over $2 billion), Dan Snyder, has defended his team's nickname, claiming that the term is used in "honor." Despite Snyder's claim, there are regular protests at stadiums where the Washington football team plays.

The issue of offensive mascots extends to representations of Black Americans as well, particularly by symbols that reference the pro-slavery Confederacy. The White supremacist arrested for a mass killing in 2015 of nine Black churchgoers in Charleston, South Carolina, promoted not only the Apartheid-era South African and Rhodesian flags but also the Confederate flag. After the massacre, people observed that while the South Carolina state flag was lowered in respect for the victims, the Confederate flag that controversially stood in front of the statehouse was not lowered. In the weeks after the massacre, some states and other institutions recoiled from public outcry about the flag and removed it. Virginia disallowed special vehicle license plates featuring the flag, Wal-Mart and Amazon.com stopped selling the flag, and the Citadel military academy voted to remove the flag from its campus chapel. The flag in South Carolina was eventually removed, as were many other Confederate flags and Confederate symbols at many U.S. high schools, including nicknames used by sports teams.

How should we understand the controversies around such symbols? First, we must acknowledge that symbols are important to people, particularly people who believe in the values and meanings with which such symbols are imbued (Blumer, 1969). Consequently, people value symbols, often treating important symbols as sacred objects, and thus tend to avoid desecrating flags, religious symbols, and other items (Durkheim, 2001). Symbols that have existed for a long time have had the opportunity to acquire intergenerational significance for many people, where their meanings are passed down, year after year, via cultural transmission.

The support for symbols is not necessarily rational but far more emotional and psychological. Thus, patriotic individuals may get angry when their country's flag is burned by others, even if the flag was not their personal property and even though the arson was of a piece of fabric and not an actual military attack on their homeland.

People interpret those symbols based on their perspectives, social positions, group memberships, and histories. And with divisive symbols, some people find themselves on the positive, self-esteem-enhancing side of the symbol while others are positioned negatively to it and find themselves insulted. This is problematic, since symbols form the ubiquitous background to our daily lives. For symbols that generate offense for some, those people may feel as though they are under attack by others or even by the entire society around them. In a country such as the United States where there are thousands of place names that are considered offensive to people of color, such names normalize the mistreatment of those groups. Subordinate groups who lack social power usually do not have control over the dominant symbols used by the powerful dominant majority (see Dennis's discussion on cultural hegemony in this volume). The offense felt by people of color from the symbols that target them serves as the unavoidable background to their everyday existence. To understand this, let's take a closer look at Native American mascots and team names.

Native American Mascots and Team Names

The many critics—Native and non-Native alike—of Native American mascots and team names point out that the common justifications ignore many important facts and social dynamics. For example, for something to be an honor, it must be a sentiment accepted by those whom it is intended to honor, not just those who are saying the words. Thus, it is important to know whether Native people consider this practice to be honoring or not, since it is largely *not* Native people who are in control of the sports teams in question. Stereotypes—even "positive" ones—minimize all other, supposedly irrelevant characteristics that many indigenous cultures also possess, such as collectivism and communalism, protection of the earth, and resistance to American expansionism. The choice of Native cultures to represent combative sports (e.g., hockey, football) is sometimes claimed to be flattering to Native people but still narrows the characteristics attributed to Native Americans to only combat skills (see Black, 2002), which is a key emphasis in the "bloodthirsty savage" stereotype (Berkhofer, 1978; King, Staurowsky, Baca, Davis, & Pewewardy, 2002). Stereotypes are problematic because they *always* reduce entire groups of people to certain limited characteristics, presuming that all members of that group share those characteristics and do not vary from that stereotype. In addition, the stereotyped personas that accompany all these mascots are troubling. For instance, the Cleveland Indians' Chief Wahoo logo is a smiling, buffoonish caricature, not much different from the historic Little Black Sambo character.

Notably, claims of honoring Native American stereotypes associated with the past also designate the contributions and very presence of Native Americans as something only from the past, thus subtly denying and ignoring their existence in the present. The Native American representations emblazoned on jerseys and logos rarely look like the actual people who live in 21st-century America but instead romanticize the so-called "noble savage" that settlers encountered when they attempted to clear the

American frontier of the Native peoples who already lived there. These mascots also exist in a sporting universe alongside other mascots that include historical relics, such as the 49ers, Pirates, Kings, Patriots, 76ers, and Yankees, as well as mythical characters, such as the Wizards and Devils, and many aggressive animals (the Lions, Tigers, Bears, Hawks, Bulls, Sharks, Coyotes, and others). Thus, in the U.S. imagination, Native Americans reside in the past and can be easily forgotten, just as easily as they can be compared to nonhuman animals and fantastical figures.

Finally, team names that represent White ethnicities and are often used as counterexamples are very different in nature from Native American mascots. First, Whites are indisputably better off than Native Americans. Whites are the dominant group and experience better health, possess substantially more political power, earn greater salaries, have nicer and safer communities, and experience far greater social status than do Native Americans. For example, Native Americans have a far higher mortality rate than Whites—715 deaths per 100,000 versus 456 per 100,000, respectively (Kunitz, 2008). In addition, only two self-identified Native Americans serve in the U.S. Congress while almost 80% of Congress is White (Bump, 2015). Moreover, the median Native American household earned $32,227 compared with $53,657 for all households (U.S. Census Bureau, 2015), and Native American reservations are significantly more likely to be sites with "extremely dangerous" unexploded military ordnance (Hooks & Smith, 2004). To compare a White mascot to a Native one is to compare a highly privileged group to one that is uniquely and profoundly disadvantaged. Second, the majority of the associated populations around those White sports teams and even the students attending those schools are overwhelmingly White and often have the same ethnic makeup of those mascots. For example, Notre Dame is a Catholic university, founded by Whites, including Irish Americans, while the Vikings football team is in a state with one of the country's heaviest concentrations of Scandinavian Americans. Native Americans, on the other hand, constitute one of the smallest racial populations in the United States and are often sequestered on reservations or isolated in urban areas. Further, most Americans perceive Native people as homogeneous and thus do not differentiate among the hundreds of different nations that possess different cultural traditions, languages, and histories. Consequently, many Native American sports mascots use the same generic appearance stereotyped in popular American culture, such as the large feathered headdress, which is more representative of certain Great Plains nations than any others. The University of North Dakota Fighting Sioux logo was at one point copied from the Chicago Blackhawks logo, with no apparent irony that the Sioux (Lakotans) are an entirely different nation of people than the Blackhawks. (That would be like representing Italians with imagery of Norwegians.)

The competition of sports dredges up the old dichotomy of "cowboys versus Indians," wherein "Indians" are an enemy to be fought by brave settlers and ranchers. Placing an entire people in a position where mockery and denigration occurs from opposing teams ought to be an immediate concern. Since the fans of other teams can be expected to chant insults during games, like "Indians suck!" (or "Braves suck!" "Chiefs suck!" "Blackhawks suck!"), how ethical is it to place an entire ethnicity or racial group in that position? This consequence is often ignored, even when claiming the nicknames are an honor. For example, the Cleveland Indians claim that their team name honors a Native American player named Louis Sockalexis. This claim is simply incorrect; the name was used to generate interest in the team and media coverage, but Sockalexis's ancestry was regularly ridiculed and insulted with slurs by fans, including fans in Cleveland (Staurowsky, 1998). The broader practice of associating Native Americans with an *entire* team expands this practice.

Even under the best of conditions and regardless of best intentions, serious and troubling problems result from the use of Native American mascots and team names. Using scientific experiments, scholars have been able to demonstrate that basic stereotypical images have psychological consequences for youth. For example, simply viewing the Cleveland Indians logo decreased Native youth's self-esteem and future aspirations while raising self-esteem and future aspirations for White youth. Essentially, it hurts Native youth—regardless of any claims of honor—while also improving White youth's sense of self, presumably because it reinforces Whites' awareness of their privileged position in the racial order (Fryberg, Markus, Oyserman, & Stone, 2008).

Confederate Symbols: Flags and Rebels

Confederate imagery is also found throughout the United States, although in greatest concentration in the Southeast. This imagery references supposedly universal aspects of Southern culture. For many, Southern culture is still related to the U.S. Civil War, which some Southerners continue to call the War of Northern Aggression. Southern cultural imagery primarily includes the Confederate flag, more specifically the Confederate battle flag, based on St. Andrew's Cross. The flag and team names such as the Rebels are symbols used by diverse groups across the United States, including White Southerners, country music fans, antigovernment activists, rural dwellers, rebellious and alternative subcultures, Southern patriots and secessionists, and others. The Confederate flag and Rebels nickname are used by many high school and collegiate sports teams and fans.

The Confederate flag is flown most frequently by Whites and is most strongly associated with working-class Whites, although advocates argue that the flag is "color-blind" and represents Southerners of all races (Reingold & Wike, 1998; see also Holyfield, Moltz, & Bradley, 2009). Consequently, advocates claim it is not a symbol of White supremacy or of racism against Blacks. Confederate flag defenders argue that it represents Southern "heritage, not hate." As such, it is a general symbol of Southern pride and not a symbol of White pride. This Southern pride often includes a belief that northern states and the federal government bully the South, brutalize Southerners, and ridicule their culture. Thus, while the flag may have an oppositional quality, advocates argue it is not a racist symbol. The more ardent supporters of the Confederate flag claim that non-Southerners have tried to erase Southern history and even tried to commit genocide against Southerners. (This final claim is most often made by secessionists such as the League of the South.)

While the Confederate flag does have broad support among many White Southerners, critics argue that it is a symbol not merely associated with general Southern culture but the Confederacy specifically. Therefore, the flag is linked directly with a White supremacist state-building project whose founding principles prioritized the enslavement of millions of people of African descent. While it is clear to everyone, including defenders of the Confederate flag, that the Civil War ended slavery, not all people admit that slavery was a central cause of the Civil War. Since many Whites are resistant to this fact, they may be unaware of or indifferent to how their advocacy for the Confederate flag sends racist messages to people of color, especially Blacks, that the South is still dominated and run by Whites. Therefore, if slavery and racial suppression of Blacks is "hate," the flag and other aspects of Confederate culture are, by definition, about a hateful heritage.

To better understand support for and opposition to Confederate symbols, it is crucial to understand that the Confederacy was a coalition of slave-owning states in the South that feared the U.S. federal government's intent to eventually end their "peculiar" and "sacred" institution of slavery, and thus they seceded from the United States. So although many current defenders of Confederate symbols deny it, the Confederacy was undeniably tied to slavery. The secession documents from the state-based conventions declaring their independence from the United States all included slavery as a key concern—a predictable outcome, considering that the convention delegates included a great number of slave owners, even though most Whites living in those states were not slave owners. This last point is one that many Confederate flag defenders mention when denying the Civil War was about slavery (e.g., "How could the war be about slavery and why would so many Whites support the war if they didn't own slaves?"). But 90% of the South Carolina convention delegates were slave owners, 86% of Georgia delegates were slave owners, and 72% of Florida delegates were slave owners (Wooster, 1962). The word *slavery* was mentioned in the secessionist declarations more often than *rights*. (The term *state rights* did not appear in the major secessionist declarations of South Carolina, Georgia, Mississippi, or Texas.) When rights *were* mentioned, it was typically in regard to one particular "right": slave owning for Whites. As for why poor, non-slave-owning Whites supported the Civil War, historian David Williams (2008) has demonstrated that there was patriotic support early on in the war but the Confederacy eventually had to resort to a draft to get more soldiers, as nearly two thirds of the Confederate army was "missing" as of 1864. Most of those missing had either abandoned the army to go home or defected. Poor Whites often fought the wealthy-led Confederacy by fighting within the ranks of the Union army or even joining Southern "layout gangs" who attacked the Confederate army, guerrilla-style. This resulting class war between rich and poor Southern Whites was a central, undeniable aspect of the Civil War that challenges the idea of a united South fighting a war that was not about slavery (Williams, 2008). The distortions that have formed since the period of Reconstruction following the Civil War have obscured the core conflicting political and economic interests in question.

After the defeat of the Confederacy, the Confederate battle flag was symbolically used to remind people of the South's resistance to the North, especially notable in regard to the White Southerners' ideal racial order. The flag was notably resurrected during the civil rights era in reaction to the protests of the civil rights movement and the federal government's intervention against Jim Crow segregation. For example, the state of Georgia embedded the flag in its flag in 1956, following the *Brown v. Board of Education* decision from the Supreme Court that ordered public schools to desegregate. The state of South Carolina put the Confederate flag on the statehouse in 1962. Thus, instead of the South being victimized by the North, this anti–civil rights reaction by Whites was meant to demand that the federal government back off its support of integration and tell Blacks to "stay in their place." Not only did states and government officials reclaim this symbol, but so did anti-integration protesters, such as those who opposed Blacks' attending White high schools and universities. The flag appeared at anti-integration rallies and was claimed as a symbol by the Ku Klux Klan. If the intensive use of the flag during this reactionary period—when Southern states defended White supremacy—did not happen, it might be possible to argue that the flag does not refer *only* to racial inequality. However, Blacks who remember the civil rights era and who have told their children about it interpret the Confederate flag in a very different way than many Whites do.

Today, numerous high schools—from Texas, Iowa, and Arkansas to Florida, Kentucky, and South Carolina—have the team name Rebels, a direct reference to the Southern army during the Civil War. At some high schools, the contemporary team names lack any imagery associated with the Confederacy, while at others the connection is undeniable. For example, at Effingham County High School in Georgia, sports fans wave Confederate flags, use "Dixie" as the school's fight song, and display Confederate soldiers on school property. Confederate flags are present at Allen Central High School in Kentucky, where the team logo is a White Confederate soldier wielding a sword. Incidentally, *The Washington Post* reported that nearly 200 schools also bear the names of Confederate leaders (Brown, 2015).

A few universities, such as Louisiana State University (LSU), have also used Confederate symbols—although fewer than those who use Native American imagery and far fewer than high schools with the Rebels team name. LSU's fans wave a gold-and-purple variation of the Confederate flag, and the team—the Fighting Tigers—is named after a famed Louisiana military regiment from the Civil War. The University of Nevada Las Vegas (a school not located in the Southeast) uses the Rebels team name and a mascot originally named Beauregard, who was dressed in a Confederate uniform, although the uniform is no longer visible in the university's sports logo. The most notorious example is the University of Mississippi (or Ole Miss), where the school fight song is "Forward Rebels," the team name is the Rebels, and the mascot was named Colonel Reb, depicted as a genteel Southern plantation owner. An Air Force veteran named James Meredith was the first Black student to attend the University of Mississippi in 1962. His enrollment sparked a violent reaction from Whites, who waved Confederate flags and rioted, resulting in the deaths of two people.

It is worth noting that these universities no longer prevent Black students from attending, as they once did. As of 2014, 15% of Ole Miss students and 12% of

LSU students are Black. Defenders of Confederate symbols point to Black inclusion as a sign of racial progress and evidence that the use of such symbols is not racist but simply about "Southern culture." However, many Blacks do not agree with these claims, as they have advocated for changing these symbols. Black students at Ole Miss have protested the nickname and logo for decades, and in 2010, the school dropped Colonel Reb in favor of a black bear, although it still retains the Rebels nickname. The state of Mississippi, which added the Confederate flag to its state flag in 1894, is now the only state in the country to have elements of the Confederate battle flag in its flag, although six other Southern states have symbolic elements from the Confederacy (Ingraham, 2015).

Claims of "tradition," "heritage," and "Southern culture" are used to neutralize the racial elements of the Confederacy while denying its White supremacist core. These terms are used reactively and are intended to end conversation and debate about the justice of using Confederate symbols. The users of these terms presume that what matters most is their *intent*, not the actual *consequences* of their actions or the *relative meaning* others will see in their actions—especially the perspectives of Blacks in the case of the Confederate flag and symbols or Native Americans in the case of sports mascots and team names. However, these claims about intention are problematic. Consider an analogy: If an abusive spouse calls their partner names, tries to control their behavior, ridicules them, diminishes their self-esteem, and physically hurts them, does it really matter what the abuser thinks about their relationship? If the abuser characterizes these actions as "loving," is that the conclusion outsiders ought to reach? Confederate symbols reimagine the "Dixieland" of the South prior to the Civil War, reinforcing the value of Whiteness over Blackness (Newman, 2007). Indeed, "old-fashioned" racist attitudes are the best predictors of support for Mississippi's Confederate-based state flag (Orey, 2004).

The Power Behind Symbols

Despite justifying Native American mascots as "honoring" and claiming Confederate symbols as "heritage," there is a system of racial hegemony operating behind these symbols, even as their defenders claim to be "color-blind." When Native Americans' cultural identities are used without their permission or the descendants of former slaves have to face symbols that heralded their enslavement and oppression, race is clearly a central component. For Native peoples, it is difficult to forget the United States' deliberate attempts at genocide. Black Americans find it equally difficult to ignore that the Confederacy was the final effort to retain a system that consciously enslaved humans for profit. The near genocide of Native Americans, which involved appropriating the land of an entire continent, and the enslavement of African peoples both helped the United States become the most powerful capitalist economy in the world (Baptist, 2014; Feagin, 2015). While the genocide and slavery have officially ended, the United States government refuses to face that history, assume responsibility for it, and make reparations with the groups it victimized for centuries.

Thus, lurking behind these sports symbols are formidable hierarchical systems whose historical legacies are more acute for people of color than for the average White American. These symbols are still used by sports teams because those who defend them fail (or refuse) to acknowledge the historical legacies they represent to Native Americans and Blacks.

The power of these institutions extends to the present day. The ownership and management of sports teams is rarely under the control of Native Americans or Blacks. The billions of dollars wrapped up in these racialized brands are thus not at the disposal of those communities who drastically need capital infusions to overcome, for instance, widespread impoverishment; 25.8% of Blacks and 27% of Native Americans were impoverished in 2011, compared with 9.9% of non-Hispanic Whites (Macartney, Bishaw, & Fontenot, 2013). The entertainment provided by these sports teams is mainly consumed by White sports fans, whose "dominant gaze" is the only real concern of owners and managers of sports teams. Indeed, most sports fans, especially those who have the money to donate to university teams as alumni or can pay for expensive stadium tickets to attend professional games, are White.

Who should have the power to dictate what an "honor" is? Whites as a group are far more supportive of racialized mascots than are people of color. Racial minorities are far more critical of the use of Native American mascots than are Whites, and Native Americans are the most critical of all (Sigelman, 1998; Williams, 2007). The criticisms of the group whose identities, tribal names, and likenesses are used for sports teams should be the most important concern, even though they are a small minority of the overall U.S. population. Native Americans (and Blacks, for that matter) are rarely consulted and are asked only when it's mandated, as with the NCAA decision that required tribal endorsements for universities to retain Native American team names and mascots. Yet their point of view is clearly important if these representations cause structural harm to their communities, without benefiting them at all.

Defenders of these representations often point out that many Native people support the practice, which is true. A number of national surveys have found a surprising amount of abstract support among people who claim Native identity (see King et al., 2002). However, most major Native American organizations (as well as other civil rights organizations, such as the NAACP, or National Association for the Advancement of Colored People) have consistently opposed the practice. Thus, while some individual Native people support the nicknames, those who have considered the group effect and have worked to defend Native interests over many decades, such as the American Indian Movement, think very differently. Also, Native Americans who do support these representations are often distant from any particular direct resulting harms. At the University of North Dakota—a school with a substantial enrollment of Native American students, in a state with many Native Americans and reservations—my own analysis (Williams, 2007) has shown that Native students were the most critical of the school's Fighting Sioux nickname, with many of those students being Sioux (Lakotan). In 2000, 21 Native American–related departments and organizations on the university's campus (ranging from student clubs to academic programs) signed a joint statement in opposition to the school's team name. There was also no significant difference among any other major tribal groups: All nations were in consensus and opposed to the nickname (Williams, 2007). Since these Native students were the ones who were geographically and socially closest to this practice, why not listen to *their* voices first and foremost? When, in 2012, the University of North Dakota dropped the nickname (as of 2015, the team is called the Fighting Hawks), the reason was mounting costs of a long legal fight and the risk of lost NCAA tournament play, not the opinions of offended Native students.

Blacks in southeastern states where Confederate symbols are most prevalent lack social power in relation to Whites. They are drastically underrepresented in public office, graduate high school and college at lower rates than Whites, are overrepresented in the criminal justice system, and earn considerably less income. For example, while Blacks are more than 12% of the U.S. population, they have only two seats in the U.S. Senate (Bump, 2015). Ninety-three percent of non-Hispanic Whites have graduated high school, and 36% have college degrees, while 87% of Blacks have graduated high school and only 23% have college degrees (Ryan & Bauman, 2016). Black males are six times more likely to be incarcerated than White males (Sentencing Project, 2013). Finally, although White median income in 2014 was $60,256 and only 10% of Whites were below the poverty line, Black median income was only $35,398 and 26% of Blacks were in poverty (DeNavas-Walt & Proctor, 2015). Some of these forms of racial inequality have diminished since the civil rights era but not all, and there are no criteria by which Blacks are doing better than Whites. Consequently, many Blacks feel that the Confederate flag serves to remind them of their "place" in the South's racial hierarchy, just as it reminds Whites of a certain idealized society in which Blacks indeed knew their "place." The "tradition" and "heritage" that Whites are celebrating with the Confederate flag is one of slavery, Jim Crow, and White supremacy. Even if this is not the intention of many Whites, they ought to ask why they would wish to offend and intimidate Blacks with these symbols, even if inadvertently. Ultimately, Confederate symbols are divisive rather than unifying, creating cleavages along racial lines (see Leib, 1995).

Changes

The long-standing traditions of using Native American and Confederate imagery have begun changing in recent decades. Largely due to protests by the affected groups, many schools have dropped the use of Native American mascots and team names and various institutions have reduced their support for Confederate flags and representations. Since universities are represented by diverse interests—and also are often public institutions—there has been considerable pressure to stop the use of Native mascots, in particular. The list of schools that have dropped them includes Stanford University, Dartmouth College, Syracuse University, Carthage College, Southern Nazarene College, the University of Illinois, St. John's University (New York), Marquette University, Miami University, Eastern Michigan University, Stonehill College,

University of West Georgia, Springfield College, Arkansas State University, the University of Massachusetts–Amherst, and the University of North Dakota. While a few university teams—such as the Florida State University Seminoles and Mississippi College Choctaw—appealed the NCAA ban and won due to positive support from nearby tribes of the same name, there is less support for these schools' nicknames among the mass of Seminole and Choctaw people, who reside in large numbers in Oklahoma due to various forced relocation campaigns in the 1800s. For example, King and Springwood (2000) report that none of the four Seminole tribes of Oklahoma have endorsed the Florida State University team, unlike the Florida-based Seminole Indian Tribe. While many high schools have changed their team names, many others have not. In Massachusetts alone, 40 high schools have Native American team names (Pohle, 2015), and nearly 500 high schools nationally use just the Indian moniker (Munguia, 2014). Perhaps the most resistant to change have been professional sports teams; none of the national teams, which are ultimately privately owned corporations with large fan bases, have changed their team names.

In the immediate aftermath of the Charleston mass killing in 2015, Alabama and South Carolina took down Confederate flags from government buildings. Virginia decided to remove the flag from specialty license plates. Tennessee's governor ordered the bust of Nathan Bedford Forrest—a general in the Confederacy, a slave trader, and the founder of the Ku Klux Klan—removed from the capital. The state of Georgia decided to rename two state holidays: Confederate Memorial Day and Robert E. Lee's Birthday. The Citadel military college took down the flag from a campus chapel in South Carolina. Some high schools also voted to change the name of their Rebels sports teams, such as Southside High School in Fort Smith, Arkansas.

Unsurprisingly, the main racial divisions for support and opposition remain between Whites and people of color. However, increasing numbers of Whites have begun changing their traditional support of offensive symbols. This is a noteworthy development, as it became increasingly difficult to honestly discuss racial issues in the Obama era, when color blindness was a central narrative. This not only made these lingering practices hard for many to stomach—considering their racist origins and conclusions—but also made it necessary for supporters of these symbols to deny any racial dimensions. Since few Whites wish to be perceived as "racist," they ultimately explain their support for Indian mascots or Confederate symbols using arguments that are race-neutral and deny historical practices such as Native American genocide, African slavery, and Jim Crow.

Dana M. Williams is an assistant professor of sociology at California State University, Chico, and teaches classes on race, social movements, research methods, statistics, and public sociology. Williams is the co-author of the book *Anarchy and Society: Reflections on Anarchist Sociology* and has published research in journals such as *Sociology of Sport Journal, Teaching Sociology, Critical Sociology*, and *Race, Ethnicity, and Education*.

SUGGESTED ADDITIONAL RESOURCES

Carstarphen, M. G., & Sanchez, J. P. (Eds.). (2012). *American Indians and the mass media.* Norman: University of Oklahoma Press.

Churchill, W. (2013). Crimes against humanity. In M. L. Andersen & P. H. Collins (Eds.), *Race, class, and gender: An anthology* (pp. 379–385). Belmont, CA: Thomson-Wadsworth.

Granderson, L. Z. (2013, February 13). Prompting mascot change. *ESPN.* Retrieved from http://espn.go.com/nfl/story/_/id/8944042/history-aloneprompt-washington-change-nfl-mascot

King, C. R. (Ed.). (2010). *The Native American mascot controversy: A handbook.* Lanham, MD: Scarecrow.

Klatell, J. (2007, February 16). Fighting Illini say goodbye to the chief. *CBS News.* Retrieved from http://www.cbsnews.com/news/fighting-illini-say-goodbye-to-the-chief

Merskin, D. (2001). Winnebagos, Cherokees, Apaches, and Dakotas: The persistence of stereotyping of American Indians in American advertising brands. *Howard Journal of Communications, 12,* 159–169.

Staurowsky, E. J. (2007). "You know, we are all Indian": Exploring White power and privilege in reactions to the NCAA Native American mascot policy. *Journal of Sport and Social Issues, 31,* 61–76.

Websites

Change the Mascot.org: http://www.changethemascot.org

Campaign led by the Oneida Indian Nation to end the use of the racial slur "redskins" as the mascot and name of the National Football League (NFL) team the Washington Redskins. Campaign calls on the NFL and its commissioner to "do the right thing and bring an end [to] the use of the racial epithet." Relatedly, see the September 8, 2013, *ABC News* article "'Change the Mascot' Campaign Hits Washington Redskins" (http://abcnews.go.com/US/sports-mascots-stir-controversy/story?id=20194389).

National Coalition on Sports & Racism in Media: http://www.aimovement.org/ncrsm/index.html
The coalition is part of the American Indian Movement.

Audio/Visual

Rosenstein, J. (Producer). (1997). In whose honor? [Television series episode]. *POV.* Brooklyn, NY: American Documentary. Further information can be found at the Public Broadcasting Service website (http://www.pbs.org/pov/inwhosehonor).

QUESTIONS FOR FURTHER DISCUSSION

1. Before reading this article, how did you feel about Native American mascots or Confederate mascots? Having read it, has your opinion changed? Why or why not?

2. Do you believe that teams with Native American names or mascots would lose fan support and funding if they changed their team names or mascots? How much should this be taken into consideration when considering changing team names or mascots?

3. Can you think of any other racist or ethnocentric traditions that we continue to uphold or celebrate? For instance, some argue that Thanksgiving is one such tradition. How should we think about these kinds of traditions? Should they be abolished altogether, or can they be modified in some way?

REACHING BEYOND THE COLOR LINE

1. Do an Internet search to find Native American tribal nations in your area. Research their histories and struggles. How does this knowledge shape your opinion of Native American mascots? Do any of the schools in your area use Native American team names or mascots? If so, what does this tell us about how we think about Native American people?

2. In small groups, research Native American team mascots in the NCAA and professional sports teams (e.g., Florida State Seminoles, Cleveland Indians, Atlanta Braves, Chicago Blackhawks, etc.). What information can you find about the origins of their mascots or team names? What do those origins tell us about how Native Americans exist in the public imagination? In your search, also look at how these teams have responded to the controversy over their mascots. What do their responses tell us about how Native Americans continue to exist in the public imagination? Has there been any change since the time when the mascot or team name was created?

REFERENCES

Baptist, E. E. (2014). *The half has never been told: Slavery and the making of American capitalism*. New York, NY: Basic Books.

Berkhofer, R. F. (1978). *The White man's Indian: Image of the American Indian from Columbus to the present*. New York: Vintage.

Black, J. E. (2002). The "mascotting" of Native America: Construction, commodity, and assimilation. *American Indian Quarterly, 26*(4), 605–622.

Blumer, H. (1969). *Symbolic interactionism: Perspective and method*. Englewood Cliffs, NJ: Prentice Hall.

Brown, E. (2015, June 24). Nearly 200 schools are named for Confederate leaders. Is it time to rename them? *Washington Post*. Retrieved from https://www.washingtonpost.com/local/education/nearly-200-schools-are-named-for-confederate-leaders-is-it-time-to-rename-them/2015/06/24/838e2cc0-1aaa-11e5-93b7-5eddc056ad8a_story.html?utm_term=.c07f003db894

Bump, P. (2015, January 5). The new Congress is 80 percent White, 80 percent male and 92 percent Christian. *Washington Post*. Retrieved from https://www.washingtonpost.com/news/the-fix/wp/2015/01/05/the-new-congress-is-80-percent-white-80-percent-male-and-92-percent-christian/?utm_term=.63f21009caf7

DeNavas-Walt, C., & Proctor, B. D. (2015). *Income and poverty in the United States: 2014*. Washington, DC: U.S. Census Bureau. Retrieved from https://www.census.gov/content/dam/Census/library/publications/2015/demo/p60-252.pdf

Durkheim, É. (2001). *The elementary forms of religious life*. Oxford, UK: Oxford University Press.

Feagin, J. (2015). *How Blacks built America: Labor, culture, freedom, and democracy.* New York, NY: Routledge.

Fryberg, S. A., Markus, H. R., Oyserman, D., & Stone, J. M. (2008). Of warrior chiefs and Indian princesses: The psychological consequences of American Indian mascots. *Basic & Applied Social Psychology, 30*(3), 208–218.

Goddard, I. (2005). "I am a red-skin": The adoption of a Native American expression (1769–1826). *European Review of Native American Studies, 19*(2), 1–20.

Holmes, B. (2014, June 18). Yes, a "redskin" does, in fact, mean the scalped head of a Native American, sold, like a pelt, for cash. *Esquire.* Retrieved from http://www.esquire.com/news-politics/news/a29318/redskin-name-update/

Holyfield, L., Moltz, M. R., & Bradley, M. S. (2009). Race discourse and the US Confederate flag. *Race, Ethnicity & Education, 12*(4), 517–537.

Hooks, G., & Smith, C. L. (2004). The treadmill of destruction: National sacrifice areas and Native Americans. *American Sociological Review, 69*, 558–575.

Ingraham, C. (2015, June 21). How the Confederacy lives on in the flags of seven Southern states. *Washington Post.* Retrieved from https://www.washingtonpost.com/news/wonk/wp/2015/06/21/how-the-confederacy-lives-on-in-the-flags-of-seven-southern-states/

King, C. R., & Springwood, C. F. (2000). Fighting spirits: The racial politics of sports mascots. *Journal of Sport and Social Issues, 24*(3), 282–304.

King, C. R., Staurowsky, E. J., Baca, L., Davis, L. R., & Pewewardy, C. (2002). Of polls and race prejudice: *Sports Illustrated*'s errant "Indian wars." *Journal of Sport & Social Issues, 26*(4), 381–402.

Kunitz, S. J. (2008). Changing patterns of mortality among American Indians. *American Journal of Public Health, 98*(3), 404–411.

Leib, J. I. (1995). Heritage versus hate: A geographical analysis of Georgia's Confederate battle flag debate. *Southeastern Geographer, 35*(1), 35–57.

Newman, J. I. (2007). Old times there are not forgotten: Sport, identity, and the Confederate flag in the Dixie South. *Sociology of Sport Journal, 24*(3), 261–282.

Macartney, S., Bishaw, A., & Fontenot, K. (2013). *Poverty rates for selected detailed race and Hispanic groups by state and place: 2007–2011.* Washington, DC: U.S. Census Bureau. Retrieved from https://www.census.gov/prod/2013pubs/acsbr11-17.pdf

Munguia, H. (2014, September 5). The 2,128 Native American mascots people aren't talking about. *FiveThirtyEight.* Retrieved from https://fivethirtyeight.com/features/the-2128-native-american-mascots-people-arent-talking-about/

Orey, B. D. A. (2004). White racial attitudes and support for the Mississippi state flag. *American Politics Research, 32*(1), 102–116.

Pohle, A. (2015, May 20). It's 2015. Why do 40 Mass. high schools still have Native American mascots? *Boston Globe.* Retrieved from https://www.boston.com/news/untagged/2015/05/20/its-2015-why-do-40-mass-high-schools-still-have-native-american-mascots

Reingold, B., & Wike, R. S. (1998). Confederate symbols, Southern identity, and racial attitudes: The case of the Georgia state flag. *Social Science Quarterly, 79*(3), 568–580.

Ryan, C. L., & Bauman, K. (2016). *Educational attainment in the United States: 2015.* Washington, DC: U.S. Census Bureau. Retrieved from http://www.census.gov/content/dam/Census/library/publications/2016/demo/p20-578.pdf

Sentencing Project. (2013, August). *Report of the Sentencing Project to the United Nations Human Rights Committee: Regarding racial disparities in the United States criminal justice system.* Washington, DC: Author. Retrieved from http://www.sentencingproject.org/wp-content/uploads/2015/12/Race-and-Justice-Shadow-Report-ICCPR.pdf

Sigelman, L. (1998). Hail to the Redskins? Public reactions to a racially insensitive team name. *Sociology of Sport Journal, 15*, 317–325.

Staurowsky, E. J. (1998). An act of honor or exploitation? The Cleveland Indians' use of the Louis Francis Sockalexis story. *Sociology of Sport Journal, 15*(4), 299–316.

U.S. Census Bureau. (2015, November 2). *American Indian and Alaska Native heritage month: November 2015*. Retrieved from http://www.census.gov/newsroom/facts-for-features/2015/cb15-ff22.html

Williams, D. (2008). *Bitterly divided: The South's inner civil war*. New York, NY: New Press.

Williams, D. M. (2007). Where's the honor? Attitudes toward the "Fighting Sioux" nickname and logo. *Sociology of Sport Journal, 24*(4), 437–456.

Wooster, R. A. (1962). *The secession conventions of the South*. Princeton, NJ: Princeton University Press.

PART III

Institutions, Policies, and Legacies of Oppression

"But What About the Children?"

Understanding Contemporary Attitudes Toward Interracial Dating and Marriage

Nikki Khanna

University of Vermont

When Beth Humphrey, a 30-year-old White account manager, and Terence McKay, a 32-year-old Black welder, decided to wed in 2009, they were stunned when the local justice refused to sign their marriage license. The justice of the peace for Tangipahoa Parish's Eighth Ward in Louisiana, Keith Bardwell, refused to do so, explaining that he had a personal policy against interracial marriage. When later questioned publicly about his controversial policy, Judge Bardwell defended himself: "I'm not a racist. . . . My main concern is for the children" (Rentas, 2009). He added, "I think those children suffer and I won't help put them through it" (Lee, 2009).

Without a doubt, Bardwell faced much public criticism. American approval of interracial marriage has increased substantially over the years—from 4% in 1958 to 87% in 2013 (Newport, 2013)—likely due to changing attitudes and generational replacement, that is, more socially progressive younger adults replacing less progressive older ones (Jones, 2011). Further, marriages between people of different races have increased steadily since the early 1960s—a time when many states criminalized interracial unions through anti-miscegenation laws. Indeed, there has been a shift in attitudes toward interracial dating, but as Judge Bardwell's statement indicates, there are still those who remain opposed to it and attempt to disguise their prejudices in alleged concerns for the children born of these unions. Looking at the history of anti-miscegenation laws can help us better understand and analyze this resistance to interracial dating and marriage.

History of Anti-Miscegenation Laws

At one time or another, 38 U.S. states criminalized interracial marriage through anti-miscegenation laws; four additional states had anti-miscegenation laws but repealed them prior to statehood (Fryer, 2007). *All* such laws prohibited marital and/or sexual unions between Whites and Blacks (Farley, 1999; Zack, 1993), clearly revealing which relationships Whites feared most. In many states, these laws were extended to other racial groups—including Native Americans, Asians (e.g., Chinese, Japanese, Koreans, Filipinos), Native Hawaiians, and in some states, *any* non-White group. For example, according to a 1927 Georgia statute, it was "unlawful for a white person to marry anyone but a white person" (Sohoni, 2007, p. 599). A *White person* was then carefully defined as anyone with "no ascertainable trace of either Negro, African, West Indian, Asiatic Indian, Mongolian, Japanese, or Chinese blood in their veins" (p. 599). Moreover, penalties for the violation of anti-miscegenation statutes varied state to state from having the marriage voided to paying a fine to imprisonment.

These laws primarily functioned to protect and preserve White racial purity; non-White "blood" was seen as a stain that corrupted White blood and defiled White racial integrity. In 1924, for instance, Virginia passed its Racial Integrity Act, which criminalized all marriages between Whites and non-Whites. Aimed at preserving White "racial integrity," it prohibited marriage between a White person and a person with *any* so-called admixture of non-White blood (Plecker, 1924). In the same year, Lonthrop Stoddard, a lawyer and eugenicist, argued, "White race purity is the cornerstone of our civilization. Its mongrelization with non-white blood . . . would spell the downfall of our civilization."[1]

Efforts to curb interracial unions often centered on the "mongrel" offspring and the threat they posed to "White racial purity." In 1878, John F. Miller, a future California senator, best articulated the West Coast anxiety regarding White–Chinese unions by saying,

> Were the Chinese to amalgamate at all with *our* people, it would be the lowest, most vile, and degraded of *our* race, and the result of that amalgamation would be a hybrid of the most despicable, a mongrel of the most detestable that has ever afflicted the earth. (Childs, 2009, p. 23; emphasis added)

In 1924, a California farmer further highlighted the problem of miscegenation in his statement before the U.S. Senate:

> Near my home is an eighty-acre tract of . . . land. On that tract lives a Japanese. With that Japanese lives a white woman. In that woman's arm is a baby. What is that baby? It isn't Japanese. It isn't white. . . . It is a germ of the mightiest problem that ever faced this state; a problem that will make the black problem of the South look white. (Kennedy, 2003, p. 268)

Anti-miscegenation laws were deemed necessary to preserve the White race and, relatedly, to keep power concentrated in the hands of Whites. Any mixing between Whites and people of color was perceived as a threat to the racial hierarchy that placed Whites comfortably at the top, and a threat to the power and resources they monopolized in their privileged position. Hence, there was little interest among White lawmakers in curbing unions between non-White groups. Instead, anti-miscegenation laws primarily criminalized relationships (e.g., marital, sexual) between Whites and non-White groups in, for example, California (which prohibited marriages between Whites and "negroes, Mongolians, members of the Malay race, or mulattoes"), Nebraska (which prohibited marriages between Whites and anyone with "1/8th or more negro, Japanese, or Chinese blood"), and Alabama (which prohibited marriage between Whites and "any negro, or the descendent of any negro"). Table 12.1 is an overview of American anti-miscegenation laws.

While rooted in colonial America, these laws flourished in the first half of the 20th century as White fears regarding miscegenation grew. Between 1900 and the late 1960s, 30 states had some form of anti-miscegenation legislation (Fryer, 2007). The taboo of interracial mixing was clearly evident even in Hollywood when the Motion Picture Association of America completely forbade the theme of miscegenation from the 1930s to the 1950s (Courtney, 2005; Sickels, 1972); in particular, depictions of sexual relationships between Whites and Blacks were strictly prohibited. In Alabama in the late 1950s, fear of Black–White marriage was readily apparent when a children's book, *The Rabbit's Wedding* by Garth Williams (1958), was removed from the shelves of the public libraries because the illustration portrayed one rabbit as White and the other as Black (Tucker, 2004). Nonetheless, the number of states with anti-miscegenation laws would decline in the 1950s and 1960s, but by 1966, 17 states still criminalized interracial marriage (all were in the southeast—as far west as Texas and Oklahoma, as far north as Maryland and Delaware, and as far south as Florida).

In 1967, a young couple from Virginia would challenge the constitutionality of such laws in the landmark case *Loving v. Virginia*. Mildred Jeter, a Black woman, and Richard Loving, a White man, married 9 years earlier in Washington, DC, where it was legal for them to do so. Upon returning to their home in Caroline County, Virginia, where they had spent most of their lives, they were arrested for violating the state's anti-miscegenation statute. After pleading guilty to the charges, they were sentenced to 1 year in jail. The trial judge, however, suspended their sentence on the condition that they leave the state of Virginia for 25 years (Zabel, 2000). In his opinion, the judge stated, "Almighty God created the races white, black, yellow, malay, and red, and he placed them on separate continents. . . . The fact that he separated the races shows that he did not intend for the races to mix" (Sollors, 2000, p. 28). Mildred Jeter and Richard Loving filed suit against the state, claiming that prohibition of marriage on the basis of race violated their Fourteenth Amendment right to equal protection under the law.

The Virginia Supreme Court upheld the state's anti-miscegenation law, claiming that the state had a right "to preserve the racial integrity of its citizens" and to prevent a "mongrel breed of citizens" (Sollors, 2000, p. 31). However, the case was soon appealed to the U.S. Supreme Court. In 1967, after nearly 10 years of marriage and the births of three children (Sickels, 1972), the court reversed the earlier decision and ruled anti-miscegenation laws unconstitutional; 16 states were affected, including

Virginia, but also Alabama, Arkansas, Georgia, Kentucky, Louisiana, Mississippi, Missouri, Tennessee, Texas, West Virginia, North Carolina, South Carolina, Florida, Oklahoma, and Delaware.

Table 12.1   Anti-Miscegenation Laws by State

State	Groups Whites Were Prohibited From	What Was Prohibited
Alabama	Negro or any descendent	Marriage, adultery, fornication
Arizona	Negro, Mongolian, Malay, Hindu	Marriage
Arkansas	Negro, Mulatto	Cohabitation, birthing a mulatto child, marriage
California	Negro, Mongolian, Malay, Mulatto	Marriage
Colorado	Negro, Mulatto	Marriage
Delaware	Negro, Mulatto	Marriage
Florida	Negro, Mulatto, anyone with 1/8 or more Negro blood	Marriage, adultery, fornication, occupy the same room at nighttime
Georgia	Any non-White person	Marriage, sexual intercourse
Idaho	Negro, Mulatto, Mongolian	Marriage
Illinois	Negro, Mulatto	Marriage
Indiana	Anyone with 1/8 or more Negro blood	Marriage
Iowa	Negro, Mulatto	Marriage
Kansas	Negro, Mulatto	Marriage
Kentucky	Negro, Mulatto	Marriage
Louisiana	Aboriginal Indian race of America, Black, Colored	Concubinage, cohabitation
Maine	Negro, Indian, Mulatto	Marriage
Maryland	Negro, a person of Negro descent (to the third generation), Malay	Marriage
Massachusetts	Negro, Indian, Mulatto	Marriage
Michigan	Negro	Marriage
Mississippi	Negro, Mulatto, Mongolian, a person with 1/8 or more of Negro or Mongolian blood	Marriage
Missouri	Negro, a person with 1/8 or more of Negro blood, Mongolian	Marriage
Montana	Negro, Chinese, a person of Negro blood or in part Negro, Japanese	Marriage

State	Groups Whites Were Prohibited From	What Was Prohibited
Nebraska	A person with 1/8 or more Negro, Chinese, or Japanese blood	Marriage
Nevada	Ethiopian or Black, Malay or brown, Mongolian or yellow	Marriage, fornication, cohabitation
New Mexico	Negro, Mulatto	Marriage, cohabitation
North Carolina	Negro, a person of Negro descent to the third generation	Marriage
North Dakota	Negro	Occupying the same room, marriage
Ohio	Negro, or any person with any distinct and visible mixture of Negro or African blood	Intercourse, marriage
Oklahoma	Any person of African descent	Marriage
Oregon	Negro, Chinese, or any person having 1/4 or more Negro, Chinese, or Kanaka blood, or any person having more than 1/2 Indian blood	Marriage
Pennsylvania	Negro	Cohabitation, fornication, adultery, marriage
Rhode Island	Negro, Indian, Mulatto	Marriage
South Carolina	Indian, Negro, Mulatto, Mestizo, or half-breed	Marriage
South Dakota	African, Korean, Malayan, Mongolian	Marriage, cohabitation
Tennessee	Negro, Mulatto	Marriage, cohabitation
Texas	Negro	Marriage
Utah	Negro, Mongolian, Malayan, Mulatto, Quadroon, Octoroon	Marriage
Virginia	Any non-White person	Marriage
Washington	Anyone with 1/4 or more Negro blood or 1/2 or more Indian blood	Marriage
West Virginia	Negro	Marriage
Wyoming	Negro, Mulatto, Mongolian, Malay	Marriage

Source: Adapted from Fryer (2007) and http://www.lovingday.org/legal-map

Note: States that never had such laws: Alaska, Connecticut, Hawaii, Minnesota, New Hampshire, New Jersey, New York, Vermont, and Wisconsin. "Mongolian" refers to Chinese, "Malay" refers to Filipino, "Hindu" refers to Asian Indian, "Mulatto" refers to anyone with Black and White ancestry, "Kanaka" refers to Native Hawaiian, "Quadroon" refers to someone who is one fourth Black, "Octoroon" refers to someone who is one eighth Black, "Mestizo" refers to someone of European and Native ancestry.

Interracial Marriage Today: Attitudes and Trends

Since *Loving v. Virginia* (1967), attitudes toward interracial marriage have become more favorable and rates of intermarriage have grown steadily, though these trends vary depending on many factors. A 2011 Gallup poll of American attitudes toward Black–White interracial marriage found that those who were 65 years or older, less educated (high school or less), conservative, and Republican were less likely to approve of such marriages, compared with their younger, more educated, liberal, moderate, Democratic, and Independent counterparts (see Table 12.2 for a break-down). The same poll revealed that the South is the least likely to approve of intermarriage, of any region in the country. Gallup polls taken from 1968 to 2013 also reveal race to be a factor shaping attitudes; according to Newport (2013), "Blacks' approval

Table 12.2 Approval of Marriage Between Blacks and Whites

Subgroup	Percentage Approve
Men	87
Women	85
18–29-year-olds	97
30–49-year-olds	91
50–64-year-olds	88
65 years +	66
East	90
Midwest	86
South	79
West	91
High school or less	78
Some college	91
College graduate only	92
Postgraduate	94
Liberal	95
Moderate	90
Conservative	78
Democrat	88
Independent	89
Republican	77

Source: Adapted from Jones (2011).

has consistently been higher than Whites' over the decades," and in 2013, 96% of Blacks approved of Black–White marriage, compared with 84% of Whites. Additionally, though attitudes have become more favorable over time, a 2012 survey of Republican voters found that 29% in Mississippi and 21% in Alabama still believed interracial marriage should be prohibited by law ("The Republican Primaries," 2012). Notably, Alabama, in 2000, was the last state to lift its unenforceable ban on interracial marriage (Yen, 2012).

Moreover, *actual* rates of intermarriage, though growing, remain low. According to Wang (2015), although interracial marriages reached a record high in 2013 (at 12% of all marriages), census data reveal that rates of intermarriage, like attitudes toward such unions, vary widely. Regarding region, Hawaii and Alaska have the highest share of mixed marriages, followed by western states such as Oklahoma, Nevada, California, Oregon, New Mexico, Colorado, and Washington (Lofquist, Lugaila, O'Connell, & Feliz, 2012; Passel, Wang, & Taylor, 2010). States with the lowest share, according to a 2012 Pew report, included southern states (e.g., Mississippi, Alabama, Louisiana)—likely because of persistent segregation and prejudicial attitudes—and homogenous, overwhelmingly White states where opportunity for outmarriage is low—for example, Vermont and Maine, both of which are 95% White ("The Republican Primaries," 2012).

Further, a Pew analysis of new marriages in 2010 revealed that the majority (43.3%) of interracial marriages were between Latinos and Whites,[2] 14.4% were between Asians and Whites, and the smallest share (11.9%) were between Blacks and Whites (Taylor et al., 2012)—no doubt reflecting the taboo still surrounding Black–White marriages. Moreover, if we look at outmarriage rates among racial groups in 2013, Native Americans were most likely to marry outside their race (58%), followed by Asians (28%), Blacks (19%), and Whites (7%) (Wang, 2015). Thus, although Whites showed a record high 84% approval rating of interracial marriage in 2011 (Jones, 2011), they remain least likely of all racial groups to actually marry outside their race. The disjuncture between the high approval rating and the low rate of outmarriage may in fact be explained by the concept of social desirability, as suggested by sociologist Daniel Lichter of Cornell University: "People don't want to reveal negative attitudes that might reflect badly on them, and they tend to tell the interviewers what they want to hear" (Jayson, 2012). Further, opportunity also influences intermarriage rates, and given that Whites are the majority group in the United States, many White Americans continue to have little day-to-day interaction with people of color in their neighborhoods, schools, and workplaces, thereby decreasing the impact of attitudes alone on actual behaviors.

Finally, Pew analyses of interracial marriages find that rates of intermarriage also vary by age, education, and gender (Passel et al., 2010). Not surprisingly, intermarriage in 2008 was strongly correlated with age; about 13% of those 25 years or younger married outside their race, compared with 3% of those 75 and older, which is likely due to generational changes in racial attitudes (also keep in mind that for many older Americans, anti-miscegenation laws and segregation were the norm in their youth). As education increases, so does the likelihood of outmarriage, though the differences are modest: 11% of those with less than a high school degree married outside their race, compared with nearly 16% of those who have attended college. For Whites, there appears to be no gender difference regarding rates of outmarriage. However, gender is correlated with intermarriage for Blacks and Asians: In 2013, Black men were much more likely to marry outside their race, compared with Black women (25% and 12%, respectively), and Asian women were far more likely to outmarry, compared with Asian men (37% and 16%, respectively; Wang, 2015). Thus, while studies reveal that attitudes toward interracial marriage have relaxed over the years, actual rates of intermarriage remain low and vary depending on many factors. These low rates point to the continuing significance of race in a "post-racial" society.

What About the Children?

Among those who disapprove of interracial marriage today, prejudicial attitudes likely play a key role, yet for some, like Judge Bardwell of Louisiana, their explanations center on the *children* of interracial marriage: *I don't approve of interracial marriage because the children suffer.* Implicit in this reasoning is the assumption that the multiracial offspring of interracial couples are mixed-up, confused, and caught between two worlds, as exemplified by a biracial guest who appeared on the *Dr. Phil* show in 2003. With falling tears, the adult woman of Black and White ancestry said before millions of Americans watching at home, "There's no place for me," "I don't know who or what I am," and described herself throughout the segment as "lonely," feeling like "trash," "torn apart inside," "not good enough," "inferior," "strange," "different," "caught in the middle," and having "no identity."[3]

Her story exemplified the "tragic mulatta" stereotype, a popular portrayal of Black–White biracial women during the slave and Jim Crow eras (also known more generally as the "tragic mulatto" stereotype). The tragic mulatta was depicted as confused, lost, self-loathing, lacking in self-esteem, and perpetually miserable (see Benshoff & Griffin, 2009). She was trapped in a permanent state of liminality—caught between two worlds, without fully belonging to either. Her character was popularized in American novels, plays, and films, and more often than not, by the end of the story, she met a tragic and heartbreaking end: She suffered loss of social status, social isolation, violence, murder, and even suicide.[4] This tragic character is best exemplified by the concept of the "marginal man," which was first introduced by sociologist Robert Park in 1928 as "one whom fate has condemned to live in two societies and in two, not merely different, but antagonistic cultures" (Stonequist, 1937/1961, p. xiiii). He believed that mixed-race people were marginal and lived "in two worlds," in both of which they were "strangers" (Park, 1928, p. 893). The question remains, however: To what extent does this "tragic marginal identity" accurately represent the experiences of multiracial people *today*? What do recent studies show?

According to Kathleen Korgen (1998), who examined identity among Black–White biracial Americans, there is an increasing acceptance of multiraciality today. Though some of her respondents sometimes felt like racial outsiders, she found that "young biracial men and women today believe that the positive attributes of biracial identity outweigh the negative" and the overwhelming majority in her study "do not wish they were born any other way" (p. 79). In fact, she found that they believed they were more objective, more open-minded, and better able to view others without "racial blinders," compared with their monoracial counterparts (p. 78). Marion Kilson (2001), in her study of multiracial Americans, similarly found that some of her respondents felt some measure of marginalization in adolescence but most viewed their biracial heritage as unique and as an "asset in which they take pride" (p. 167). In a more recent study, I found that most of my Black–White respondents expressed pride in their biracial backgrounds, and they claimed that their backgrounds made them feel "different and unique" (Khanna, 2011, p. 118).

Moreover, though studies frequently predict that mixed-race people suffer lower self-esteem, higher rates of depression, lower academic performance, and poor peer relations, empirical research actually shows that multiracial people tend to be "as well-adjusted as their monoracial peers on most psychological outcomes" (Shih & Sanchez, 2005, p. 569). In a review of more than 40 studies of multiracial Americans, Shih and Sanchez (2005) found very little evidence that multiracial individuals were dissatisfied, unhappy, or uncomfortable with their racial identities. Upon closer inspection, an analysis of the qualitative studies revealed both challenges and benefits for those with multiracial backgrounds; in some cases, they felt rejected by others because of their racial identity, while others cited benefits such as having access to and support from a larger number of racial and cultural communities. While the authors cited numerous studies that revealed issues with identity development, depression, problem behaviors (e.g., early sexual activity, alcohol or drug use), poor academic performance, and low self-esteem, the majority of these studies sampled clinical populations. This is problematic given the selectivity of the samples in question (i.e., study participants were already being treated in a clinical setting— often in therapy). Studies that sampled nonclinical populations generally found positive outcomes, such as pride in one's racial identity, happiness, success in school, and high self-esteem.

When reviewing quantitative studies, Shih and Sanchez (2005) found mixed results (see also Kahn & Denmon's 1997 review). For instance, they found that multiracial adolescents exhibited slightly higher levels of problem behaviors (e.g., delinquency, marijuana use) than their monoracial counterparts, though this finding was based on a small number of studies and must, they warn, be interpreted with caution. Regarding school performance, some studies found no differences between multiracial adolescents and their White counterparts, and often studies suggested that multiracial adolescents fared better academically than their monoracial minority counterparts. Quantitative studies further revealed that multiracial adolescents develop good peer relations in terms of popularity and feeling accepted (which challenges the stereotype that they are socially isolated and marginalized), but there were mixed results regarding measures of self-esteem and depression. Some studies found that multiracial individuals show lower levels of self-esteem than their monoracial counterparts, while others found higher levels of self-esteem or no difference at all.

And studies that looked at depression suggest that multiracial individuals may possibly fare worse than their White peers, but not when compared with their monoracial minority peers—though this was based on only four studies, and hence the trend should be viewed with caution.

Thus, according to Shih and Sanchez's (2005) review, previous studies reveal *no clear patterns* regarding the social and psychological adjustment of multiracial Americans. The mixed results are likely due to the fact that many studies drew respondents from clinical and therapeutic settings (which led to an early emphasis on problems); many relied on small, nonrepresentative samples; and some studies focused on one multiracial group while others grouped all multiracials together regardless of racial background (Campbell & Eggerling-Boeck, 2006). The research, however, is ongoing, and in a more recent study of multiracial adolescents, Campbell and Eggerling-Boeck (2006) also asked, "What about the children?" Examining the mental health and social adjustment of more than a thousand multiracial adolescents of varying racial backgrounds in a large, nationally representative, nonclinical sample, they found "no pervasive disadvantage associated with a multiracial heritage" and they "do not find evidence that Park's 'marginal man' hypothesis is true today" (p. 168). They were able to examine multiracial groups separately (e.g., Black–White, Asian–White, American Indian–White) and together as a group, and they found no evidence that multiracial Americans differed significantly from their White counterparts in terms of depression, seriously considering suicide, feeling socially accepted, feeling close to others at school, and participating in extracurricular activities.[5] While many Americans might hold particular concern for Black–White multiracial children, Campbell and Eggerling-Boeck (2006) add, "It is especially noteworthy that Black-Whites face no pattern of particular hardships" given that "it is this group for whom most of the theories regarding the 'difficulty' of biracial status were developed" (p. 168). Clearly, more research is needed, though it appears from these data that we cannot assume that multiracial Americans today are the identity-confused, socially isolated, tragic characters commonly portrayed in early American history.

Conclusion

America has a 300-year history of anti-miscegenation legislation. Although these laws have since vanished and attitudes toward interracial marriage have relaxed, intermarriage rates remain low—even more so among certain segments of the American population. Attitudinal resistance to interracial marriage undoubtedly reflects lingering prejudicial attitudes, though frequently explanations center on the children of such marriages and the belief that they suffer as multiracial people living in a racialized world. Undeniably, multiracial Americans face unique challenges (and research does bear this out), yet studies also suggest that they are not necessarily maladjusted or psychologically troubled, as often believed. Though some studies do point to some negative social or psychological issues and these findings should not be ignored, studies also show that multiraciality is becoming more commonly accepted, and multiracial Americans are increasingly pointing to the positive aspects of having a multiracial ancestry. Moreover, as intermarriage becomes more common and less taboo and as the number of Americans with multiracial ancestry grows (as is projected), the traditional challenges for children of multiracial ancestry will likely fade as well. During the height of the Jim Crow era and racial segregation, their experiences likely mirrored the "tragic mulatto" stereotype, but recent scholarly evidence suggests that their experiences look quite different today.

These findings raise two important concerns. First, persistent negative stereotypes of multiracial people may be driving some of the observed disapproval ratings for interracial relationships even in the present day. Lingering "tragic" stereotypes of multiracial children as confused and socially isolated, even if uncorroborated in research, may discourage many Americans from exploring interracial relationships and accepting those relationships in their families and the larger society. Certainly, some may object to interracial relationships out of apprehension for multiracial children and obstacles they perceive they might face in society.

Second, these findings also raise the question: To what extent do some Americans rely on the "multiracial-kids-suffer" argument to *mask* their own personal prejudices against these unions? In other words, objections to interracial marriage under the pretense of concern for the well-being of multiracial children may very well be another form of hidden racism—a way to disguise one's true feelings toward interracial relationships in an era where overt racism has the potential to be met with backlash and criticism. Sociologist Eduardo Bonilla-Silva (2010) examines what he calls "color-blind racism," a new type of racism in contemporary America that, unlike earlier Jim Crow racism, which was overt and in-your-face (e.g., racial slurs, open discrimination), is by contrast "subtle" and "apparently nonracial" (p. 3). Yet, like Jim Crow racism, this new type of seemingly innocuous racism functions to maintain the racial status quo. Bonilla-Silva writes:

> Compared to Jim Crow racism, the ideology of color blindness seems like "racism lite." Instead of relying on name calling (niggers, Spics, Chinks), color-blind racism otherizes softly ("these people are human, too"); instead of proclaiming God placed minorities in the world in a servile position, it suggests that they are behind because they do not work enough; instead of viewing interracial marriage as wrong on a straight racial basis, it regards it as "problematic" because of concerns over the children, location, or the extra burden it places on couples. Yet this new ideology has become a formidable political tool for the maintenance of the racial order. (p. 3)

Thus, for some Americans, concern for multiracial children may provide a scapegoat explanation for their own unfavorable attitudes toward interracial relationships and marriage. By focusing on the offspring of interracial unions, they can, as Bonilla-Silva puts it, "safeguard their racial interests without sounding 'racist'" (p. 4).

Nikki Khanna received her PhD in sociology from Emory University and is currently an associate professor of sociology at the University of Vermont. Her work looks at multiracial identity, race and adoption, and colorism among Asian Americans, and has been published in outlets such as *Social Psychology Quarterly, Ethnic and Racial Studies, Sociological Spectrum, Sociological Quarterly, Sociology Compass,* and *Teaching Sociology.* Her recent book, *Biracial in America: Forming and Performing Racial Identity,* looks at Black–White biracial Americans and the underlying processes shaping their racial identities.

NOTES

1. See the Facing History website at https://www.facinghistory.org/resource-library/eugenics-race-and-marriage.

2. It must be noted, however, that "Latino/Hispanic" is a panethnic label, and in census data, those of Latino/Hispanic ancestry could be of any race, including White. Thus, these figures are somewhat misleading.

3. Aired on the *Dr. Phil* show on March 15, 2003.

4. To read more about this stereotype, see http://www.ferris.edu/htmls/news/jimcrow/mulatto.

5. Only American Indian/Native American–White adolescents showed some negative outcomes compared with White students, but they resembled the outcomes of monoracial American Indians. Other multiracial groups (e.g., Black–White, Asian–White) were not shown to be disadvantaged compared with Whites.

SUGGESTED ADDITIONAL RESOURCES

Childs, E. C. (2005). *Navigating interracial borders: Black-White couples and their social worlds.* New Brunswick, NJ: Rutgers University Press.

Dalmage, H. M. (2000). *Tripping on the color line: Black-White multiracial families in a racially divided world.* New Brunswick, NJ: Rutgers University Press.

Kennedy, R. (2003). *Interracial intimacies: Sex, marriage, identity, and adoption.* New York, NY: Vintage Books.

Sollors, W. (2000). *Interracialism: Black-White intermarriage in American history, literature, and law.* New York, NY: Oxford University Press.

QUESTIONS FOR FURTHER DISCUSSION

1. In 1968, only 20% of Americans approved of interracial marriage, but by 2011 those numbers jumped to 86%. How might we explain these changing attitudes over time? (That is, how can we explain declining prejudicial attitudes?) Furthermore, rates of intermarriage have also increased over time. Other than declining prejudicial attitudes, what might be additional explanations for this trend?

2. Interracial couples may face unique challenges compared with their same-race counterparts. What types of challenges, if any, might they face? In addition, what factors may affect the degree to which they face these challenges? (Hint: Think social context and the social characteristics of the couple, such as their racial mix, social class, etc.)

3. To what extent do you think lingering negative stereotypes about multiracial people exist today? To what extent do you think they might contribute to some Americans' attitudes toward interracial marriage? Finally, the author argues that some Americans may rely on the "multiracial-kids-suffer" argument to mask their own personal prejudices against interracial unions. To what extent, if at all, do you think some use this argument as a form of hidden racism or color-blind racism?

4. Anti-miscegenation laws varied state to state, and in 1967, the Supreme Court ruled these laws unconstitutional because they violated the Fourteenth Amendment to the U.S. Constitution. What parallels, if any, exist between interracial marriage and same-sex marriage regarding the controversy and legislation?

REACHING BEYOND THE COLOR LINE

1. As a class, explore contemporary attitudes toward interracial dating and marriage by collectively constructing a survey and distributing it to other students on campus (e.g., students in another course, in the student center). In particular, ask questions about their attitudes toward interracial dating and marriage for various racial groups (e.g., Whites, Blacks, Asians or Asian Americans, Native Americans), and collect information about the respondents—such as their race, gender, and political affiliation (and any other factor you deem potentially important). What do you find? Are there racial groups that students are more or less open to dating, marrying, or both? Are there differences in student perceptions of interracial dating versus interracial marriage? Are certain characteristics of the students (such as race, gender, or political affiliation) correlated with their attitudes?

2. For further research, go to http://www.lovingday.org/legal-map to view an interactive map of where interracial marriage was prohibited by law. Click on each state to read the anti-miscegenation legislation. Looking at the state you were born in and another state of your choosing, answer the following questions: Did an anti-miscegenation law exist? If not, why do you think this state was one of the nine states that never had such laws? If yes, when was it created and repealed? If any, what type of union was prohibited in your state? Which racial groups were prohibited from intermarrying? What was the penalty for violating the law?

3. Consider one or more of the following questions for an in-class free-write activity: (a) What are your thoughts regarding interracial dating and marriage? What is beneficial about interracial unions? What is problematic about them? (b) Often people say they support interracial relationships until it comes to a member of their

family dating or marrying outside his or her race. How do you think your family might react if you dated or married outside your race? How might you react if a sibling or other family member dated or married outside his or her race? Explain.

4. The portrayal of interracial relationships has a long history in Hollywood (though notably, the portrayal of Black–White relationships was prohibited from the 1930s to 1950s). Choose a film that features an interracial couple and answer the following questions in a short response paper: What year do the events of the movie take place? How is the relationship portrayed (is it problematized or glamorized)? What is the family and societal reaction to the relationship (positive, negative, or neutral)? How closely do you imagine the movie's portrayal of the relationship and reactions mirrors reality during that time period and why? And finally, how might the portrayal look different today? Explain. Possible movies to analyze include *Guess Who's Coming to Dinner* (1967), *Jungle Fever* (1991), *The Bodyguard* (1992), *Mississippi Masala* (1992), *Zebrahead* (1992), *Made in America* (1993), *Corrina, Corrina* (1994), *Monster's Ball* (2001), *Save the Last Dance* (2001), *Guess Who?* (2005), *Something New* (2006), and *Lakeview Terrace* (2008).

REFERENCES

Benshoff, H. M., & Griffin, S. (2009). *America on film: Representing race, class, gender and sexuality at the movies.* Malden, MA: Blackwell.

Bonilla-Silva, E. (2010). *Racism without racists: Color-blind racism & racial inequality in contemporary America.* Lanham, MD: Rowman & Littlefield.

Campbell, M. E., & Eggerling-Boeck., J. (2006). What about the children? The psychological and social well-being of multiracial adolescents. *Sociological Quarterly, 47*(1), 147–173.

Childs, E. C. (2009). *Fade to Black and White: Interracial images in popular culture.* Lanham, MD: Rowman & Littlefield.

Courtney, S. (2005). *Hollywood fantasies of miscegenation: Spectacular narratives of gender and race.* Princeton, NJ: Princeton University Press.

Farley, R. (1999). Racial issues: Recent trends in residential patterns and intermarriage. In N. J. Smelser & J. C. Alexander (Eds.), *Diversity and its discontents: Cultural conflict and common ground in contemporary American society* (pp. 85–128). Princeton, NJ: Princeton University Press.

Fryer, R. G. (2007). Guess who's been coming to dinner? Trends in interracial marriage over the 20th century. *Journal of Economic Perspectives, 21*(2), 71–90.

Jayson, S. (2012). U.S. rate of interracial marriage hits record high. *USA Today.* Retrieved September 16, 2012, from http://usatoday30.usatoday.com/news/health/wellness/marriage/story/2012-02-16/US-rate-of-interracial-marriage-hits-record-high/53109980/1

Jones, J. (2011, September 12). Record-high 86% approve of Black-White marriages. *Gallup.* Retrieved from http://www.gallup.com/poll/149390/Record-High-Approve-BlackWhite-Marriages.aspx

Kahn, J. S., & Denmon, J. (1997). An examination of social science literature pertaining to multiracial identification: A historical perspective. *Journal of Multicultural Social Work, 6,* 117–138.

Kennedy, R. (2003). *Interracial intimacies: Sex, marriage, identity, and adoption.* New York, NY: Vintage Books.

Khanna, N. (2011). *Biracial in America: Forming and performing racial identity.* Lanham, MD: Lexington Books.

Kilson, M. (2001). *Claiming place: Biracial young adults of the post-civil rights era.* Westport, CT: Bergin & Garvey.

Korgen, K. (1998). *From Black to biracial: Transforming racial identity among biracial Americans.* New York, NY: Praeger.

Lee, P. (2009). Interracial couple is refused marriage license by justice of peace over concern for future children. *New York Daily News.* Retrieved April 18, 2017, from http://www.nydaily news.com/news/national/interracial-couple-refused-marriage-license-justice-peace-concern-future-children-article-1.382084

Lofquist, D., Lugaila, T., O'Connell, M., & Feliz, S. (2012). *Households and families: 2010.* Washington, DC: U.S. Census Bureau. Retrieved September 16, 2012, from http://www.census.gov/prod/cen2010/briefs/c2010br-14.pdf

Loving v. Virginia, 388 U.S. (1967).

Newport, F. (2013). *In U.S., 87% approve of Black-White marriage, vs. 4% in 1958.* Gallup. Retrieved May 23, 2016, from http://www.gallup.com/poll/163697/approve-marriage-blacks-whites.aspx?version=print

Park, R. (1928). Human migration and the marginal man. *American Journal of Sociology, 33*(6), 881–893.

Passel, J. S., Wang, W., & Taylor, P. (2010). *Marrying out: One-in-seven new U.S. marriages is interracial or interethnic.* Washington, DC: Pew Research Center. Retrieved September 16, 2012, from http://www.pewsocialtrends.org/files/2010/10/755-marrying-out.pdf

Plecker, W. A. (1924, March). *Virginia health bulletin.* Retrieved from https://www.dnalc.org/view/10431--The-New-Virginia-Law-to-Preserve-Racial-Integrity-by-W-A-Plecker-Virginia-Health-Bulletin-vol-16-2-.html

Rentas, K. (2009). Removing a justice of the peace in Louisiana no cakewalk. *CNN.* Retrieved January 15, 2013, from http://www.cnn.com/2009/CRIME/10/19/louisiana.interracial.marriage/index.html?iref=allsearch

The Republican primaries: Miscegenation and the South. (2012, March 13). *The Economist.* Retrieved May 23, 2012, from http://www.economist.com/blogs/democracyinamerica/2012/03/republican-primaries

Shih, M. D., & Sanchez, T. (2005). Perspectives and research on the positive and negative implications of having multiple racial identities. *Psychological Bulletin, 131,* 569–591.

Sickels, R. J. (1972). *Race, marriage, and the law.* Albuquerque: University of New Mexico Press.

Sohoni, D. (2007). Unsuitable suitors: Anti-miscegenation laws, naturalization laws, and the construction of Asian identities. *Law & Society Review, 41*(3), 587–618.

Sollors, W. (2000). *Interracialism: Black-White intermarriage in American history, literature, and law.* New York, NY: Oxford University Press.

Stonequist, E. (1961). *The marginal man.* New York, NY: Russell & Russell. (Original work published 1937)

Taylor, P., Wang, W., Parker, K., Passel, J. S., Patten, E., & Motel, S. (2012). *The rise of intermarriage: Rates, characteristics vary by race and gender.* Washington, DC: Pew Research Center. Retrieved May 23, 2016, from http://www.pewsocialtrends.org/files/2012/02/SDT-Intermarriage-II.pdf

Tucker, W. H. (2004). "Inharmoniously adapted to each other": Science and racial crosses. In A. S. Winston (Ed.), *Defining difference: Race and racism in the history of psychology* (pp. 109–128). Washington, DC: American Psychological Association.

Wang, W. (2015). Interracial marriage: Who is marrying out? *Pew Research Center.* Retrieved May 23, 2016, from http://www.pewresearch.org/fact-tank/2015/06/12/interracial-marriage-who-is-marrying-out/

Williams, G. (1958). *The rabbits' wedding*. New York, NY: HarperCollins.

Yen, H. (2012, February 16). Interracial marriage in the US hits new high: 1 in 12. *NBC News*. Retrieved April 18, 2017, from http://www.nbcnews.com/id/46409832/ns/us_news-life/#.WPYf6oWcHIU

Zabel, W. D. (2000). Interracial marriage and the law. In W. Sollors (Ed.), *Interracialism: Black-White intermarriage in American history, literature, and law* (pp. 54–60). New York, NY: Oxford University Press.

Zack, N. (1993). *Race and mixed race*. Philadelphia, PA: Temple University Press.

"Black People Don't Value Marriage as Much as Others"

Examining Structural Inequalities in Black Marriage Patterns

Dawne M. Mouzon

Rutgers University–New Brunswick

Most social scientists agree that there have been tremendous changes in what sociologist Dorothy Smith (1993) coined the SNAF, or Standard North American Family. This ideological concept refers to a married heterosexual man and woman who live together with their biological children under one roof. However, contemporary families exhibit a far wider range of forms and flexibility. What we formerly viewed as "the family" has transformed into a mosaic of configurations, including stepfamilies, children raised by gay and lesbian couples, adoptive families, and interracial and interethnic unions, like those represented in popular TV shows such as *Modern Family* and *Grey's Anatomy*.

By far, the most important demographic change in the social institution of marriage over the past 50 years is the dramatic decline in marriage. Roughly 72% of all Americans were married in 1960, but only half (51%) of all Americans were married in 2010 (Pew Research Center, 2011). This decline was also demonstrated among Whites; 74% of Whites were married in 1960, but only 55% were married in 2010. Latinos exhibit similar patterns (72% and 48%, respectively). However, the marriage decline has been far steeper among Blacks than for any other racial or ethnic group in the United States. Almost 61% of Blacks were married in 1960, but this figure dropped to 31% by 2010 (Pew Research Center, 2011). Blacks also experience higher divorce rates and lower remarriage rates than Whites (Livingston, 2014; Stykes,

Gibbs, & Payne, 2014). Scholars and the public have understandably been concerned about the universal marriage decline. After all, marriage historically provides myriad benefits to families. Individuals who are married tend to have better physical and mental health, have higher household incomes, have more social integration, accumulate more wealth, and raise children with more positive health and social outcomes than those who are unmarried (Carr & Springer, 2010; Ribar, 2015). Because the marriage decline has been most pronounced among Blacks, greater scrutiny has been directed toward this group in an effort to understand the fundamental question, "Why aren't more Black people married?" In part, this can be answered by looking at trends in marriage among Blacks over time.

A Brief History of Black Marriage

The history of Black marriage in the United States is a complicated one. The Transatlantic Slave Trade was initiated by European settlers in the early 17th century. During this process, White colonists enslaved and forcibly sent millions of Africans to the United States (among other places in the African Diaspora) to extract their free labor to aid in the agricultural and economic development of the new colonies. Because slavery was purely an economic system, African families were often forcefully separated from each other based on the specific labor and reproductive needs of plantation owners. Slaves were not considered citizens (or even fully human) and therefore were not legally eligible to marry. However, some plantation owners permitted their slaves to engage in symbolic Christian or African marriage ceremonies, often including rituals such as "jumping the broom." After almost 250 years of bondage, the institution of North American slavery was formally abolished at the end of the Civil War in 1865. Slavery was immediately followed by the development of new economic systems during Reconstruction (1865–1877) and the social marginalization of Blacks that characterized the Jim Crow Era (1877–1965).

In his landmark book, *The Black Family in Slavery and Freedom, 1750–1925*, historian Herbert Gutman (1977) analyzed an impressive array of data from sources such as birth records, census data, and marriage records from six large plantations. He concluded that during the period from 1850 to 1930, Black families were either equally likely or more likely to reside in married-couple households than native-born Whites. Moreover, roughly three quarters of slave unions were legally formalized after manumission (Gutman, 1977). Although recent work has suggested more modest marriage rates during this time, these data also show that at least half of Blacks were married between 1880 and 1940 (Ruggles, 1994). Taken together, these findings prove the unmistakable value that most Blacks placed on forging marital bonds both during and after slavery.

Influential scholars of Black family life have rightfully pointed out the historical strengths of Black families, including the incorporation of extended family members, strong biological and fictive kinship bonds, and flexible and egalitarian family roles, among other characteristics (R. Hill, 2003; S. Hill, 2005; Stack, 1974). Newer research suggests that historically abundant and supportive Black family networks have been partially eroded due to structural factors such as deindustrialization caused by globalization (and the ensuing flight of blue-collar jobs to developing countries), the disincentive to marry under restrictions imposed by mid-1990s welfare reform, and the war on drugs, all of which primarily targeted Blacks and other people of color (Roschelle, 1997).

Marriage is a fundamental mechanism underlying health and social inequities, a major point that students learn in my courses. When asked to brainstorm about the factors underlying the contemporary Black marriage decline, one student will inevitably declare, "Black people don't value marriage as much as Whites," a simple statement that echoes the sentiments of many scholars, many policymakers, and much of the media. In other words, the assertion is that Blacks have certain cultural beliefs that devalue the importance of marriage to individuals, families, and society as a whole. One of the first individuals to offer this argument was Daniel Patrick Moynihan, a sociologist turned Democratic senator who served the state of New York between 1976 and 2000.

Moynihan's theoretical framework—later coined the *culture of poverty* or the *tangle of pathology*—was first laid out in his 1965 research report titled *The Negro Family: The Case for National Action*. In this report, Moynihan argued that social problems among Blacks could be easily traced to Black women's presumed preference for the matriarchal family, an argument he supported by citing their disproportionately higher rates of nonmarital childbearing and low prevalence of marriage. At the outset of his chapter on "The Negro American Family," Moynihan professes this philosophy in no uncertain terms:

> At the center of the tangle of pathology is the weakness of family structure. Once or twice removed, it will be found to be the principal source of most of the aberrant, inadequate, or antisocial behavior that did not establish, but now serves to perpetuate, the cycle of poverty and deprivation.

In other words, because Blacks did not conform to the SNAF ideological code of a nuclear family consisting of a married man and woman and their biological children co-residing in a single household, Moynihan predicted that they would be doomed to continue suffering from high rates of social ills such as crime, incarceration, and presumed welfare dependency. The tangle of pathology approach is cultural determinism at its very worst and yet is still widely believed. Unfortunately, despite more substantial sections of the report underscoring the contribution of broader structural factors (i.e., public policy, labor market marginalization, and the legacy of slavery) in undermining Black family structure, Moynihan is best remembered for his brief musings on the cultural values of Black people regarding family formation and maintenance.

Answering the Question: Do Blacks Value Marriage Less Than Whites?

Given the pervasiveness of belief in this idea, how well do empirical data support this culture of poverty argument? Do Blacks really value marriage less than Whites? M. Belinda Tucker, a social psychologist from the University of California–Los Angeles, used data from Whites, Blacks, and Mexican Americans residing in 21 U.S. cities to definitively answer this long-standing question. After examining 10 different values related to marriage (e.g., importance of marrying one day, importance of being married when having children, etc.), she found no race or ethnic differences among Whites, Blacks, and Mexican Americans on half of the measures. All groups had similar levels of values regarding the expectation of marriage, the importance of marrying someday, and the importance of being married when having children. Where there were differences, *Blacks actually valued marriage more than Whites* (Tucker, 2000).

The culture of poverty approach supposes that Black women prefer to head single-mother families—in other words, that they devalue the nuclear family. Yet findings from the Pew Research Center (2010) cast serious doubt on that assumption. Blacks and Whites are equally critical of the trend of single motherhood; 74% of Blacks and 70% of Whites—yet only 58% of Latinos—reported that women having children without a male partner is "a bad thing for society" (Pew Research Center, 2010). When asked whether a child needs a home with both a mother and a father to grow up happily, 57% of Whites agreed with that statement. Despite their higher rates of nonmarital childbearing, more Blacks and Latinos agreed with that statement (65% and 72%, respectively). Moreover, among cohabiters, Blacks and Latinos are more likely than Whites to report that they intend to marry but less likely than Whites to ultimately marry their cohabiting partners (Guzzo, 2008).

If surveys indicate Blacks value marriage as much as or more than Whites, what types of partners are they seeking? The Pew Research Center (2010) asked respondents to rate the importance of various factors when choosing a mate. When asked how important it is that a "good husband or partner provide a good income," 67% of Black women believed that it is very important, compared with half of Latinas and only 35% of White women. Roughly 55% of Black women and 54% of Latinas said it was very important for a husband or partner to be well educated, compared with only 28% of White women. When asked whether financial stability should be an important criterion for people to get married, 50% of Black women and 46% of Latina women agreed, versus only 25% of White women (Pew Research Center, 2010). A highly acclaimed ethnography from sociologists Kathryn Edin and Maria Kefalas, titled *Promises I Can Keep: Why Poor Women Put Motherhood Before Marriage* (2005), found that low-income Black and Latina mothers value marriage highly but perceive myriad financial barriers to becoming married. The fact that Black women place more emphasis on the role of socioeconomic status (SES) in deciding to marry yet many Black men experience socioeconomic disadvantage is one piece of the puzzle that can help explain the Black–White marriage gap.

Over the past 30 years, there has been a strong countermovement that seeks to change pervasive cultural assumptions about Black families. The crux of this movement focuses on structural—rather than cultural—impediments that hinder Blacks from becoming and remaining married. The underpinning of this argument is that the SNAF ideal was (and still is) harder for Blacks to attain given their continued marginalization in most mainstream social institutions.

Essentially, marriage stands at the intersection of many other social institutions. In other words, marriage and marital rates are greatly affected by the structure of the labor force, the educational system, and the criminal justice system. If, as we have just learned, Blacks value marriage and express a desire and intent to be married just as much as (if not more than) Whites, what explains their increasingly lower rates of marriage? In other words, are structural inequalities a more significant driving force behind the Black marriage decline than presumed cultural beliefs that devalue marriage?

Many scholars attribute the Black marriage decline to an imbalanced gender ratio. When considering the ratio of available (i.e., alive and noninstitutionalized) Black men to Black women, there are roughly 91 Black men for every 100 Black women (U.S. Census Bureau, 2012). The corresponding gender ratio for Whites is 99 White men for every 100 White women. The gender ratio is actually reversed among Latinos, resulting in a gender ratio of 107 Latino men for every 100 Latina women. An analysis of low-income cities (Harknett & McLanahan, 2004) found that after taking employment into account, there were only 46 employed Black men for every 100 Black women (vs. a roughly 82:100 ratio of employed White men to employed White women; corresponding figures for Mexicans and those of other Hispanic descent were 83 and 69 per 100, respectively).

Ralph Richard Banks (2011), a Stanford Law professor, recently offered a methodologically rigorous examination of the marriage decline (both overall and by race). In addition to pointing out these glaring disparities, he suggests that interracial marriage may be one solution to increase the especially low rates of marriage among Black women. Although intermarriage is becoming a more common phenomenon across all groups, it is important to note that in 2010, more than twice as many Black men (24%) as Black women (9%) married interracially (Wang, 2012; see Khanna in this volume for further discussion on interracial marriage). Therefore, an imbalanced gender ratio (further perpetuated by higher rates of interracial marriage among Black men) is an important contributor to the Black–White marriage gap. There are simply fewer Black men physically available for Black women to marry. This begs the question, where are Black men?

Where Are Black Men? Gender Ratios and "Marriageability"

There are two primary mechanisms to explain the relative dearth of available Black men in the community. First, Black men have the highest rate of incarceration of any other group. Black men had an incarceration rate of 4,347 per 100,000 in 2010, a rate that was six times higher than that of White men (678 per 100,000). The incarceration rate of Hispanic/Latino men was 1,775 per 100,000, half as high as that of Black men (U.S. Bureau of Justice Statistics, 2011; see also Doude in this volume). Even when prisoners are released from custody, they face extremely high levels of discrimination in the labor force, reflecting one of the most enduring stigmas and barriers to upward mobility in the United States. Given the high priority women of color place on the financial viability of potential partners, those with a criminal history will be considered less attractive by potential partners, further driving down marriage rates in these groups.

Disproportionately high mortality rates and low life expectancy among Black men can also help explain the imbalanced gender ratio (Xu, Kochanek, Murphy, & Tejeda-Vera, 2010). Black men die earlier than any other racial or ethnic and gender group. For example, White men and women can expect to live roughly 79 and 84 years, respectively. But Black women's life expectancy is roughly 78 years and Black men's life expectancy is only 71. Black men have a much higher age-adjusted death rate than White men (890 and 1,151 per 100,000, respectively) and a homicide death rate roughly 10 times higher than White men (37.1 and 3.7 per 100,000, respectively). Indeed, homicide—an important way in which bodies are prematurely removed from the marriage market—is the fourth leading cause of death for Black men and the eighth leading cause of death for Latino men but does not rank in the top 10 for White men (Miniño & Murphy, 2012; Xu et al., 2010).

Clearly, there are fewer "warm bodies" for Black women to marry, but what about the quality of Black men who *are* physically present in the dating and marriage markets? In his groundbreaking book, *The Truly Disadvantaged: The Inner City, the Underclass, and Public Policy* (1987/1990), sociologist William Julius Wilson set forth the argument that Black marriage decline was due to a shortage of "marriageable Black men." Marriageable men are those who exhibit qualities that are attractive to potential romantic partners in the marriage market. Women of all races and ethnicities prefer to date and marry men who are educated, earn a good income, and have a stable job (although, as described earlier, these characteristics are ironically most important to Black women; see Pew Research Center, 2010; Tucker, 2000). In a direct test of this theory, Wilson and Kathryn Neckerman (1986) found an inverse relationship between male employment and marriage rates; as male unemployment increased, marriage rates decreased. A similar study using longitudinal data from 1990 through 2009 found a strong inverse relationship between the rates of families headed by women and the quantity and the quality of men (Craigie, Myers, & Darity, 2012). In focusing on structural factors, William Julius Wilson's work (and subsequent work using this framework) stands in direct contrast to Moynihan's cultural argument.

Are there really fewer marriageable Black men than White men? Let's first consider unemployment rates. In 2013, 6.8% of White men were unemployed, compared with 14.2% of Black men (U.S. Bureau of Labor Statistics, 2014). Sociologists are well aware of the overlap between race or ethnicity and social class, a relationship that would imply that most of the race disparities in SES (in this case, unemployment) are because

Blacks have less education than Whites. However, race disparities in unemployment persist even at the highest levels of education. Among the college educated, 2.6% of White men but 4.4% of Black men were unemployed in 2013. This means that even after holding education constant—that is, comparing "apples to apples," or Black men and White men with the same level of education—Black men are still more likely to be unemployed than White men. When coupled with the aforementioned findings that Blacks place heavy emphasis on the role of finances when deciding whether to marry, these trends can help explain the Black–White marriage gap. It is quite clear that cultural values are not the problem; structural inequality is.

In examining the "marriageability" of Black men in terms of income, not surprisingly, there is a race divide in median weekly earnings among men. In 2013, White men earned roughly $935 per week, while Black men earned $700 per week (U.S. Bureau of Labor Statistics, 2014). Can race differences in educational attainment explain why Black men earn so much less? That is, do Black men earn less than White men because they have lower educational attainment? As was the case with unemployment, the race wage gap persists when comparing highly educated Black men with highly educated White men. In fact, the largest race wage gaps among men occur at the highest levels of education; college-educated White men earn $1,416 per week, while college-educated Black men earn only $1,045. Indeed, at the high school diploma level and higher, Black men earn between 27% and 36% less than White men (U.S. Bureau of Labor Statistics, 2014).

How does the socioeconomic standing of Black men compare with their likely romantic partners, Black women? For most racial and ethnic groups, women typically have lower SES than men. However, the socioeconomic standing of Black women is either equal to or higher than that of Black men. As an illustrative example, the gender wage gap is smaller among Blacks than Whites. Although White women earn only 81.7% of White men's annual earnings, Black women earn 91.3% of Black men's annual earnings, a much smaller gender difference (U.S. Bureau of Labor Statistics, 2014). Black women generally have higher educational attainment than Black men, a pattern not found among Whites. For example, a similar proportion of White men and White women hold at least a bachelor's degree (30.8% and 29.9%, respectively), but more Black women than Black men hold at least a bachelor's degree (21.4% and 17.7%, respectively; U.S. Census Bureau, 2012). Given their similar or higher levels of economic standing relative to Black men, Black women may perceive less economic benefit to marriage, which is another potential explanation for the Black–White marriage gap.

In an innovative study, Harknett and McLanahan (2004) simultaneously tested the cultural and structural arguments for why Black women are less likely than White women to marry after a nonmarital birth. They found that Black women had the strongest pro-marriage attitudes. Moreover, the overall gender ratio and an undersupply of employed men fully explained the Black mothers' lower likelihood of marriage. This analysis directly tested the culture–structure debate and provides convincing evidence that structure matters most and, in fact, that Blacks neither suffer from nor perpetuate cultural-deficiency mores that devalue marriage.

Conclusion

As the above empirical findings suggest, Blacks place similar or higher value on the institution of marriage, which definitively overturns the cultural argument that Blacks are less likely to get married because they don't value marriage as much as Whites. There instead appears to be strong evidence in support of two sets of structural factors to explain the Black marriage gap. First, the imbalanced gender ratio (due to higher incarceration and mortality rates among Black men) results in fewer Black men physically present in the marriage market. Second, the lower "marriageability" of Black men (who experience high rates of unemployment and lower earnings and educational attainment) reduces the economic benefit of marriage for Black women. Future research should put the cultural argument to rest and focus on finding policy solutions to increase the socioeconomic standing of Black men (Darity & Hamilton, 2012).

Dawne M. Mouzon, PhD, is a sociologist and assistant professor at the Edward J. Bloustein School of Planning and Public Policy at Rutgers University–New Brunswick. She is also a member of the core faculty at the Institute for Health, Health Care Policy, and Aging Research at Rutgers University. Her work largely focuses on physical and mental health disparities facing low-income communities and communities of color. Her current research focuses on identifying causal mechanisms to explain the Black–White paradox in mental health, or the unexpected finding that Blacks typically exhibit better mental health outcomes than Whites despite their lower socioeconomic standing and greater exposure to discrimination.

SUGGESTED ADDITIONAL RESOURCES

Banks, R. R. (2011). *Is marriage for White people? How the African American marriage decline affects everyone.* New York, NY: Dutton.

Chambers, A. L., & Kravitz, A. (2011). Understanding the disproportionately low marriage rate among African Americans: An amalgam of sociological and psychological constraints. *Family Relations, 60*(5), 648–660.

Marsh, K., Darity, W. A., Cohen, P. N., Casper, L. M., & Salters, D. (2008). The emerging Black middle class: Single and living alone. *Social Forces, 86,* 735–762.

Patterson, O. (1999). *Rituals of blood: The consequences of slavery in two American centuries.* New York, NY: Basic Civitas Books.

Raley, R. K., & Sweeney, M. M. (2009). Explaining race and ethnic variation in marriage: Directions for future research. *Race and Social Problems, 1*(3), 132–142.

QUESTIONS FOR FURTHER DISCUSSION

1. Black marriage decline is often depicted as a function of cultural beliefs that devalue marriage. There has also been a similar culture–structure debate in the area of education, with some proposing that Blacks have worse educational

outcomes because they value education less than Whites, an argument that has also been disproven (see also Patel, Meanwell, & McClure in this volume). Why do you think scholars and the media continue to attribute Blacks' lower social standing to the notion that they have counterproductive cultural values?

2. Is the Black marriage decline/Black–White marriage gap a trend that deserves public policy attention? Based on the findings outlined in this chapter, what might be some effective policy solutions to address this gap?

3. Emerging sociological research (e.g., Marsh, Darity, Cohen, Casper, & Salters, 2008) has identified "The Love Jones Cohort," a relatively affluent group of Black Americans (primarily women) who are single and living alone (SALA), with neither a spouse nor children in the household. Research indicates that these households increasingly comprise a large proportion of the Black middle class. What are the implications of this cohort for companionship, childbearing, and caregiving across the life course? How might public policy best address this burgeoning segment of the Black population?

4. Other industrialized nations (e.g., Sweden) have begun the legal recognition of cohabiting unions, as opposed to the prior universal focus on implementing public policies that only benefit or protect couples who are legally married. Might this be a more appropriate solution for increasing the stability of Black romantic unions than universal marriage promotion policies? Why or why not?

5. In his 2011 book, *Is Marriage for White People? How the African American Marriage Decline Affects Everyone*, Stanford Law professor Ralph Richard Banks makes a strong case that structural barriers have caused the Black marriage decline. He proposes that Black women (who often face a lack of available or quality potential partners) should consider dating outside of their race. How do you feel about this recommendation? Would that solve the problem? What are the advantages and disadvantages of this approach?

6. Recent work finds that marriage rates are also declining among those with lower education. What might be some reasons for that decline? Does it deserve policy attention, and if so, why?

REACHING BEYOND THE COLOR LINE

1. Go to www.census.gov. Research the rates of interracial marriage. Which race or gender group has the highest rates of interracial or interethnic marriage? Which race or gender group has the lowest rates of interracial or interethnic marriage? How well do your findings mesh with Banks's (2011) recommendation that Black women consider marrying outside of their race?

2. Download data from the Pew Research Center (2010) report "The Decline of Marriage and Rise of New Families." Section 2 outlines racial and ethnic differences in perceptions of what makes a good partner. This chapter reviewed the

findings regarding the importance of providing a good income. What other factors are important to Black, White, and Latina women? Are there similar findings for Black, White, and Latino men?

3. Pair up with a classmate. Research the marriage rates of Asians and Hispanics/ Latinos over time. Compare them to the rates for Blacks. Are the patterns similar or different? What do you think makes these racial and ethnic groups distinct from Blacks?

REFERENCES

Banks, R. R. (2011). *Is marriage for White people? How the African American marriage decline affects everyone.* New York, NY: Dutton.

Carr, D., & Springer, K. W. (2010). Advances in families and health research in the 21st century. *Journal of Marriage and Family, 72,* 743–761.

Craigie, T. L., Myers, S. L., & Darity, W. A. (2012). *The decline of marriageable males and female family headship revisited.* Retrieved from http://lgi.umn.edu/centers/rwc/conferences/fourth/pdf/craigie_myers_darity_draft8d.pdf

Darity, W. A., & Hamilton, D. (2012). Bold policies for economic justice. *Review of Black Political Economy, 39*(1), 79–85.

Edin, K., & Kefalas, M. J. (2005). *Promises I can keep: Why poor women put motherhood before marriage.* Berkeley: University of California Press.

Gutman, H. (1977). *The Black family in slavery and freedom, 1750–1925.* New York, NY: Vintage Books.

Guzzo, K. B. (2008). Marital intentions and the stability of first cohabitations. *Journal of Family Issues, 30*(2), 179–205.

Harknett, K., & McLanahan, S. (2004). Explaining racial and ethnic differences in marriage among new, unwed parents. *American Sociological Review, 69*(6), 790–811.

Hill, R. B. (2003). *The strengths of Black families* (2nd ed.). Lanham, MD: University Press of America.

Hill, S. A. (2005). *Black intimacies: A gender perspective on families and relationships.* Walnut Creek, CA: AltaMira Press.

Livingston, G. (2014). *Four-in-ten couples are saying "I do," again.* Washington, DC: Pew Research Center.

Marsh, K., Darity, W. A., Cohen, P. N., Casper, L. M., & Salters, D. (2008). The emerging Black middle class: Single and living alone. *Social Forces, 86,* 735–762.

Miniño, A. M., & Murphy, S. L. (2012). *Death in the United States, 2010* (NCHS Data Brief No. 99). Hyattsville, MD: Centers for Disease Control & Prevention, National Center for Health Statistics.

Moynihan, D. P. (1965). *The Negro family: The case for national action.* Washington, DC: U.S. Department of Labor, Office of Planning and Research.

Pew Research Center. (2010, November 18). *The decline of marriage and rise of new families.* Washington, DC: Author. Retrieved from http://www.pewsocialtrends.org/2010/11/18/the-decline-of-marriage-and-rise-of-new-families/

Pew Research Center. (2011, December 14). *Barely half of U.S. adults are married: A record low.* Washington, DC: Author.

Ribar, D. C. (2015). Why marriage matters for child wellbeing. *Future of Children, 25,* 11–27.

Roschelle, A. R. (1997). *No more kin: Exploring race, class, and gender in family networks.* Thousand Oaks, CA: Sage.

Ruggles, S. (1994). The origins of African American family structure. *American Sociological Review, 59*, 136–151.

Smith, D. E. (1993). The Standard North American Family: SNAF as an ideological code. *Journal of Family Issues, 14*(1), 50–65.

Stack, C. B. (1974). *All our kin: Strategies for survival in a Black community.* New York, NY: Basic Books.

Stykes, B., Gibbs, L., & Payne, K. K. (2014). *First divorce rate, 2012* (FP-14-09). Bowling Green, OH: National Center for Family & Marriage Research. Retrieved from https://www.bgsu .edu/content/dam/BGSU/college-of-arts-and-sciences/NCFMR/documents/FP/FP-14- 09-divorce-rate-2012.pdf

Tucker, M. B. (2000). Marital values and expectations in context: Results from a 21-city survey. In L. J. Waite & C. Bachrach (Eds.), *The ties that bind: Perspectives on marriage and cohabitation* (pp. 166–187). New York, NY: Aldine de Gruyter.

U.S. Bureau of Justice Statistics. (2011). *Correctional population in the United States, 2010.* Washington, DC: U.S. Department of Justice.

U.S. Bureau of Labor Statistics. (2014). *Labor force characteristics by race and ethnicity, 2013* (Report 1050). Washington, DC: U.S. Department of Labor.

U.S. Census Bureau. (2012). *The statistical abstract of the United States: The national data book.* Washington, DC: U.S. Department of Commerce. Retrieved from http://www.census.gov/ compendia/statab/2012edition.html

Wang, W. (2012, February 16). *The rise of intermarriage: Rates, characteristics vary by race and gender.* Washington, DC: Pew Research Center.

Wilson, W. J. (1990). *The truly disadvantaged: The inner city, the underclass, and public policy.* Chicago, IL: University of Chicago Press. (Original work published 1987)

Wilson, W. J., & Neckerman, K. M. (1986). Poverty and family structure: The widening gap between evidence and public policy issues. In S. H. Danziger & D. H. Weinberg (Eds.), *Fighting poverty: What works and what doesn't* (pp. 232–259). Cambridge, MA: Harvard University Press.

Xu, J., Kochanek, K. D., Murphy, S. L., & Tejeda-Vera, B. (2010, May 20). Deaths: Final data for 2007. *National Vital Statistics Reports, 58*(19). Hyattsville, MD: Centers for Disease Control and Prevention, National Center for Health Statistics.

"Well, That Culture Really Values Education"

Culture Versus Structure in Educational Attainment

Hersheda Patel

Georgia State University

Emily Meanwell

Indiana University

Stephanie M. McClure

Georgia College

Public education is one of the most important institutions in American society and is considered a key mechanism of social mobility (Urban & Wagoner, 1996). Discussions of racial inequality in the United States frequently point to persisting differences in educational attainment (see Figure 14.1). When attempting to explain these persisting differences, students often reach for cultural explanations, including the idea that high attainment on the part of Asian Americans is explained by shared cultural values. This belief is evident in popular culture and media discourse. From children's shows such as *The Suite Life of Zack and Cody,* where Cody's Asian girlfriend, Barbara, takes "A.P. Lunch," to *The Network Guys,* a commercial campaign by AT&T, in which an Indian network tech is able to analyze complex network data but is inept at understanding social situations, stereotypical portrayals of highly academic Asian Americans appear, often in hyperbolized forms. When Asians

Figure 14.1   Educational Attainment of the Population Aged 25 and Over by Race, Hispanic Origin, and Nativity Status: 2015 (in percent)

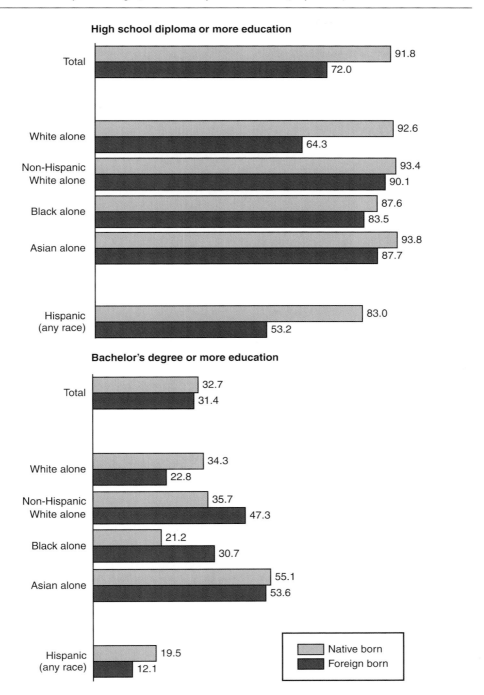

Source: U.S. Census Bureau, Current Population Survey, 2015.

aren't being used as stereotypical main or supporting characters, they are usually nothing more than shadows of the stereotype, such as the Asian nerds in the movie *Mean Girls* (2004), the technology-producing Asians of District Three in *The Hunger Games* (2012), and the NBC TV show *Community*'s all-Asian Math Club.

These popular portrayals of Asian Americans are also reflected in media discourse. Harkaran Singh (2011), a writer for the *Berkeley Political Review* (a magazine from the University of California), writes that Asians value education more than Americans because of the importance of gaining respect for one's family in "Asian society." He also asserts that Americans do not value education and are more likely to idolize the class clown than the scholar (Singh, 2011). Similarly, after a 2012 Pew research report found that Asian Americans are more educated, wealthier, and value work, marriage, and family more than average Americans, a *USA Today* article attempted to use these findings to argue that so-called Asian American cultural values are responsible for their success rather than historical and structural explanations. For example, as Paul Taylor, the executive vice president of the Pew Research Center, says in the original research report, "recent Asian arrivals are the most highly educated . . . immigrants in U.S. history" (Nasser, 2012). Research shows that the skills and education immigrants bring with them are more likely to account for the high levels of education and wealth found in the study, yet even those who have access to these data use cultural arguments to explain these educational and wealth trends.

These seemingly positive portrayals of Asian American educational values are meant to create a juxtaposition with the supposed lack of positive educational values in Blacks and Latinos. The myth of Asian Americans as having superior values that lead to their academic success suggests that poor values are to blame for the persisting educational attainment gap experienced by Blacks and Latinos, thus making invisible the structural factors that lead to this gap.

To consider whether Asian educational attainment can be explained by the idea that "Asian culture really values education," and the corresponding belief that lower levels of attainment among Blacks and Latinos are explained by the absence of these values, we must first define and unpack some key terms used in these claims: *education, Asian, Black, Latino, culture,* and *value*. While at first glance these terms may appear straightforward and easily definable, upon further examination, we see that their meanings are often quite murky, which significantly complicates the nature of these claims and ultimately debunks them.

Clarifying the Terms

To begin, in most of the research that has engaged these issues, either *education* has been defined as "educational attainment" and measured by category (high school, college, post-college) or with a continuous measure (years of education), or it has been defined as "achievement" and measured using standardized test scores. But on both of these measures, it is true that Blacks and Latinos have lower levels of education, whether defined by attainment, category of education, or years of education.

The question is: Why is this the case? And what can further examination of terms such as *Asian, Black, Latino,* and *culture* tell us about the differences in how racial groups really think about education?

Terms such as *Asian, Black,* and *Latino* require further examination because these are socially constructed categories that contain individuals from widely different backgrounds. For instance, the term *Asian* refers most overtly to the world's largest continent, from which many people who have immigrated to the United States originate. It is important to note that on the Asian continent, almost no one refers to themselves as "Asian"; they may refer to themselves by national identity (e.g., Chinese, Japanese, Korean) or by a more specific regional identity (e.g., Han, Zhuang, or Man). The use of the term *Asian* to refer to this widely diverse group is most often deployed in the United States, where it is attached to *American* to form the panethnic label *Asian American.* This label was originally developed by the U.S. government (particularly the Census Bureau) but has subsequently come to be used by people within the group as well. The process of panethnic identity development has been explored in some depth by several authors (Espiritu, 1993; Liu, 1998; Wu, 2003) and is well worth exploring further (see suggestions for further reading at the end of this chapter). For our purposes, it is important to note that the label *Asian American* is socially constructed, generated by the immigrant experience, and encompasses an incredibly diverse group of people with different histories, backgrounds, and immigration experiences (see also Zhou in this volume).

Thus, one of the problems with the stereotype that all Asians as a panethnic group are high educational achievers is that it obscures the fact that this stereotype does not hold across all Asian students. For example, Baker, Keller-Wolff, and Wolf-Wendel (2000) find that Asian and Pacific Islander students have higher math performance than Whites but that there are major differences between subgroups of Asian students—with Filipino and Pacific Islander students (e.g., students of indigenous Hawaiian heritage, Samoans, Guamanians, and Tahitians) showing significantly lower levels of math achievement (though Filipino students outperform other Asian subgroups in reading achievement). Another analysis finds that Pacific Islanders are falling behind other Asian groups in obtaining bachelor's degrees (UC AAPI Policy Initiative, 2006; see also Lee & Kumashiro, 2005). These differences are important to consider when looking at differences in educational attainment and how Asian Americans have fared as a whole.

The terms *Black* and *Latino* are equally complicated and also reflect panethnic racial categories that include individuals from very different places whose reasons for being in the United States can be quite distinct. Further discussions of the development and diversity of these groups are available in Omi and Winant (1994), Davis (1991), De Genova and Ramos-Zayas (2003), and Rodriguez (2000); more of this diversity is also discussed below. All these terms form a sort of racial shorthand that can be deployed for various purposes (e.g., government data collection, social science description, political collective action), most of which are somewhat neutral. Nonetheless, it is important to keep in mind their internal diversity and socially constructed nature. This variation is particularly salient as we move to the next term: *culture.*

Culture has been defined by social scientists in diverse ways. For our purposes, we will use one of the most common definitions, which fits with what is implied by the myth itself: that culture is a set of attitudes, values, beliefs, and practices that form a way of life for a particular group of people. With that definition in hand, and given our previous discussion of the panethnic racial labels, we see the first problem with this myth. Given the great variation contained in the group we call "Asian Americans," it isn't reasonable to assume that all the people within it share the same attitudes, values, beliefs, and practices. The assumption of within-group homogeneity is one of many problems with shorthand racial labels as they are used in everyday conversation. Determining who "values" education and how we can detect that "valuing" through data collection is even more difficult. When we try to decide who values education and who doesn't using racial group categories, we are required to account for some of that within-group variation.

Additionally, while people in a given group may share certain experiences, there are many individual-level differences that greatly affect their values, lifestyle, and educational achievement. These variables include, but are not limited to, parents' occupations, parenting styles, educational attainment of parents, family structure, number of books and other resources in the home, and Internet access (Fuligni, 1997; Kao, 1995; Portes & Zhou, 1993; Teachman, 1987). Two parents with well-paying jobs and college degrees who encourage positive educational practices in a nice house with books and Internet access form the ideal background for promoting high levels of educational achievement, but the presence of these characteristics varies both by group and within groups (Kao, 1995). Therefore, the idea that all people in any group value or do not value education and that the presence or absence of such values alone can account for educational attainment becomes problematic.

Finally, the positive educational outcomes often attributed to "Asian values" have been found in other immigrant groups. For example, West Indian immigrants show higher levels of education, higher socioeconomic status, and higher standards of living than nonimmigrant Americans (Model, 1995, 2011). One can hardly make the argument that West Indian immigrants share Asian culture and values. It is more plausible that we find higher levels of educational success among immigrant groups due to the nature of individuals who self-select into the immigration process and possibly the nature of immigration itself (Xie & Goyette, 2003). In fact, some evidence suggests that the risks and challenges associated with immigration may contribute to increased pressure on first-, 1.5-, and second-generation immigrants to succeed academically to achieve upward social mobility. This pressure can come directly from families or through shared knowledge of the hardships that accompany immigration (Waters, 1996). This pressure crosses racial and ethnic lines and is evident in all American immigrant groups across time (Portes & Rumbaut, 2001). Over generations, we find that descendants of immigrants show equal levels of academic success as nonimmigrant Americans. It seems that once the intensity of the immigrant experience becomes diluted, the pressure associated with it lessens, leading to "normal" levels of academic achievement. This finding allows us to consider other variables that may explain differing levels of academic achievement across groups that do not rely on culturally essentialist explanations.

Determining who values education ultimately requires collecting data at two levels: (1) the individual level—such as information on family economic resources, parental educational attainment, and immigrant status (e.g., first or second generation, age at time of immigration, legal vs. undocumented, or visa status)—and (2) the collective or group level, which takes into consideration, for example, whether the group is a voluntary or an involuntary immigrant group, the historical timing of their arrival in the United States, reception on arrival, geographic concentration, and overt structural barriers to education. When we take these factors into account, simplistic narratives of which group values education more, and how that valuing is causally related to educational attainment, become more complex. For example, what were the resources immigrants brought with them from their country of origin (including money, education, connections to people already in the United States). What kinds of aid did they receive, and what structural barriers did they face upon arrival? These factors are rarely taken into account when considering who values education, and instead, we have come to rely on cultural explanations. In doing so, we conflate perceived valuing of education with the actual causes of educational attainment disparities. Even if we could determine if an entire group values education, we could not make the argument that valuing education alone is enough to explain the racial gap in educational attainment. To explain this gap, we must account for structural factors. This is particularly evident in the discourse surrounding Black Americans and education.

Cultural Explanations of Black Educational Achievement

The persistent differences in academic achievement between Black students and their peers are particularly troubling. Despite the centrality of education to the civil rights movement's agenda, one of the most common ways this achievement gap has been explained is by pointing to *cultural factors* and a supposed devaluing of education among Blacks. Even President Obama has employed detrimental cultural explanations. For example, in a speech on July 27, 2004, then-Senator Obama stated:

> Go into any inner city neighborhood, and folks will tell you that government alone can't teach kids to learn. . . . Children can't achieve unless we raise their expectations and . . . eradicate the slander that says a Black youth with a book is acting White.

Obama's reference to the idea that Black students who put forth academic effort are derided by peers for "acting White" connects to a theory that has been researched and debated by scholars for over 30 years, under the umbrella of *oppositional culture theory*.

Anthropologist John U. Ogbu's oppositional culture explanation for racial differences in academic achievement emphasizes academic disengagement among Blacks (Fordham & Ogbu, 1986; Ogbu, 1978). Ogbu distinguished between different types of minorities in the United States, particularly between voluntary immigrant minorities who came to America in search of prosperity and involuntary, subordinate minorities such as Blacks who were brought to the United States against their will. While members of voluntary immigrant groups have an optimistic attitude toward schooling, Ogbu argued, Blacks do not. Faced with and frustrated by substandard schools, discrimination, and limited opportunities for success in the job market, he argued that Blacks, over generations, developed coping mechanisms and adaptations—including a cultural orientation toward education that leads to a lack of effort and underachievement. Fordham and Ogbu (1986) argued that academic achievement was further discouraged by negative sanctioning from Black peers, who labeled academic effort and good grades as "acting White."

As this cultural explanation of academic achievement gaps between different racial and ethnic groups became more popular, some of its original points became muddied or lost. While Ogbu emphasized that oppositional culture was an adaptation to social structural conditions, subsequent discussions tended to focus on problematic Black culture while overlooking the structural roots Ogbu emphasized. Thus, there was a tendency to explain racial achievement gaps by attributing them to a lack of valuing of education while ignoring the societal conditions that Ogbu said produced academic disengagement in the first place. This is a history and structure that must be taken into account when looking at Blacks' and also Latinos' relationship with education.

Beyond Cultural Explanations: The Role of History and Structure in Education

Therefore, a major problem with cultural explanations of educational achievement is that they disregard structural barriers to achieving success. *Structure* refers to the patterns and relationships among social institutions, social networks, and other participants in a society that affect the behaviors of all members of the society. Structure is both created by and regulates the actions, behaviors, attitudes, and beliefs of individuals. Therefore, structural barriers are those roadblocks enacted by social institutions, social networks that are outside of the immediate control of any single person in any racial or ethnic group.

Different racial and ethnic groups within the United States have faced these structural barriers with varying levels of resources (such as education and occupational training and skills). For example, most documented Asians that have come to America in the past 60 years have possessed high levels of education and training and have been able to replicate their success in America both in terms of education and occupation (Steinberg, 2001). Similarly, in the late 19th century and early 20th century, White ethnic groups were able to successfully assimilate and integrate into mainstream society because of the industrial skills they brought with them from Europe (Blauner, 2001; Steinberg, 2001). On the other hand, Blacks were heavily concentrated in the South during this time and mainly had agricultural skills. During the Industrial Revolution, Blacks moved to the North equipped with the most basic of skills and facing a 200-year-old system of racism and prejudice (Blauner, 2001; Steinberg, 2001). In the North, White ethnics were hired at higher rates than Blacks. When Blacks were hired in large numbers, it was a result of strikes by White ethnic groups, which meant Blacks were paid much lower wages (Steinberg, 2001). All these historical and structural factors contributed to the inability of Blacks to achieve success and overcome the economic barriers to gaining widespread access to higher education at the same levels as White ethnics and Asians.

College educations were long reserved for White, upper-class, Protestant men (Rudolph, 1962/1990). While times have changed and other groups have gained access to higher education, many college campuses, particularly the most prestigious universities, remain predominantly White (U.S. Census Bureau, 2012). Historical research indicates that many early Asian immigrant populations achieved educational parity with Whites between the first and second world wars due to the highly restrictive immigration laws of the era and lack of specific anti-Asian policies at American universities (Hirschman & Wong, 1986; Wong, 1980). Race-based immigration quotas restricted the granting of new visas to as low as 2% of the current population of certain Asian immigrant groups, creating a selection effect in which only the wealthiest, most educated, and highly connected individuals were granted U.S. visas. Furthermore, most American universities during this time were focused on preventing mass Black enrollment, leading to the creation and implementation of specific anti-Black admissions and enrollment policies. Although these institutions did not desire other minority groups, including Asian and Jewish immigrants, people from those groups were able to enroll due to loopholes in admissions policies that were written specifically to exclude Blacks (Wallenstein, 1999). Census data suggest that there was no educational disadvantage between Whites and native-born Japanese Americans at least as far back as 1910. For Chinese Americans, parity seems to have arrived by 1920, and for Filipino Americans, by 1940 (Hirschman & Wong, 1986). This early parity significantly influences intergenerational patterns at the group level today. In other words, higher educational attainment for any group is intimately connected to the educational attainment of previous generations.

On the other hand, prior to the mid-20th-century civil rights movement, Black participation in predominantly White institutions across the country was extremely limited. Between 1865 and 1895, about 194 Blacks graduated from northern colleges, 75 from Oberlin College in Ohio alone, with the other 119 attending 52 other schools, for an average of little more than 2 per school. There is also evidence of some Blacks graduating from southern colleges before their admittance was made illegal at the end of this period (Bowles & DeCosta, 1971). This southern restriction was relatively consistent through 1953, with the exception of some minimal movement among primarily border state universities after key court cases in the 1930s

(Bowles & DeCosta, 1971). However, Bowles and DeCosta (1971) write that northern schools were not much better in this period:

> The difference between the passive discrimination of the Northern colleges which, while permitting a few Negro students to enter, were by reason of financial requirements or social isolation, or both, discouraging to most Negro prospective students, and the active discrimination of the white Southern colleges was, essentially, only a difference in degree. (p. 40)

Despite the strong discrimination Blacks faced at White universities, their determination to educate themselves did not waver. Dating back to the early 19th century, free Blacks were attempting to create their own higher education institutions, which were often met with White resistance. In 1831, the First Annual Convention of the People of Color voted to create a college for scientific, mechanical, and agricultural education in New Haven, Connecticut (Bowles & DeCosta, 1971). Before the plans could be carried out, the White citizens of New Haven voted against the creation of the college, calling colleges aimed at educating "colored people" an "unwarrantable and dangerous undertaking," and claimed they would resist the establishment of the college in Connecticut "by every lawful means" (p. 23). The group later attempted to fulfill their goal of educating Blacks by partnering with an existing White college in Canaan, New Hampshire, but that school was forcibly removed from the town for enrolling Black students (Bowles & DeCosta, 1971). This history of exclusion from White colleges and barriers in creating and funding Black colleges is evidence of the structural racism that has served to prevent Blacks from closing the achievement gap despite the long history of valuing and fighting for access to education.

Beginning in the 1960s and influenced by a changing political climate, universities exhibited a rising concern with the participation of people of color in higher education. This led to the development of admissions policies designed to increase the number of students of color on campus, which was relatively successful at increasing Black student enrollment (Allen, Epps, & Haniff, 1991; see also Poon in this volume). However, this varied significantly by region. Many southern states adopted a position of "massive resistance" to integration, including the signing of the Southern Regional Education Compact on February 8, 1948, by 14 states trying to avoid the desegregation of their institutions of higher education and the Southern Manifesto on March 12, 1956, by more than 100 southern senators, which denounced the 1954 *Brown v. Board of Education* decision that declared separate as inherently unequal.

In spite of this history, the idea that a group's valuing of education explains differences in attainment persists. In particular, the idea that Blacks and Latinos do not value education has been present both in American society generally and in academic research (see Coontz, 1992, on myths about Black families' culture more generally). As mentioned above, this myth does not square with the emphasis on access to education that has been central throughout Blacks' long fight for equality (Anderson, 1988; Bowles & DeCosta, 1971). For example, the landmark decision in *Brown v. Board of Education,* in which the Supreme Court ruled that separate schools could not be equal, was one of the most important steps in the civil rights movement (see Tushnet, 1987). This decision removed some of the most crucial structural barriers that denied Black children equal educational opportunity and set in motion the long process of integrating schools. Yet more than 50 years later, the promise of equal education hasn't come to fruition, and due to the abandonment of specific integration programs and persisting neighborhood racial segregation, schools have lost much of the integration progress that was made from 1970 to 1990 (Orfield, Frankenberg, & Lee, 2002).

What the Research Shows: Lack of Support for Cultural Explanations

Scholars have researched the oppositional culture theory for more than a quarter century. Researchers have looked at attitudes toward education among different racial groups, as well as evidence of stigmatization of high-achieving Black students as "acting White." This work has produced mixed findings but, overall, little empirical support for the cultural explanations of differences in academic achievement proposed by Ogbu's theory. First, researchers have found that Black students hold positive attitudes toward education. Research has found that education is valued by Blacks as the chief pathway to upward social mobility (Cole & Omari, 2003). Theoharis (2009) similarly finds that Black and Latino students are committed to education and see it as holding promise even as they attend a failing urban school where they perceive there are adults who think them incapable of success. In one study that used data from a national survey, Black students reported more pro-school attitudes than White students (Ainsworth-Darnell & Downey, 1998; for similar findings see Cook & Ludwig, 1997; A. L. Harris, 2006, 2008). While these studies used survey data of older students, another study using ethnographic data found positive attitudes toward education among younger Black students at two all-Black elementary schools (Tyson, 2002).

Second, research has also explored the idea that Black students' peer culture stigmatizes academic success. Ainsworth-Darnell and Downey (1998) found that Blacks who were seen by their peers as good students were *more* likely to be popular than Whites seen as good students; Datnow and Cooper (1996) found similar results for Black students at a predominantly White elite school. These findings contradict the idea that successful Black students are stigmatized by peers as "acting White." Some research has, though, found an increased likelihood for Black students who report being "very good" students to also report being put down by peers (Farkas, Lleras, & Maczuga, 2002; see also a response from Downey & Ainsworth-Darnell, 2002). Other research found that in some schools, Black students may be mildly socially penalized for certain public expressions of academic engagement or effort in the classroom—a "weak" version of the "acting White" hypothesis (Wildhagen, 2011).

Recent work on the "acting White" phenomenon gives a nuanced view that is instructive for considering the daily lived experiences of students. One study found that when students talk about "acting Black," "acting Spanish," and "acting White," they are referring to ethnic or racial cultural tastes and styles and not really opposition to education or stigmatizing academic achievement (see also C. A. Harris, 2013). Another study found some evidence that high achievement among Blacks is stigmatized, but only in one of the eight schools the researchers studied (Tyson, Darity, & Castellino, 2005). In addition to being relatively uncommon, the researchers also found that while the stigma of "acting White" was a painful experience for high-achieving Black students, it did not keep those students from pursuing academic achievement.

Tyson et al. (2005) in fact found important similarities between the experiences of high-achieving Black *and* White students. The authors found three types of oppositional culture to high academic achievement: a general type, labeling high-achieving students of any race as "nerds"; a racialized version (with race-based labels like "acting White" or "Oreo," i.e., Black on the outside but White on the inside); and a class-based version that stigmatized high-achieving students of any race as "high and mighty" or acting like they're better than others (Tyson et al., 2005). This work highlights the similar experiences of high-achieving students across different racial and even class groups.

Additionally, in the few cases where the racialized version of oppositional culture was present, the authors found that it was related to particular school environments and experiences: The "acting White" stigma occurred in the context of racially mixed (but predominantly White) schools where high-achieving Black students in advanced classes were isolated from other Black students (Tyson, 2011) and is more likely to be part of local school culture when students see stark differences in socioeconomic status between Blacks and Whites and perceive them as corresponding to academic achievement and class placement within the school (Tyson et al., 2005). This research thus points to the importance of the school context and structural factors—such as tracking or ability grouping and the resulting racial isolation in some schools—in shaping the "acting White" phenomenon more than the cultural values students bring with them to school. Instead of attitudes toward education shaping achievement, then, Tyson et al. (2005) emphasize how experiences at school can shape attitudes toward education.

Ogbu's theory of oppositional culture has also been used to discuss academic achievement gaps between White and Latino students, particularly Mexican American students. Ogbu (1978) argued that they were involuntary minorities conquered in what is now the southwest United States, with later immigrants from Mexico being given the same status as a conquered minority. Research on oppositional culture among Mexican Americans has been less widespread but has thus far found little support for the idea that Mexican American or Latino youth do not value education (see Valencia, 2011; Valencia & Black, 2002). For example, alongside the Black civil rights movement was a Mexican American fight for equal schools (Donato, 1997; San Miguel, 1987). Studies found that in actuality, Mexican American and Latino parents value education, hold high expectations for their children's educational attainment, and may even emphasize higher education more than White parents (Immerwahr & Foleno, 2000; Valencia & Black, 2002). Carter (2005) found heterogeneous experiences but overall high rates of pro-school attitudes among low-income Latino youth; while students did talk about "acting White" versus "acting Spanish," these ideas were not related to academic achievement and instead tended to focus on dress and linguistic style.

Conclusion

As a whole, this work challenges the myth that racial differences in academic achievement simply result from differences in the value placed on education across racial and ethnic cultures. The lack of empirical evidence for cultural explanations suggests that educators and policymakers need to look at other factors to understand and close the achievement gap. Tyson's (2011) work points to the importance of structural arrangements of schooling in America—including the racialized nature of ability tracking in many schools—and their impact on student cultures. Research also shows Black students are significantly more likely to be taught by inexperienced teachers than their White peers, contributing to differences in achievement (Clotfelter, Ladd, & Vigdor, 2005). A. L. Harris and Robinson (2007) point to racial differences in prior skills—cognitive skills developed before students enter high school—as the key underlying factor contributing to poor achievement among Black students in high school, regardless of their behaviors during high school (while in comparison, Asian American students' achievement in high school is statistically explained mostly by their behaviors during high school).

As these brief paragraphs indicate, access to and success in education has a long and complex racial history. Belief that culture itself is a sufficient explanatory variable in regard to education requires a vast oversimplification of the concept of culture itself, as well as blindness to the impact of history and structural opportunity that shape the outcomes of individuals and groups. It may be a comforting simplification, and it is certainly widespread, but it does not square with empirical reality. Continued commitment to the idea of a monolithic Asian culture or a monolithic Black or Latino culture does little to forward our understanding of variation in intergroup educational attainment or our efforts toward educational equity.

Hersheda Patel is a graduate student in the sociology program at Georgia State University. Her research interests are in the sociology of education, particularly the college choice process and the nature of campus racial composition.

Emily Meanwell is the director of the Social Science Research Commons at Indiana University. She is also the study director for the Sociological Research Practicum. Her research focuses on culture and inequality, particularly political culture surrounding educational policies designed to reduce inequality. She has also explored the experiences of homeless shelter residents.

Stephanie M. McClure is a professor of sociology at Georgia College. She teaches classes on racial stratification, social theory, and the sociology of education.

Her research interests are in the area of higher education, with a focus on college student persistence and retention across race, class, and gender, and a special emphasis on post-college student experiences that increase student social and academic integration. She has published in the *Journal of Higher Education, Symbolic Interaction,* and the *Journal of African American Studies.*

SUGGESTED ADDITIONAL RESOURCES

Carter, P. L. (2005). *Keepin' it real: School success beyond Black and White.* New York, NY: Oxford University Press.

Liu, E. (1998). *The accidental Asian: Notes of a native speaker.* New York, NY: Vintage Books.

Tyson, K. (2011). *Integration interrupted: Tracking, Black students, and acting White after Brown.* New York, NY: Oxford University Press.

Wu, F. (2003). *Yellow: Race in America beyond Black and White.* New York, NY: Basic Books.

Audio/Visual

Hampton, H., Vecchione, J., Fayer, S., Bagwell, O., Crossley, C., DeVinney, J. A., . . . Bond, J. (2006). *Eyes on the prize* [Television series; American Experience special broadcast]. Alexandria, VA: Public Broadcasting Service. (Especially "Fighting Back," on school desegregation post-*Brown,* and "The Keys to the Kingdom," on school desegregation in Boston in 1974)

Palos, A. L. (Director). (2011). *Precious knowledge* [Documentary]. Tucson, AZ: Dos Vatos Productions.

QUESTIONS FOR FURTHER DISCUSSION

1. Why do you think this myth that some cultures simply value education more than others has persisted, despite evidence to the contrary?

2. If cultural differences did explain differences in educational attainment, what kinds of policy changes would be necessary? If, on the other hand, the authors are correct in asserting that culture is not a sufficient explanation, how does that change the kinds of policies necessary to decrease group-level differences in educational attainment?

REACHING BEYOND THE COLOR LINE

1. The authors give several examples of these myths in popular culture. Choose a television show or movie mentioned in the essay and analyze the portrayal of the myth that some cultures just value education more than others. Look at the portrayals of race, inequality, and structural and cultural factors. Where do cultural factors come into play? What about structure? You can find examples at the following website (which also assumes a cultural explanation): http://tvtropes.org/pmwiki/pmwiki.php/Main/AsianAndNerdy

REFERENCES

Ainsworth-Darnell, J. W., & Downey, D. B. (1998). Assessing the oppositional culture explanation for racial/ethnic differences in school performance. *American Sociological Review, 63*(4), 536–553.

Allen, W. R., Epps, E. G., & Haniff, N. G. (Eds.). (1991). *College in Black and White: African American students in predominantly White and in historically Black public universities.* Albany: State University of New York Press.

Anderson, J. D. (1988). *The education of Blacks in the South 1860–1935.* Chapel Hill: University of North Carolina Press.

Baker, B. D., Keller-Wolff, C., & Wolf-Wendel, L. (2000). Two steps forward, one step back: Race/ethnicity and student achievement in education policy research. *Educational Policy, 14*(4), 511–529.

Blauner, B. (2001). *Still the big news: Racial oppression in America.* Philadelphia, PA: Temple University Press.

Bowles, F., & DeCosta, F. A. (1971). *Between two worlds: A profile of Negro higher education.* New York, NY: McGraw-Hill.

Brown v. Board of Education, 347 U.S. (1954).

Carter, P. L. (2005). *Keepin' it real: School success beyond Black and White.* New York, NY: Oxford University Press.

Clotfelter, C., Ladd, H., & Vigdor, J. (2005). Who teaches whom? Race and the distribution of novice teachers. *Economics of Education Review, 24*(4), 377–392.

Cole, E. R., & Omari, S. R. (2003). Race, class and the dilemmas of upward mobility for African Americans. *Journal of Social Issues, 59*(4), 785–802.

Cook, P. J., & Ludwig, J. (1997). Weighing the "burden of 'acting white'": Are there race differences in attitudes toward education? *Journal of Policy Analysis and Management, 16*(2), 256–278.

Coontz, S. (1992). *The way we never were: American families and the nostalgia trap.* New York, NY: Basic Books.

Datnow, A., & Cooper, R. (1996). Peer networks of African American students in independent schools: Affirming academic success and racial identity. *Journal of Negro Education, 656*(4), 56–72.

Davis, J. F. (1991). *Who is Black? One nation's definition.* University Park: Pennsylvania State University Press.

De Genova, N., & Ramos-Zayas, A. (2003). Latino racial formations in the United States: An introduction. *Journal of Latin American Anthropology, 8*(2), 2–17.

Donato, R. (1997). *The other struggle for equal schools: Mexican Americans during the civil rights era.* Albany: State University of New York Press.

Downey, D. B., & Ainsworth-Darnell, J. W. (2002). The search for oppositional culture among Black students. *American Sociological Review, 67*(1), 156–164.

Espiritu, Y. L. (1993). *Asian American panethnicity: Bridging institutions and identities.* Philadelphia, PA: Temple University Press.

Farkas, G., Lleras, C., & Maczuga, S. (2002). Does oppositional culture exist in minority and poverty peer groups? *American Sociological Review, 67*(1), 148–155.

Fordham, S., & Ogbu, J. U. (1986). Black students' school success: Coping with the "burden of 'acting White.'" *Urban Review, 18*(3), 176–206.

Fuligni, A. (1997). The academic achievement of adolescents from immigrant families: The roles of family background, attitudes, and behavior. *Child Development, 68*(2), 351–363.

Harris, A. L. (2006). I (don't) hate school: Revisiting oppositional culture theory of Blacks' resistance to schooling. *Social Forces, 85*(2), 797–833.

Harris, A. L. (2008). Optimism in the face of despair: Black–White differences in beliefs about school as a means for upward social mobility. *Social Science Quarterly, 89*(3), 629–651.

Harris, A. L., & Robinson, K. (2007). Schooling behaviors or prior skills? A cautionary tale of omitted variable bias within oppositional culture theory. *Sociology of Education, 80*(2), 139–157.

Harris, C. A. (2013). *The Cosby cohort: Blessings and burdens of growing up Black middle class.* Lanham, MD: Rowman & Littlefield.

Hirschman, C., & Wong, M. (1986). The extraordinary educational attainment of Asian-Americans: A search for historical evidence and explanations. *Social Forces, 65*(1), 1–27.

Immerwahr, J., & Foleno, T. (2000). *Great expectations: How the public and parents—White, African American, and Hispanic—view higher education.* New York, NY: Public Agenda.

Kao, G. (1995). Asian Americans as model minorities? A look at their academic performance. *American Journal of Education, 103*(2), 121–159.

Lee, S., & Kumashiro, K. (2005). *A report on the status of Asian Americans and Pacific Islanders in education: Beyond the "model minority" stereotype.* Washington, DC: National Education Association.

Liu, E. (1998). *The accidental Asian: Notes of a native speaker.* New York, NY: Vintage Books.

Model, S. (1995). West Indian prosperity: Fact or fiction? *Social Problems, 42*(4), 535–553.

Model, S. (2011). *West Indian immigrants: A Black success story?* New York, NY: Russell Sage Foundation.

Nasser, H. E. (2012, June 19). Study: Asian Americans value hard work, family. *USA Today.* Retrieved from http://usatoday30.usatoday.com/news/nation/story/2012-06-18/asian-american-study/55677050/1

Ogbu, J. U. (1978). *Minority education and caste: The American system in cross-cultural perspective.* New York, NY: Academic Press.

Omi, M., & Winant, H. (1994). *Racial formation in the United States: From the 1960s to the 1990s.* New York, NY: Routledge.

Orfield, G., Frankenberg, E. D., & Lee, C. (2002). The resurgence of school segregation. *Educational Leadership, 60*(4), 16–20.

Portes, A., & Rumbaut, R. (2001). *Legacies: The story of the immigrant second generation.* Berkeley: University of California Press and Russell Sage Foundation.

Portes, A., & Zhou, M. (1993). The new second generation: Segmented assimilation and its variants. *Annals of the American Academy of Political and Social Science, 530,* 74–96.

Rodriguez, C. E. (2000). *Changing race: Latinos, the census, and the history of ethnicity in the United States.* New York: New York University Press.

Rudolph, F. (1990). *The American college & university: A history.* Athens: University of Georgia Press. (Original work published 1962)

San Miguel, G., Jr. (1987). *"Let all of them take heed": Mexican Americans and the campaign for educational equality in Texas, 1910–1981.* Austin: University of Texas Press.

Singh, H. (2011, November 22). Why do Asian Americans dominate education? *Berkeley Political Review.* Retrieved from https://web.archive.org/web/20120521093059/http://bpr.berkeley.edu:80/2011/11/why-do-asian-americans-dominate-education/

Steinberg, S. (2001). *The ethnic myth: Race, ethnicity, and class in America* (3rd ed.). Boston, MA: Beacon Press.

Teachman, J. (1987). Family background, educational resources, and educational attainment. *American Sociological Review, 52*(4), 548–557.

Theoharis, J. (2009). "I hate it when people treat me like a fxxx-up": Phony theories, segregated schools, and the culture of aspiration among African American and Latino teenagers. In G. Alonso, N. S. Anderson, C. Su, & J. Theoharis (Eds.), *Our schools suck: Students talk back to a segregated nation on the failures of urban education* (pp. 69–112). New York: New York University Press.

Tushnet, M. (1987). *The NAACP's legal strategy against segregated education, 1925–1950.* Chapel Hill: University of North Carolina Press.

Tyson, K. (2002). Weighing in: Elementary-age students and the debate on attitudes toward school among Black students. *Social Forces, 80*(4), 1157–1189.

Tyson, K. (2011). *Integration interrupted: Tracking, Black Students, and acting White after Brown.* New York, NY: Oxford University Press.

Tyson, K., Darity, W. A., Jr., & Castellino, D. (2005). "It's not a Black thing": Understanding the burden of acting White and other dilemmas of high achievement. *American Sociological Review, 70*(4), 582–605.

UC AAPI Policy Initiative. (2006). *Pacific Islanders lagging behind in higher educational attainment: Analytical brief of new Census data.* Retrieved from http://npien.com/images/teachers/PIEducationAttainBrief_Nov14th.pdf

Urban, W. J., & Wagoner, J. L., Jr. (1996). *American education: A history.* New York, NY: Routledge.

U.S. Census Bureau. (2012). Table 5: Type of college and year enrolled for college students 15 years old and over, by sex, age, race, and Hispanic origin: 1980 to 2009 [Chart]. Retrieved from http://www.census.gov/hhes/school/data/cps/2012/tables.html

Valencia, R. R. (Ed.). (2011). *Chicano school failure and success: Past, present, and future* (3rd ed.). New York, NY: Routledge.

Valencia, R. R., & Black, M. S. (2002). "Mexican Americans don't value education!"—On the basis of the myth, mythmaking, and debunking. *Journal of Latinos and Education, 1*(2), 81–103.

Wallenstein, P. (1999). Black Southerners and non-black universities: Desegregation of higher education, 1935–1967. *History of Higher Education Annual, 19*, 121–148.

Waters, M. (1996). Ethnic and racial identities of second-generation Black immigrants in New York City. In A. Portes (Ed.), *The new second generation* (pp. 171–196). New York, NY: Russell Sage Foundation.

Wildhagen, T. (2011). What's oppositional culture got to do with it? Moving beyond the strong version of the acting White hypothesis. *Sociological Perspectives, 54*(3), 403–430.

Wong, M. G. (1980). Changes in socioeconomic status of the Chinese male population in the United States from 1960 to 1970. *International Migration Review, 14*(4), 511–524.

Wu, F. (2003). *Yellow: Race in America beyond black and white.* New York, NY: Basic Books.

Xie, Y., & Goyette, K. (2003). Social mobility and the educational choices of Asian Americans. *Social Science Research, 32*, 467–498.

"They Don't Want to Be Integrated; They Even Have Their Own Greek Organizations"

History, Institutional Context, and "Self-Segregation"

Stephanie M. McClure

Georgia College

When discussing issues of race on campus, students often correctly recognize that racial segregation in residence halls, dining halls, and student organizations on campus indicates the amount of work that needs to be done around race in society as a whole (Saenz, Ngai, & Hurtado, 2007). Such segregation is the result of a range of social forces connected to many of the topics discussed in this book. However, in a search for easy scapegoats for this segregation, students often turn their attention to campus sororities and fraternities—Greek-letter organizations, or GLOs (Collison, 1987; Crain & Ford, 2013; Dziadosz, 2006; Vendituoli & Grant, 2013). On most campuses throughout the United States, the composition of GLOs is noticeably racially homogenous. While this is true across the color line, many students single out and question those groups that are historically Black. These questions regularly come up on college campuses and in introductory courses on race, including in the comments of my own students, as is referenced in the quote in the title of this essay. Yet the history of Black Greek-letter organizations (BGLOs) on campuses and their impact on their members is rarely familiar to college administrators, much less to college students themselves (Hughey, 2007). It is worth considering this history and impact in more depth to understand common misperceptions. We will consider the reasons White students often call attention to these specific organizations, even as racial segregation occurs in many other on-campus settings.

College is potentially a time of great intellectual and personal growth. Students spend their days on campus not only engaging in the process of attaining a degree but also learning about who they are as individuals and figuring out who they want to become (Astin, 1993; Pascarella & Terenzini, 2005). Research shows that this process is most successful where students are able to develop meaningful friendships and get involved in clubs and organizations they enjoy (Braxton, 2000). That is, to gain the full value of a college experience, all students must be able to locate a group of people with whom they feel safe and valued, and through whom they feel connected to the wider campus community. This process is known as social integration and not only is necessary for identity development but is in fact fundamental to successful college completion (Braxton, 2000; Tinto, 1993, 2006). This is true for all students, but research has clearly demonstrated that successful social integration can be particularly challenging for students of color on predominantly White campuses (Black, Belknap, & Ginsberg, 2005; Feagin, Vera, & Imani, 1996; Patton, Bridges, & Flowers, 2011). Social integration has recently been related to a concept called "sense of belonging," which several studies have demonstrated is an important predictor of student retention through graduation (Museus & Maramba, 2011). Self-reported "sense of belonging" is often lower for Black, Latino, and Asian American students on predominantly White campuses (Johnson et al., 2007).

As any college student can tell you, campuses are made up of a variety of subcultures or communities that welcome different types of students into the life of the college. The greater the variety of campus communities available, the more likely it is that a greater range of students "will be able, if they so desire, to become integrated and establish competent intellectual and social membership" in the institution (Tinto, 1993, p. 124). The integrative effectiveness of these various communities is largely dependent on having a critical mass of diverse students on campus, including students with different social class backgrounds, geographic origins, unique interests, and racial or ethnic group membership (Tinto, 1993; Willie, 2003). But involvement in extracurricular organizations is unequivocally linked to higher levels of student satisfaction and college graduation (Fischer, 2007; Jackson & Swan, 1991).

For example, Samuel D. Museus (2008) conducted an interview study with 24 Black and Asian American undergraduate students at a large public university that was 85% White. His data revealed that for students in both groups, their membership in "ethnic student organizations" gave them connections, emotional support, and space for identity exploration, which increased their sense of comfort on campus. Museus did not find that this membership also facilitated increased contact with faculty, another important factor for student success, although this has been a finding in other research (e.g., Guiffrida, 2003).

For students of all racial backgrounds, Greek membership is one way to achieve this kind of beneficial social integration. All GLOs are characterized by restricted membership, as a specific type of voluntary association (Knoke, 1986). The student organizations that evolved to become the GLOs we know today were literary and study groups that attempted to provide avenues for discussion, academic development, and social outlets within a pretty restrictive, almost monastic, higher education environment (Jones, 2004; Rudolph, 1962/1990). These organizations also provided students with housing, built-in study groups, and social support, as well as the benefit of helping students find others who shared common interests and goals. Beginning in the late 19th century, sororities were organized along the same lines, with the first collective organization being formally founded in 1902. These Greek organizations were also always race and class selective at a time when American higher education itself was primarily, although not exclusively, available to a select proportion of the U.S. population, namely upper-class Whites (Handler, 1995). Early GLOs particularly remained closed to the small numbers of African Americans on predominantly White campuses at the turn of the 20th century (Kimbrough, 2003; Washington & Nuñez, 2005).

While most fraternities or sororities moved to rid themselves of overtly racially restrictive clauses around the middle of the past century, this was a complex and controversial process. It most often took the form of conflict between current members who were in favor of removing official clauses, but without changing racially marked pledging practices, and national offices that were run by alumni who resisted any policy change whatsoever, particularly when it was demanded by campus administrators (Hughey, 2007). This was the case for the University of Minnesota and the University of Michigan, and for the Theta Chi fraternity at Dartmouth during this time (Lee, 1955). It was in 1963 that all social organizations were mandated to remove any remaining racially restrictive membership clauses (Whipple, Baier, & Grady, 1991). It is important to keep in mind that, under whatever circumstances, the removal of specific clauses was rarely associated with change in new member recruitment practices or the overall racially marked character of these organizations (Crain & Ford, 2013; Hughey, 2010; Lee, 1955). For example, Deborah Williams, an African American student at the University of Georgia, participated in sorority rush in 1968 at a time when organizations were completely White. Williams described the shock of the White members who greeted her at the various sorority houses. Although she was invited back to three sororities, she did not receive an invitation to join any of them (Baugh, 1968).

Presently, while none of the national governing organizations collect official data on the racial composition of their chapters, single institution data from a range of studies confirms racial homogeneity observed by students on campus (Hughey, 2010; Stains, 1994; Vendituoli & Grant, 2013). Black GLOs were founded, starting at the turn of the 20th century, in part to offer a Greek option for Black students who were banned from joining those existing White organizations. However, they differ significantly from their historically White counterparts not only in their history of racial restrictions but also in mission. There are currently nine national Black Greek organizations under the National Pan-Hellenic Council. Black students on the campuses of both historically Black colleges and universities (HBCUs) and predominantly White institutions founded fraternal organizations to enhance their college experiences and to deal with political and social issues facing the Black community (Rodriguez, 1995). While the major breeding ground for BGLOs was Howard University, an HBCU where five of the nine organizations were founded, three of the nine were founded on predominantly White campuses. These are Alpha Phi Alpha fraternity (Cornell University in 1906), Kappa Alpha Psi fraternity (Indiana University in 1911), and Sigma Gamma Rho sorority (Butler University in 1922).

BGLOs have from the start been more focused on sociopolitical goals, including racial equality and community service. This activism can be clearly seen in many of the initial major service programs that were established as the organizations grew to be national and international in scope. These include Phi Beta Sigma's Bigger and Better Business Program, which was established in the 1920s and worked to empower Black business owners; the Guide Right program established by Kappa Alpha Psi in 1922, which works to encourage academic achievement among high school seniors; the Voting Rights Program developed by Alpha Phi Alpha, which worked to register African Americans to vote at a time of widespread disenfranchisement; the National Library Project created in 1937 by Delta Sigma Theta, which helped develop local libraries for African Americans; and the Zeta Phi Beta housing project of 1943, where the sorority worked with the National Housing Association to locate housing vacancies for WWII war workers (Berkowitz & Padavic, 1999; Ross, 2000). Moreover, it is important to note that there are many cases where White students who shared these goals have joined these groups (Hughey, 2007).

For many Black students on predominantly White campuses, even those who are not Greek members, BGLOs are a primary source of social activities, in a setting where few such resources are available (Kimbrough & Hutcheson, 1998). White students often respond to this information by suggesting that social clubs and events that are predominantly White are in fact open to students of all races and that students of color are welcome at these events. While this is nominally the case, research suggests that at many such events, particularly those where alcohol is involved, the risk of racist comments and behavior can be quite high, creating an unwelcoming, even hostile environment in a nominally race-neutral setting (Black et al., 2005). Research on the impact of campus racial climate, defined as a combination of the racial history of an institution, its racial demography, and the average attitudes and behaviors of current students, confirms what my own students report (Hurtado, Enberg, Ponjuan, & Landremann, 2002). As a White student of mine wrote of his adjustment to the college party scene [and why he left it], "I used to hear so much racist language from other people at the parties. I remember being shocked." The experience of social integration may be virtually impossible for a Black student who has multiple experiences with discrimination on campus. It is difficult to come to share the norms and values of a community when those seem to include a lack of value for someone from your racial background (see Mendoza-Denton, Downey, Purdy, Davis, & Pietrzak, 2002). This kind of discrimination often takes organizational form in White GLOs, particularly in the form of racially insensitive party themes, including "ghetto" parties and "tacos and tequila" (Hughey, 2010; Stains, 1994; Whaley, 2009).

In addition, as discussed above, several studies found that participation in same-race organizations did not increase isolation for Black and other minority students, as commonly believed, but actually made them feel more a part of the campus community (McClure, 2006; Moran, Yengo, & Algier, 1994; Murguia, Padilla, & Pavel, 1991; Taylor & Howard-Hamilton, 1995). Students use these enclaves to scale down a large campus and deal with it more effectively, particularly as that relates to issues of discrimination on campus. It is in this function that the Black Greek organization can most clearly be seen as unique from White Greek organizations. Based on the overall campus environment and the needs and experiences of students of color, same-race organizations create a unique integrating niche for these students.

As these organizations often function as a kind of supportive enclave for minority students, they can actually facilitate increased cross-race interaction for their members. Because they generate a sense of meaningful membership in the larger campus community, members are encouraged to participate in other, non-Black student organizations that promote equal-status contact (McClure, 2006; Murguia et al., 1991). Equal-status contact is one of the most effective prejudice-reduction mechanisms and requires long-term contact among individuals of equal social status who voluntarily work toward a cooperative goal under the supervision of a legitimate authority (Wittig & Grant-Thompson, 1998).

Conclusion

For White students who believe race does not play a role in campus life and who believe they are open to being friends with students of all races, several questions should be considered. First, while you may not say negative things about students of other races, do you ever hear them in all-White social settings, particularly where alcohol is involved? If yes, when you hear these things, are they immediately followed by negative social sanctions (glares, verbal recrimination, stony silence), which indicate they are not approved of by other White students? Or do you and your peers often do as the student quoted above admitted: "Most of the time I took the path of least resistance and ignored it"?

It is also worth reflecting on why the question of "self-segregation" repeatedly comes up in campus discussions of race. Often, the question itself is a distancing mechanism. For those of us who were and are members of predominantly White Greek organizations (including this author), arguing that people of color simply don't want to be integrated into these organizations justifies their racial homogeneity and lets us off the hook for taking action to change that reality. For non-Greek White students, the question may be related to a wider strategy of denial and resistance, which seeks to define a problem as the result of someone else's choices. The issue then becomes unrelated to any action or inaction we may take in our own day-to-day college activities. This is in spite of the fact that on many campuses, students of color regularly spend time in environments where they are the minority, while this happens only rarely for White students.

Given the apparent openness of most campus events, it is possible for White students with a sincere interest in moving past highly segregated social spaces to take the initiative to attend alone, or with a few friends, events that are sponsored or organized by minority student groups on campus, including BGLOs. This decision is a powerful individual act that moves past verbal and written accusation into the realm of action. Instead of using the existence of minority-marked events as a justification and rationalization for our own racially homogeneous social networks, White people have the opportunity to put into action the very same integration that they indicate they desire in people of color.

Stephanie M. McClure is a professor of sociology at Georgia College. She teaches classes on racial stratification, social theory, and the sociology of education. Her research interests are in the area of higher education, with a focus on college student persistence and retention across race, class, and gender, and a special emphasis on post-college student experiences that increase student social and academic integration. She has published in the *Journal of Higher Education, Symbolic Interaction,* and the *Journal of African American Studies.*

SUGGESTED ADDITIONAL RESOURCES

On the History of Greek Organizations

Kimbrough, W. M. (2003). *Black Greek 101: The culture, customs, and challenges of Black fraternities and sororities.* Madison, NJ: Fairleigh Dickinson University Press.

Ross, L. C., Jr. (2000). *The divine nine: The history of African American fraternities and sororities.* New York, NY: Kensington.

Syrett, N. L. (2009). *The company he keeps: A history of White college fraternities.* Chapel Hill: University of North Carolina Press.

On the Experiences of Students of Color on Predominantly White Campuses

Aries, E. (2008). *Race and class matters at an elite college.* Philadelphia, PA: Temple University Press.

Chavous, T. M. (2000). The relationships among racial identity, perceived ethnic fit, and organizational involvement for African American students at a predominantly White university. *Journal of Black Psychology, 26*(1), 79–100.

Feagin, J. R., Vera, H., & Imani, N. (1996). *The agony of education: Black students at White colleges and universities.* New York, NY: Routledge.

Hu, S., & St. John, E. P. (2001). Student persistence in a public higher education system: Understanding racial and ethnic differences. *Journal of Higher Education, 72*(3), 265–286.

Willie, S. S. (2003). *Acting Black: College, identity and the performance of race.* New York, NY: Routledge.

Websites

North-American Interfraternity Conference: http://www.nicindy.org
National Panhellenic Conference: http://www.npcwomen.org/index.aspx
National Pan-Hellenic Council: http://www.nphchq.org

QUESTIONS FOR FURTHER DISCUSSION

1. Have you ever thought about the concept of "self-segregation" as it relates to your campus? What information in the essay do you believe best challenges the assumption that minority student organizations self-segregate? What other information do you think might be useful?

2. If BGLOs do not exist (or do not exist in great numbers) on your campus, consider organizations like the Black Student Union or the Latino Alliance. How are they different from the Greek organizations discussed here or from other student organizations on campus? How and why might this vary with campus racial composition?

3. What (if any) student organizations are you involved with? What is the overall racial composition of these groups? Does it reflect the racial composition or social dynamics described in this essay? How or why?

REACHING BEYOND THE COLOR LINE

1. For White students, following this discussion, locate and attend an on-campus event where you believe you will be one of the few White people in attendance. For students of color, if you are involved in a student organization like those described above (where there may be relatively few White people in attendance), ask a White friend or classmate to attend an organizational event or meeting with you. For all students, take some time to reflect on how you felt about this experience and whether or not you would likely do the same thing again. Why or why not?

REFERENCES

Astin, A. W. (1993). *What matters in college? Four critical years revisited.* San Francisco, CA: Jossey-Bass.

Baugh, C. (1968). Describes reactions as "priceless." *Red & Black, 11*, 1–68.

Berkowitz, A., & Padavic, I. (1999). Getting a man or getting ahead: A comparison of Black and White sororities. *Journal of Contemporary Ethnography, 27*(4), 530–557.

Black, T., Belknap, J., & Ginsberg, J. (2005). Racism, sexism, and aggression: A study of Black and White fraternities. In T. L. Brown, G. S. Parks, & C. M. Phillips (Eds.), *African American fraternities and sororities: The legacy and the vision* (pp. 363–392). Lexington: University Press of Kentucky.

Braxton, J. M. (Ed.). (2000). *Reworking the student departure puzzle.* Nashville, TN: Vanderbilt University Press.

Collison, M. N. E. (1987, April 22). Black fraternities on White campuses, accused of separatism, say they are just misunderstood. *Chronicle of Higher Education, 33*, 35.

Crain, A., & Ford, M. (2013, September 11). The final barrier: 50 years later, segregation still exists. *Crimson White.* Retrieved from http://now.dirxion.com/Crimson_White/library/Crimson_White_9_11_2013.pdf

Dziadosz, A. (2006, November 30). After years of self-segregation, Greeks say it's time to shake up the system. *Michigan Daily.* Retrieved from http://www.michigandaily.com/content/after-years-self-segregation-greeks-say-its-time-shake-system?page=0,1

Feagin, J. R., Vera, H., & Imani, N. (1996). *The agony of education: Black students at White colleges and universities.* New York, NY: Routledge.

Fischer, M. J. (2007). Settling into campus life: Differences by race/ethnicity in college involvement and outcomes. *Journal of Higher Education, 78*(2), 125.

Guiffrida, D. A. (2003). African American student organizations as agents of social integration. *Journal of College Student Development, 44,* 304–319.

Handler, L. (1995). In the fraternal sisterhood: Sororities as gender strategy. *Gender & Society, 9*(2), 236–256.

Hughey, M. W. (2007). Crossing the sands, crossing the color line: Non-Black members of Black Greek letter organizations. *Journal of African American Studies 11,* 55–75.

Hughey, M. W. (2010). A paradox of participation: Nonwhites in White sororities and fraternities. *Social Problems, 57*(4), 653–679.

Hurtado, S., Enberg, M., Ponjuan, L., & Landremann, L. (2002). Students' pre-college preparation for participation in a diverse democracy. *Research in Higher Education 43*(2), 163–186.

Jackson, K., & Swan, L. (1991). Institutional and individual factors affecting African American undergraduate student performance. In W. R. Allen, E. G. Epps, & N. Z. Haniff (Eds.), *College in Black and White: African American students in predominantly White and in historically Black public universities* (pp. 127–142). Albany: State University of New York Press.

Johnson, D. R., Solder, M., Leonard, J. B., Alvarez, P., Inkelas, K. K., Rowan-Kenyon, H. T., & Longerbeam, S. D. (2007). Examining sense of belonging among first year undergraduates from different racial/ethnic groups. *Journal of College Student Development, 48*(5), 525–542.

Jones, R. L. (2004). *Black haze: Violence, sacrifice, and manhood in Black Greek-letter fraternities.* Albany: State University of New York Press.

Kimbrough, W. M. (2003). *Black Greek 101: The culture, customs, and challenges of Black fraternities and sororities.* Madison, NJ: Fairleigh Dickinson University Press.

Kimbrough, W. M., & Hutcheson, P. A. (1998). The impact of membership in Black Greek-letter organizations on Black students' involvement in collegiate activities and their development of leadership skills. *Journal of Negro Education, 67*(2), 96–105.

Knoke, D. (1986). Associations and interest groups. *Annual Review of Sociology, 12,* 1–21.

Lee, A. M. (1955). *Fraternities without brotherhood: A study of prejudice on the American campus.* Boston, MA: Beacon Press.

McClure, S. M. (2006). Facilitating student involvement and cross-race contact: The impact of membership in a Black Greek organization. In R. M. Moore III (Ed.), *African Americans and Whites: Changing relationships on college campuses* (pp. 77–88). Lanham, MD: University Press of America.

Mendoza-Denton, R., Downey, G., Purdy, V., Davis, A., & Pietrzak, J. (2002). Sensitivity to status-based rejection: Implications for African American students' college experience. *Journal of Personality and Social Psychology, 83,* 896–918.

Moran, J., Yengo, L., & Algier, A. (1994). Participation in minority oriented co-curricular organizations. *Journal of College Student Development, 35,* 143.

Murguia, E., Padilla, R. V., & Pavel, M. (1991, September). Ethnicity and the concept of social integration in Tinto's model of institutional departure. *Journal of College Student Development, 32,* 433–439.

Museus, S. D. (2008). The role of ethnic student organizations in fostering African American and Asian American students' cultural adjustment and membership at predominantly White institutions. *Journal of College Student Development, 49*(6), 568–586.

Museus, S. D., & Maramba, D. C. (2011). The impact of culture on Filipino American students' sense of belonging. *Review of Higher Education, 34*(2), 231–258.

Pascarella, E. T., & Terenzini, P. T. (2005). *How college affects students: Volume 2. A third decade of research.* San Francisco, CA: Jossey-Bass.

Patton, L. D., Bridges, B. K., & Flowers, L. A. (2011). Effects of Greek affiliation on African American students' engagement: Differences by college racial composition. *College Student Affairs Journal, 29*(2), 113–123, 177–179.

Rodriguez, R. (1995, November 30). Pledging relevance: From the Million Man March to education budget cuts, Black and Latino fraternities and sororities lock step with their communities. *Black Issues in Higher Education,* 32–34.

Ross, L. C. (2000). *The divine nine: The history of African American fraternities and sororities.* New York, NY: Kensington.

Rudolph, F. (1990). *The American college & university: A history.* Athens: University of Georgia Press. (Original work published 1962)

Saenz, V. B., Ngai, H. N., & Hurtado, S. (2007). Factors influencing positive interactions across race for African American, Asian American, Latino, and White college students. *Research in Higher Education, 48*(1), 1–38.

Stains, L. A. (1994). Black like me. *Rolling Stone, 678,* 69.

Taylor, C. M., & Howard-Hamilton, M. F. (1995). Student involvement and racial identity attitudes among African American males. *Journal of College Student Development, 36*(4), 330–336.

Tinto, V. (1993). *Leaving college: Rethinking the causes and cures of college student attrition.* Chicago, IL: University of Chicago Press.

Tinto, V. (2006). Research and practice of student retention: What next? *Journal of College Student Retention, 8*(1), 1–19.

Vendituoli, M., & Grant, M. (2013, September 19). College changes sorority rush process amid racism claims. *USA Today College.* Retrieved from http://www.usatoday.com/story/news/nation/2013/09/18/sorority-rush-changed-racism/2833079

Washington, M., & Nuñez, C. L. (2005). Education, racial uplift, and the rise of the Greek-letter tradition: The African American quest for status in the early twentieth century. In T. L. Brown, G. S. Parks, & C. M. Phillips (Eds.), *African American fraternities and sororities: The legacy and the vision* (pp. 137–179). Lexington: University Press of Kentucky.

Whaley, D. E. (2009). Links, legacies, and letters: A cultural history of Black Greek-letter organizations. In C. L. Torbenson & G. S. Parks (Eds.), *Brothers and sisters: Diversity in college fraternities and sororities* (pp. 46–82). Cranbury, NJ: Associated University Presses.

Whipple, E. G., Baier, J. L., & Grady, D. L. (1991). A comparison of Black and White Greeks at a predominantly White University. *NASPA Journal, 28*(2), 140–148.

Willie, S. S. (2003). *Acting Black: College, identity and the performance of race.* New York, NY: Routledge.

Wittig, M. A., & Grant-Thompson, S. (1998). The utility of Allport's conditions of intergroup contact for predicting perceptions of improved racial attitudes and beliefs. *Journal of Social Issues, 54*(4), 795–812.

"I Had a Friend Who Had Worse Scores Than Me and He Got Into a Better College"

The Legal and Social Realities of the College Admissions Process

OiYan Poon

Colorado State University

A college degree, especially from a selective postsecondary institution, is commonly valued as a means toward upward mobility. With limited seats available, selective institutions have their pick of an overabundance of highly qualified students each year. In selective college admissions, many qualified applicants denied admissions may question the fairness of the selection process. For example, a YouTube video[1] presents the following scenario, in which a White female applicant is denied admission to a college where her Black acquaintance with lower grades and test scores was admitted, drawing the unfounded conclusion that the Black applicant was racially privileged in the admissions process:

> Look at Sara, a white female high school student applying for college. Throughout high school, she achieved good grades in challenging classes and earned good test scores. She applied to one of the best universities in her state, only to be denied admission a few weeks later. She later found out that her friend Emily, an African American student, was accepted to the same school with lower grades and test scores. Unfortunately, Sara was negatively affected by affirmative action. If the standard college application simply did not include race, there would be no room for inequality.

Two key misconceptions underlie the video's argument. First, it presumes that affirmative action is an unfair system of racial quotas that defies principles of equality. It incorrectly frames the goal of the civil rights movement as color blindness and thus race-conscious admissions policies as counter to principles of racial justice. Second, it assumes that selective institutions use a simplistic process of college admissions that applies basic criteria of test scores and grades for evaluating student achievement, aptitude, and merit. In this misconception, test scores and grades are incorrectly viewed as unquestionably reliable measures of achievement.

In reality, admissions processes are complex evaluation methods that necessarily include criteria beyond tests and grades to gauge the fit between students and a given selective institution. Admissions committees begin by answering the question: How does this university or college define "merit" in the admissions process? Among selective higher education institutions, there are many ways to define merit for admissions. According to *Merriam-Webster*, *merit* is defined as "character or conduct deserving reward" (Merit, 2011). Although "merit" is commonly assumed to mean high test scores and grades, students' character and conduct extend beyond simplistic, and questionable, measures of academic achievement and promise. Indeed, selective institutions include more than test scores and grades in determining selection criteria that align with how they define "merit," because students are more than just what numbers can reveal. Research demonstrates that test scores and grades are significantly limited in their ability to predict how successful a student will be in college and beyond (Sedlacek, 2005). They are also inadequate measures of student talents, gifts, achievements within specific contexts of opportunity, and other unquantifiable characteristics.

Unique institutional missions and interests inform each college's and university's admissions policies and procedures, resulting in the development and use of a large array of selection criteria. Given the complexities and diversity of institutional interests, it is false to assume that test scores, grades, and race are, or even should be, the *only* three criteria considered. It is also problematic to assume that tests and grades are objective, reliable, and race-neutral measures of a student's achievements and aptitude (Santelices & Wilson, 2010).

Common Misconceptions

Myths surrounding race-conscious admissions policies often emerge from underlying concerns over fairness in the generally opaque process of admissions in top schools. Anxiety over the mysterious selective college admissions process is understandable given the intense public discourse on increasing competition in selective college admissions (Steinberg, 2003). Moreover, this anxiety can be fed by a general perception that the prestige of the institution attended can have direct effects on one's future well-being and earning potential (Lareau, 2011).

Misconception 1: Affirmative Action Consists of Racial Quotas and Reverse Discrimination

Contemporary opponents of affirmative action policies misleadingly claim that it is a system of racial quotas. *Quotas* are defined as an articulated allotment of a limited resource assigned to specific groups—in this case, a finite number of enrollment offers at selective colleges. Quotas have historically acted as a cap limiting certain groups from accessing elite institutions, such as those placed on Jews by Ivy League schools in the early 20th century (Karabel, 2005). Conversely, quotas are also minimum targets for certain groups, as in the case of the Ivy League Jewish quota, where the limitation of Jews allowed for the assurance of a minimum target allotment of admission for White Anglo-Saxon Protestants. The practice of using quotas in college admissions was declared unconstitutional by the U.S. Supreme Court in the 1978 *Regents of the University of California v. Bakke.* However, the court distinguished between the use of quotas and the consideration of race in selective admissions. In selecting students, admissions offices cannot legally use racial quotas, but they can continue to consider race as one of many factors in reviewing applications, especially in an effort to produce a diverse campus environment that can allow students of all backgrounds to realize valuable educational benefits (Garces & Jayakumar, 2014). The rejection of quotas in favor of a very limited consideration of race as one of many factors in admissions for the advancement of diversity and its educational benefits on campus has been reaffirmed by the Supreme Court decisions in both *Grutter v. Bollinger* (2003) and *Fisher v. University of Texas at Austin* (2016). Therefore, claims that current-day practices of affirmative action are applied as racial quotas, or even as racial preferences, are misleading and false.

Opponents of race-conscious admissions also argue that affirmative action represents "reverse discrimination," which defies values of hard work and merit. According to a 1974 opinion piece published in *The Harvard Crimson,* affirmative action "provoked an outcry of 'reverse discrimination' from whites who say blacks and other minorities don't have to work as hard to get into college" (Leonard, 1974). Arguing that affirmative action actually serves as a source of racism, a more recent opinion piece in *The Daily Texan* states, "The biggest problem with affirmative action is simple. Using discrimination to combat discrimination encourages racial hatred in our society" (McGarvey, 2012). While Whites have been the supposed targets of "reverse discrimination," some also claim that Asian Americans are harmed by affirmative action policies (Bernhard & Delwiche, 2015). Inherently, this view stereotypes Whites and Asian Americans as hard workers entitled to admissions at top schools while stereotyping Black, Latinx,[2] and other students of color as undeserving students who do not work hard.

While some have claimed that the elimination of affirmative action would lead to overwhelming Asian American majorities in elite college undergraduate enrollments (Espenshade & Chung, 2005), such studies do not account for the removal of suspected negative action[3] practices that would increase admissions for Asian Americans (Kidder, 2005). Unlike affirmative action, negative action limits the admission of Asian Americans in favor of White applicants (Kang, 1996), similar to earlier Ivy League quotas against Jews (Golden, 2007). Moreover, studies like Espenshade's often assume that admissions criteria include only test scores and grades, which is an incomplete and deficient understanding of the admissions selection process. Even Espenshade has expressed that his research is not a "smoking gun" of anti-Asian discrimination in admissions processes that consider race (Jaschik, 2009), because there is insufficient "empirical evidence to support that claim" (Bernhard & Delwiche, 2015).

Opponents of race-conscious admissions policies also argue that affirmative action is a system of unfair racial preferences. At least as early as 2003, conservative student organizations have staged "anti-affirmative action bake sales," charging different prices determined by customers' racial identity (Potter, 2003). They compare the unequal pricing schema to admissions policies that include race as a factor. Ward Connerly, a prominent Black affirmative action opponent, has explained that his stance emerged from his commitment to civil rights. Invoking the words of Dr. Martin Luther King Jr., Connerly (2005) states, "The success of [Dr. King's] children should be based on their individual accomplishments and merit and their right to equal treatment" (see also Thornhill in this volume for further discussion). The misappropriation of Dr. King's words is disturbing, since the late reverend was clearly not color-blind in leading a movement that acted to affirmatively confront systems of racial inequality (Turner, 1996). Bonilla-Silva (2006) has incisively argued how color-blind ideology serves to maintain racism by ignoring persistent systematic racial injustices. Furthermore, the assumption that affirmative action in selective admissions operates as a racial preference, or a proverbial thumb on the scales, is inaccurate because Supreme Court decisions have considerably limited the ways admissions processes can account for race in seeking to achieve diversity, as will be discussed later in this chapter.

Misconception 2: Race-Blind Admissions Policies Are Fair

Second, opponents of affirmative action believe that a race-blind admissions process is both possible and the only fair system of college admissions. They argue that race-blind admissions policies would be tantamount to charging everyone the same price for a cupcake regardless of social identity. In reference to the *Fisher v. University of Texas* U.S. Supreme Court case (2013), Megyn Kelly, then a correspondent on *The O'Reilly Factor,* stated, "In this case you have a White student who was denied admission to the University of Texas saying, 'The reason I didn't get in is because kids who have lower GPAs, lower test scores than I did were admitted because of the color of their skin'" (O'Reilly, 2012).

In addition to incorrectly assuming that test scores, grades, and race are the only admissions criteria, anti-affirmative action advocates also presume that tests and grades are racially neutral in their evaluative power. However, these quantitative measures can be tainted by bias, making them unfair gauges of student potential, especially if they are the only factors for admissions. The evaluative power of high school GPA can be limited by implicit and explicit biases influencing how schools and teachers treat diverse students, creating barriers to high school academic achievement by race (Conchas, 2006; Tenenbaum & Ruck, 2007). Moreover, SAT results have been found to correlate with socioeconomic backgrounds of test takers, undermining the reliability of such tests to fairly evaluate applicants' academic achievement and potential (Geiser, 2008; Santelices & Wilson, 2010). Consequently, some highly competitive colleges have even decided to deemphasize or not require test scores, including Bates College, Colby College, New York University, and Pitzer College.

Ultimately, it is essential to understand that selective evaluation methods for admissions are constructed to fit the unique interests of diverse institutions in how they define what merits a student's admission and to help them achieve their educational missions. Therefore, narrow quantitative measures such as test scores and grades are severely limited in what they can tell admissions officers about students. Taken alone, they can hinder admissions review processes from a fair and full evaluation of fit between a student and institution. Below is a glimpse into the selective college admissions process, which is a systemic approach to evaluating large numbers of highly qualified applicants for student–institutional fit.

What Goes Into an Admissions Process and Why?

The first step to constructing an informed opinion about the fairness of admissions review criteria is to gain a basic understanding of the complicated nuts and bolts of selective college admissions. A wide range of selection criteria are used in the admissions process to evaluate whether a student will help an institution fulfill its specific interests and goals, which may include the advancement of financial health, campus traditions, athletic teams, and geographic, economic, cultural, and racial diversity. Subsequently, criteria for admissions may include preferences for geographic locations of hometowns, legacies and relatives of donors, and student athletes, among many other criteria. Race can serve as one of many factors in the process of admissions review, but legally it cannot serve as a singular criterion.

In the next section, I present an overview of the role and function of admissions offices, a brief description of some selection criteria connected to institutional goals, and key legal principles that limit how race can be used in admissions decisions.

Evaluating for Institutional Interests and "Fit"

Specific institutional values, missions, and interests determine the methods and criteria for undergraduate admissions at selective postsecondary institutions (Steinberg, 2003). Admissions officers represent and apply their respective institutional missions, values, and goals in recruiting applicants, constructing criteria and review procedures for the evaluation of applicants, and enrolling students (Hossler, 2011). They work to ensure a strong fit between their institution's characteristics and interests and those of incoming students. Much like in a healthy relationship, student and institution should complement each other's interests.

Admissions processes at different schools reflect the diversity of institutional values and interests, resulting in different mixes and weighting of multiple criteria in admissions policies and practices (Steinberg, 2003). These factors and their weighting are subject to change depending on specific institutional interests and goals (Rashid, Hurtado, Brown, & Agronow, 2009). While it is impossible to provide a comprehensive list of admissions criteria at both private and public institutions, because private schools are not obligated to release details on their selection criteria, it is interesting to note the similarities in criteria between selective public universities such as the University of California (UC) and the University of Texas (UT). Based on the highly selective nature of these two revered institutions, it is possible to speculate that the criteria used at these two universities might share some similarities with those at elite private institutions.

The UC (2012), which consists of nine undergraduate campuses, has defined 14 criteria for admissions review for undergraduate admissions:

- Academic grade point average
- Test scores
- Number of, content of, and performance in academic courses
- Number of and performance in honors or advanced placement classes
- High school class ranking
- Quality of the senior-year program, including the number and type of academic classes in progress or planned
- Quality of academic performance relative to the educational opportunities offered at the student's high school
- Outstanding work in one or more subjects
- Outstanding work in one or more special projects in any academic field of study
- Recent, marked improvement in academic performance as demonstrated by GPA and quality of courses completed or in progress
- Special talents, achievements, or awards in a particular field
- Completion of special projects undertaken in the context of a student's high school curriculum or in conjunction with special school events, projects, programs
- Academic accomplishments in light of student's life experiences and special circumstances
- Location of student's secondary school and residence

The admissions offices at each undergraduate UC campus work with their respective campus leaders to determine the evaluation method for each criterion in accordance with their individual university ethos. Therefore, how UC Davis, UCLA, or UC San Diego engages in a comprehensive review of applicants to evaluate quality of senior-year program or special talents may greatly differ. Due to the passage of Proposition 209 in 1996, affirmative action practices are not allowed by state law in California.

Unlike UC, UT continues to legally consider race among many other factors in its admissions process, but only for a small proportion of the applicant pool. In 1997, the State of Texas established a law that required the university to automatically offer admission to Texas high school seniors who ranked in the top 10% of their high school classes. In 2009, the state amended the law to admit enough Texas high school graduates to fill 75% of available slots for Texas residents based on class rank. With state population outpacing available slots for new students in the state's higher education system, Texas adjusted the class ranking threshold to the top 8% in 2013. For the remaining 25% of incoming classes, UT engages in a holistic review of qualifications for every applicant. In holistic review, the university considers a variety of both academic and personal achievement factors, as well as "special circumstances that can help to put an applicant's achievement into context" (UT, 2017). To evaluate academic achievement, UT considers students' class ranks, test scores, and high school coursework. To assess personal achievement, the university reviews students' written essays, information about student activities, and letters of recommendation. It also considers special circumstances, "to get a clearer picture of the applicant's qualifications." These include socioeconomic status of family, single-parent home, language spoken at home, family responsibilities, overcoming adversity, cultural background, race and ethnicity, and other information included in student files. This information can be provided by students in an optional essay or letters of reference. It allows reviewers to conduct a comprehensive and humanistic evaluation of each applicant's accomplishments within his or her personal context of achievement.

By taking a look at these two universities' admissions criteria, we can see they recognize that prospective college students are much more than just their test scores and grades. In constructing complex evaluation methods, selective colleges and universities intentionally select the mix of information they require to holistically evaluate applicants, informed by a constellation of information. Indeed, tests and grades are not the only means for evaluating academic merit, and are limited in their capacity to evaluate and understand who students are and the characteristics they bring to a campus community.

In constructing an admissions review method, it is important to understand what each item adds to the process and how it contributes to the evaluation of a student according to institutional criteria for determining a student's merit. While some assume that test scores are the best measures of academic merit, research has found that standardized tests are reliable in predicting only about 6% of the variance in a student's GPA in the first year of college (Atkinson & Geiser, 2009; Sedlacek, 2005). In other words, the SAT and ACT have the power to predict a very small amount of difference in students' academic potential. High school grades have been found to be a stronger predictor of college freshman-year grades than test scores but are also limited in what they say about a student (Hoffman & Lowitzki, 2005).

Logically, then, tests and grades should not be the only standards of merit. Given the severe inadequacies of tests and grades, a fair assessment of merit must include a wide range of criteria to provide a holistic assessment of applicants. Even "the College Board has long felt that the SAT was limited in what it measured and should not be relied upon as the only tool to judge applicants" (Sedlacek, 2005, p. 177; see also Balf, 2014). A range of criteria should be used to understand who students are and what they bring to a campus environment, through a process that holistically accounts for the unique profile of each applicant. These criteria, such as those used by UC and UT, may include place of residence and secondary school, language spoken at home, socioeconomic background (including race), ability to overcome adversity, special talents, and accomplishments.

In pursuit of fairness in selective college admissions, opponents of affirmative action are often silent about the ways U.S. systems of education are riddled with racial and class barriers (McDonough, 1994) that prevent fairness in college access. While some criticize the use of race and ethnicity even as a limited factor for admissions, few of these critics are as vocal about the use of legacy preference, which privileges children of alumni in admissions. Legacy applicants at Harvard have been found to have a 40% admission rate, compared with the 11% admission rate for the general applicant pool, even with lower test scores and grades than other applicants (Howell & Turner, 2004; Shadowen, Tulante, & Alpern, 2009). Private institutions may defend the use of legacy preference in admissions as a tool for preserving institutional tradition and to encourage alumni donations supporting institutional financial interests (Golden, 2007; Howell & Turner, 2004).

Generally, a student's chances of admission at a given institution depend on a number of factors that represent institutional interests. In any given year, an institution may be seeking particular types of students to contribute to the campus character. In addition to academic interests, colleges and universities may want to satisfy alumni demands in exchange for financial donations. For institutions with competitive NCAA sports teams, talented student-athletes may be evaluated for their academic promise as well as their athletic talents. Therefore, the captain of a state championship volleyball team or a nationally or internationally ranked tennis player might have lower test scores and grades than his or her peers yet be admitted to contribute his or her unique talents to the campus. Indeed, much more than just tests, grades, and race go into admissions decisions to evaluate fit between students and selective institutions.

Racial Diversity: A Compelling Interest

Among the various institutional interests to be met in the college admissions process, campus racial diversity is but one interest. Legally, race can be one of many factors in college admissions processes through affirmative action practices. In the 1978 *Bakke* decision, the U.S. Supreme Court allowed for the use of race as one of many factors in college admissions and banned the use of racial quotas. This practice of affirmative action was reinforced in the 2003 Supreme Court decision in *Grutter v. Bollinger*. In that case, the University of Michigan Law School successfully demonstrated that the educational benefits of racial diversity represented a compelling state interest that justified the use of race as one factor in admissions decisions. Notably, in *Gratz v. Bollinger* (2003), the Supreme Court ruled that the use of a fixed point system is unconstitutional. Taken together, the *Grutter* and *Gratz* decisions reaffirmed the importance of advancing campus diversity for the realization of valuable educational benefits, but further limited how selective institutions could account for race as one of many factors in admissions. Based on a large and growing body of empirical research, racial diversity on campus can lead to positive educational outcomes for all students (Gurin, Dey, Hurtado, & Gurin, 2002), can contribute to student growth and development in skills for democratic citizenship and participation (Gurin, Nagda, & Lopez, 2004), and is generally linked to the educational and civic mission of higher education (Hurtado, 2007). Therefore, to fulfill legitimate educational goals, some selective institutions justifiably implement a limited consideration of race, alongside a number of other preferences and criteria, in their admissions processes.

Consequently, affirmative action practices in college admissions are legally justified as long as they pass the strict scrutiny test. According to Winkler (2006), strict scrutiny consists of a two-prong test in which

> courts first determine if the underlying governmental ends, or objectives, are "compelling." . . . If the governmental ends are compelling, the courts then ask if the law is a narrowly tailored means of furthering those governmental interests. Narrow tailoring requires that the law captures within its reach no more activity (or less) than is necessary to advance those compelling ends. (p. 800)

According to the 2016 U.S. Supreme Court *Fisher v. University of Texas* (*Fisher II*) decision, diversity remains a compelling state interest justifying affirmative action, or a limited use of race as one of many factors, in admission. Citing its ruling in the 2013 *Fisher* (*Fisher I*) case, the Supreme Court reaffirmed that "the educational benefits that flow from student body diversity" validated the continued consideration of race in admissions. Within this legal context, diversity is a dynamic and fluid notion that focuses institutional attention "on the interactions among students within a particular context and under appropriate environmental conditions needed to realize the educational benefits of diversity . . . the term *dynamic diversity* cannot be reduced to a generalizable number" (Garces & Jayakumar, 2014, p. 116). Accordingly, the court in *Fisher II* allowed colleges and universities some liberty in determining whether their admissions criteria and process sufficiently advance valuable educational benefits that flow from diversity. Because diversity is a flexible concept, the Supreme Court also concluded that "regular evaluation of data and consideration of student experience" is necessary for "the University [to] tailor its [admissions] approach in light of changing circumstances, ensuring that race plays no greater role than is necessary to meet its compelling interest" of diversity as compulsory to educational goals (*Fisher II*, 2016, p. 11). In other words, diversity is not a fixed idea, nor does it suggest a specific campus demographic profile. Instead, diversity is essential for educational institutions to advance educational goals, and what is required for a campus to be a diverse learning environment will be different at various institutions depending on context. University leaders will need to continually assess their campus environments to determine whether they have achieved diversity for their educational missions (Garces & Jayakumar, 2014).

The current legal precedent according to the U.S. Supreme Court *Fisher II* (2016) case recognizes that admissions processes and criteria are necessarily flexible and adaptive to meeting ever-changing social contexts that inform the educational missions of colleges and universities.

Conclusion

The inclusion of race as one of many criteria in selective college admissions processes is legally justified in fulfilling institutional and public interests in racial diversity and equity. Without racial diversity, college campuses can be hindered from preparing and educating all students to become socially responsible leaders, socially engaged citizens with cultural competencies in an increasingly global society faced with significant challenges. Given the educational interests and benefits of racial diversity, the compelling public interest in addressing persistent racial inequalities (Zamani-Gallaher, Green, Brown, & Stovall, 2009), and traditional civil rights principles of advancing racial justice and equity, the use of race as one factor in admissions is necessary. It is important to note that the U.S. Supreme Court has severely limited how colleges and universities can account for race in their admissions decisions. The court has declared the use of quotas and the explicit boosting of applicant scores based on race (i.e., directly adding points to an applicant's score based on race) unconstitutional but has maintained that diversity is important enough to the nation to justify continued, but very limited, consideration of race in admissions decisions.

Aspiring college students come from all walks of life. Their varied life experiences, which result from social differences, can endow them with an array of unique perspectives, talents, and skills representing the strengths of diversity in the United States. Many college applicants are proven community leaders, budding scientists, talented artists, gifted athletes, brilliant musicians, future teachers, and caring and integral members of their families and communities. They have passions, talents, and vocational callings that span an immense range of fields. Test scores and GPAs cannot fairly represent the totality of any given student's qualities and strengths. With such divergent qualifications found among large and talented pools of applicants, selective colleges and universities have the difficult task of constructing methods to understand and evaluate how each student would fit into the specific school's mission.

Thus, "merit" becomes the demonstration of characteristics that fit an institution's values, interests, and educational goals. Merit is not measured in a uniform way. Consequently, selective colleges and universities determine their own mix of criteria for assessing applications. These criteria are chosen for their relevance and reliability in evaluating students for fit with institutional values and goals. While test scores and high school grades serve as limited tools in predicting college GPAs, colleges and universities that value racial diversity, equity, diverse student skills, talents, and potential above and beyond book learning and multiple-choice test taking must include other criteria.

Accordingly, selective admissions processes represent complex methods of student evaluation involving multiple measures. Returning to the video presented at the beginning of this essay, the narrator's assertion that Sara was negatively impacted by affirmative action is groundless, given the wide range of goals and criteria in college admissions at different schools. Moreover, the full details of Sara's and Emily's applications are not provided. Did Emily win a statewide academic award? Has she been recognized for leading a successful countywide service project? Was Emily's grandfather an important donor to the university? Many factors may have contributed to the decision to admit Emily and reject Sara, but we don't know what those factors are. There are many factors that lead to various outcomes in selective college admissions. The inclusion of race as one among many factors in admissions has become a tepid policy to advance racial equity and diversity foundational to the achievement of important educational goals, and yet affirmative action remains under attack. In an effort to prepare future college graduates for a multicultural and racially diverse world and to confront pervasive and persistent racial inequalities in U.S. education systems, selective institutions are justified in using race as one of many criteria in their efforts to affirmatively and intentionally pursue racial diversity and equity.

OiYan Poon is an assistant professor in the higher education leadership program at Colorado State University. Her research interests include Asian Americans in education, affirmative action, and the racial politics of college access and admissions policies. She has served as an undergraduate admissions reviewer at University of California–Davis and a scholarship application reviewer for the Gates Millennium Scholars Program.

NOTES

1. See http://www.youtube.com/watch?v=UdBMWpu2Opo.

2. I use the term *Latinx* because it allows for a more gender identity–inclusive paradigm for recognizing the diversity within this ethnic population (Scharrón-Del Río & Aja, 2015).

3. According to Kang (1996), "negative action against Asian Americans is in force if a university denies admission to an Asian American who would have been admitted had that person been white" (p. 3). For example, since the 1980s, there have been notable controversies and concerns that elite institutions restrict the admission of Asian Americans to maintain and increase the admissions rates of White applicants (Kang, 1996; Liu, 2007; Nakanishi, 1995; Poon, 2009).

SUGGESTED ADDITIONAL RESOURCES

Asian American Civil Rights. (2017). Retrieved from http://asianamericancivilrights.org/

Guinier, L. (2015). *The tyranny of the meritocracy: Democratizing higher education in America.* Boston, MA: Beacon Press.

Jayakumar, U. M., & Garces, L. M. (Eds.). (2015). *Affirmative action and racial equity: Considering the* Fisher *case to forge the path ahead.* New York, NY: Routledge.

Park, J. J. (2013). *When diversity drops: Race, religion, and affirmative action in higher education.* New Brunswick, NJ: Rutgers University Press.

Zamani-Gallaher, E. M., & Green, D. O. (2009). *The case for affirmative action on campus: Concepts of equity, considerations for practice.* Sterling, VA: Stylus.

REACHING BEYOND THE COLOR LINE

You are a member of the admissions committee at Catalina College, a selective institution that values the pursuit of knowledge, social justice, leadership in service to humanity, and advancing a diverse democracy. Based on this mission, construct criteria with which you will evaluate the following five applicants. Using the criteria you construct, create a scoring rubric. Using this rubric, evaluate the following students for admission.

Student 1

- Captain of tennis team; lettered in three sports (tennis, basketball, and cheerleading)
- 3.7 GPA (weighted)
- Has taken 7 of 23 (30%) AP courses offered by high school
- SAT: 740 (CR); 690 (Math); 780 (Writing)
- Attended Middlebury College summer school (costs $8,000 for 8 weeks)
- Grandparents are alumni of Catalina who have contacted the institution because they are considering giving the school a large donation
- White female; upper middle class

Essay: Ever since I was very young, I have had the privilege of traveling all over the world. By the time I was 15, I had been to over 25 countries. I've always been amazed by the diversity of cultures, and had the opportunity to try all kinds of foods that I wouldn't normally have had the chance to. When I entered high school, I knew I wanted to better understand the world around me through an academic lens. I also wanted to serve people who are not as privileged as me. So during the summer after my junior year of high school, I was accepted to Middlebury College Summer School. It was a chance to practice being a college student. I took great classes on philosophy and biology. Most importantly, I was able to confront and overcome the adversity of having a roommate with Multiple Sclerosis. She was wheelchair bound, and depended on people to help her in and out of bed. A lot of that responsibility fell on me. At first it was really burdensome for me because it took away from my time in the morning and at night to get my work done. After a while, I realized that I was lucky to not have a physical disability, and learned to help my roommate when I had time. Even though I had a lot on my plate, I came to an epiphany that it is important to help people. It helped me learn to balance responsibilities, and most importantly it made me feel good.

Student 2

- Works 35 hours a week at a fast-food restaurant to save money for college
- 3.75 GPA (weighted)
- Has taken 3 of 3 (100%) AP courses offered by high school
- SAT: 620 (CR); 750 (Math); 690 (Writing)
- Asian American (Pakistani) female; working class; first-generation college student

Essay: I haven't always been someone who thought college was possible. My parents were constantly struggling to make ends meet, and fighting over finances. They worked all the time to keep their store open. My earliest memories are of playing on the floor of their convenience store. The other memories after that are of being physically and verbally abused by my parents. They were always mad about not being able to make ends meet, about rude customers, and about how life in America wasn't a dream. When I was 12, the abuse I took at home became apparent at school, and I was taken away from my parents, and placed in the foster care system. Over the last six years, I've lived in 5 different homes. Thankfully, they've all been in the same city, close to the high school I go to now. When I started high school, I met Mrs. Kane who somehow saw something in me, and took me under her wing. She told me about Upward Bound, and for the next few years I learned how college offered a pathway for a better life. To make ends meet, I started working 35 hours a week, so I could save money for college. I'm grateful that I had some great teachers who cared and a stable school community, where I started the South Asian Student Association. Last year, we raised money to support the earthquake victims in northern India. I know that I've benefited from support from people like Mrs. Kane and the staff at Upward Bound. Without people like them, I would not have been prepared to succeed in college. I probably wouldn't have even known the first thing about applying to college. In my future, I plan to "pay it forward." In college, I want to be a tutor and mentor underprivileged youth, and give back to the Upward Bound program. After college, I'm thinking about pursuing a career that would allow me to help young people in the foster care system. I hope to also find reconciliation with my parents, and let them know that I forgive them.

Student 3

- 4.1 GPA (weighted)
- Has taken 9 of 15 (60%) AP courses offered by high school
- SAT: 770 (CR); 800 (Math); 760 (Writing)
- Elected leader in eight different activities—Key Club, Spanish Club, Chess Club, school newspaper, student government, speech and debate, Academic Decathlon, and band
- Asian American (Chinese) male; middle class

Essay: For as long as I can remember, my parents have been my heroes. They immigrated to the U.S. with almost nothing, and have become very successful in providing everything that my siblings and I would need. They're even founders and leaders of our church, which keeps growing every year. My parents came to the U.S. as international graduate students. Shortly after they arrived, they found out my mother was pregnant with my older sister. Life as graduate students was very difficult, and raising a child on grad student salaries was going to be even harder. Several years later, when I was 3, my parents graduated from their doctoral programs, and we moved to northern California. Even with their limited English skills and cultural barriers, they knew they had to find a place to live that had good schools for their children. Last year, when we visited the ancestral villages in China on both sides of my family, I was struck by their humble beginnings. The villages were extremely poor, and only a few houses had modern plumbing. My parents' story, where they've come from and how they've made themselves into community leaders, inspires me to be the best that I can be. They've taught me that hard work in America is always rewarded.

Student 4

- 3.4 GPA (weighted)
- Has taken 5 of 15 (33%) AP courses offered by high school
- Member of a U.S. Olympic team; came in fifth place in event
- SAT: 580 (CR); 610 (Math); 550 (Writing)
- Mixed-race African American, American Indian, and White; middle class

Essay: It's 4 a.m., and my alarm has gone off. I feel like I just went to bed a couple hours ago, and well . . . I actually did. It's time for practice again. My schedule looks like this: 3 hours of practice every day before school; school; 4 hours of practice after school; dinner; homework until about 1 a.m.; and sleep. On Saturdays, I have 6 hours of practice. I have one rest day—Sunday. You could say I don't have a normal teenage schedule, but I have a dream. Ever since I first saw the Olympics on television, I knew that I wanted to be an Olympian. I have been competing nationally and internationally since I was ten years old, and finally became an Olympian. I try to bring the same intensity to my academics, but with my schedule it's been a challenge. However, I know that the skills I've developed as an Olympian have cultivated strong leadership skills and a commitment to achieving all my goals in life. College will be the first time I will be able to control my schedule and explore non-athletic endeavors. I am excited about the possibilities of being involved in campus leadership programs, studying abroad, and even just meeting new people with diverse interests. I bring a unique perspective to my classes and to the campus community and am anxious to learn from my peers and accomplished faculty.

Student 5

- 3.5 GPA (weighted)
- Has taken 6 of 10 (60%) AP courses offered by high school
- Founder of Rainbow Alliance (LGBT organization) in metropolitan region
- SAT: 680 (CR); 790 (Math); 650 (Writing)
- Latinx transgender; Catholic; middle class

Essay: When I was younger, I thought being Mexican American meant feeling ashamed that members of my family, including my grandparents, had been undocumented immigrants who had a weird culture. So I tried to hide my heritage from classmates and teachers in my predominantly White community. In denial of who I was, I avoided talking about my culture, made jokes about Mexicans, and never invited friends to my house. Because of the way politicians and media talked about Mexicans, I internalized a prejudice against my own culture. This shame contributed toward the depression I experienced during my first and second years in high school, when I also started coming to terms with what it meant to be transgender and Catholic. At times, I considered taking my own life. I didn't want to disappoint my family and my church community, but I also didn't know how I could continue to deny who I was inside. These personal challenges led to the poor grades I had during my first years in high school. Thankfully, the youth minister in my church encouraged me to open up and talk with him about my struggles. He was accepting of who I am, and helped me talk with my family, who also amazingly reminded me of their love and grace for me. During my junior year, I also took a community college class on social movements, to learn about LGBT activism. Thankfully, I also learned about the history and legacy of Latinx social justice movements and Latinx leaders, some of whom were queer. The class helped validate my intersectional identity as a queer Latinx leader dedicated to the betterment of society. Today, I'm not ashamed of any part of who I am. I am especially thankful to have been blessed by my family, which has blessed me with a rich history, traditions, compassion, and love for community.

Questions for Discussion

1. What criteria and institutional interests did you use to review and select students for admission?

2. How did you evaluate and score each student? Why?

3. Did you admit students with lower grades or test scores than another applicant? Why or why not?

4. Was your process fair to all students and did it meet institutional interests?

5. Do you feel that anyone can understand who you are, your accomplishments, and your potential by just looking at your test scores and high school grades? Why or why not?

REFERENCES

Atkinson, R. C., & Geiser, S. (2009). *Reflections on a century of college admissions tests* (No. CSHE.4.2009). Research and Occasional Papers Series (pp. 1–21). Berkeley, CA: Center for Studies in Higher Education. Retrieved from http://www.cshe.berkeley.edu/sites/default/files/shared/publications/docs/ROPS-AtkinsonGeiser-Tests-04-15-09.pdf

Balf, T. (2014, March 6). The story behind the SAT overhaul. *New York Times Magazine.* Retrieved from http://www.nytimes.com/2014/03/09/magazine/the-story-behind-the-sat-overhaul.html?_r=0

Bernhard, M. P., & Delwiche, N. J. (2015, May 16). Groups file federal complaint alleging discrimination in Harvard admissions process. *Harvard Crimson.* Retrieved from http://www.thecrimson.com/article/2015/5/16/complaint-federal-harvard-admissions/

Bonilla-Silva, E. (2006). *Racism without racists: Color-blind racism and the persistence of racial inequality in the United States.* Lanham, MD: Rowman & Littlefield.

Conchas, G. Q. (2006). *The color of success: Race and high-achieving urban youth.* New York, NY: Teachers College Press.

Connerly, W. (2005, April 15). On the defensive: Quota defenders are having a tough time. *National Review.* Retrieved from http://www.nationalreview.com/article/214196/defensive-nro-primary-document

Espenshade, T. J., & Chung, C. Y. (2005). The opportunity cost of admission preferences at elite universities. *Social Science Quarterly, 86*(2), 293–305.

Fisher v. University of Texas at Austin, 570 U.S. ___ (2013).

Fisher v. University of Texas at Austin, 579 U.S. ___ (2016).

Garces, L. M., & Jayakumar, U. M. (2014). Dynamic diversity: Toward a contextual understanding of critical mass. *Educational Researcher, 43*(3), 115–124.

Geiser, S. (2008). *Not so fast! A second opinion on a University of California proposal to endorse the new SAT* (No. CSHI.16.2008). Research and Occasional Papers Series (pp. 1–11). Berkeley, CA: Center for Studies in Higher Education. Retrieved from http://www.cshe.berkeley.edu/not-so-fast-second-opinion-university-california-proposal-endorse-new-sat

Golden, D. (2007). *The price of admission: How America's ruling class buys its way into elite colleges—and who gets left outside the gates.* New York, NY: Three Rivers Press.

Gratz v. Bollinger, 539 U.S. 244 (2003).

Grutter v. Bollinger, 539 U.S. 306 (2003).

Gurin, P., Dey, E. L., Hurtado, S., & Gurin, G. (2002). Diversity and higher education: Theory and impact on educational outcomes. *Harvard Educational Review, 72*(3), 330–366.

Gurin, P., Nagda, B. A., & Lopez, G. E. (2004). The benefits of diversity in education for democratic citizenship. *Journal of Social Issues, 60*(1), 17–34.

Hoffman, J. L., & Lowitzki, K. E. (2005). Predicting college success with high school grades and test scores: Limitations for minority students. *Review of Higher Education, 28*(4), 455–474.

Hossler, D. (2011). From admissions to enrollment management. In N. Zhang (Ed.), *Rentz's student affairs practice in higher education* (4th ed., pp. 63–95). Springfield, IL: Charles C Thomas.

Howell, C., & Turner, S. (2004). Legacies in Black and White: The racial composition of the legacy pool. *Research in Higher Education, 45*(4), 325–351.

Hurtado, S. (2007). Linking diversity with the educational and civic missions of higher education. *Review of Higher Education, 30*(2), 185–196.

Jaschik, S. (2009, November 3). The power of race. *Inside Higher Ed.* Retrieved from https://www.insidehighered.com/news/2009/11/03/elite

Kang, J. (1996). Negative action against Asian Americans: The internal instability of Dworkin's defense of affirmative action. *Harvard Civil Rights-Civil Liberties Law Review, 31*, 1–48.

Karabel, J. (2005). *The chosen: The hidden history of admission and exclusion at Harvard, Yale, and Princeton.* New York, NY: Houghton Mifflin.

Kidder, W. C. (2005). Negative action versus affirmative action: Asian Pacific Americans are still caught in the crossfire. *Michigan Journal of Race & Law, 11*, 605–624.

Lareau, A. (2011). *Unequal childhoods: Class, race, and family life.* Berkeley: University of California Press.

Leonard, H. J. (1974, February 8). The "reverse discrimination" backlash. *Harvard Crimson.*

Liu, A. (2007). Affirmative action & negative action: How Jian Li's case can benefit Asian Americans. *Michigan Journal of Race & Law, 13*, 391–432.

McDonough, P. M. (1994). Buying and selling higher education: The social construction of the college applicant. *Journal of Higher Education, 65*(4), 427–446.

McGarvey, S. (2012, March 19). Affirmative action: Racist by nature. *Daily Texan.* Retrieved from http://www.dailytexanonline.com/opinion/2012/03/19/affirmative-action-racist-by-nature

Merit. (2011). *Merriam-Webster.com.* Retrieved from http://www.merriam-webster.com/dictionary/merit

Nakanishi, D. T. (1995). A quota on excellence? The Asian American admissions debate. In D. T. Nakanishi & T. Nishida (Eds.), *The Asian American educational experience* (pp. 273–284). New York, NY: Routledge.

O'Reilly, B. (2012, February 23). Supreme Court to hear affirmative action case. *The O'Reilly Factor.* Fox News. Retrieved from http://www.foxnews.com/transcript/2012/02/24/supreme-court-hear-affirmative-action-case.html

Poon, O. (2009). Haunted by negative action: Asian Americans, admissions, and race in the "colorblind era." *Harvard University Asian American Policy Review, 18.*

Potter, W. (2003, February 28). Chewing over affirmative action. *Chronicle of Higher Education,* p. A8.

Rashid, M., Hurtado, S., Brown, M., & Agronow, S. (2009). *A response to: "Not so fast! A second opinion on a University of California proposal to endorse the new SAT."* Research and Occasional Paper Series. Berkeley, CA: Center for Studies in Higher Education.

Regents of the University of California v. Bakke, 438 U.S. 264 (1978).

Santelices, M. V., & Wilson, M. (2010). Unfair treatment? The case of Freedle, the SAT, and the standardization approach to differential item functioning. *Harvard Educational Review, 80*(1), 106–134.

Scharrón-Del Río, M. R., & Aja, A. A. (2015). The case for "Latinx": Why intersectionality is not a choice. *Latino Rebels.* Retrieved from http://www.latinorebels.com/2015/12/05/the-case-for-latinx-why-intersectionality-is-not-a-choice/

Sedlacek, W. E. (2005). The case for noncognitive measures. In W. Camara & E. W. Kimmel (Eds.), *Choosing students: Higher education admissions tools for the 21st century* (pp. 177–194). Mahwah, NJ: Lawrence Erlbaum.

Shadowen, S. D., Tulante, S. P., & Alpern, S. L. (2009). No distinctions except those which merit originates: The unlawfulness of legacy preferences in public and private universities. *Santa Clara Law Review, 49*, 51–136.

Steinberg, J. (2003). *The gatekeepers: Inside the admissions process of a premier college.* New York, NY: Penguin Books.

Tenenbaum, H. R., & Ruck, M. D. (2007). Are teachers' expectations different for racial minority than for European American students? A meta-analysis. *Journal of Educational Psychology, 99*(2), 253–273.

Turner, R. (1996). The dangers of misappropriation: Misusing Martin Luther King, Jr.'s legacy to prove the colorblind thesis. *Michigan Journal of Race & Law, 2,* 101–130.

University of California. (2012). *How applications are reviewed.* Retrieved from http://www .universityofcalifornia.edu/admissions/freshman/how-applications-reviewed/index.html

University of Texas. (2017). Freshman application review. Retrieved from https://admissions .utexas.edu/apply/decisions/freshman-review

Winkler, A. (2006). Fatal in theory and strict in fact: An empirical analysis of strict scrutiny in the federal courts. *Vanderbilt Law Review, 59,* 794–871.

Zamani-Gallaher, E. M., Green, D. O., Brown, M. C., & Stovall, D. O. (2009). *The case for affirmative action on campus: Concepts of equity, considerations for practice.* Sterling, VA: Stylus.

"We Need to Take Care of 'Real Americans' First"

Historical and Contemporary Definitions of Citizenship

Kara Cebulko

Providence College

> *When Mexico sends its people, they're not sending their best. They're not sending you. They're not sending you. They're sending people that have lots of problems, and they're bringing those problems with us. They're bringing drugs. They're bringing crime. They're rapists. And some, I assume, are good people.*
>
> —Donald Trump (June 2015)

L aunching his bid for the Republican nomination to be president of the United States, Donald Trump pointed to the crowd, which was overwhelmingly White, and told them in no uncertain terms that Mexican immigrants are a threat to Americans. But it is not just people crossing the U.S.–Mexico border whom Donald Trump positions as threats. After the terrorist attacks in Paris by ISIL members on November 13, 2015, and a separate terrorist attack by Syed Rizwan Farook and Tashfeen Malik in San Bernardino, California, on December 2, 2015, Donald Trump called for a ban on all Muslims entering the United States and a halt to the resettlement of refugees from the Middle East.

He escalated his rhetoric during a speech in Warwick, Rhode Island, in the spring of 2016, telling the mostly White crowd that Syrian refugees had been resettled in Rhode Island and that folks needed to "lock [their] doors":

> Lock your doors, folks, okay, lock your doors. . . . There's no documentation, we have our incompetent government people letting them in by the thousands, and who knows, maybe it's ISIS. You see what happens with two people that became radicalized in California, where they shot and killed all their coworkers. Not with me, folks, it's not happening with me.

Importantly, there is no evidence to support his claims of rampant criminality among foreign-born Mexicans, an unsafe vetting process for refugees, or widespread domestic terrorism by Muslims. Using 2000 census data, Rumbaut and Ewing (2007) found that foreign-born Mexican immigrant men (as well as foreign-born Guatemalans and Salvadorans) have the lowest incarceration rates of all Latin American immigrants. They also found that the incarceration rate for Mexican men (0.7%) Was even lower than the incarceration rate for native-born non-Hispanic White men (1.7%).

And despite claims to the contrary by Trump and others, the refugee vetting process is extremely arduous, taking 18 to 24 months to complete and requiring several background checks. As Kathleen Newland (2015) of the Migration Policy Institute argues, "the refugee resettlement program is the least likely avenue for terrorists to choose" because of the "painstaking, many-layered review" in which "the FBI, Department of Homeland Security, State Department and national intelligence agencies independently check refugees' biometric data against security databases." Indeed, of the 748,000 refugees settled through the refugee resettlement program since September 11, 2011, only three have been arrested for planning terrorist attacks and two of them were planning an attack abroad, not in the United States (Newland, 2015).

Moreover, most Americans would be surprised to learn that the Triangle Center on Terrorism and Homeland Security reported in June 2015 that most law enforcement agencies believe that antigovernment extremists, not al-Qaeda and other like-minded extremist groups, pose the greatest threat for political violence in the United States (Kurzman & Schanzer, 2015). Of the 382 law enforcement agencies surveyed, 74% reported antigovernment extremism as one of the top three threats in their jurisdictions, while only 39% listed extremism connected with al-Qaeda or other similar terrorist organizations.

Despite these facts, however, the fear of Mexicans and Muslims strikes deep in the minds of some Americans. This has been especially true in the wake of 9/11, as the media and politicians have conflated migration from Latin America with terrorism (Chavez, 2013).[1] Not surprisingly, perhaps, anti-immigrant laws have increased throughout the country since 9/11, capitalizing on fears that we must protect "real Americans" from an "invasion" of terrorists and criminals.

But who, exactly, are "real" Americans? And is the fear of "outsiders" as a threat really new? As we will see, defining *who is, who can be, and who should be* an American has been a reoccurring theme throughout American history (Daniels, 1998;

Hing, 2004; Ngai, 2004). Because members of a nation-state cannot possibly know everyone in their national community, the nation-state is an "imagined community" (Anderson, 1983/1991). Importantly, this "imagined community"—the collective vision of who we are—shapes (and is shaped by) immigration policies that decide entry and removal, access to citizenship and rights, and ultimately, the composition of the American community (Zolberg, 2006). Throughout history, race, ethnicity, and religion have played a large role in this collective vision of who we are and our immigration policies.

"Illegal Aliens," Presidents, and "Real Americans"

Posing for a photo op in 2007, then-leading Democratic candidate for president Hillary Rodham Clinton held up a T-shirt that read, "Legalize the Irish!" Four years later, Donald Trump, contemplating a 2012 presidential bid, told media outlets that he had sent private investigators to Hawaii, the place of President Obama's birth, to investigate "the truth" of Obama's birthplace. Despite the fact that rumors claiming Obama was not a U.S.-born citizen had long since been discredited, the resulting uproar from Trump's announcement of an "investigation" led the White House to release the long form of President Barack Hussein Obama's birth certificate on April 27, 2011.

What do these two seemingly different events have in common? Together, they say a lot about the roles that race, ethnicity, and religion play in the collective vision of who we are as a nation. The contrast is striking. On the one hand, an influential politician, Hillary Clinton, poses for a photo op with "illegal aliens"—persons who exist at the outermost edge of American society—calling for their formal, legal inclusion in the national community.[2] Notably, there was no media or political firestorm denouncing her photo op with the *White, Irish* "illegal aliens." On the other hand, the 44th president of the United States, Barack Obama, continued to face allegations that he was not, in fact, a "real American." The irony, of course, is that Obama's own biography seems to be the quintessential American immigrant success story: the son of an immigrant who worked hard, overcame obstacles, and became one of the most powerful men in the world. But of course, he is not the son of an Irish man. He is the son of a Kenyan man. Moreover, his middle name is *Hussein*. Thus, in the eyes of some, President Obama could not possibly be an American, even if he was the 44th president of the United States. It is hard to imagine these stories playing out in similar fashion had the "illegal aliens" been Mexican rather than Irish and had President Obama been White rather than Black with Hussein as a middle name. Together, these two examples remind us that despite the diversity in contemporary America and the racial progress we have made, the collective vision of who we are (and who we should be) remains one of a White, Christian nation.

The stories we tell about our nation's past and, specifically, stories of voluntary White European immigrants also reflect this collective vision of ourselves (Chomsky, 2007). After all, largely excluded in the White European immigrant narrative are the experiences of people of color, experiences that often include forced migration, enslavement, or exclusion. The narrative also obscures the ways Whiteness has always provided advantages in access to entry, to citizenship, and to the full rights and privileges of citizenship. Moreover, it serves as a false and unattainable measuring stick against which today's immigrants, who largely hail from Latin America and Asia, are compared. Thus, it is important to debunk the White European immigrant narrative. When we do, we can see the ways becoming an American largely included "becoming White" and were aided by laws, public policy, government programs, unions, self-distancing by immigrants themselves, and by a time of economic expansion and decreased migration from Europe. But the question remains: Is Whiteness still key to becoming an American? Not only in regard to the law but in the eyes of the public?

The Stories We Tell: The Great (White) Immigrant Narrative and the Immigrant Threats of Today

Look, I'm the son of an Italian immigrant. I think immigration is one of the great things that has made this country the dynamic country that it continues to be. . . . And so we should not have a debate talking about how we don't want people to come to this country, but we want them to come like my grandfather and my father came here. They made sacrifices. They came in the 1920s. There were no promises. There were no government benefits.

—Former senator Rick Santorum (R-PA, September 2011, Republican primary presidential debate)

The story that many Americans tell—especially White Americans—resembles the story Senator Rick Santorum told (above) during a 2011 debate. It is a story that contrasts a nostalgic, romanticized immigrant past with a threatening story of an immigrant present. Thus, on one hand, many Americans celebrate the stories of past European immigrants who, according to the narrative, came to the United States "legally," pulled themselves up by their own bootstraps, and were quick to culturally and structurally assimilate—learning English, quickly adopting norms, beliefs, and values of American society, and ultimately, achieving the American dream. But on the other hand, these same Americans fear that today's immigrants, mostly immigrants of color, are poor "invaders/aliens" who migrate "illegally," refuse to assimilate, take jobs and resources away from "real" Americans, and ultimately threaten our national identity as a (White) Anglo-Saxon Christian nation (Huntington, 2004, 2009). Yet as we will see, the United States has a history of viewing immigrants as threats and seeking restrictions on their migration and citizenship.

A History of Restriction and Exclusion of the "Other"

While many Americans assume that the United States has always welcomed immigrants as long as they work hard and assimilate, the reality is that from the colonial era to the present day, some nativist groups have pushed for restrictive and exclusionary laws and policies to protect "real Americans" from "threatening Others." At the heart of these historical and present-day fears lies the belief that America's national identity as a White, Anglo-Saxon, and Christian (Protestant) nation is in peril. For example, political scientist Samuel Huntington (2009) argued that "the persistent inflow of Hispanic immigrants threatens to divide the United States into two peoples, two cultures, and two languages," since Latino immigrants are "rejecting the Anglo-Protestant values that built the American dream." Momentarily setting aside the claim that Latino immigrants are failing to assimilate, Huntington's fears are remarkable for their similarity to Benjamin Franklin's in 1751:

> Why Should Pennsylvania, founded by the English, become a Colony of Aliens, who will be so numerous as to Germanize us instead of our Anglicizing them, and will never adopt our Language or Customs, any more than they can acquire our Complexion. (Quoted in Daniels, 1998, p. 38)

Germans then, Latinos now. The message is clear in both examples. Germans and Latinos are too numerous, incapable of assimilating (i.e., "will never adopt our Language or Customs"; see Rudolph in this volume for further discussion on language acquisition), and threaten America's Anglo-Protestant culture. Today, of course, the idea of Germans posing a threat to America's national identity seems absurd. But in the eyes of many in 1751, the German threat was real, as was the Irish Catholic threat and the subsequent Italian threat. In all cases, these groups were seen as too numerous, incapable of assimilating, and as taking jobs from "real Americans." The hostility also led to restrictive immigration laws, such as the literacy law of 1917 and the National Origins Quota laws in the 1920s, which aimed to reduce the migration of southern and eastern Europeans (Hing, 2004).

The hostility and restrictions European groups faced were harsh but paled in comparison with the exclusion, conquest, and extermination faced by Asians, Mexicans, other Latin Americans, Blacks, and Native Americans. Although the founding fathers wrote "All Men are Created Equal," the first Congress in 1790 limited citizenship through naturalization to "free White persons" of good moral character who had been in the United States for two years.[3] For persons who were of color and born in the United States, their access to citizenship depended on individual state laws (Daniels, 1998). Thus, although some White ethnic groups were subjected to xenophobic restriction laws, most who did arrive were allowed to become citizens through a relatively easy naturalization process (Ngai, 2004).[4]

With citizenship, White ethnics gained access to other opportunities in achieving the American dream. In contrast, many (indeed, most) Blacks and Native Americans were enslaved, exterminated, pushed onto reservations, and later (once granted citizenship) subjected to years of formal segregation and institutional discrimination. Meanwhile, xenophobia and racism led to laws that excluded Asian immigration altogether (on the grounds that they were "racially ineligible for citizenship") and relegated Mexican Americans to second-class citizenship in the American Southwest, their original homeland.

Racial requirements for citizenship were not fully lifted until 1952. But if Whiteness was so important for citizenship, *who* exactly was White? Whiteness, like all racial categories, was constructed over time, including through laws. The Johnson-Reed Act of 1924 and the Supreme Court decisions of *Takao Ozawa v. United States* (1922) and *United States v. Bhagat Singh Thind* (1923) were particularly instrumental in setting the legal boundaries of Whiteness (Ngai, 2004). Following on the heels of previous restriction and exclusion laws, the Johnson-Reed Act of 1924 sought to restrict southern and eastern European migration (on the grounds that they were inferior to northern and western Europeans) and ban all Asian migration (on the grounds that Asians were racially ineligible for citizenship). Ironically, while the law was discriminatory and reduced southern and eastern European migration, it also helped these very groups over time, as the law placed boundaries around Whiteness, boundaries that included them (Ngai, 2004).

The Supreme Court also played a large role in setting the legal boundaries of Whiteness. In 1922, in *Takao Ozawa v. US*, Takao Ozawa, a Japanese man, argued that the Japanese should be eligible for citizenship under the Naturalization Act of 1906—which limited citizenship to Whites and Blacks—because the Japanese were highly assimilable and their "dominant strains are 'White persons,' speaking an Aryan tongue and having Caucasian root stock" (Ngai, 2004, p. 44). The Supreme Court ruled, however, that the Japanese were of the Mongolian race, not the "Caucasian" race. Thus, the Japanese were not White and were ineligible for citizenship. Just months later, however, the Supreme Court reversed its own logic of using science as the basis of deciding Whiteness. In *U.S. v. Bhagat Singh Thind* (1923), Thind, a U.S. army veteran and Indian immigrant, used scientific evidence to claim that Indians were part of the Aryan race and thus should be eligible for citizenship. But then, according to the Supreme Court, "Whiteness" was not based in science but in what "the common man" said Whiteness was (Ngai, 2004).

Thus, the "law establishe[d] Whiteness as American identity" (Carbado, 2005, p. 637) and had very real effects on who became American and who had access to social and civil rights. Between 1907 and 1924, about 1.5 million immigrants became citizens, most all of whom were European immigrants (Ngai, 2004). Meanwhile, no amount of assimilation through socialization—adopting American customs and values—was enough to make Asians real Americans. "Real Americans" were those who not only adopted American values but who could "become White" (Ngai, 2004). Without citizenship, Asians were denied other rights, including land ownership in most states (Hing, 2004; Ngai, 2004).

If Asians were deemed non-White, what about Mexicans? Per terms of the Treaty of Guadalupe Hidalgo in 1848, which ended the Mexican–American War, Mexico gave up the land that is now the American Southwest. Mexicans who remained on the land were allowed to become U.S. citizens. Since citizenship was restricted to "Whites," Mexican Americans were technically considered "White." But while legally White and legally citizens, Mexican Americans were "socially non-White" and the American public treated them as second-class citizens in their schools and communities—treatment akin to what Blacks experienced under Jim Crow segregation (Donato & Hanson, 2012).

The Historical "Rules" of Migration and the Production of Illegality

Some Americans state that they are not against immigration, just "illegal" immigration. This assertion is often accompanied by the claim that their ancestors came "legally" and, thus, new immigrants should "play by the rules like my ancestors did." As Chomsky (2007) argues, this claim is "one of the most oft repeated—and most puzzling comments" in the immigration debate (p. 53). It is puzzling and problematic for a number of reasons. First, as previously detailed, historically, the "rules" for migration have generally favored Europeans over other groups. Furthermore, the rules have changed over time. Thus, many White ethnics' ancestors would not be eligible to migrate under today's restrictions, which generally require family or employer sponsorships for migration (American Immigration Council, 2008). During the Open Door Era of Immigration, from 1776 until the late 1800s, there was no "line" for Europeans "to get in" because there generally were no restrictions on any migration (Bernard, 1998). When restrictions did emerge, Europeans continued to fare better than other groups. In contrast, today's restrictions on entry mean that there are few legal channels for entry; thus, there is no "line" for many immigrants around the world (American Immigration Council, 2008).

Second, this claim is problematic because it ignores the fact that some Europeans entered or stayed in the country "illegally" (and continue to do so). Restrictions on entry reduced but did not stop the flows of southern and eastern Europeans. Rather, the new laws made previously legal acts (i.e., migration) illegal or changed the route they took to come to America. But the sheer number of "illegal" Europeans never grew as large as the number of Mexicans. The question is, *Why*? Part of the answer lies in policies that allowed Europeans to circumvent restriction laws *and* the selective application of (1) legalization policies and (2) enforcement policies.

Following the quota laws of 1921 and 1924 that restricted southern and eastern Europeans' entry at sea ports, thousands started arriving illegally into the United States through Canada and, especially, Mexico. It was their unlawful entry (and the unlawful entry of the Chinese), not the migration of Mexicans, that prompted the U.S. government to start heavily patrolling its land borders and increasing deportation efforts. By the late 1920s, the flow of "illegal" Europeans had already declined. While enforcement policies (including the threat of deportation) may have deterred some migration, many Europeans actually circumvented the national origins restrictions through a different legal route: They migrated to Canada, and after 5 years of living in Canada, they were legally allowed to migrate to the United States. Once in the United States, they could easily become U.S. citizens and then legally apply to bring relatives into the United States as nonquota immigrants (Ngai, 2004).

Furthermore, Europeans benefited disproportionately from discretionary policies, which allowed certain "illegal" immigrants to legalize their status. Between 1925 and 1965, through various administrative policies and discretions, about 200,000 undocumented Europeans successfully adjusted their legal status (Ngai, 2004). The discourse painted White Europeans as "deserving" and as "good persons" whose lives should not be ruined for *minor* mistakes. These administrative policies and discretions, however, rarely benefited Mexicans, who were seen as poor criminals and racialized as "other" lying outside the "real American" community. Under this racialized construction, Mexicans became the main targets of enforcement policies (De Genova & Ramos-Zayas, 2003; Hing, 2004; Ngai, 2004). Moreover, it was not just unauthorized Mexicans targeted for removal but also lawfully present Mexicans and Mexican Americans. After the stock market crash of 1929, nativist alarm called for programs that encouraged Mexicans and Mexican Americans, often through scare tactics, to return to Mexico. According to the U.S. Department of Labor, over 15 months, more than 2 million persons of Mexican descent returned to Mexico (Hing, 2004). While Mexicans were welcomed (by some) as laborers during economic booms, they were never welcomed as persons, as citizens, or as "real Americans."

Today, it is not just Mexicans but all Latinos who are lumped together as "the threat" to American national identity (Chavez, 2013) and are the main targets of enforcement. Although the Department of Homeland Security emphasizes national security in the wake of 9/11 (implying a focus on counterterrorism), very few persons from countries the government associates with terrorism are deported. Instead, Afro-Caribbean drug peddlers (who often are lawful permanent residents) and Latino undocumented workers are disproportionately targeted (through racial profiling) for detention and deportation (Golash-Boza, 2012).

Immigrants, Past and Present, and Assimilation

Many Americans also assert that unlike previous waves of immigrants, today's immigrants do not want to assimilate. As Pat Buchanan (2002) says,

> Unlike the immigrants of old, who bade farewell forever to their native lands when they boarded the ship, for Mexicans, the mother country is right next door. Millions have no desire to learn English or to become citizens. America is not their home: Mexico is; and they wish to remain proud Mexicans. They come here to work. Rather than assimilate, they create Little Tijuanas in U.S. cities. With their own radio and TV stations, newspapers, films, and magazines, the Mexican Americans are creating an Hispanic culture separate and apart from America's larger culture. (pp. 125–126)

Thus, for Buchanan and many other Americans, the assertion that today's immigrants, unlike past immigrants, do not assimilate means that they refuse to learn English, do not adopt American culture, and have no desire to become American citizens. Instead, they retain their own culture, live among themselves, and only come "to work" or "to take advantage of us," as one White woman told Lillian Rubin (1994) during the course of her research.

There are a few problems, however, with this contrasting assimilation narrative. First, it is simply not the case that past immigrants who came to the United States "bade farewell forever" to their homelands. In fact, some Europeans could be characterized as "Birds of Passage" (Piore, 1979), never intending to settle in the United States. Rather, they hoped to make money and return to their homelands. An estimated 20% to 30% of Italian men who immigrated to the United States eventually returned permanently to Italy (Mintz & McNeil, 2012). Furthermore, the reality is that assimilation—becoming more culturally, linguistically, socially, and socioeconomically integrated into the host society—rarely took place within one generation for past waves of European immigrants (Alba & Nee, 2003). For example, the language shift to English usually occurred over the course of three generations rather than within one generation (Veltman, 1983).

Scholarship suggests, however, that descendants of European immigrants did assimilate (Alba & Nee, 2003). But what is the story of more recent immigrants and their children? Contrary to claims that they are not learning English, scholarship suggests that children of immigrants, including all Asian and Latino ethnic groups, have shifted to English (Portes & Rumbaut, 2001; Tran, 2010). Importantly, however, learning English and speaking another language are not mutually exclusive, and bilingualism may be advantageous in an increasingly globalized world (Portes & Rumbaut, 2001; Tran, 2010).

Some scholars argue that the question of assimilation is not *whether* children of immigrants will assimilate, but to *which segment of society* they will assimilate (Portes & Rumbaut, 2001; Portes & Zhou, 1993). According to the segmented assimilation framework, factors in the contexts of exit and reception, including race, will shape specific integration patterns. While some immigrants may experience upward assimilation (and assimilate to the White mainstream), others might experience downward assimilation (as they assimilate to stigmatized groups of color and experience systematic disadvantages). Still other immigrants may experience mostly upward assimilation through *selective acculturation,* or by selectively combining norms and values of both the dominant society and the immigrant community. Some research, however, finds little evidence of downward assimilation (Kasinitz, Mollenkopf, Waters, & Holdaway, 2008; Smith, 2003; Waldinger & Feliciano, 2004). For example, drawing on a large study of second-generation immigrants in adulthood in New York City, Kasinitz et al. (2008) find that most immigrant children, when compared with their native-born peers of the same race (rather than Whites), are doing quite well, having higher levels of education and labor force participation. Furthermore, they have had success by joining the mainstream economy rather than immigrant economic niches.

Achieving the American Dream: Structural Opportunities and the Bootstrap Myth

Another repeated claim by many White Americans is that their ancestors, unlike today's immigrants, "never asked for government handouts" and instead achieved upward mobility through their hard work alone. Yet, importantly, Whiteness not only provided advantages in entry and access to citizenship, it was a privileged status that allowed European ethnics access to opportunities, including government programs denied to non-Whites. Historians have shown that upward mobility for European ethnics was rarely achieved by hard work alone (Brodkin, 1998; Ignatiev, 1995; Roediger, 1991, 2005). Whiteness provided access to all sorts of social citizenship benefits, including union membership (which helped achieve safer working conditions and better wages); Social Security benefits (which initially excluded agricultural and domestic service workers—sectors that were overwhelmingly Black and Mexican); GI bills that helped subsidize the cost of higher education; and federal loans for housing, which subsidized Whites in homeownership and accumulation of wealth. Furthermore, southern and eastern European immigrants often distanced themselves from stigmatized people of color as they pursued new opportunities—opportunities available only because they were classified as racially White (Roediger, 2005; see also Ioanide and Moore in this volume).

Conclusion

Contemporary political rhetoric and anti-immigrant policies about protecting real Americans are nothing new. Both the rhetoric and the policies reflect—and hope to maintain—a vision of the United States as an "imagined community" (Anderson, 1983/1991) of White Anglo-Saxon Americans. The rhetoric and policies are not always explicitly racist. For example, Arizona's controversial Senate Bill 1070, passed in 2010, requires police to check the papers of persons they have a "reasonable suspicion" of being present unlawfully. But what visible indicators exist of "illegality"? As critics point out, this law necessarily encourages racial profiling. Whites are rarely suspected of being foreigners, let alone "illegal aliens."

What lies at the heart of anti-immigrant policies? A failure to assimilate seems unlikely. Undocumented youth who came to the United States as children often cite their assimilation to American society as evidence of their deservingness of being granted American citizenship. Yet, at the time of this writing, Congress continues to deny them a pathway to citizenship. The claim that immigrants "break our laws" also seems insufficient, particularly when Americans break laws all the time. Furthermore, when we examine the past and present laws that created high numbers of undocumented immigrants among some populations but not others, we can raise the question of whether these laws are or were just. Additionally, "illegality" does not explain why Latino and (lawfully present) Black immigrants are disproportionately targeted in deportation and detention policies. According to Douglas S. Massey (1995), the "real nature of the anti-immigrant reaction among non-Hispanic Whites" is "a fear of cultural change and a deep seated worry that European Americans will be displaced from their dominant position in American life" (p. 632). Eduardo Bonilla-Silva (2004) argues, however, that Whites are not being displaced. While he claims that the United States is moving from a biracial order to a triracial order, Whites—including some immigrants who can be considered "White"—will remain on top of the racial hierarchy. Thus, Whiteness continues to be constructed and to be important in gaining the full benefits of citizenship and belonging.

Kara Cebulko is an associate professor of sociology and global studies at Providence College. Her current research focuses on how legal status shapes the transition to and experience of young adulthood for 1.5-generation immigrants. She teaches courses on migration, borders, and globalization and has published in the *Sociological Quarterly,* the *Journal of Marriage and Family,* the *Journal of Family Studies,* and *Sociological Perspectives.* Her first book, *Documented, Undocumented and Something Else: The Incorporation of Children of Brazilian Immigrants,* was published in 2013 by LFB Scholarly.

NOTES

1. The most explicit and vitriolic rhetoric of protecting "real Americans" from immigrants appears in the comment sections of online news articles and anti-immigrant websites. But the discourse is also present in mainstream media. See Chavez (2013) for a full discussion on the construction of the present-day Latino threat narrative in the media and public discourse.

2. *Illegal immigrant* and *illegal alien* are dehumanizing terms. Indeed, no human being is "illegal." Illegality is not an inherent condition of a person; it is produced by immigration laws—laws that change in each historical time period, reflecting the sociopolitical context of the time (De Genova, 2002; Ngai, 2004). Furthermore, *illegality* suggests criminality. Being in the United States without documents, however, is a civil—not a criminal—offense.

3. Citizenship in the United States is granted in three ways: (1) through birth on U.S. soil; (2) through naturalization, the process by which foreign nationals become citizens after meeting certain requirements; or (3) through being born to U.S. parents abroad.

4. For most of the 19th century, 5 years of residence and no criminal record were required for citizenship (Ngai, 2004). It was not until 1906 that English language ability was required for naturalization.

SUGGESTED ADDITIONAL RESOURCES

Hing, B. O. (2004). *Defining America through immigration policy.* Philadelphia, PA: Temple University Press.

Ngai, M. M. (2004). *Impossible subjects: Illegal aliens and the making of modern America.* Princeton, NJ: Princeton University Press.

Portes, A., & Zhou, M. (1993, November). The new second generation: Segmented assimilation and its variants. *Annals of the American Academy of Political and Social Science, 530,* 74–96.

Roediger, D. (2005). *Working toward Whiteness: How America's immigrants became White; The strange journey from Ellis Island to the suburbs.* New York, NY: Basic Books.

QUESTIONS FOR FURTHER DISCUSSION

1. What does it mean to be *an American*? What do you think of when you imagine a *quintessential American*? What does it mean to be a *citizen*? In what ways are—or should—these concepts be related to one another?

2. How has race, historically, played a role in defining who is—and who can become—an American? Did any of these past events surprise you? Why?

3. How might the collective vision of "who we are" help explain our response to tragedy? Consider the following: in the summer of 2012, two tragedies happened within a few weeks of each other. In the first case, a White man opened fire in a movie theater in Aurora, Colorado, killing 12 persons and injuring 56. In the second tragedy, a White supremacist went into a Sikh Temple and murdered six persons. In comparison with the Aurora shooting, very little public attention was paid to the Sikh temple shooting. Why is that? Could we imagine so little attention being paid to the second tragedy if it involved a person of color or non-Christian background walking into a White Christian church? Or consider gun violence and the death of children. In December 2012, a gunman opened fire on an elementary school in Newtown, Connecticut, killing 27 persons, mostly White children. It was a horrific mass murder. Yet children, especially children of color, die every night in many of our nation's cities. There were about 500 murders in Chicago around the same time, many more deaths than in the Newtown tragedy. Yet their deaths do not result in the same public media outcry. How do we make sense of these varying reactions from the public?

4. Similarly, how might the collective vision of who we are explain our response to what we view as potential threats? For example, in early 2016, a militia of mostly White, gun-yielding protestors seized land in a federal wildlife refuge in Oregon to protest the "tyranny" of the federal government. They encouraged other "patriots" to grab their guns and join them. What was your reaction to this event? How did others react? How do you think the collective reaction to this would have been different had the "patriots" been Black? Or Muslim? Or Latino?

5. Donald Trump's campaign slogan in 2016 was "Make America Great Again." Keeping this chapter in mind, what are the implications of this slogan?

6. What are some potential viable solutions for the issues discussed in this chapter?

REACHING BEYOND THE COLOR LINE

1. Read the essay "My Life as an Undocumented Immigrant," by Jose Antonio Vargas (http://www.nytimes.com/2011/06/26/magazine/my-life-as-an-undocumented-immigrant.html). After reading this essay, reflect on the following: What does it mean to be an American? In what ways does Vargas's story both challenge and reinforce our ideas of what a real American is?

2. We are often surprised when we examine the ways Irish, Italians, and others were depicted in popular media throughout history. Do your own research. Go to the Internet and find old political cartoons and media depictions of the Irish and Italians throughout history. Analyze them. What do these images and cartoons convey about conceptions of race, citizenship, and the possibilities to become American?

3. After collecting political cartoons depicting Italian and Irish immigrants, collect some contemporary images and cartoons of Latinos and undocumented immigrants. What do these images and cartoons convey about conceptions of race, citizenship, and the possibilities for these groups to become American? Compare and contrast the depictions and messages they convey.

REFERENCES

Alba, R., & Nee, V. (2003). *Remaking the American mainstream: Assimilation and contemporary immigration.* Cambridge, MA: Harvard University Press.

American Immigation Council. (2008). *Deromanticizing our immigrant past: Why claiming "my family came legally" is often a myth.* Washington, DC: Immigration Policy Center. Retrieved from http://ilw.com/articles/2009,0116-kelley.shtm

Anderson, B. (1991). *Imagined communities: Reflections on the origin and spread of nationalism.* London, UK: New Left Books. (Original work published 1983)

Bernard, W. S. (1998). Immigration: History of U.S. policy. In D. Jacobson (Ed.), *The immigration reader: America in a multi-disciplinary perspective* (pp. 48–71). Malden, MA: Blackwell.

Bonilla-Silva. E. (2004). From bi-racial to tri-racial: Towards a new system of racial stratification in the USA. *Ethnic and Racial Studies, 27*(6), 931–950.

Brodkin, K. (1998). *How Jews became White folks: And what that says about race in America.* New Brunswick, NJ: Rutgers University Press.

Buchanan, P. J. (2002). *The death of the West: How dying populations and immigrant invasions imperil our country and civilization.* New York, NY: St. Martin's Press.

Carbado, D. W. (2005). Racial naturalization. *American Quarterly, 57*(3), 633–658.

Chavez, L. R. (2013). *The Latino threat: Constructing immigrants, citizens, and the nation.* Stanford, CA: Stanford University Press.

Chomsky, A. (2007). *They take our jobs! And 20 other myths about immigration.* Boston, MA: Beacon Press.

Daniels, R. (1998). What is an American? Ethnicity, race, the Constitution and the immigrant in early American history. In D. Jacobson (Ed.), *The immigration reader: America in a multi-disciplinary perspective* (pp. 29–47). Malden, MA: Blackwell.

De Genova, N. P. (2002). Migrant "illegality" and deportability in everyday life. *Annual Review of Anthropology, 31,* 419–447.

De Genova, N. P., & Ramos-Zayas, A. Y. (2003). *Latino crossings: Mexicans, Puerto Ricans, and the politics of race and citizenship.* New York, NY: Routledge.

Donato, R., & Hanson, J. S. (2012). Legally White, socially "Mexican": The politics of de jure and de facto school segregation in the American Southwest. *Harvard Educational Review, 82*(2), 202–225.

Golash-Boza, T. M. (2012). *Immigration nation: Raids, detentions, and deportations in post 9/11 America.* Boulder, CO: Paradigm.

Hing, B. O. (2004). *Defining America through immigration policy.* Philadelphia, PA: Temple University Press.

Huntington, S. P. (2004). *Who are we? The challenges to America's national identity.* New York, NY: Simon & Schuster.

Huntington, S. P. (2009). The Hispanic challenge. *Foreign Policy.* Retrieved from http://www.foreignpolicy.com/articles/2004/03/01/the_hispanic_challenge

Ignatiev, N. (1995). *How the Irish became White.* New York, NY: Routledge.

Kasinitz, P., Mollenkopf, J. H., Waters, M. C., & Holdaway, J. (2008). *Inheriting the city: The children of immigrants come of age.* New York, NY: Russell Sage Foundation.

Kurzman, C., & Schanzer, D. (2015). *Law enforcement assessment of the violent extremism threat*. Durham, NC: Triangle Center on Terrorism and Homeland Security. Retrieved from https://sites.duke.edu/tcths/files/2013/06/Kurzman_Schanzer_Law_Enforcement_Assessment_of_the_Violent_Extremist_Threat_final.pdf

Massey, D. S. (1995). The new immigration and ethnicity in the United States. *Population and Development Review, 21*(3), 631–652.

Mintz, S., & McNeil, S. (2012). Italian immigration. *Digital History*. Retrieved from http://www.digitalhistory.uh.edu/voices/italian_immigration.cfm

Newland, K. (2015). The U.S. record shows that refugees are not a threat. Migration Policy Institute. Retrieved from http://www.migrationpolicy.org/news/us-record-shows-refugees-are-not-threat

Ngai, M. M. (2004). *Impossible subjects: Illegal aliens and the making of modern America*. Princeton, NJ: Princeton University Press.

Piore, M. (1979). *Birds of passage: Migrant labor and industrial societies*. Cambridge, UK: Cambridge University Press.

Portes, A., & Rumbaut, R. G. (2001). *Legacies: Stories of the immigrant second generation*. Berkeley: University of California Press.

Portes, A., & Zhou, M. (1993, November). The new second generation: Segmented assimilation and its variants. *Annals of the American Academy of Political and Social Science, 530*, 74–96.

Roediger, D. (1991). *The wages of Whiteness*. New York, NY: Verso.

Roediger, D. (2005). *Working toward Whiteness: How America's immigrants became White; The strange journey from Ellis Island to the suburbs*. New York, NY: Basic Books.

Rubin, L. (1994). *Families on the fault line: America's working class speaks about the family, the economy, race and ethnicity*. New York, NY: HarperCollins.

Rumbaut, R. G., & Ewing, W. A. (2007). *The myth of immigrant criminality and the paradox of assimilation: Incarceration rates among native and foreign-born men*. Immigration Policy Center Special Report. Washington DC: American Immigration Law Foundation.

Smith, J. (2003). Assimilation across the Latino generation. *American Economic Review, 93*, 315–319.

Takao Ozawa v. United States, 260 U.S. 178 (1922).

Tran, V. (2010). English gain vs. Spanish loss? Language assimilation among second-generation Latinos in young adulthood. *Social Forces, 89*(1), 257–284.

United States v. Bhagat Singh Thind, 261 U.S. 204 (1923).

Veltman, C. (1983). *Language shift in the United States*. The Hague: Walter De Gruyter.

Waldinger, R., & Feliciano, C. (2004). Will the second generation experience "downward assimilation"? Segmented assimilation reassessed. *Ethnic and Racial Studies, 27*, 376–402.

Zolberg, A. (2006). *A nation by design: Immigration policy in the fashioning of America*. New York, NY: Russell Sage Foundation.

"If Black People Aren't Criminals, Then Why Are So Many of Them in Prison?"

Confronting Racial Biases in Perceptions of Crime and Criminals

Sara Buck Doude

Georgia College

When discussing race in relation to crime, students often focus on a few observations to support their idea that racism ended with the civil rights movement and that therefore the criminal justice system is without racial bias. Each semester, I ask criminology students to anonymously write down their picture of the typical criminal. Responses vary. Often, recently publicized crime stories come to mind, such as the 2012 mass shooting at a screening of *The Dark Knight Rises* in Colorado or the Sandy Hook Elementary School tragedy in Connecticut. However, the general picture of a criminal is a young Black male who, in the process of drug dealing or gang banging, commits murder via drive-by shooting. Recent examples from this assignment reveal that students' perceptions are veiled in stereotypes associated with Black males. For example, one student writes "hooded male with baggy clothes." Another student writes "thugs," while another writes "Black male, sweatpants, and hoodie" (for further discussion on race and perception, see Ray in this volume). Although this is anecdotal evidence, I have received these types of responses over the course of many years of teaching criminology.

Generally, students do not recognize racial disparities in those arrested and convicted of crimes until they are pointed out through this assignment. They may recognize this perception subconsciously but do not acknowledge it until they have to write or verbalize their picture of the typical criminal. When and if they do recognize such disparities, they argue that they aren't due to racism, because the justice system is color-blind and racism isn't as bad today as it was in the past. As Rose M. Brewer and Nancy A. Heitzeg (2012b) argue, for many, "the issue then is crime, not race, and certainly not racism" (p. 383). Thus, many look at the "personal responsibility" involved in those who commit crime, rather than at a racially biased justice system. Others make group-based arguments, but about the culture of the perceived criminals and not about the system—that it just so happens certain groups of people (specifically Black males) are crime-prone, have bad values, and choose to commit crimes. The possibility that racism is institutionalized in the justice system is met with deep hostility. If students consider such a fact, they propose that there may be racist individuals among those enforcing laws but the legal system itself is not a racist entity. Student responses to these questions are a reflection of social perceptions of crime and criminals, and research reveals that this is not a recent phenomenon.

According to Katheryn K. Russell (1996), "'race and crime' is almost always a negative referent for 'Blacks and crime'" (p. 595). Analysis of race and crime coverage in media has been extensively studied (e.g., Feagin, 2000; Loury, 2008; Rome, 2006; Tonry, 1995; Western, 2006). Britto and Dabney's (2010) analysis of three political talk shows on cable television reveals that people of color were presented as offenders nearly 10 times more frequently than they were presented as victims and were 7.5 times more likely to be shown as evil, compared with Whites (pp. 210–211). However, when White violent offenders—such as mass shooters, who are predominately White males—are discussed, they are presented as mentally ill and coming from good families and neighborhoods (see, e.g., media coverage regarding *The Dark Knight Rises* and Sandy Hook shooters; Mingus & Zopf, 2010). Meanwhile, people of color—specifically Black Americans—who commit crimes are presented as having bad values and no role models, as coming from bad families, and as living in bad neighborhoods (read: urban inner city). These portrayals heighten fear of crime in neighborhoods with higher proportions of non-Whites and those perceived to have Blacks or Latinos living nearby (Chiricos, McEntire, & Gertz, 2001). These messages are absorbed by the public through the media, which has a horrid history of portraying the typical criminal as a person of color (more specifically, a Black man) with White female victims—a stereotypical portrayal that is not consistent with offending and victimization data (Britto & Dabney, 2010).

Incarceration data also support this perception of the Black criminal. State prisons house disproportionately poor, uneducated Black men (Loury, 2008; Western, 2006). About two thirds of all inmates are serving time for drug and property offenses, while one third are serving time for violent crimes (Loury, 2008). When analyzing the ratios of incarceration, Black men are imprisoned at seven times the rate of White men, and Black women are imprisoned at three times the rate of White women (Guerino, Harrison, & Sabol, 2012).

How should we interpret the overrepresentation of Blacks in crime statistics? As Loury (2008) argues, "the nation's social policy—intimately connected with public rhetoric about responsibility, dependency, social hygiene, and the reclamation of public order—can be fully grasped only when viewed against the backdrop of America's often ugly and violent racial history" (p. 11).

Fear of the Black Male

Throughout American history, the behavior of Black men has been strictly policed through both formal (e.g., the criminal justice system) and informal (e.g., vigilantism) social control and for the purposes of maintaining a White patriarchal society. We can see this most specifically when we look at the crime of rape. As Susan Brownmiller (1975) states, "The White man has used the rape of 'his' women as an excuse to act against Black men" (p. 255). Prior to the mid-1900s, in cases of rape when the offender was Black and the victim was White, White male juries and judges assumed that a White woman would not consent to sexual relations with a Black man (Allison & Wrightsman, 1993; Estrich, 1987). Ample historical evidence has shown, however, that rapes of White women committed by Black men were very rare and often fabricated by Whites as an excuse to lynch a Black man, where this "explanation" was frequently applied *after* the alleged assailant had already faced a horrific death at the hands of White mobs (Chasteen, 1998). Lynchable offenses related to rape included "whistling at a White woman, entering a White woman's home or talking 'inappropriately' around White women" (p. 30).

Historically, Black men were more likely to serve a heavier sentence for rape, which is still the case today. In addition, Black men were more likely than White men to be executed by the state or lynched if they raped a White woman or were merely suspected of doing so. Punishment during the colonial South was especially harsh. In Virginia, the punishment for a slave who raped a White woman was dismemberment. Indeed, a Black man raping a White woman was perceived as the "ultimate purpose of the slaves' revenge" (Brownmiller, 1975, p. 237), where Black men were perceived as being determined to get back at White men for a variety of injustices by raping "their" White women (see also Chasteen, 1998). After slavery, the lynching of Black men increased as Whites sought new ways to police the behavior of Black men in the absence of institutionalized slavery.

Black men have felt the brunt of the vigilante justice system as well as the criminal justice system throughout the history of the United States; at many points in history, these two systems were one and the same. The perception of the criminality of the Black male still prevails with the stereotype of the Black rapist and has subsequently transformed into the Black criminal or drug dealer. This perception has been accepted by governmental agencies and the public, specifically the White public.

The criminal stereotype has fallen squarely on young African American men, the repercussions of which are deadly. It prevails in American history and popular culture and was a possible contributing factor in the 2012 shooting death of unarmed teenager Trayvon Martin and many others since, including Philando Castile and Alton Brown. Since 2012, police use of force and shootings of unarmed Black men have flooded the media. In many of these incidents, cell-phone video captured officers shooting men in the back or shooting as they reached for their wallets while sitting in their cars, among many other encounters. The Federal Bureau of Investigation (FBI) 2014 Uniform Crime Report (UCR) supplementary homicide data show that 31.8% of individuals shot by the police were African American. Indeed, Blacks are overrepresented given their smaller population in comparison with Whites (*Guardian*, 2016). This has created a national conversation on race and the criminal justice system, which acknowledges that the system is experienced in a very different way depending on one's race. After the shooting of Trayvon Martin and the acquittal of his shooter, the media began to question the notion of an equal justice system. The existence of structural racism and subconscious bias in the criminal justice system began to be seen as a possible contributor to the overcriminalization of Black men prior to and during arrest (where use of force is a distinct possibility) and during the sentencing process.

The Evolution of the Stereotype of the Black Criminal

From the fear of the Black rapist, the stereotype of the Black criminal as a drug dealer or a violent criminal has evolved. It has yet to be determined as a cause or an effect in relation to, say, racial hoaxes, although correlations exist. A *racial hoax* is the accusation that a person of color committed a crime—usually murder, rape, or assault—when in fact the crime was committed by the one making the accusation, usually a White person (Russell, 1996, 2009). The Black male criminal stereotype is thus used as a method to hide the real crime (Russell, 2009), usually a violent crime. Examples of racial hoaxes include Susan Smith's 1994 claim that a Black male carjacked her and fled with her two children, when in fact she had killed her two children. In a more recent example, in 2016, a New York firefighter was charged with second-degree arson for burning down his own house. He claimed that the supporters of the Black Lives Matter movement set it aflame and graffitied "Lie with pigs, fry like bacon" in response to a Blue Lives Matter flag hanging in his yard (CBS News, 2016). These hoaxes are ultimately believable because Americans' perceptions of crime include the criminal having a Black face.

Another way we see this is through racial profiling. Racial profiling is the use of race in conjunction with the profile of a criminal suspect. It encompasses many activities, such as "driving while Black," wherein drivers are stopped because of their race and not because of illegal activity. The term *racial profiling* didn't become a part of the lexicon until 1994, when minority drivers were subject to a disproportionate number of stops, searches, and arrests along the New Jersey Turnpike (Withrow & Dailey, 2012). Stopping someone exclusively based on race is discrimination, yet it is often difficult to ascertain if race is the determinant for a traffic stop. For a stop or arrest to be legal, race must be only one of several descriptors of an individual suspect. Race and other factors constitute "reasonable suspicion," which is cause for a lawful stop (Walker, Spohn, & DeLone, 2007; Withrow & Dailey, 2012). That is, if a tall young Black man committed robbery in a red T-shirt and drove away in a red car, stopping all Black men in the area not fitting the rest of that description would be illegal according to the U.S. Supreme Court (Withrow & Dailey, 2012).

Racial profiling has primarily occurred in the context of the war on drugs, which has come to be interpreted as a war on Black Americans (Tomaskovic-Devey & Warren, 2009; Withrow & Dailey, 2012). Tomaskovic-Devey and Warren (2009) describe the Drug Enforcement Administration's Operation Pipeline, which began in 1984. Officers were trained to recognize profiles of drug couriers, which included drivers who didn't "fit" their cars (i.e., drivers in cars that appeared to be above their economic means), drivers with dark skin, drivers who wore gold jewelry, and drivers belonging to racial groups involved in the drug trade. Thus, racial profiling became a practice endorsed by the federal government. Further, the Department of Justice (DOJ) has insisted that racial profiling is a more effective strategy to control crime than random stops (Tomaskovic-Devey & Warren, 2009). Withrow and Dailey (2012) elaborate on this practice along the New Jersey Turnpike: "More than 250 troopers are assigned to patrol this stretch of highway. Most of them . . . are heavily influenced by intelligence reports of the U.S. Drug Enforcement Agency indicating the increased probability that racial and ethnic minorities are drug couriers" (pp. 134–135). This profile is a contributor to the overrepresentation of Black men in state and federal prison systems for drug-related crimes. Indeed, Tonry (1995) argues that "urban Black Americans have borne the brunt of the War on Drugs" and "the recent Blackening of America's prison population is the product of malign neglect of the war's effects on Black Americans" (p. 105).

Allegations of racial profiling have led to lawsuits involving traffic stops in the states of New Jersey and Maryland (Walker et al., 2007; Withrow & Dailey, 2012). More recently, research from Philadelphia and New York City law enforcement agencies has found that people of color are stopped and frisked at far higher rates than Whites (Buettner & Glaberson, 2012). Stop and frisks, or Terry stops, occur when police officers stop and detain individuals for a short period of time. Stops are based on reasonable suspicion, and officers are required to articulate the suspicion for said search, or the suspicion that someone is breaking the law, has likely committed a crime, or is in the process of committing a crime (Withrow & Dailey, 2012; again, see Ray in this volume). Police are required to have reasonable suspicion that a person is about to or has just committed a penal code violation before stopping that person (Goldstein, 2012). However, what constitutes reasonable suspicion is highly subjective, which causes much disagreement in the courts.

The New York Police Department's (NYPD's) stop-and-frisk policy led to 685,724 stops in 2011, of which people of color represented more than 80%, despite the fact that they represent only about half of the New York City population. Only 1.9% of those stops resulted in a weapon confiscation, and Whites were more likely to possess a weapon. Young people of color experienced more than 40% of the stops, despite being only 4.7% of the city's population. Shockingly, young Black men were stopped 168,124 times, which exceeded the population of 158,406 young Black men in the city (Baker, 2012). Some were likely stopped more than once. In the August 2013 ruling on the constitutionality of the policy, U.S. District Court judge Shira A. Scheindlin asserted that the policy was unconstitutional and in violation of protections provided by the Fourth and Fourteenth Amendments.[1]

Coining the term *indirect racial profiling*, she explained how the department's reliance on data indicating that Black men committed a disproportionate amount of crime amounted to a constitutional violation (Goldstein, 2013). Her decision was partially based on a commander's testimony on the "right people" to stop, in which he was specifically referring to people of color. The NYPD defended this policy by asserting that specific people (read: people of color) were committing violent crimes in specific neighborhoods and needed additional police scrutiny. The police commissioner allegedly stated that young Black and Latino men were the focus of the stops because the commissioner "wanted to instill fear in them, [that] every time they leave their home, they could be stopped by the police" (Goldstein, 2013).

Despite the nation's falling crime rates over the past decade, this increasingly punitive response is partially based on the stereotype of the African American criminal. This perception is reflected in statistics from the FBI UCR, where Blacks are overrepresented in crime statistics. While Whites compose 77% of the U.S. population and are underrepresented in arrest and incarceration data, Blacks compose 13% of the U.S. population and are overrepresented in arrest and incarceration data (FBI, 2014; U.S. Census Bureau, 2010). In 2014, 69.4% of all persons arrested for violent crime were White, and 27.8% were Black (FBI, 2014). In nearly all categories of crime recorded by the UCR, with the exception of gambling, Blacks are overrepresented as per their population (FBI, 2014). These statistics indicate the pervasiveness of the stereotype, which carries real-life consequences for many Black Americans.

Recent Police Brutality Cases

Data on police use of force and race are not consistent, thereby making generalizations difficult. Consistency is lacking in wording of variables, such as "killing" versus "shooting"; the range of perspectives (i.e., officer versus suspect); and the use of citizen complaints. An analysis of the NYPD stop-and-frisk data from 2003 to 2013, for example, indicates that police are 24% more likely to point a weapon at a Black person compared with a White person in a similar situation and that Blacks stopped by police are 17% more likely to experience police use of force. The same study used two other data sets from a Houston, Texas, police department and found no racial differences in officer-related shootings. In addition, Blacks are 24% less likely to be shot at in comparison with Whites (Bui & Cox, 2016; Fryer, 2016).

However, recent cases have proven just how deadly Black men's interactions with the police can be. The 2014 police shooting of Michael Brown in Ferguson, Missouri, triggered a DOJ investigation into the Ferguson Police Department. The police officer who shot Brown, Darren Wilson, was not indicted by the grand jury in the criminal case. This outcome and the subsequent protests drew the DOJ's attention. Their investigation revealed a pattern of abuses of Black citizens that permeated the city's culture and illustrate the power of police subculture and systemic racism.

The department found that the Ferguson Police Department regularly conducted stops without reasonable suspicion and made arrests without probable cause, in violation of the Fourth Amendment; interfered with the right to free expression, in violation of the First Amendment; and frequently used unreasonable force, in violation of the Fourth Amendment. These violations were part of a larger problem of systemic racism within the city of Ferguson. For example, the DOJ found that the Ferguson Municipal Court had a pattern of focusing on revenue over public safety, thus leading to court practices that violated the Fourteenth Amendment's due process and equal protection requirements. Moreover, the court exhibited practices that exacerbated the harm of Ferguson's unconstitutional police practices and imposed particular hardship on Ferguson's most vulnerable residents, especially those living in or near poverty. The DOJ found that minor offenses often generated crippling debts, resulted in jail time because of inability to pay, and led to the loss of driver's licenses, employment, and/or housing. Finally, the department found that the harms of Ferguson's police and court practices were borne disproportionately by Blacks and that this disproportionate impact was avoidable, in part because Ferguson's harmful court and police practices were partially due to intentional discrimination, as demonstrated by direct evidence of racial bias and stereotyping of Blacks by certain Ferguson police and municipal court officials (U.S. Department of Justice, 2015).

The 2015 death of Freddie Gray also spurred a DOJ investigation, this time into the Baltimore, Maryland, police department. On April 12, 2015, Freddie Carlos Gray Jr. was approached by Baltimore police officers and proceeded to flee. After he was detained, Gray was arrested for allegedly having an illegal switchblade, which was later found to be a legal knife. Gray was handcuffed and, despite pleas for his inhaler, was placed in the police van without receiving medical attention. During the ride to the police station, the officers claimed that Gray became "irate," which led them to place him in ankle cuffs. He was then loaded "on his stomach head first into the wagon" ("Freddie Gray's Death," 2016). During the ride to the station, the officers picked up a suspect from a different case. The van made a total of four stops between the arrest of Freddie Gray and arrival at the police station. After the police arrived at the station, they requested paramedics to take Gray to the hospital. When he arrived at the hospital he was in critical condition. His spine was 80% severed at the neck. Gray's family stated that the hospital performed surgeries on Gray to treat three broken vertebrae and an injured voice box. Mr. Rodriguez, the other suspect in the van, stated, "I know that when Mr. Gray was placed inside that van, he was able to talk, he was upset, and when Mr. Gray was taken out of that van he could not talk and he could not breathe." On May 1, 2015, the state prosecutor brought criminal charges against the six police officers involved in the case. State Attorney Marilyn Mosby charged the six Baltimore officers days later with offenses ranging from second-degree depraved-heart murder to manslaughter, reckless endangerment, and misconduct in office. All six officers were acquitted (Rector, 2016). Mosby has subsequently faced significant negative backlash, including a malicious prosecution suit from several of the officers (Fenton, 2017).

The Baltimore report revealed similar findings to those in Ferguson: regular violations of Black citizens' First and Fourth Amendment rights. Essentially, the department found reasonable cause to believe that the Baltimore Police Department engaged in a pattern or practice of

- conducting stops, searches, and arrests without meeting the requirements of the Fourth Amendment;
- focusing enforcement strategies on Blacks, leading to severe and unjustified racial disparities in violation of Title VI of the Civil Rights Act and the Safe Streets Act;
- using unreasonable force in violation of the Fourth Amendment;
- interacting with individuals with mental health disabilities in a manner that violates the Americans with Disabilities Act; and
- interfering with the right to free expression in violation of the First Amendment (U.S. Department of Justice, 2016).

Another significant concern identified by the department was transport practices that place detainees at significant risk of harm. In the Gray case, the officers were accused of giving him a "rough ride," which is a long-standing police tactic in which the arrestee is injured without having direct physical contact with the officer. A rough ride is accomplished by not securely placing arrestees in the vehicle and then driving recklessly so they injure themselves. For Gray, this included being handcuffed, shackled at the ankles, and placed in the transport van on his stomach, with no safety belt restraint, in violation of police policy. This DOJ report further supports the notion of systemic racism engrained in the policing subculture, which is highly protective of its members. It also points to the dehumanization of Blacks—Black men in particular—who often become victims of this stereotype in a way that leads to higher arrest rates and the overrepresentation of Black men in the correctional system.

Race and Incarceration

Unsurprisingly, Black men are substantially overrepresented in jail and prison populations. This is often the result of compounding racial biases throughout the whole criminal justice process—arrest, courts, adjudication, and corrections (Brewer & Heitzeg, 2012a, 2012b; Walker et al., 2007). It is also the result of the idea of neutral application of law, which presumes White innocence and ignores the cultural context in which people of color live, a context shaped by America's racially charged past (Loury, 2008; Ross, 1996).

Essentially, Black Americans now experience "the new plantation—in the prison industrial complex" (Brewer & Heitzeg, 2012b, p. 380), where they are victimized by the unequal protection of law, greater police surveillance, and ultimately, greater rates of incarceration. After incarceration, they often become inmate labor (which closely aligns with slave labor) within the confines of the penitentiary and are thoroughly under the control of the state (Alexander, 2010; Davis, 2003). Inmate labor has been used through the inmate lease system (Blackmon, 2008). Throughout the early 20th century, the inmate lease system (which was primarily composed of Blacks) was used to build mines in Birmingham, Alabama, and pave the streets in Atlanta, Georgia (Blackmon, 2008). These inmates had often been charged with crimes specifically created to target Blacks, such as "carrying a weapon, riding on empty freight train cars, or violation of racial etiquette such as speaking loudly in the presence of white women" (p. 67). Douglas Blackmon (2008) asserts that throughout the late 1860s and 1870s, "every southern state enacted an array of interlocking law essentially intended to criminalize Black life" (p. 53). The inmate lease system still exists and is currently used by several companies, including Walmart, Hewlett-Packard, McDonald's, BP Oil, Chevron, Bank of America, AT&T, and IBM (Fraser & Freeman, 2012; Thompson, 2012). This labor is cheap; federal inmates are paid $0.12 to $1.15 per hour, while state inmates are paid $0.13 to $0.32. Some states compensate inmates by decreasing the length of their sentences (Thompson, 2012). In addition, child support and victim compensation are frequently deducted from federal inmates' wages. According to Fraser and Freeman (2012), "the caste nature of the South's convict lease system should remind us of the unbalanced racial profile of America's bloated prison population today" (p. 96).

While "national security" and "crime control" are often given as reasons for the mass imprisonment of Blacks (Brewer & Heitzeg, 2012a, 2012b), incarceration actually functions as a way to segregate Blacks from the rest of American society. Brewer and Heitzeg (2012a, 2012b) and Western (2006) argue that a variety of factors contribute to the overrepresentation of people of color in corrections. Specifically, the political economy of the correctional industry, which includes the prison construction boom and development of private prisons, as well as economic decline and fewer low-skilled jobs, has contributed to harsher sentences. Policies such as "three strikes" laws, "truth in sentencing" laws as opposed to indeterminate sentencing, the end of rehabilitation as a correctional philosophy, incarceration for nonviolent crimes as a result of the war on drugs, and a general increase in the use of incarceration in response to criminal behavior are all contributing factors to the number of people of color under correctional supervision. These factors have led to an attitude of resignation on behalf of young men of color toward the criminal justice system, given the oppressive realities listed above: "For many young males, especially African Americans and Hispanics, the threat of going to prison or jail is not a threat at all but rather an expected or accepted part or life" (Irwin & Austin, 1997, p. 156, as quoted in Western, 2006).

Conclusion

As Loury (2008) states, "crime and punishment has a color in America" (p. 22). Americans' conceptualization of the rapist, drug dealer, and general criminal have more often than not involved people of color and, specifically, Black males.

This conceptualization is representative of a long history of racial biases prevalent within American society and is well reflected in our justice system—from arrest rates to corrections to the death penalty. How do we rid ourselves of this harmful ideal? Evidence is abundant that racial biases begin before stop-and-frisk stops and traffic stops. If race is part of the American perception of crime, then it is no wonder that it is a consideration in the first stage of the criminal justice process (e.g., a stop), which can only mean that it is compounded toward the end of the criminal justice process (e.g., corrections and imprisonment). In the end, Loury (2008) raises a key question:

> Who is to blame for the domestic maladies that beset us? We have constructed a national narrative. We have created scapegoats, indulged our need to feel virtuous, and assuaged our fears. We have met the enemy and the enemy is them. Incarceration keeps them away from us. (p. 25)

Essentially, as Loury indicates, public safety has come to mean keeping the public (presumably, the White public) "safe" from people of color.

Sara Buck Doude is an associate professor of criminal justice at Georgia College. Her scholarship focuses on radical criminological theory, gender and racial biases within criminal justice, and interpersonal violence within marginalized groups. Her work has appeared in the *Encyclopedia of Theoretical Criminology* (2010), the *Encyclopedia of Women and Crime*, and the *Sexual Assault Report*. Her forthcoming work focuses on perceptions of rape based on the sexuality of the victim and offender.

NOTE

1. The order also froze the stop-and-frisk cases until further appellate rulings. However, New York City challenged the ruling under former mayor Michael Bloomberg. Current mayor Bill de Blasio hasn't yet dropped the city's challenge to Scheindlin's ruling.

SUGGESTED ADDITIONAL RESOURCES

Alexander, M. (2010). *The new Jim Crow: Mass incarceration in the age of color blindness.* New York, NY: New Press.

Blackmon, D. A. (2008). *Slavery by another name: The re-enslavement of Black Americans from the Civil War to World War II.* New York, NY: Random House.

Daniels, J. (2014). White women and the defense of lynching. *Racism Review.* Retrieved from http://www.racismreview.com/blog/2014/02/11/white-women-defense-lynching/

Feagin, J. R. (2000). *Racist America: Roots, current realities, and future reparations*. New York, NY: Routledge.

Federal Bureau of Investigation. (2015). *Uniform crime reports: Hate crime statistics*. Retrieved from http://www.fbi.gov/about-us/cjis/ucr/ucr-publications#Hate

Federal Bureau of Investigation. (2016). Crime in the U.S. Retrieved from https://ucr.fbi.gov/crime-in-the-u.s/2016

Guardian. (2016). The counted: People killed by the police in the US. Retrieved from http://www.theguardian.com/us-news/ng-interactive/2015/jun/01/the-counted-police-killings-us-database

Irwin, J., & Austin, J. (1997). *It's about time: America's imprisonment binge* (2nd ed.). Belmont, CA: Wadsworth.

Loury, G. C. (2008). *Race, incarceration, and American values*. Cambridge, MA: Boston Review.

New York Times. (2017). Police brutality, misconduct and shootings. Retrieved from http://www.nytimes.com/topic/subject/police-brutality-misconduct-and-shootings

Parsons-Pollard, N. (2011). *Disproportionate minority contact: Current issues and policies*. Durham, NC: Carolina Academic Press.

Rios, V. (2011). *Punished: Policing the lives of Black and Latino boys*. New York: New York University Press.

Tonry, M. (1995). *Malign neglect: Race, crime, and punishment in America*. New York, NY: Oxford University Press.

U.S. Department of Justice. (2015, March 4). *Justice Department announces findings of two civil rights investigations in Ferguson, Missouri* [Press release]. Retrieved from https://www.justice.gov/opa/pr/justice-department-announces-findings-two-civil-rights-investigations-ferguson-missouri (See also www.justice.gov/sites/default/files/opa/press-releases/attachments/2015/03/04/ferguson_police_department_report.pdf)

U.S. Department of Justice. (2016). *Justice Department announces findings of investigation into Baltimore Police Department* [Press release]. Retrieved from https://www.justice.gov/opa/pr/justice-department-announces-findings-investigation-baltimore-police-department (See also https://www.justice.gov/opa/file/883366/download)

Western, B. (2006). *Punishment and inequality in America*. New York, NY: Russell Sage Foundation.

Western, B. (2012). The social impact of the U.S. penal system. Retrieved from http://scholar.harvard.edu/brucewestern/publications/term/3695

Audio/Visual

Blackmon, D. A., Allan, C. (Executive Producers), & Pollard, S. (Director). (2012). *Slavery by another name* [Documentary]. United States: Public Broadcasting Service. Retrieved from http://www.pbs.org/tpt/slavery-by-another-name/watch

CBS News. (2012). "Stop and frisk": Fighting crime or racial profiling? [Video]. Retrieved from https://www.youtube.com/watch?v=sVaD0Aljx0k

DuVernay, A. (Producer & Director). (2016). *13th*. United States: Netflix.

Orr, M. (2010, July 12). Stop and frisk in Brownsville, Brooklyn [Video]. *New York Times*. Retrieved from https://www.nytimes.com/video/nyregion/1247468422062/stop-and-frisk-in-brownsville-brooklyn.html

Reuters. (2012, June 29). Stories of "stop and frisk"—Reuters Investigates [Video]. Retrieved from http://www.reuters.com/video/2012/06/29/stories-of-stop-and-frisk-reuters-invest?videoId=236276763

QUESTIONS FOR FURTHER DISCUSSION

1. Are arrest and incarceration data a reflection of true and actual amounts of crime? Why or why not? What do you believe official crime data tell us about the nature of crime in America? How would you explain the overrepresentation of people of color at all stages of the criminal justice system?

2. According to the essay, how has the history of America contributed to the Black criminal stereotype? Is the criminal stereotype applied to other groups? (How) is the stereotype of the Black rapist still prevalent in current American society? Why were White women seen as entities to be protected? Are White women still portrayed this way in regard to crime?

REACHING BEYOND THE COLOR LINE

1. Select a popular television crime show or procedural (e.g., *Law & Order*, *CSI*, *Criminal Minds*). Conduct a content analysis of four to six episodes. Is the Black criminal stereotype prevalent? If yes, what are the crimes portrayed? Who are the victims?

2. As a class, construct a survey instrument about perceptions of the police. Gather data from a representative sample of the student body at your college and compare the findings across racial and ethnic groups.

REFERENCES

Alexander, M. (2010). *The new Jim Crow: Mass incarceration in the age of colorblindness.* New York, NY: New Press.

Allison, J. A., & Wrightsman, L. S. (1993). *Rape: The misunderstood crime.* Newbury Park, CA: Sage.

Baker, A. (2012, May, 12). New York Police release data showing rise in number of stops on streets. *New York Times.* Retrieved from http://www.nytimes.com/2012/05/13/nyregion/new-york-police-data-shows-increase-in-stop-and-frisks.html

Blackmon, D. A. (2008). *Slavery by another name: The re-enslavement of Black Americans from the Civil War to World War II.* New York, NY: Doubleday.

Brewer, R. M., & Heitzeg, N. A. (2012a). The racialization of crime and punishment: Criminal justice, color-blind racism and the political economy of the prison industrial complex. *American Behavioral Scientist, 51,* 625–644.

Brewer, R. M., & Heitzeg, N. A. (2012b). The racialization of crime and punishment: Criminal justice, color-blind racism and the political economy of the prison industrial complex. In H. T. Greene & S. L. Gabbidon (Eds.), *Race and crime: A text/reader* (pp. 380–388). Thousand Oaks, CA: Sage.

Britto, S., & Dabney, D. A. (2010). "Fair and balanced?" Justice issues on political talk shows. *American Journal of Criminal Justice, 35*(4), 198–218.

Brownmiller, S. (1975). *Against our will: Men, women, and rape.* New York, NY: Fawcett Columbine.

Buettner, R., & Glaberson, W. (2012, July 10). Courts putting stop-and-frisk policy on trial. *New York Times.* Retrieved from http://www.nytimes.com/2012/07/11/nyregion/courts-putting-stop-and-frisk-policy-on-trial.html

Bui, Q., & Cox, A. (2016, July 11). Surprising new evidence shows bias in police use of force but not shootings. *New York Times.* Retrieved from https://www.nytimes.com/2016/07/12/upshot/surprising-new-evidence-shows-bias-in-police-use-of-force-but-not-in-shootings.html

CBS News. (2016, December 9). Firefighter accused of setting own house ablaze, shifting blame to anti-cop graffiti. *Crimesider.* Retrieved from http://www.cbsnews.com/news/jason-stokes-firefighter-accused-of-setting-own-house-ablaze-shifting-blame-with-anti-cop-graffiti/

Chasteen, A. L. (1998). *Rape narratives in the United States: Feminism, culture and the construction of rape as a social problem* (Doctoral dissertation). Retrieved from ProQuest Digital Dissertations database. (Publication No. AAT 9825180)

Chiricos, T. G., McEntire, R., & Gertz, M. (2001). Perceived racial and ethnic composition of neighborhood and perceived risk of crime. *Social Problems, 48*(3), 322–340.

Davis, A. Y. (2003). *Are prisons obsolete?* New York, NY: Seven Stories Press.

Estrich, S. (1987). *Real rape: How the legal system victimizes women who say no.* Cambridge, MA: Harvard University Press.

Feagin, J. R. (2000). *Racist America: Roots, current realities, and future reparations.* New York, NY: Routledge.

Federal Bureau of Investigation. (2014). *Crime in the United States.* Retrieved from https://ucr.fbi.gov/crime-in-the-u.s/2014/crime-in-the-u.s.-2014/cius-home

Fenton, J. (2017, January 6). Freddie Gray case: Judge allows malicious prosecution lawsuit against Mosby to proceed. *Baltimore Sun.* Retrieved January 10, 2017, from http://www.baltimoresun.com/news/maryland/freddie-gray/bs-md-ci-mosby-lawsuit-to-proceed-20170106-story.html

Fraser, S., & Freeman, J. B. (2012). In the rearview mirror. *New Labor Forum, 21*(3), 94–98.

Freddie Gray's death in police custody—what we know. (2016, May 23). BBC News. Retrieved January 09, 2017, from http://www.bbc.com/news/world-us-canada-32400497

Fryer, R. G., Jr. (2016). *An empirical analysis of racial differences in police use of force* (NBER Working Paper No. 22399). Retrieved from http://www.nber.org/papers/w22399

Goldstein, J. (2012, September 25). Prosecutor deals blow to stop-and-frisk tactic. *New York Times.* Retrieved from http://www.nytimes.com/2012/09/26/nyregion/in-the-bronx-resistance-to-prosecuting-stop-and-frisk-arrests.html

Goldstein, J. (2013, August 14). Police dept's focus on race is at core of ruling against stop-and-frisk tactic. *New York Times.* Retrieved from http://www.nytimes.com/2013/08/15/nyregion/racial-focus-by-police-is-at-core-of-judges-stop-and-frisk-ruling.html

Guardian. (2016). The counted: People killed by the police in the US. Retrieved from http://www.theguardian.com/us-news/ng-interactive/2015/jun/01/the-counted-police-killings-us-database

Guerino, P., Harrison, P. M., & Sabol, W. J. (2012). *Prisoners in 2010* (NCJ 236096). U.S. Department of Justice, Office of Justice Programs, Bureau of Justice Statistics. Retrieved from http://www.bjs.gov/content/pub/pdf/p10.pdf

Irwin, J., & Austin, J. (1997). *It's about time: America's imprisonment binge* (2nd ed.). Belmont, CA: Wadsworth.

Loury, G. C. (2008). *Race, incarceration, and American values.* Cambridge, MA: Boston Review.

Mingus, W., & Zopf, B. (2010). White means never having to say you're sorry the racial project in explaining mass shootings. *Social Thought and Research, 31*, 57–77. Retrieved from https://kuscholarworks.ku.edu/handle/1808/10073

Rector, K. (2016, July 28). Charges dropped, Freddie Gray case concludes with zero convictions against officers. *Baltimore Sun.* Retrieved January 09, 2017, from http://www.baltimoresun.com/news/maryland/freddie-gray/bs-md-ci-miller-pretrial-motions-20160727-story.html

Rome, D. M. (2006). The social construction of the African American criminal stereotype. In M. Zatx, C. Mann, & N. Rodriguez (Eds.), *Images of color: Images of crime* (3rd ed., pp. 78–88). Los Angeles, CA: Roxbury.

Ross, T. R. (1996). *Just stories: How the law embodies racism and bias.* Boston, MA: Beacon Press.

Russell, K. K. (1996). The racial hoax as crime: The law as affirmation. *Indiana Law Journal, 71*(3), 594–621.

Russell, K. K. (2009, June 8). Racial hoaxes: Black men and imaginary crimes [Radio series program]. In M. Martin (Host), *Tell Me More.* Washington, DC: National Public Radio. Retrieved from http://www.npr.org/templates/story/story.php?storyId=105096024

Thompson, H. (2012). The prison industrial complex. *New Labor Forum, 21*(3), 38–47.

Tomaskovic-Devey, D., & Warren, P. (2009). Explaining and eliminating racial profiling. *Contexts.* Retrieved from https://contexts.org/articles/explaining-and-eliminating-racial-profiling/

Tonry, M. (1995). *Malign neglect: Race, crime, and punishment in America.* New York, NY: Oxford University Press.

U.S. Census Bureau. (2010). *U.S. Census 2010.* Retrieved from http://www.census.gov/2010census

U.S. Department of Justice. (2015, March 4). *Justice Department announces findings of two civil rights investigations in Ferguson, Missouri* [Press release]. Retrieved from https://www.justice.gov/opa/pr/justice-department-announces-findings-two-civil-rights-investigations-ferguson-missouri

U.S. Department of Justice. (2016). *Justice Department announces findings of investigation into Baltimore Police Department* [Press release]. Retrieved from https://www.justice.gov/opa/pr/justice-department-announces-findings-investigation-baltimore-police-department

Walker, S., Spohn, C., & DeLone, M. (2007). *The color of justice: Race, ethnicity, and crime in America* (4th ed.). Belmont, CA: Thompson Wadsworth.

Western, B. (2006). *Punishment and inequality in America.* New York, NY: Russell Sage Foundation.

Withrow, B. L., & Dailey, J. D. (2012). Racial profiling litigation: Current status and emerging controversies. *Journal of Contemporary Criminal Justice, 28*(2), 122–145.

ESSAY 19

"What's the Point of 'Black Lives Matter' Protests?"

Black Lives Matter as a Movement, Not a Moment

Keeanga-Yamahtta Taylor

Princeton University

> *What happened to my daughter was unjust. It was unjust. It was really unjust. I've been through all the range of emotions that I can go through, concerning this. But I will not stop, as all of the rest of the mothers have said, until I get some answers.*
>
> —Cassandra Johnson, mother of Tanisha Anderson, killed by Cleveland police in 2014

Every movement needs a catalyst, an event that captures people's experiences and draws them out from their isolation into a collective force with the power to transform social conditions. Few could have predicted that White police officer Darren Wilson shooting Mike Brown would ignite a rebellion in a small, largely unknown Missouri suburb called Ferguson. For reasons that may never be clear, Brown's death was a breaking point for the African Americans of Ferguson—but also for hundreds of thousands of Black people across the United States. Perhaps it was the inhumanity of the police leaving Brown's body to fester in the hot summer sun for four and a half hours after killing him, keeping his parents away at gunpoint, and with dogs. "We was treated like we wasn't parents, you know?" Mike Brown Sr. said. "That's what I didn't understand. They sicced dogs on us. They wouldn't let us identify his body. They pulled guns on us."[1] Maybe it was the military hardware the police brandished when protests against Brown's death arose. With tanks and machine guns and a never-ending supply of tear gas, rubber bullets, and swinging batons, the Ferguson police department declared war on Black residents and anyone who stood in solidarity with them.

Since then, hundreds more protests have erupted. As the United States celebrates various fiftieth anniversaries of the Black freedom struggles of the 1960s, the truth about the racism and brutality of the police has broken through the veil of segregation that has shrouded it from public view. There have been periodic ruptures in the domestic quietude that is so often misinterpreted as the docility of American democracy: the brutal beating of Rodney King, the sodomy of Abner Louima, the execution of Amadou Diallo. These beatings and murders did not lead to a national movement, but they were not forgotten. As Ferguson protestor Zakiya Jemmott said, "My first protest was in 1999, when Amadou Diallo was murdered by police. I haven't seen any changes and have not changed my perception of police officers."[2]

It is impossible to answer, and perhaps futile to ask, the question "why Ferguson?" just as it's impossible ever to accurately calculate when "enough is enough." The transformation of Mike Brown's murder from a police killing into a lynching certainly tipped the scales. Writer Charles Pierce captured what many felt: "Dictators leave bodies in the street. Petty local satraps leave bodies in the street. Warlords leave bodies in the street. Those are the places where they leave bodies in the street, as object lessons, or to make a point, or because there isn't the money to take the bodies away and bury them, or because nobody gives a damn whether they are there or not."[3] In the hours after Brown's body was finally moved, residents erected a makeshift memorial of teddy bears and memorabilia on the spot where police had left his body. When the police arrived with a canine unit, one officer let a dog urinate on the memorial. Later, when Brown's mother, Lesley McSpadden, laid out rose petals in the form of his initials, a police cruiser whizzed by, crushing the memorial and scattering the flowers.[4] The next evening, McSpadden and other friends and family went back to the memorial site and laid down a dozen roses. Again, a police cruiser came through and destroyed the flowers.[5] Later that night, the uprising began.

The police response to the uprising was intended to repress and punish the population, who had dared to defy their authority. It is difficult to interpret in any other way their injudicious use of tear gas, rubber bullets, and persistent threats of violence against an unarmed, civilian population. The Ferguson police, a 95 percent White and male force, obscured their badges to hide their identities, wore wristbands proclaiming "I AM DARREN WILSON," and pointed live weapons at unarmed civilians engaged in legal demonstrations. The municipality resembled a rogue state, creating arbitrary rules governing public protests and assaulting the media, as both an act of revenge and an attempt to hide the sheer brutality of its operation. In the twelve days following Brown's death, 172 people were arrested, 132 of whom were charged only with "failure to disperse." At one point during the demonstrations, a Ferguson officer pointed his AR-15 semiautomatic rifle in the direction of a group of journalists and screamed, "I'm going to fucking kill you!" When someone asked, "What's your name, sir?" He screamed, "Go fuck yourself!"[6] For a moment, the brutal realities of Black life in Ferguson were exposed for all to see.

Indeed, as the daily protests went on, the Ferguson police's escalating brutality and lawlessness seemed to arise out of frustration that they could not make the Black men and women of Ferguson submit. Quentin Baker, a nineteen-year-old from St. Louis, observed that "all of these things happen after the police provoke it. What they want to do is impose their will."[7] Just as residents rebuilt the memorials for Mike Brown within hours every time the police tried to destroy them, the same dynamic held for the protests. Every night the police used tear gas and rubber bullets to disperse the crowd; the next day, the crowds would reemerge. Ferguson activist Johnetta Elzie described how the protestors were changing even in the face of "unthinkable" police violence:

> I became less of a peaceful protester and more of an active one. Using my voice to chant loudly along with other protesters seemed to be enough but it wasn't. Instead, I decided to yell directly at the police. I decided to dare the police to look at the faces of the babies and children their dogs were so ready to chase down. As more people began to look directly at the police and yell their grievances, the more aggravated they became.[8]

Protestor Dontey Carter said, "I've been down here since the first day. . . . We all had the same pain and anger about this. We all came together that day. . . . They're killing us, and it's not right."[9]

Carter's words addressed the urgency of a summer that had turned into a killing season. Just weeks before Mike Brown was shot, the world had watched video of New York City cop Daniel Pantaleo choking the life out of Eric Garner. Four days before Brown was killed, the police struck in a suburb of Dayton, Ohio. John Crawford III, a twenty-two-year-old, unarmed African American man, was killed in the aisle of a Walmart while he talked on the phone with the mother of his children. Crawford had been holding a toy gun. Even though Ohio is an "open carry" state where citizens are allowed to carry unconcealed guns, local police opened fire on Crawford with little to no warning, killing him.[10] Two days after Brown's murder, police in Los Angeles shot unarmed Ezell Ford three times in the back as he lay facedown on the sidewalk. The following day, elsewhere in California, Dante Parker, a thirty-six-year-old African American man, was detained by police and tasered multiple times before dying in police custody.[11] The Ferguson rebellion became a focal point for the growing anger in Black communities across the country.

For almost the entire fall, the Ferguson movement focused on winning an indictment of Darren Wilson. Prosecutors worked to drag out the grand jury proceedings as long as possible, believing that colder weather would edge the movement off the streets. Undoubtedly, given the level of repression, the intensity of the August protests was not sustainable over time. But when that level of intensity waned, the *persistence* of the protests kept the movement alive. Activists and others from around the country were also important in helping sustain the local movement. In late August 2014, Darnell Moore and Patrisse Cullors of #BlackLivesMatter organized a "freedom ride" to bring people from all around the country to the suburb in solidarity with the local movement. Moore described the breadth of the mobilization:

> More than 500 people traveled from across the United States and Canada to provide various forms of support to the activists on the ground in Ferguson. Those who traveled with us represented a new and diverse contingent of black activists. We weren't all the same age, nor did we share the same political viewpoints. We weren't all heterosexual or documented or free from past involvement with the criminal justice system. Some of us were transgender, disabled or bisexual.[12]

Local activists held vigils, picketed the Ferguson police department, and blocked traffic on Interstate 70, which runs through Ferguson, in a dogged effort to maintain pressure on local officials to indict Wilson. Continued police harassment was also critical to sustaining the movement. In late September, Mike Brown's memorial was doused with gasoline and ignited. The flames revitalized the protests: more than two hundred people gathered in an angry protest that saw five people arrested.[13]

When local officials began to speculate that the grand jury decision would be made public in October, local activism picked up. A multiracial protest erupted in the solidarity song "Which Side Are You On?" during a performance of the St. Louis Symphony. When the protestors marched out, chanting "Black lives matter," many in the audience—including symphony musicians—applauded. On October 8, an off-duty St. Louis police officer fired at Black teenager Vonderrit Myers seventeen times, hitting him with eight bullets and killing him. Days after Myers's death, two hundred students marched from Myers's neighborhood, called Shaw, to join hundreds more students in an occupation of St. Louis University (SLU). For several days more than a thousand students occupied the campus, harkening back to the days of the Occupy movement.[14] The occupation of SLU coincided with Ferguson October, in which hundreds of people traveled to Ferguson—in solidarity with the local movement, but also to register their own protest. As protestor Richard Wallace from Chicago put it, "Everybody here is representing a family member or someone that's been hurt, murdered, killed, arrested, deported."[15]

Black Women Matter

Most murders of Black people at the hands of the state go unnoticed by the public and unreported by the mainstream media. The few cases—compared to the significantly larger number of people killed—that do come into the public spotlight often involve

Black men or boys. This was certainly true in Ferguson and Baltimore. This is not entirely surprising since, when police shoot to kill, they are usually taking aim at African American men. But Black women who are partnered with, have children with, or parent Black men and boys also suffer the effects of violence against them. The erasure of this particular way that Black women experience police violence minimizes the depth and extent of the harm caused by the abusive policing state. Black men falling under the control of the criminal justice system has a deleterious impact on their families and neighborhoods. Ex-convict status increases rates of poverty and unemployment, and the formerly incarcerated are banned from access to federal programs intended to blunt the worst effects of poverty, including housing vouchers, student loans, and other forms of financial aid. These policies affect not only Black men but also Black women who have Black men in their lives.

Black women, however, are also the victims of the policing state, including police violence and imprisonment. While Trayvon Martin became a household name, most people are not familiar with the case of Marissa Alexander, a Black woman who was a victim of domestic violence. After using a firearm to keep her abuser at bay, Alexander invoked Florida's "stand your ground" statute as a defense. Although George Zimmerman, who killed Martin, succeeded in using this defense, Alexander was sentenced to twenty years in prison. Even though Alexander would eventually be released from jail, the contrast was a stark reminder of the dual system of justice in the United States.

The police also kill Black women. The names of Rekia Boyd, Shelly Frey, Miriam Carey, and Alberta Spruill are less familiar than those of Mike Brown and Eric Garner, but their killings were motivated by the same dehumanizing factors. Police also view Black women's lives with suspicion and ultimately as less valuable, making their death and brutalization more likely, not less. It is hardly even newsworthy when Black women, including Black transwomen, are killed or violated by law enforcement—because they are generally seen as less feminine or vulnerable. Consider the case of Tulsa, Oklahoma, police officer Daniel Holtzclaw, who was convicted of raping thirteen Black women while on duty. Holtzclaw is believed to have targeted Black women because they were of "lower social status," meaning that they were less likely to be believed and fewer people would care.[16] Indeed, Holtzclaw's crimes barely made a ripple in the national news.

Even though Black women have always been susceptible to violence from the police and the criminal justice system, where organizing and struggle have emerged, they have, for the most part, had a male face. For cases that develop a national profile, a male lawyer or reverend or civil rights leader—such as Al Sharpton—is usually the most visible face. Of course, mothers and other women in the lives of the (typically male) victims are heard from, but the activism has been seen as male-led and organized—until Ferguson.

In fact, the media have been particularly cognizant of the "women of Ferguson" as central to turning "a string of protests into a movement, by seamlessly shifting between the roles of peace-keepers, disrupters, organizers and leaders."[17] Indeed, the women who played an indispensable role in keeping the Ferguson movement together through the summer until the early winter were also aware of their role. As Brittney Ferrell points out,

> The media has left out that if it were not for Black women, there would be no movement. We have seriously carried this to where it is now, not to say there are no men out here doing their thing because there are. What I am saying is that women have been here since day one, we are willing to lay our lives on the line to keep up the good fight without the support from anyone or any organization, hence why we built our own.[18]

To ask why Black women have played such a central role in this movement is to assume that they have played a lesser role in other movements. It should go without saying that Black women have always played an integral role in the various iterations of the Black freedom struggle. Whether it was Ida B. Wells, who risked her life to expose the widespread use of lynching in the South, or the mothers of the wrongfully accused Scottsboro Boys, who toured the world to build the campaign to free their sons, Black women have been central to every significant campaign for Black rights and freedom. Black women, including Ella Baker, Fannie Lou Hamer, Diane Nash, and countless and unknown others, were critical to the development of the civil rights movement, but that movement is still primarily known by its male leaders.

Today, though, the face of the Black Lives Matter movement is largely queer and female. How has this come to be? Female leadership may actually have been an outcome of the deeply racist policing Black men have experienced in Ferguson. According to the US Census Bureau, while there are 1,182 African American women between the ages of twenty-five and thirty-four living in Ferguson, there are only 577 African American men in this age group. More than 40 percent of Black men in both the 20–24 and 35–54 age groups in Ferguson are missing.[19]

It's not just Ferguson. Across the United States, 1.5 million Black men are "missing"—snatched from society by imprisonment or premature death. To put it starkly, "More than one out of every six Black men who today should be between 25 and 54 years old have disappeared from daily life."[20] This does not mean that, if the 40 percent of Black men missing from Ferguson were present, they would be playing the same role that women have played in building, organizing, and sustaining the movement, but it does provide a concrete example of the impact of the hyperaggressive, revenue-generating approach to policing in Ferguson. It is more likely that these women have stepped into leadership roles because of the absolutely devastating impact of policing and police violence in Black people's lives in general. But whatever the reasons, their presence has contributed more than just gender balance.

The Black women leading the movement against police brutality have worked to expand our understanding of the broad impact of police violence in Black communities. Sometimes this is articulated through the straightforward demand that society as a whole recognize that the police victimize Black women. "The media is excluding the fact that the police brutality and harassment in our communities impacts the women just as much as the men," says Zakiya Jemmott, adding, "They're highlighting black male lives and pushing the black female lives lost to police violence to the side. I want for the media to understand that *all* black lives matter."[21] But Black women have also made a much more deliberate intervention to expose police brutality as part of a much larger system of oppression in the lives of all Black working-class and poor people. Charlene Carruthers of Black Youth Project 100 explains,

> It's important because we are really serious about creating freedom and justice for all black people, but all too often black women and girls, black LGBTQ folks, are left on the sidelines. And if we're going to be serious about liberation we have to include all black people. It's really that simple. And it's been my experience that issues of gender justice and LGBT justice have been either secondary or not recognized at all.[22]

The Black women who created the hashtag #BlackLivesMatter—Patrisse Cullors, Opal Tometi, and Alicia Garza—articulate most clearly the overlapping oppressions confronting Black people in the struggle to end police violence and win justice. In an essay that captures the expansive nature of Black oppression while arguing that the movement cannot be reduced only to police brutality, Alicia Garza writes,

> It is an acknowledgment Black poverty and genocide is state violence. It is an acknowledgment that 1 million Black people are locked in cages in this country—one half of all people in prisons or jails—is an act of state violence. It is an acknowledgment that Black women continue to bear the burden of a relentless assault on our children and our families and that assault is an act of state violence. Black queer and trans folks bearing a unique burden in a hetero-patriarchal society that disposes of us like garbage and simultaneously fetishizes us and profits off of us is state violence; the fact that 500,000 Black people in the US are undocumented immigrants and relegated to the shadows is state violence; the fact that Black girls are used as negotiating chips during times of conflict and war is state violence; Black folks living with disabilities and different abilities bear the burden of state-sponsored Darwinian experiments that attempt to squeeze us into boxes of normality defined by White supremacy is state violence.[23]

The focus on "state violence" strategically pivots away from a conventional analysis that would reduce racism to the intentions and actions of the individuals involved. The declaration of "state violence" legitimizes the corollary demand for "state action." It demands more than the removal of a particular officer or the admonishment of a particular police department, but calls attention to the systemic forces that allow the individuals to act with impunity. Moreover, these organizers are "intersectional" in their approach to organizing—in other words, they start from the basic recognition that the oppression of African Americans is multidimensional and must be fought on different fronts. The analytic reach of these organizers is what really underlies the tension between the "new guard" and the "old guard." In some ways, it demonstrates that today's activists are grappling with questions similar to those Black radicals confronted in the Black Power era, questions bound up with the systemic nature of Black oppression in American capitalism and how that shapes the approach to organizing.

Placing police brutality into a wider web of inequality has largely been missing from the more narrowly crafted agendas of the liberal establishment organizations, like Sharpton's National Action Network (NAN), which have focused more on resolving the details of particular cases than on generalizing about the systemic nature of police violence. This has meant that mainstream civil rights organizations tend to focus on legalistic approaches to resolve police brutality, compared to activists who connect police oppression to other social crises in Black communities. Of course, that approach has not been fully supplanted; a significant focus of the Ferguson movement was voter registration and increasing the presence of African Americans in local governing bodies. But the movement in Ferguson has also validated those who embraced a much wider view by showing how the policing of African Americans is directly tied to the higher levels of poverty and unemployment in Black communities through the web of fees and fines and arrest warrants trapping Black people in a never-ending cycle of debt. The gravity of the crisis confronting Black communities, often stemming from these harmful encounters with the police, legitimizes the need for a more encompassing analysis. It allows people to generalize from police violence to the ways that public funding for police comes at the expense of other public institutions, and creates the space to then ask why. Not only do the "new guard's" politics stand in sharp contrast to those of the "old guard" but so does their approach to organizing. Beyond being led by women, the new guard is decentralized and is largely organizing the movement through social media. This is very different from national organizations like the NAACP, NAN, or even Jackson's Operation PUSH, whose mostly male leaders make decisions with little input or direction from people on the ground. This strategy is not simply the product of male leadership, but of an older model that privileged leveraging connections and relationships within the establishment over street activism—or using street protests to gain leverage within the establishment. The newness of the Ferguson movement and the incipient movement against police violence have temporarily prevented that kind of political shortcut.

From Moment to Movement

On November 24, 2014, a grand jury in Ferguson decided not to indict Darren Wilson for the murder of Mike Brown. Angry protests ripped through the suburb in the dead of night when the decision was announced. Rows of riot police protected City Hall and the police department while the commercial section of Black Ferguson was allowed to burn. There was little surprise about the decision not to indict, but there was anger at the completion of a legal lynching. President Obama returned to the airwaves to counsel patience and respect for the law. He reminded his audience that "we are a nation built on the rule of law," a concept rendered hollow and meaningless by months of witnessing the lawlessness of the Ferguson police department.[24] Obama implored protestors to channel their concerns "constructively" and not "destructively," but the split screens of several networks showed the president's words were falling on deaf ears as fires burned through the night in Ferguson. This was not, however, a revival of the previous August, when the fires were igniting a new movement against police brutality; these were the flames of resignation and exhaustion.

As happened so often in 2014, at the moment when it appeared that the momentum of activism had swung back in the other direction, there was a new death at the hands of the police, like kindling on a fire. Two days before the Wilson decision was announced, young Tamir Rice, only twelve, was shot and killed by police in a playground in Cleveland, Ohio. Rice had been playing with a toy gun. Police shot and killed the boy within two seconds of their arrival—so quickly that the police car had not even stopped. Nine days earlier, Tanisha Anderson, also of Cleveland, had been killed when an officer performed a "judo" move to take her to the ground and in the process slammed her head into the concrete.[25] Days later, a Staten Island grand jury returned a decision not to indict Daniel Pantaleo, the officer who choked Eric Garner to death. Where the Ferguson decision seemed like an endpoint to the months-long struggle for justice there, these deaths and the Garner decision opened up an entirely new chapter. The continuation of the protests, however, was fraught with the tensions of going from "moment to movement."[26]

Obama quickly organized a meeting of some of the more visible activists from Ferguson and around the country to discuss police violence. James Hayes from the Ohio Student Union was one of the participants. "We appreciate that the president wanted to meet with us, but now he must deliver with meaningful policy," Hayes reported. "We are calling on everyone who believes that Black lives matter to continue taking to the streets until we get real change for our communities."[27] That such a meeting ever convened was proof alone that this was no longer just about Ferguson. The nation's political establishment was concerned about containing the movement.

This was no ordinary meeting; it included the president and vice president of the United States as well as the attorney general. But just as they were attempting to get in front of the anger over Ferguson, two days later the decision not to indict Pantaleo produced even larger protests than those that had greeted the Wilson decision. Tens of thousands of people across the United States clogged the streets in disgust, if not rage, over the refusal to punish another White police officer for the death of an unarmed Black man. In Garner's case, the evidence was incontrovertible. Hundreds of thousands of people had watched the video of him pleading for his life and repeating, eleven times, "I can't breathe" while Pantaleo squeezed the life out of his body. Yet the grand jury found no fault. In the aftermath of the Garner decision Obama shelved the talk about "a nation of laws" and announced the formation of a new task force charged with creating "specific recommendations about how we strengthen the relationship between law enforcement and communities of color and minority communities that feel that bias is taking place."[28]

Black Lives Matter

In December and January, "Black Lives Matter" was the rallying cry from every corner. A week after the Garner decision several hundred congressional aides, most of them Black, walked off the job in protest.[29] Black professional athletes wore T-shirts adorned with the slogan "I Can't Breathe." Soon after, high school and college students began wearing the shirts as well. Thousands of college, high school, and even middle school students began organizing and participating in die-ins, walkouts, marches, and other forms of public protest.[30] At Princeton University, more than four hundred students and faculty participated in a die-in. The protest included mostly African American students, but a number of White, Latino/a, and Asian students participated in the direct action. Students at Stanford blocked the San Mateo Bridge across San Francisco Bay. Students at seventy medical schools organized die-ins under the slogan "White Coats for Black Lives."[31] Public defenders and other lawyers organized their own actions, including die-ins.[32] Protests were sweeping the nation and politicians raced to keep up. Presidential hopeful Hillary Clinton, who had never publicly mentioned Mike Brown's name, was forced to say "Black Lives Matter" when she spoke in New York three days after the march.[33]

Even Obama began to change his tune. When talking about young African Americans, he was speaking less about morality and "instead focused on African American concerns about unfair treatment and called them part of the American family—which makes it awfully hard to single them out as the problem child in need of some tough love."[34] Garza of #BlackLivesMatter spoke to the significance of the actions: "What's happening right now is that a movement is growing. We are building relationships and connections, exercising new forms of leadership, new tactics, and learning lessons from our elders—people like Bayard Rustin, Diane Nash, Linda Burnham, Assata Shakur and Angela Davis—who have been part of social movements before us."[35]

Ferguson Action's statement echoed this sentiment when it described the movement as "coordinated" and "organized" but "decentralized." In some sense, the futility of organization had been confirmed by their wild success in organizing protests and demonstrations on the fly. For months, Twitter and other social media platforms *were* successful in organizing large and influential protests. The December 13 march in New York City was organized by two relatively novice activists on Facebook; within hours thousands of people had "liked" it and committed to attending. Upward of fifty thousand people actually showed up for the rally. But how would the movement go from direct action, die-ins, highway closures, and walkouts to ending police brutality without dedicated spaces to meet, strategize, and engage in democratic decision-making? Considering the demands and "vision" that Ferguson Action put forward, everything from ending racial profiling to full employment and ending mass incarceration, it is impossible to imagine any of this happening only online.

These debates over organization resemble some of the hostility to organization that emerged in the Occupy movement from 2011. In both cases, the absence of formal structures and formal leadership was described as "giving everyone a voice." If there is no organization, then no one can take over control. DeRay McKesson acknowledged this when he said, "But what is different about Ferguson . . . what makes that really important, unlike previous struggle, is that—who is the spokesperson? The people. The people, in a very democratic way, became the voice of the struggle."[36]

McKesson is one of the most visible actors in the movement and his insights are influential. He elaborates:

> It is not that we're anti-organization. There are structures that have formed as a result of protest that are really powerful. It is just that you did not need those structures to begin protest. *You* are enough to start a movement. Individual people can come together around things that they know are unjust. And they can spark change. Your body can be part of the protest; you don't need a VIP pass to protest. And Twitter allowed that to happen. . . . I think that what we are doing is building a radical new community in struggle that did not exist before. Twitter has enabled us to create community. I think the phase we're in is a community-building phase. Yes, we need to address policy, yes, we need to address elections; we need to do all those things. But on the heels of building a strong community.[37]

Not everyone rejects the need for organization. The fight against police terror has produced many new organizations and networks. At a forum at the historic Riverside Church in New York City, Asha Rosa of the Black Youth Project 100 spoke passionately on the need to be not only radical but also organized:

> Organizations are longer lasting than an action, longer lasting than a campaign, longer lasting than a moment. Organizations are where we can build structures that reflect our values, and build communities that help us sustain ourselves in this work and sustain the work itself. We saw 60,000 people in the streets in New York City [for the December protest]. . . . I won't be surprised if we don't see 60,000 people in the streets again until it's warm, and that's okay. . . . There are phases in these movements. We have to sustain that and make sure there are organizations for people to get plugged into.[38]

The Demands: This Is What We Want

The absence of an independent movement organization has meant that the actual demands of the movement have been muddled. Some of this arises from the difficulty of the task itself. Police violence is a part of the DNA of the United States. As I have argued earlier, there has been no golden age of policing in which violence and racism were not central to the job. But that does not mean that nothing can be done to rein in the policing state. The Ferguson Action website has compiled the most comprehensive list of movement demands, including demilitarizing the police, passing anti-racial-profiling legislation, and collecting data documenting police abuse, among other measures.[39] Hands Up United, based in Ferguson and St. Louis, has called for the "immediate suspension without pay of law enforcement officers that have used or approved excessive use of force."[40] #BLM has called on the attorney general to release the names of police who have killed Black people over the last five years "so they can be brought to justice—if they haven't already."[41]

The demands of different organizations in the movement overlap, but what is the mechanism for acting on these demands when they are disconnected from any structure coordinated through the movement? How can we pay systematic attention to the progress made in achieving these demands or determining whether or not the demands have to be recalibrated? Connecting police violence to the vast effects of institutional racism is a strength of the current movement, but there is also a danger of submerging reforms that are attainable now into a much broader struggle to transform the very nature of American society. In other words, fighting around the demand to be "free" does not clarify the steps it will take to achieve that goal.

Demanding everything is as ineffective as demanding nothing, because it obscures what that struggle looks like on a daily basis. It can also be demoralizing, because when the goal is everything, it is impossible to measure the small but important steps forward that are the wellspring of any movement. This is not an argument for thinking small or abandoning the struggle to completely transform the United States; it is an argument for drawing a distinction between the struggle for reforms that are possible today and the struggle for revolution, which is a longer-term project. To be sure, there is definitely a relationship between the two. The struggle to reform various aspects of our existing society makes people's lives better in the here and now; it also teaches people how to struggle and organize. Those are the building blocks that can lead to larger and more transformative struggles. In the process, people in the movement develop politically, gain experience and expertise, and become leaders. It is impossible to conceive of leaping from inactivity to changing the world in a single bound.

For example, many Black people in the South who were radicalized in the 1950s in the struggle against Jim Crow would probably not have recognized themselves ten years later. Many people whose politics began with narrow demands to end Jim Crow eventually concluded that a government invested in racism could never achieve justice for Black people. Consider the experiences of the activists who made up SNCC, who in 1964 arrived at the Democratic National Convention in Atlantic City with the hope of seating Black delegates from their Mississippi Freedom Democratic Party as the delegation from Mississippi. The point was to expose and embarrass the national party for allowing the all-White Democratic Party to seat its delegation, knowing full well that Black people in Mississippi were violently disenfranchised. The SNCC activists believed if they were successful, they could break the grip of the Dixiecrats—the White Democratic Party of the South—on the electoral process throughout the South. But there was no way that Lyndon Johnson and the national Democratic Party were going to risk Southern White votes by acquiescing to the demands of civil rights activists. In the end, Johnson forced a deal down the activists' throats that left the convention and the White supremacist wing of the Democratic Party basically intact. James Forman, the executive director of SNCC, spelled out the meaning of the defeat:

> Atlantic City was a powerful lesson. . . . No longer was there any hope . . . that the federal government would change the situation in the Deep South. The fine line of contradiction between the state governments and the federal

government, which we had used to build a movement, was played out. Now the kernel of opposites—the people against both the federal and state governments was apparent.[42]

Narrowing the demands of the movement in order to retain focus does not mean narrowing its reach. The brilliance of the slogan "Black Lives Matter" is its ability to articulate the dehumanizing aspects of anti-Black racism in the United States. The long-term strength of the movement will depend on its ability to reach large numbers of people by connecting the issue of police violence to the other ways that Black people are oppressed.

This process is already under way, as "new guard" activists have worked to make those connections. The best example of this involves the struggle of low-wage workers to raise the minimum wage to $15 an hour. Twenty percent of fast-food workers are Black and 68 percent of them earn between $7.26 and $10.09 an hour.[43] In Chicago, fast-food restaurants employ 46 percent of Black workers—in New York it's 50 percent.[44] Twenty percent of Walmart's 1.4 million workers are African American, making it the largest employer of Black Americans. There is a logical connection between the low-wage workers' campaigns and the Black Lives Matter movement. The overrepresentation of African Americans in the ranks of the poor and working class has made them targets of police, who prey on those with low incomes. Black and Latino/a workers are also more likely to suffer the consequences of the mounting fees and fines discussed in chapter 4 [of *From #BlackLivesMatter to Black Liberation*]. Mwende-Katwiwa of the BYP 100 in New Orleans explains the relationship between economic and racial justice:

> Too often Black youth are trapped in a singular narrative about their lived experience that does not address the structural and social conditions. . . . The #BlackLivesMatter movement goes beyond a call to end police brutality and murder against Black people—it is a recognition that Black life is valuable while it is still being lived. Valuing Black life means Black people should have access to their basic human dignity at their workplace—especially Black youth who are disproportionately impacted by unemployment and are over-represented in low-wage jobs.[45]

The movement today is in a much better position to nurture and develop a relationship with the growing low-wage-worker struggle than has been possible with the civil rights establishment. For years, Walmart and McDonald's have been reliable contributors to the CBC, NAACP, and NAN.[46]

The Black Lives Matter movement has the potential to make deeper connections to and create relationships with organized labor. Black workers continue to be unionized at higher rates than White workers. The reason is simple: Black union workers make far above and beyond what nonunion Black workers make, in salary and benefits. Black workers also tend to be concentrated in the sectors most under attack by the state—federal, state, and local government, including education and other municipal jobs. Throughout the winter of 2015, Black Lives Matter activists all over the country organized actions to "shut it down," including highways, public transportation, shopping establishments—even brunch! Developing alliances with organized labor could lead to workers exercising their power to shut down production, services, and business as usual as pressure for concrete reforms concerning the policing state. The pathway for this has already been trodden. On May 1, 2015, tens of thousands of activists rallied across the country under the banner of Black Lives Matter—and in Oakland, California, the International Longshore and Warehouse Union, Local 10, conducted a work stoppage that halted the flow of millions of dollars' worth of goods and prevented them from being loaded onto cargo ships. This was the first time a major union had initiated a work stoppage in solidarity with the Black Lives Matter movement. The coalition that helped to organize the action said in a statement:

> Labor is one sector of the community that can truly shut this country down. If workers refuse to work, product doesn't get made, and money doesn't exchange hands. The only way this country is going to take us seriously is if we interrupt their commerce and impact their bottom line. Simply appealing to their humanity doesn't work. If that was the case, the epidemic of Black genocide at the hands of police would have ended decades ago.[47]

Broadening the reach of the movement also belies the notion that the movement is divided between old and young. Collaborating with Black workers, including Black teachers and other trade unionists, cuts across age groups and demonstrates that working-class African Americans of all generations have a vested interest in the success of the movement.

Solidarity

One important frontier of the movement also involves its capacity to develop solidarity with other oppressed groups of people. African Americans have always felt the most punishing aspects of life under American capitalism acutely. This has not meant, however, that Black people are alone in their desire to transform the harshness of society. The oppression of Indigenous people, immigrants, and non-White people more generally pervades American society. In profound ways, it is the secret to the conundrum of how the 1 percent can dominate a society where the vast majority has every interest in undoing the existing order. Basic math would seem to indicate that 12 or 13 percent of the population, which is what African Americans constitute, would have no realistic capacity to fundamentally transform the social order of the United States.

The challenge for the movement is transforming the goal of "freedom" into digestible demands that train and organize its forces so that they have the ability to fight for more; the movement must also have a real plan for building and developing solidarity among the oppressed. This means building networks and alliances with Latinos in opposition to attacks on immigrant rights, connecting with Arabs and Muslims campaigning against Islamophobia, and organizing with Native organizations that fight for self-determination within the United States. This is not an exhaustive list; it is only a beginning.

The struggle to build solidarity between oppressed communities, however, is not obvious. For example, when three young Muslims, Deah Barakat, Razan Abu-Salha, and Yusor Abu-Salha, were shot and killed by a White man in Chapel Hill, North Carolina, and activists began the hashtag #MuslimLivesMatter, there was a backlash. Some activists described the hashtag as an "appropriation" of the ongoing Black movement:

> This is not at all to undermine or belittle the injustices that other minority groups in this country deal with every day; in fact, it is quite the opposite. Every community deserves to be able to think critically about their own positions in America, about their own challenges, about their own experiences, and in their own terms. Of course Muslim lives are under fire in our American systems. There is no question about that. However, building off the #BlackLivesMatter trend equates struggles that are, though seemingly similar, drastically different.[48]

It is one thing to respect the organizing that has gone into the movement against police violence and brutality, but quite another to conceive of Black oppression and anti-Black racism as so wholly unique that they are beyond the realm of understanding and, potentially, solidarity from others who are oppressed.

In the contest to demonstrate how oppressions differ from one group to the next, we miss how we are connected through oppression—and how those connections should form the basis of solidarity, not a celebration of our lives on the margins. The American government demonizes its enemies to justify mistreating them, whether it is endless war, internment, and torture or mass incarceration and police abuse. There is a racist feedback loop, in which domestic and foreign policies feed and reinforce each other. This is why US foreign policy in the Middle East has reverberated at home. The cynical use of Islamophobia to whip up support for continued American interventions in Arab and Muslim countries inevitably has consequences for Muslim Americans. And the ever-expanding security state, justified by the "War on Terror," becomes the pretext for greater police repression at home—which, of course, disproportionately affects African Americans and Latino/as in border regions.

Conclusion

Protests can expose these conditions and their relationship to the policing state; protests can draw in larger numbers of people; protests can compel public figures to speak against those conditions. Protests can do many things, but protests alone cannot end police abuse and the conditions that are used to justify it. The movement against police brutality, even in its current inchoate state, has transformed how Americans see and understand policing in the United States. Over the course of a year, Black people from coast to coast have led a struggle to expose the existence of an urban police state with suburban outposts. It has shown the country the depths of the lie that we live in a colorblind or postracial country. Eighty-three percent of Americans say racism "still poses a problem," up 7 percent from 2014. Sixty-one percent of Whites and 82 percent of Blacks agree that "there's a need for a conversation about racism in American life."[49] In less than a year, the number of White Americans who view police killings as "isolated incidents" has fallen from 58 percent to 36 percent.[50] At the same time, in July 2015 alone, the police killed an astonishing 118 people, the most that had been killed over the entire year thus far.[51] By mid-August they had killed another fifty-four. On the anniversary of Mike Brown's death, Ferguson police shot and critically injured another Black teenager. In New York City, where there was a vibrant anti-police-brutality movement for years before the most recent iteration of the national movement, liberal mayor Bill DeBlasio has pledged to hire a thousand new police officers. This was surprising, since DeBlasio rode the success of the campaign to end stop-and-frisk into office in 2013. This is only one example of how resilient the police are as an institution, but it also shows elected officials' reluctance to discipline them.

The movement is confronted with many challenges, but it has also shown that it will not go away easily. This has less to do with the organizing genius of organizers than with deep anger among ordinary Blacks who have been beaten, imprisoned, humiliated, and abused, all the while being blamed for their own victimization. The power of ordinary African Americans to push the movement forward was seen in June 2015 in McKinney, Texas, when the police attacked several Black children at a swimming party, including fifteen-year-old Dajerria Becton, who was manhandled by one officer in particular.

> In years past, a story like this would have resulted in little if any attention. Instead, a few days later, hundreds of Black and white protestors filled the street of the small suburban development where the children had been set upon, chanting, "We want to go swimming" and "No swimming, no driving." It must have been a powerful scene to everyone who witnessed it—and for different reasons. Many of the suburban white neighbors who supported the police were outraged but could do nothing about it; they had been rendered powerless. The police were undoubtedly intimidated by the action, so much so that the most aggressive cop, who had attacked Becton, was forced to resign days later. Most importantly, though, for the Black children who had been abused and threatened at gunpoint by the police and for their parents, to have hundreds of people show up to insist that their lives mattered must have repaired some part of the damage. For them to see the solidarity of hundreds of white people must have given them some hope that not all whites are racist and that some would even stand up and fight alongside them. The demonstration may have also validated their right to resist and stand up to racism and racist violence and affirmed that they were right to protest from the very beginning.

The Black Lives Matter movement, from Ferguson to today, has created a feeling of pride and combativeness among a generation that this country has tried to kill, imprison, and simply disappear. The power of protest has been validated. For it to become even more effective, to affect the policing state, and to withstand opposition and attempts to infiltrate, subvert, and undermine what has been built, there must be more organization and coordination in the move from protest to movement.

Keeanga-Yamahtta Taylor is author of *From #BlackLivesMatter to Black Liberation*, published by Haymarket Books in January 2016. Her interests are in race and public policy, Black politics, and racial inequality in the United States. She is assistant professor of African American studies at Princeton University. Taylor's writing has been published in *Souls: A Critical Journal of Black Politics, Culture and Society, The Guardian, Boston Review, The New Republic, AlJazeera America, Jacobin, In These Times, New Politics, International Socialist Review,* and other publications. She is currently working on a book manuscript titled *Race for Profit: Black Housing and the Urban Crisis in the 1970s,* under contract with the University of North Carolina Press in their Justice, Power, and Politics series. Taylor received her PhD in African American studies at Northwestern University in 2013 and is currently an assistant professor in African American studies at Princeton University.

NOTES

1. John H. Richardson, "Michael Brown Sr. and the Agony of the Black Father in America," *Esquire*, January 5, 2015, http://www.esquire.com/features/michael-brown-father-interview-0115.

2. Kristin Braswell, "#FergusonFridays: Not All of the Black Freedom Fighters Are Men: An Interview With Black Women on the Front Line in Ferguson," Feminist Wire, October 3, 2014, http://www.thefeministwire.com/2014/10/fergusonfridays-black-freedom-fighters-men-interview-black-women-front-line-ferguson/.

3. Charles P. Pierce, "The Body in the Street," *Esquire*, August 22, 2014, http://www.esquire.com/blogs/politics/The_Body_In_The_Street.

4. Mark Follman, "Michael Brown's Mom Laid Flowers Where He Was Shot—and Police Crushed Them," *Mother Jones*, August 27, 2014, http://www.motherjones.com/politics/2014/08/ferguson-st-louis-police-tactics-dogs-michael-brown.

5. Richardson, "Michael Brown Sr."

6. Amnesty International USA, "On the Streets of America: Human Rights Abuses in Ferguson," October 24, 2014, http://www.amnestyusa.org/research/reports/on-the-streets-of-america-human-rights-abuses-in-ferguson.

7. Joel Anderson, "Ferguson's Angry Young Men," BuzzFeed, August 22, 2014, http://www.buzzfeed.com/joelanderson/who-are-fergusons-young-protesters.

8. Johnetta Elzie, "When I Close My Eyes at Night, I See People Running From Tear Gas," *Ebony* (September 2014), http://www.ebony.com/news-views/ferguson-forward-when-i-close-my-eyes-at-night-i-see-people-running-from-tear-ga.

9. Anderson, "Ferguson's Angry Young Men."

10. Jon Swaine, "Ohio Walmart Video Reveals Moments Before Officer Killed John Crawford," *Guardian*, September 24, 2014, http://www.theguardian.com/world/2014/sep/24/surveillance-video-walmart-shooting-john-crawford-police.

11. Josh Harkinson, "4 Unarmed Black Men Have Been Killed by Police in the Last Month," *Mother Jones*, August 13, 2014, http://www.motherjones.com/politics/2014/08/3-unarmed-black-african-american-men-killed-police.

12. Darnell L. Moore, "Two Years Later, Black Lives Matter Faces Critiques, but It Won't Be Stopped," Mic, August 10, 2015, http://mic.com/articles/123666/two-years-later-black-lives-matter-faces-critiques-but-it-won-t-be-stopped.

13. Associated Press, "Five Arrested in Ferguson After Protests Break Out Over Burned Memorial," *Guardian*, August 12, 2015, http://www.theguardian.com/world/2014/sep/24/ferguson-protest-michael-brown-memorial-fire-police.

14. Trymaine Lee, "Why Vonderrit Myers Matters," MSNBC, October 18, 2014, http://www.msnbc.com/msnbc/why-vonderrit-myers-matters.

15. Democracy Now!, "Ferguson October: Thousands March in St. Louis for Police Reform and Arrest of Officer Darren Wilson," Pacifica Radio, October 13, 2014, http://www.democracynow.org/2014/10/13/thousands_march_in_ferguson_for_police.

16. Ella Baker, "Bigger Than a Hamburger," *Southern Patriot*, June 18, 1960, History Is a Weapon, http://www.historyisaweapon.com/defcon1/bakerbigger.

17. Amanda Sakuma, "Women Hold the Front-Lines of Ferguson," MSNBC, October 12, 2014, http://www.msnbc.com/msnbc/women-hold-the-front-lines-ferguson.

18. Braswell, "#FergusonFridays."

19. Stephen Bronars, "Half of Ferguson's Young African-American Men Are Missing," *Forbes*, March 18, 2015, http://www.forbes.com/sites/modeledbehavior/2015/03/18/half-of-fergusons-young-african-american-men-are-missing/.

20. Justin Wolfers, David Leonhardt, and Kevin Quealy, "1.5 Million Missing Black Men," *New York Times*, April 20, 2015, http://www.nytimes.com/interactive/2015/04/20/upshot/missing-black-men.html?abt=0002&abg=1.

21. Braswell, "#FergusonFridays."

22. Katherine Mirani, "Nurturing Black Youth Activism," *Chicago Reporter*, October 6, 2014, http://chicagoreporter.com/nurturing-black-youth-activism/.

23. Alicia Garza, "A Herstory of the #BlackLivesMatter Movement," Feminist Wire, October 7, 2014, http://thefeministwire.com/2014/10/blacklivesmatter-2/.

24. Barack Obama, "Remarks on Ferguson Grand Jury Decision," *Washington Post*, November 24, 2014, http://www.washingtonpost.com/politics/transcript-obamas-remarks-on-ferguson-grand-jury-decision/2014/11/24/afc3b38e-744f-11e4-bd1b-03009bd3e984_story.html.

25. M. David and Jackson Marciana, "Tanisha Anderson Was Literally Praying for Help as Cops Held Her Down and Killed Her," CounterCurrent News, February 28, 2015, http://countercurrentnews.com/2015/02/tanisha-anderson-was-literally-praying-for-help/.

26. Fredrick Harris, "Will Ferguson Be a Moment or a Movement?" *Washington Post*, August 22, 2014, http://www.washingtonpost.com/opinions/will-ferguson-be-a-moment-or-a-movement/2014/08/22/071d4a94-28a8-11e4-8593-da634b334390_story.html.

27. Ferguson Action, "Breaking: Ferguson Activists Meet With President Obama to Demand an End to Police Brutality Nationwide," press release, December 1, 2014, http://fergusonaction.com/white-house-meeting/.

28. Tanya Somanader, "President Obama Delivers a Statement on the Grand Jury Decision in the Death of Eric Garner," White House press release, December 3, 2014, https://www.whitehouse .gov/blog/2014/12/03/president-obama-delivers-statement-grand-jury-decision-death-eric-garner.

29. Tim Mak, "Capitol Hill's Black Staffers Walk Out to Do 'Hands Up, Don't Shoot!'" Daily Beast, December 10, 2014, http://www.thedailybeast.com/articles/2014/12/10/black-congressional-staffers-plan-ferguson-garner-walkout.html.

30. Nicole Mulvaney, "Princeton University Students Stage Walkout in Protest of Garner, Ferguson Grand Jury Decisions," NJ.com, December 4, 2014, http://www .nj.com/mercer/index.ssf/2014/12/princeton_university_students_stage_black livesmatter_walkout_protest_of_garner_ferguson_decisions.html.

31. WhiteCoats4BlackLives, "About," n.d., accessed June 21, 2015, http://www.white coats4blacklives.org/.

32. Malaika Fraley and Gary Peterson, "Bay Area Public Defenders Rally for 'Black Lives Matter,'" San Jose Mercury News, December 18, 2014, http://www.mercury news.com/ci_27163840/bay-area-public-defenders-stand-up-black-lives.

33. Jill Colvin, "Hillary Clinton Denounces Torture, Says Black Lives Matter," Huffington Post, December 16, 2014, http://www.huffingtonpost.com/2014/12/16/hillary-clinton-torture-blacks_n_6338154. html.

34. Nia-Malika Henderson, "'Black Respectability' Politics Are Increasingly Absent From Obama's Rhetoric," Washington Post, December 3, 2014, http://www.washington post.com/blogs/the-fix/wp/2014/12/03/black-respectability-politics-are-increasingly-absent-from-obamas-rhetoric/.

35. Marcia Chatelain, "#BlackLivesMatter: An Online Roundtable With Alicia Garza, Dante Barry, and Darsheel Kaur," Dissent, January 19, 2015, http://www.dissent magazine.org/blog/blacklivesmatter-an-online-roundtable-with-alicia-garza-dante-barry-and-darsheel-kaur.

36. Noah Berlatsky, "Hashtag Activism Isn't a Cop-Out," Atlantic, January 7, 2015, http:// www.theatlantic.com/politics/archive/2015/01/not-just-hashtag-activism-why-social-media-matters-to-protestors/384215/.

37. Ibid.

38. Danny Katch, "#BlackLivesMatter Looks to the Future," Socialist Worker, February 4, 2015, http://socialistworker.org/2015/02/04/blacklivesmatter-looks-ahead.

39. Ferguson Action, "Demands," n.d., accessed June 24, 2015, http://fergusonaction .com/demands/.

40. Hands Up United, "Hands Up," n.d., accessed June 24, 2015, http://www.handsup united.org/.

41. #BlackLivesMatter, "Demands," n.d., accessed June 24, 2015, http://blacklivesmatter .com/demands/.

42. James Forman, The Making of Black Revolutionaries: A Personal Account (New York: Macmillan, 1972), 395–96.

43. Annie-Rose Strasser, "The Majority of Fast Food Workers Are Not Teenagers, Report Finds," ThinkProgress, August 8, 2013, http://thinkprogress.org/economy/2013/08/08/ 2433601/fast-food-workers-young/.

44. BYP 100, "Racial Justice Is Economic Justice," n.d., accessed June 24, 2015, http://byp100 .org/ff15signup/.

45. CopyLine, "Black Youth Project 100 (BYP100) Declares #BlackWorkMatters at Protests in Chicago, New Orleans & New York City," April 20, 2015, http://www.copylinemagazine .com/2015/04/20/black-youth-project-100-byp100-declares-blackworkmatters-at-protests-in-chicago-new-orleans-new-york-city/.

46. Peter Waldman, "NAACP's FedEx and Wal-Mart Gifts Followed Discrimination Claims," *Bloomberg BusinessWeek*, May 8, 2014, http://www.bloomberg.com/news/ articles/2014-05-08/naacp-s-fedex-and-wal-mart-gifts-followed-discrimination-claims.

47. Alessandro Tinonga, "Black Lives Matter on the Docks," Socialist Worker, April 30, 2015, http://socialistworker.org/2015/04/30/black-lives-matter-on-the-docks.

48. Sabah, "Stop Using #MuslimLivesMatter," Muslim Girl, February 12, 2015, http://muslimgirl .net/10302/solidarity-mean-appropriation/.

49. Ariel Edwards-Levy, "Americans Say Now Is the Right Time to Discuss Racism, Gun Control," Huffington Post, June 22, 2015, http://www.huffingtonpost.com/2015/06/22/ charleston-poll_n_7640026. html.

50. Terrell Jermaine Starr, "New Study: More White People See Systemic Problems in Policing After Freddie Gray, but Racial Gulf Remains," AlterNet, May 5, 2015, http://www.alternet .org/civil-liberties/new-study-more-white-people-see-systemic-problems-policing-after-freddie-gray-racial.

51. *Guardian*, "The Counted: People Killed by Police in the United States in 2015," interactive database, June 1, 2015, http://www.theguardian.com/us-news/ng-interactive/2015/jun/01/ the-counted-police-killings-us-database.

SUGGESTED ADDITIONAL RESOURCES

Camp, J. T., & Heatherton, C. (Eds.). (2016). *Policing the planet: Why the policing crisis led to Black Lives Matter*. London: Verso Books.

Davis, A. Y., & Barat, F. (2016). *Freedom is a constant struggle: Ferguson, Palestine, and the foundations of a movement*. Chicago, IL: Haymarket Books.

Lowery, W. (2016). *They can't kill us all: Ferguson, Baltimore, and a new era in America's racial justice movement*. New York, NY: Little, Brown.

Powell, A. J. (2016, September 29). Problem-oriented policing in an age of protest. *Society Pages*. Retrieved from https://thesocietypages.org/trot/2016/09/29/problem-oriented-policing-in-an-age-of-protest/

Taylor, K. (2016). *From #BlackLivesMatter to Black liberation*. Chicago, IL: Haymarket Books.

Williams, J. (Producer), & Grant, L. (Director). (2016). *Stay woke: The Black Lives Matter movement* [Documentary]. United States: BET.

QUESTIONS FOR FURTHER DISCUSSION

1. What previous knowledge or information did you have about the Black Lives Matter movement? How does the essay change your perception and understanding of Black Lives Matter?

2. What do you remember about the cases discussed by Taylor when they occurred? How does the additional knowledge offered by Taylor shape your opinion of these cases?

3. Many critics have suggested that the Black Lives Matter movement doesn't have any goals. What information from this essay provides a response to that critique?

4. What other questions do you have about the Black Lives Matter movement?

REACHING BEYOND THE COLOR LINE

1. In small groups, research cases of police brutality that have involved victims from other racial and ethnic groups. What examples can you find? What are the similarities and differences between these cases and those reviewed by Taylor?

2. Consider the emergence of #SayHerName and how it connects to the #Black LivesMatter movement, using the video from Democracy Now: "Say Her Name: Families Seek Justice in Overlooked Police Killings of African-American Women" (https://www.youtube.com/watch?v=jMV5_lyYR6Y&feature=youtu.be).

3. Research the case of Emmett Till. Write a three-to-five-page paper on the similarities between Till's relationship to the civil rights movement and Trayvon Martin's relationship to the Black Lives Matter movement. What do these cases tell us about what sparks social movements?

4. Consider the national anthem protests by Colin Kaepernick and other athletes and celebrities. Research the reactions to these protests. What do these reactions tell us specifically about our perceptions of Black protests? What can these reactions tell us about the importance of social movements?

"If Only They Would Make Better Choices . . . "

Confronting Myths About Ethnoracial Health Disparities

Dawne M. Mouzon

Rutgers University–New Brunswick

With a few important exceptions, people of color in the United States face numerous health inequities. Non-Hispanic Blacks (hereafter referred to as Blacks) have the lowest life expectancy of all groups at 74.6 years, followed by Native Americans at 76.9; however, non-Hispanic Whites (hereafter referred to as Whites) can expect to live between 2 to 4 years longer, to 78.9 years. Latino life expectancy is 82.8 years and Asians have the longest life expectancy of all groups at 86.5 years (Lewis & Burd-Sharps, 2015).

The lower life expectancies of Blacks and Native Americans lead many to believe that these outcomes are due to poor lifestyle choices. In the general discourse on obesity, for instance, Blacks are characterized as overweight due to "cultural traditions" that devalue the importance of healthy eating or exercise. Similarly, Native Americans and Alaska Natives are often presumed to lack the control to avoid heavy alcohol use. These beliefs suggest that people of color, and low-income ones in particular, lead lifestyles conducive to early death. As the conventional wisdom suggests, "If they would just make better food choices/stop smoking/go to the doctor more often, they would be able to live as long as Whites." However, a sociological examination of disease among groups of color reveals myriad structural causes for these health inequities.

In the next section, I briefly review epidemiological patterns of illness for hypertension, diabetes, heart disease, and stroke/cardiovascular disease—patterns that indicate there is nothing random about who gets sick and who remains well in this country.

A Brief Epidemiological Profile of the United States

To get a better understanding of some of the health problems that plague groups of color in the United States, we can explore patterns for hypertension, diabetes, heart disease, and stroke based on race/ethnicity. Figure 20.1 displays age-adjusted prevalence of these illnesses. *Prevalence* refers to the proportion of existing cases of illness in a population. In addition, it is important to note that differences in health conditions exist based not only on racial or ethnic background but also on gender, differences I will highlight throughout this chapter whenever possible.[1]

Hypertension. Hypertension (i.e., high blood pressure) can harden the arteries and lead to decreased blood and oxygen flow to the heart, potentially causing a heart attack. Hypertension can also affect the brain (potentially causing a stroke) or the kidneys (potentially leading to chronic kidney disease; Centers for Disease Control and Prevention, 2014). Hypertension prevalence is highest among Blacks (33.2%) and Native Hawaiians/Other Pacific Islanders (36.5%).[2] Essentially, roughly 1 in 3 Blacks and 1 in 3 Native Hawaiians/Other Pacific Islanders meet the criteria for hypertension. Hypertension prevalence for other ethnoracial groups is lower, hovering around 21% to 25%, or between 1 in 5 and 1 in 4 cases (Blackwell, Lucas, & Clarke, 2014; see Figure 20.1).

Diabetes. Diabetes is a disease in which the pancreas fails to release insulin after the body turns food into sugars (i.e., glucose). In a normally functioning system, insulin opens the body's cells so glucose can enter and be used for energy. With diabetes, that system fails and can lead to damage of the eyes, kidneys, nerves, and heart (Diabetes Research Institute, 2016). Diabetes ranks as the seventh-leading cause of death for all adults living in the United States (Xu et al., 2016). American Indians/Alaska Natives have the highest age-adjusted prevalence of diabetes (17.9%), followed by Blacks (13.2%) and Latinos (12.2%). Conversely, diabetes prevalence is notably lower among Asians (9.0%), Native Hawaiians/Other Pacific Islanders (7.3%), and Whites (7.6%) (Blackwell et al., 2014; see Figure 20.1). Race/ethnicity also strongly patterns age-adjusted mortality rates due to diabetes. Despite having the second-highest prevalence of diabetes, Blacks have the highest diabetes mortality rates (38.2 per 100,000), more than twice those of Whites (18.6 per 100,000). Diabetes mortality rates are also higher among American Indians/Alaska Natives (31.3 per 100,000) and Latinos (25.1 per 100,000) relative to Whites; however, Asians/Native Hawaiians and other Pacific Islanders have diabetes mortality rates that are slightly lower than those for Whites (15.0 per 100,000) (National Center for Health Statistics, 2016; see Figure 20.2).

Heart Disease. Heart disease (i.e., cardiovascular disease) is the leading cause of death for all adults living in the United States, regardless of race/ethnicity (Xu et al., 2016). The term is actually used to describe a number of conditions, including coronary artery disease and heart rhythm problems. Narrowed or blocked blood vessels can lead to heart attack, chest pain (angina), or stroke (Mayo Clinic Staff, 2014). Prevalence of heart

Figure 20.1 Age-Adjusted Prevalence of Selected Conditions, by Race/Ethnicity, United States, 2012

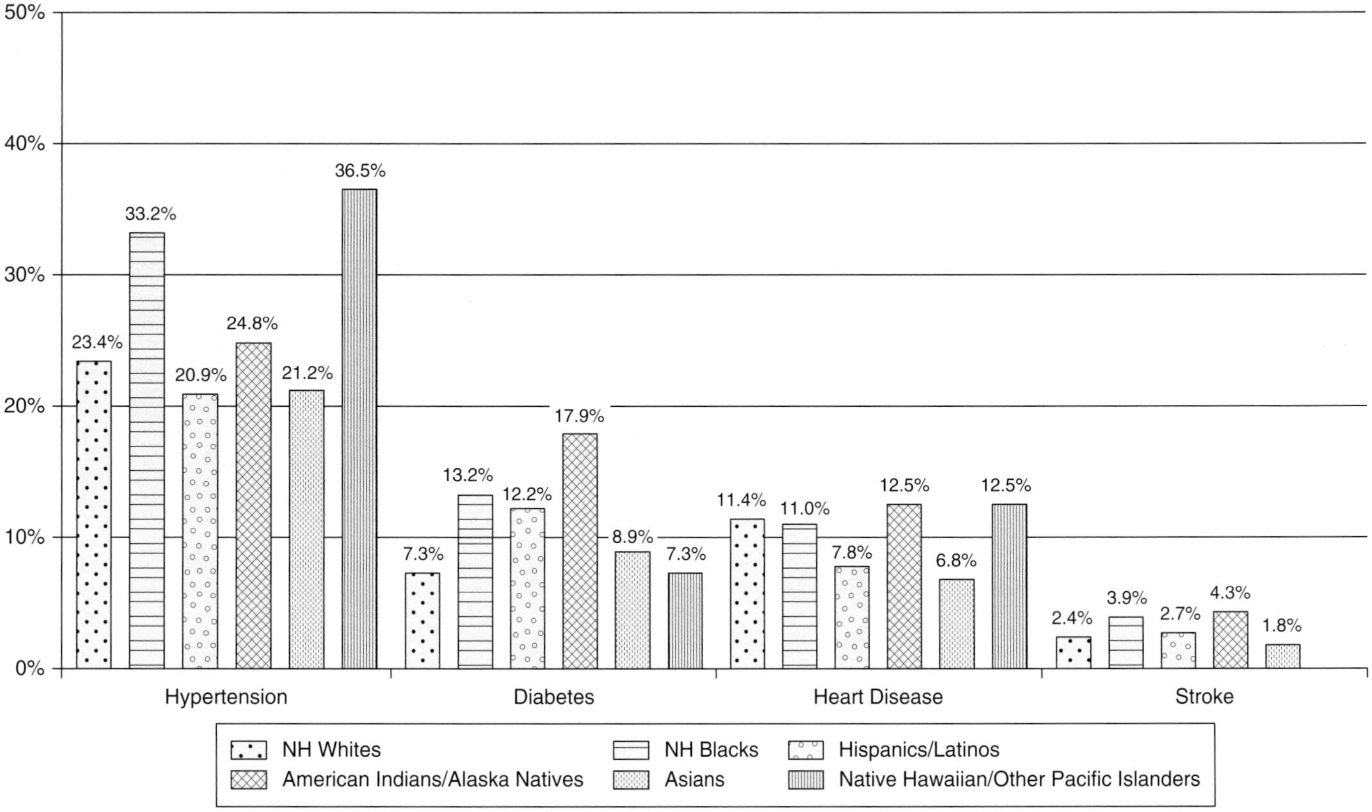

Source: Blackwell, Lucas, and Clarke (2014).

Note: For Stroke category, too few cases/data not available for Native Hawaiian/Other Pacific Islanders.

Figure 20.2 Age-Adjusted Mortality Rates (per 100,000) for Selected Conditions, by Race/Ethnicity, United States, 2014

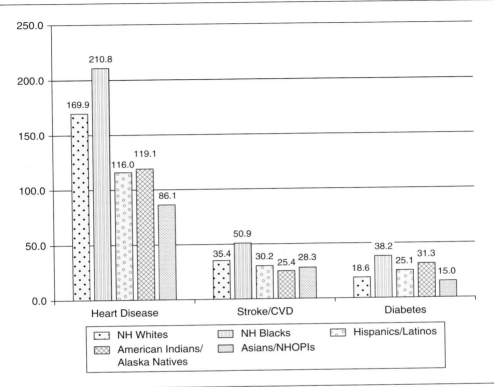

Source: National Center for Health Statistics (2016, Tables 16 and 17).

disease is relatively similar among Whites (11.4%), Blacks (11.0%), American Indians/ Alaska Natives (12.5%), and Native Hawaiians/Other Pacific Islanders (12.5%) (Blackwell et al., 2014). Heart disease prevalence is markedly lower among Latinos (7.8%) and Asians (6.8%) (see Figure 20.2). However, disparities in heart disease become vividly apparent when considering mortality due to this illness (National Center for Health Statistics, 2016). Blacks have the highest age-adjusted mortality rate due to heart disease, which causes 210.8 deaths per 100,000 Blacks (National Center for Health Statistics, 2016). Whites have the second-highest mortality rate due to heart disease (169.9 per 100,000), followed by American Indians/Alaska Natives (119.1 per 100,000) and Latinos (116.0 per 100,000). Heart disease mortality rates among Asians (86.1 per 100,000) are half those of Whites and Blacks (National Center for Health Statistics, 2016; see Figure 20.2).

Stroke. Stroke is a type of cerebrovascular disease that affects blood supply to the brain. It occurs when a blood vessel that carries oxygen and nutrients to the brain is blocked by a clot or bursts, which prevents blood and oxygen from getting to brain cells, thus causing those brain cells to die. A stroke can damage parts of the brain that control specific activities (e.g., speech, mobility), causing parts of the body not to work as they did before (American Stroke Association, 2017). Although the prevalence of stroke is relatively low in the adult U.S. population (ranging from 1.8% among Asians to 4.3% among American Indians/Alaska Natives and 3.9% among Blacks), cerebrovascular disease/stroke ranks as the fifth-leading cause of death in the U.S. population (Xu et al., 2016). Blacks face an overwhelmingly disproportionate burden of death due to stroke, however (50.9 per 100,000; National Center for Health Statistics, 2016). Conversely, stroke mortality rates are lower not only among Whites (35.4) but among all other groups of color besides Blacks (30.2 for Latinos, 28.3 for Asians/Native Hawaiians and other Pacific Islanders, and 25.4 for American Indians/Alaska Natives; National Center for Health Statistics, 2016; see Figure 20.2).

The above patterns reveal that health represents a form of systematic inequality that disproportionately burdens people of color (especially those who are socioeconomically disadvantaged). The question is: Why do these disparities exist? Below, I investigate three common explanations of ethnoracial health disparities in the United States: socioeconomic status, health behaviors, and institutional racism.

Common Explanations for Ethnoracial Health Disparities

Argument 1: Health Disparities Are Due to Differences in Socioeconomic Status

The landmark Whitehall studies are part of a longitudinal data collection effort that seeks to investigate social determinants of health and mortality among British civil servants. The first cohort (Whitehall I) began in 1967 and was composed of more than 18,000 White men aged 20 to 64 who were followed over a 10-year period to identify risks for morbidity (illness) and mortality (death) due to heart disease and other causes. The second Whitehall cohort (Whitehall II) included more than 10,000 male *and* female British civil servants aged 35 to 55 and began in 1985. Follow-up data collection is ongoing.

The major contribution of the Whitehall studies was its discovery of a trend called the *social gradient in health,* or the empirical finding that as socioeconomic status (SES) rises, health status improves. The primary finding from Whitehall I was that men in the lowest occupational grade had the highest risk of 10-year mortality, with the lowest mortality rates among men in the highest occupational grade and intermediate mortality rates along the middle of the spectrum (Marmot, Shipley, & Rose, 1984). In other words, men with lower-status jobs (i.e., men in blue-collar or manual-labor jobs characterized by high levels of demand and low levels of control) had the highest risk of death within 10 years. Conversely, men with the highest-status jobs had the lowest risk of death and those men with middle-class jobs had an intermediate level of risk. The social gradient in mortality was later replicated for both physical and mental health morbidity in Whitehall II (Ferrie, Shipley, Smith, Stansfeld, & Marmot, 2002; Marmot et al., 1991) and in a multitude of U.S. studies using indicators of SES that are more standard in the U.S. context (e.g., income, educational attainment, and wealth; Adler & Ostrove, 1999).

Based on the social gradient in health, the common reasoning is that disadvantaged people of color experience higher rates of illness and mortality because they have lower SES than Whites. For example, more than 1 in 4 Blacks (25.8%), American Indians/Alaska Natives (23.9%), and Latinos (23.2%) live below the poverty line, more than twice the rate of Whites (9.9%) (Macartney, Bishaw, & Fontenot, 2013). However, as a whole, Asians have similar or higher SES compared with Whites (i.e., 11.6% living below the poverty line). Therefore, they are the only group of color that does not face socioeconomic disadvantage as a whole, although many face substantial racial discrimination—experiences that are also detrimental to health (Gee, Ro, Shariff-Marco, & Chae, 2009).

Unemployment rates are highest among Blacks (9.6%) and American Indians/Alaska Natives (9.9%), with roughly half the rates of unemployment found among Whites (4.6%), Asians (3.8%), and Native Hawaiians/Other Pacific Islanders (5.7%). Roughly 6.6% of Latinos are also currently unemployed (U.S. Bureau of Labor Statistics, 2016). Educational attainment patterns show a very similar pattern; although half (50.2%) of Asians and 30.9% of Whites have earned at least a bachelor's degree, only 17.7% of Blacks, 13.0% of Latinos, 13.0% of American Indians/Alaska Natives, and 14.4% of Native Hawaiians/Other Pacific Islanders have at least a bachelor's degree (Ogunwole, Drewery, & Rios-Vargas, 2012). Finally, the racial wealth gap has reached unprecedented highs. In 2009, Whites had 19 times the net worth of Blacks, 15 times the net worth of Latinos, and more than twice the net worth of Asians (Pew Research Center, 2011).

What do these statistics on income, employment, educational attainment, and wealth mean for one's health status? Among other things, higher SES typically affords the material resources to practice a healthy lifestyle. This may include having enough disposable income to purchase healthier but often costlier food options or the ability to afford a gym membership. In addition, higher SES status means one might live in a "safe" neighborhood where one feels comfortable jogging or walking, or a neighborhood that has ready access to grocery stores where fresh fruits and vegetables can be purchased (Gordon-Larsen, Nelson, Page, & Popkin, 2006; more on these things later in the essay). When we consider access to these kinds of resources, health disparities look less like the result of poor choices and more like a systemic issue reflecting race and class inequalities.

Although the focus of health disparities research has traditionally been on the goods and services that tangible resources such as money can buy, increasing attention has been directed toward the physiological burden imposed by the stress of having low SES. In a normal stress response, when encountering a perceived threat, the body activates itself through mechanisms such as increased blood flow and the release of hormones such as cortisol and norepinephrine (adrenaline). In the short term, the stress response is adaptive, with its heighted physiological resources making either a "fight" response (face the threat) or a "flight" response (flee the threat) possible. But when one is constantly assailed by chronic stressors such as poverty and racial discrimination, the stress response remains activated, leading to wear and tear on the body, measured in part by biomarkers for accelerated aging, or *allostatic load* (McEwen & Stellar, 1993). Poverty is a common chronic stressor for disadvantaged people of color; important recent studies find that although allostatic load levels are similar among Blacks and Whites at age 20, Blacks accumulate allostatic load at a more rapid rate than Whites across the life course. This is evidence of cumulative disadvantage that results in the "weathering" (accelerated aging) of Black bodies (Geronimus, Hicken, Keene, & Bound, 2006). Similar weathering was found among low-income individuals relative to those with higher income. Although this study did not include other groups besides Whites and Blacks, it is reasonable to believe that these biological processes also operate among other people of color.

Following the social gradient argument, we would expect that controlling for SES—that is, comparing apples to apples (high-status Whites to high-status people of color)—would eliminate the persistent ethnoracial disparities we have witnessed for decades. In other words, the argument is often made that *people of color experience worse health outcomes relative to Whites because they are more likely to be poor and have lower educational attainment; if that weren't the case, ethnoracial health inequities would disappear.* But is this true?

A simple and customary way to answer this question is by comparing the earnings of Whites and people of color *at the same level of education.* All things being equal, if SES can explain the worse health profiles of people of color relative to Whites, then there should be no health differences between low-SES Whites and low-SES people of color.

Using the argument that lower SES accounts for health inequities facing disadvantaged people of color, we would expect that people of color with at least a bachelor's degree would have the same earnings as Whites with at least a bachelor's degree; in essence, (high) educational similarity would erase the negative health consequences associated with being a person of color. But does this argument hold weight? Among those with the highest education (at least a bachelor's degree), White men and Asian men earn $1,448 and $1,495 per week, respectively, compared with far lower earnings among the highest-educated Black men ($1,103) and Latino men ($1,167). Similar but weaker patterns exist among women; the highest-educated White and Asian women outearn the highest-educated Black women (U.S. Bureau of Labor Statistics, 2016). In other words, achieving advanced education does not afford the same economic benefits for Blacks and Latinos as it does for Whites and Asians.

The "diminishing returns" pattern between SES and health has been detailed extensively by others (Farmer & Ferraro, 2005; Williams & Sternthal, 2010). After controlling for SES indicators such as educational attainment and income, Blacks (and to a less consistent degree, Latinos) still have more negative health profiles than Whites (Braveman, Cubbin, Egerter, Williams, & Pamuk, 2010; Kawachi, Daniels, & Robinson, 2005; Williams, 2012). In other words, when comparing high-SES people of color with high-SES Whites, health disparities persist. Taken together, the body of evidence for this argument is weak at best. The data clearly debunk the notion that disadvantaged people of color exhibit poor health outcomes simply because they are more likely to rank low on indicators of SES. Ethnoracial disparities persist even after accounting for lower SES among people of color.

Argument 2: Health Disparities Are Due to Unhealthy Behaviors Among People of Color

Another common trope to explain poor health outcomes among disadvantaged people of color is that they are more likely to engage in unhealthy behaviors than Whites are. Many of these behaviors (e.g., smoking, unhealthy eating, drinking, and lack of exercise) are indeed major risk factors for many of the chronic illnesses discussed in the epidemiological overview above. Below, I detail the evidence for the health behaviors argument, using both data from federal governmental agencies (e.g., Centers for Disease Control and Prevention) and empirical evidence from the longitudinal Whitehall studies.

Smoking. Data on age-adjusted prevalence of current cigarette smoking by race/ethnicity and gender can be found in Figure 20.3 (National Center for Health Statistics, 2016). Among men, White men have similar age-adjusted prevalence of current smoking compared to Blacks and American Indians/Alaska Natives (21.3% vs. 21.9% and 23.1%, respectively). Latino men (15.7%) and Asian men (14.8%) are far less likely to smoke. Among women, White women are the most likely to smoke (18.7%), though American Indian/Alaska Native women also have high prevalence of current smoking (18.2%). Smoking prevalence is considerably lower among Black women (14.4%) and Latina women (14.4%) and drastically lower among Asian women (5.2%).

Figure 20.3   Age-Adjusted Prevalence of Current Cigarette Smoking by Race/Ethnicity and Gender, United States, 2012 to 2014

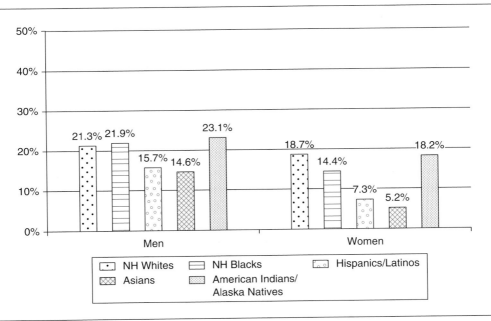

Source: National Center for Health Statistics (2016, Table 49).

As a whole, this means that although American Indians/Alaska Natives often have the highest rate of current smoking (fitting squarely within the health behaviors argument), smoking prevalence among Whites is also quite high. Among men, current smoking prevalence among White men is similar to that of Black men and much higher than that of their Latino and Asian counterparts. Among women, White women have the highest prevalence of current smoking, with similar prevalence among American Indian/Alaska Native women. However, current smoking prevalence among White women is substantially higher than that of Black women and especially Latina and Asian women. Given these rates, smoking does not appear to be an important driver of ethnoracial health inequities.

Healthy Eating. Diet is a well-known risk factor for virtually every single chronic illness. People who eat healthfully have markedly lower risk of mortality, heart disease, cardiovascular disease, diabetes, some cancers, and a host of other chronic conditions. Obesity is the most common measure of healthy eating and is an important independent risk factor; people who eat in an unhealthy fashion are more likely to both acquire and die from these chronic illnesses.[3] Body weight categories are typically constructed based on body mass index, or BMI (weight in pounds/height in inches * 703). *Overweight* is defined as having a BMI between 25 and 29.9, and *obesity* is defined as having a BMI of 30 or larger. Roughly 1 in 3 Americans are currently overweight, and another 1 in 3 are obese (U.S. Department of Health and Human Services, 2012).

Are there ethnoracial differences in the prevalence of overweight/obesity? If so, the logic goes, these differences could help explain the enduring ethnoracial health disparities in this country. Based on the age-adjusted prevalence data in Figure 20.4, there are important differences in healthy eating among men, though perhaps not as stark as expected (National Center for Health Statistics, 2016). Among men, almost 80% (79.6%) of Latinos are either overweight or obese, but notably, White men have the second-highest prevalence of overweight/obesity (73.7%). Much like the case with cigarette smoking, although one group of color (in this case, Latinos) has a higher prevalence of the behavior, Whites rank second highest in the prevalence of that behavior, followed by other groups of color (Black men at 69.6% and Asian men at only 46.9%). The trends in overweight/obesity for women are starker, however. More than 80% of Black women are obese, followed by 77.1% of Latina women. This trend fits well with the health behaviors argument. However, White women rank in the middle of the pack; 63.5% of them are either overweight or obese. Prevalence among Asians (who rank lowest in overweight/obesity) is about half that of Whites (who rank second lowest). Only roughly one third (34.4%) of Asian women are either overweight or obese.

Taken together, there is little evidence that overweight/obesity (measured as a proxy for the health behavior of healthy eating) can account for ethnoracial health inequities among men, although the patterns for women suggest that these may represent important risk factors for Black and Latina women.

Figure 20.4 Prevalence of Age-Adjusted Overweight or Obese Adults, by Race/Ethnicity and Gender, United States, 2011 to 2014

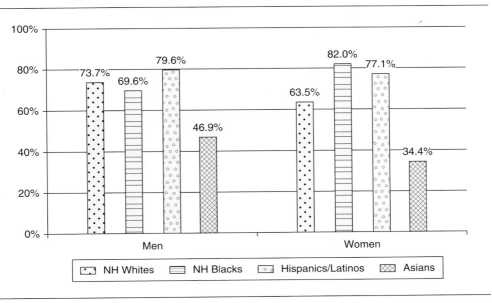

Source: National Center for Health Statistics (2016, Table 58).

Exercise. Similar to unhealthy eating, lack of exercise is a major risk factor for many chronic illnesses. Based on guidelines from the federal government, adults in the United States should engage in 150 minutes per week of moderate-intense activity (e.g., brisk walking, gardening) or 75 minutes per week of vigorous-intense activity. In 2012, more than half of Whites (53.7%) and 47.5% of Asians met aerobic activity guidelines. Rates of exercise were somewhat lower for American Indians (44.1%), Blacks (43.6%), and Latinos (42.9%) (Blackwell et al., 2014). These patterns suggest moderately lower rates of physical activity among disadvantaged people of color than among Whites.

Substance Use. Data on heavy drinking, illicit drug use, and exercise can be found in Figure 20.5 (National Center for Health Statistics, 2016). Heavy alcohol use is defined as drinking five or more drinks on the same occasion on each of 5 or more days in the past 30 days.[4] Roughly 9.1% of American Indians/Alaska Natives meet the criteria for heavy drinking in the past month, the highest prevalence of all groups, though Whites ranked second highest at 7.1%. Heavy drinking is less common among Latinos (5.1%), Native Hawaiians/Other Pacific Islanders (4.6%), and Blacks (4.5%) and is extremely rare among Asians (2.0%). This means that Whites are actually *more likely* to be heavy drinkers than disadvantaged groups of color.

Figure 20.5 also displays data on any illicit drug use within the past month (National Center for Health Statistics, 2016). Native Hawaiians/Other Pacific Islanders have the highest prevalence of any illicit drug use (15.6%), followed by American Indians/Alaska Natives (14.9%). Drug use prevalence is somewhat lower among Blacks (12.4%),

Figure 20.5 Prevalence of Heavy Drinking, Illicit Drug Use, and Aerobic Activity, by Race/Ethnicity, United States, 2011 to 2014

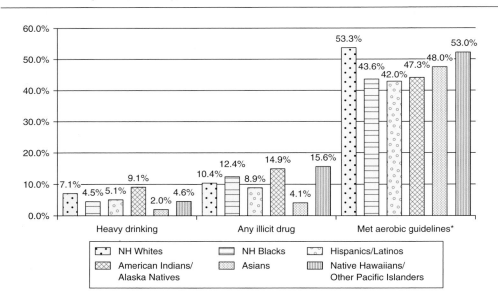

Sources: Heavy drinking and illicit drug use were derived from National Center for Health Statistics (2016, Table 50). Aerobic guidelines were derived from National Center for Health Statistics (2015, Table PA-1a).

Whites (10.4%), and Latinos (8.9%); rates are lowest among Asians (4.1%). It is also important to note that the recent opioid abuse epidemic is almost exclusively concentrated among Whites. A total of 82% of opioid overdose deaths in 2014 occurred among Whites, while only 8% of such deaths occurred among Blacks and only 7% occurred among Hispanics (Kaiser Family Foundation, 2015). In fact, the unprecedented recent drop in life expectancy among Americans has almost wholly been attributed to the opioid epidemic, a phenomenon that occurs far more often among Whites than among people of color. As a whole, the available data suggest that substance use is *not* consistently higher among people of color than among Whites; as such, it is highly unlikely that substance use accounts for the intractable racial/ethnic disparities in health in the United States.

Health Behaviors in the Whitehall Studies. In addition to documenting the social gradient in health, findings from the Whitehall studies have offered essential contributions to our understanding of the extent to which health behaviors can explain health inequities. A study using 25 years of Whitehall data found that health behaviors accounted for only one third of the socioeconomic difference in mortality. In other words, two thirds of mortality differences between those of low SES and those of higher SES were explained *by causes other than health behaviors* (van Rossum, Shipley, van de Mheen, Grobbee, & Marmot, 2000). These patterns were subsequently replicated in the United States using nationally representative data from the Americans' Changing Lives survey. Even after controlling for cigarette smoking, alcohol drinking, BMI, and physical activity, those with high income had far lower risk of mortality over 7 years than those of the lowest and middle income (Lantz et al., 1998). Although these findings are based on socioeconomic disparities in health (rather than ethnoracial health disparities, specifically), the findings are instructive and suggest that, given the large overlap between race and SES, health behaviors contribute modestly (at best) to ethnoracial health disparities.

Overall, the epidemiological evidence for the health behaviors argument is mixed. Although people of color sometimes exhibit poorer health behaviors than Whites (e.g., lower rates of exercise and higher rates of overweight/obesity), Whites are either equally likely or more likely to engage in certain unhealthy behaviors (e.g., cigarette smoking, heavy drinking, and illicit drug use) than most groups of color. Another problem with the health behaviors argument is that it presumes a moral failing among people of color—that people of color could easily choose to engage in healthy behaviors but simply opt not to. Before falling into such simplistic thinking, however, it is imperative to consider the social context in which these health behaviors arise, by considering characteristics of the social and economic environment that often preclude disadvantaged people of color from making healthier "choices." I undertake this argument in the following section.

Argument 3: Health Disparities Are Due to Unequal Neighborhoods That Constrain Healthy Choices for People of Color

The World Health Organization defines *social determinants of health* as "the conditions in which people are born, grow, live, work and age," further stating that these conditions "are shaped by the distribution of money, power and resources at global, national and local levels." SES and health behavior—the focus of the two previous arguments for understanding ethnoracial health disparities—are social determinants of health that largely operate at the individual level. To be clear, it certainly matters whether or not people smoke, exercise, or eat a high-fat diet. Yet a singular focus on individual-level factors will do little to address health injustices facing communities of color. This is because individual characteristics such as health behaviors and SES are largely shaped by broader, more wide-ranging social determinants of health that influence, for example, the opportunities to achieve high SES or engage in healthy behaviors. Unequal neighborhoods—and the historical forces that shaped their development (e.g., residential segregation)—better explain the ethnoracial health disparities than do individual-level factors such as health behaviors.

The legacy of residential segregation has relegated many people of color to living in underresourced neighborhoods characterized by concentrated poverty.[5] Residential segregation is an example of institutionalized racism, or unfair treatment toward people of color that is embedded in social systems such as the labor market, the criminal justice and educational systems, and public policy broadly speaking (as opposed to discriminatory acts that occur at the individual level, between people). Of all racial/ethnic groups, rates of Black–White residential segregation show the starkest patterns. For example, in 2010, 59% of Blacks would have had to move to another neighborhood for Whites and Blacks to be evenly distributed across neighborhoods. Conversely, 49% of Hispanics and 41% of Asians would have had to move to achieve equal racial composition across neighborhoods (Logan, 2013).

Neighborhoods directly pattern life opportunities in a multitude of ways that influence health (LaVeist, Gaskin, & Trujillo, 2011). For one, the built environment of neighborhoods determines the availability of amenities and resources that can impact health. For example, the ability to exercise is strongly influenced by whether or not a neighborhood has safe parks, sidewalks, and recreational facilities. The ability to seek health care—preventive or otherwise—depends largely on a neighborhood's availability of health care facilities and providers. The ability to eat healthy foods is strongly contingent on the presence of large-scale supermarkets in a neighborhood, stores that are far more likely to carry a wide range of fresh fruits and vegetables than corner stores or bodegas. In addition to these healthy neighborhood resources, neighborhoods can also be characterized by the presence of negative resources that are harmful to health. Density of liquor stores and fast-food outlets is also known to negatively impact rates of alcohol use and unhealthy eating (LaVeist, Pollack, Thorpe, Fesahazion, & Gaskin, 2011).

While neighborhood parks, recreational facilities, health care facilities, and supermarkets can directly affect the opportunity to achieve good health, other neighborhood characteristics and institutions can indirectly affect health disparities. For example, the quality of public schools available in a community largely predicts college readiness and later economic success. Given the aforementioned links between SES and health, the inability to attain higher education has important implications for future health status. Likewise, employment opportunities or lack thereof (another indicator of SES) matter for health. Sociologist William Julius Wilson has studied the "spatial mismatch" at length, finding a direct link between the flight of jobs from urban communities and long periods of Black joblessness, especially among men (Wilson, 1990).

Policing is another neighborhood social determinant of health that has recently gained traction both in the popular media and in the scientific literature. Police violence contributes to unnecessary and unfair loss of life among men and women in communities of color. Notably, "legal intervention" (*deaths caused* by police and other persons with *legal* authority to use deadly force, excluding *legal* executions) was a leading cause of death for Black, Latino, and Native American men aged 20 to 24 in 2014. Beyond police violence, over-policing and aggressive policing tactics within disadvantaged communities can lead to hypervigilance and other negative mental health consequences for people of color (Sewell, Jefferson, & Lee, 2016). Mass incarceration—a trend largely targeting disadvantaged communities of color—also has lifelong consequences for health (Schnittker, Massoglia, & Uggen, 2011).

Unfortunately, health-promoting features of neighborhoods (e.g., sidewalks and safe parks, recreational facilities, health care services, supermarkets, quality educational systems, access to employment opportunities) are far more prevalent in affluent White communities, while health-damaging characteristics (e.g., liquor stores, fast-food outlets, failing public schools, over-policing, unemployment and underemployment) are far more prevalent in poor communities of color (LaVeist, Pollack, et al., 2011). Therefore, disadvantaged people of color often face an insidious combination of lack of health-promoting resources and an abundance of health-depleting characteristics, which decreases the range of healthful options available to them.

A useful (ecological) theoretical model for understanding social determinants of health can be found in Figure 20.6. SES, health behavior, and medical care (the innermost circles) are examples of social determinants of health at the individual level. These downstream factors are most proximal to health outcomes and, as such, are often targeted as the main causes of health disparities. Such an approach is extremely shortsighted, however. These factors are shaped by broader upstream forces, such as living and working conditions at the meso level (the intermediate set of circles) and economic and social opportunities and resources at the macro level (the largest overlapping concentric circles). The macro level shapes social conditions at the meso level, which also helps determine opportunities and constraints at the individual level. Put simply, individual-level characteristics (e.g., health behavior) do not occur in a vacuum.

Relatedly, although initially developed to explain health disparities based on gender, the *theory of constrained choices* can and should be applied to the study of ethnoracial health disparities. This theory takes as its starting point the notion that not all subgroups have the same range of opportunities to live a healthy lifestyle (Bird & Rieker, 2008). Put simply, health education approaches that seek to teach disadvantaged people of color either the value of healthy eating or how to eat in a healthy fashion will fail spectacularly in communities that lack supermarkets. Teaching the value of physical

Figure 20.6 Upstream and Downstream Social Determinants of Health

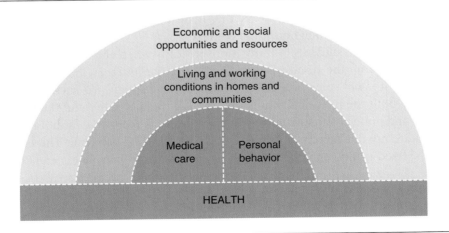

Source: Adapted from Braveman et al. (2010).

activity (more pointedly, assuming that people of color do not already value exercise) will do little to improve rates of physical inactivity when there are no sidewalks on which to walk, safe parks in which to walk or jog, or affordable recreation centers or gyms in which to exercise.

What is the evidence supporting neighborhoods as the key driver of ethnoracial health inequities? Data from the Exploring Health Disparities in Integrated Communities (EHDIC) study provide a prime site to test this argument directly. EHDIC is a multisite cohort study of health disparities in racially integrated communities across the United States. Its first site in southwest Baltimore (EHDIC-SWB) features a community in which Blacks and Whites have similar household incomes, effectively isolating racial (i.e., Black–White) differences in health disparities by controlling for SES. Therefore, studies from the EHDIC data collection effort allow for the comparison of Blacks and Whites with similar SES (both individual and community) who live under identical neighborhood conditions.

One important EHDIC study found that Black–White disparities in hypertension, diabetes, obesity (among women only), and the use of health care services were either wholly eliminated or narrowed substantially in this neighborhood (LaVeist, Pollack, et al., 2011). Other EHDIC studies compared Black–White health disparities in southwest Baltimore (again, where Whites and Blacks live in equal residential contexts) to Black–White health disparities in national datasets (that are unable to make neighborhood adjustments). When considering health behaviors such as binge drinking and physical activity and health outcomes such as diabetes and hypertension, EHDIC studies show minimal or no health disadvantage among Blacks relative to Whites. Conversely, Black–White health disparities are sizable in national datasets that control for individual SES and health behaviors but do not consider neighborhood context (Fesahazion, Thorpe, Bell, & LaVeist, 2012; LaVeist, Thorpe, Galarraga, Bower, & Gary-Webb, 2009; Thorpe, Brandon, & LaVeist, 2008; Wilson-Frederick et al., 2014). Findings from the EHDIC studies strongly support the notion that ethnoracial health disparities are due neither to individual-level SES differences nor differences in individual human behaviors. Instead, they are strongly patterned by systematic differences in neighborhood context.

I always encourage students to think more critically when encountering or offering solutions that blame the disadvantaged for their circumstances. Inequality is not a natural event. It is not some benign outcome that just happens. As such, it is imperative to study both the historical events that created the inequality and the contemporary social and political circumstances that perpetuate it over time. Ethnoracial health disparities are not due merely to differences in SES or health behavior. Therefore, they will not be fixed using simplistic approaches such as health awareness and education programs. Likewise, policy initiatives based on the faulty premise that poor health outcomes among people of color are due to their poor choices (e.g., the recently proposed American Health Care Act) will greatly exacerbate health inequities that already exist, further fueling these stereotypes. Unless and until this country musters the political will to address inequitable neighborhoods, disadvantaged people of color will continue to unfairly live shorter and sicker lives than their White counterparts.

Dawne M. Mouzon, PhD, is a sociologist and assistant professor at the Edward J. Bloustein School of Planning and Public Policy at Rutgers, the State University of New Jersey. Her research largely focuses on identifying causal mechanisms to explain the *Black–White paradox in mental health*, or the unexpected finding that African Americans and Afro-Caribbeans typically exhibit better mental health outcomes than Whites despite their lower socioeconomic standing and greater exposure to discrimination. She directs the undergraduate Health Disparities Certificate Program at Rutgers University, where she teaches introductory and advanced courses in health disparities.

NOTES

1. Also, where possible, I present rates for non-Hispanic Whites and non-Hispanic Blacks (as opposed to including those of Hispanic origin in these groups).

2. The Native Hawaiian/Other Pacific Islander group has conventionally been combined with the Asian racial category, despite considerably higher socioeconomic status among Asians. In light of this awareness, the OMB Directive 15 (1997) called for the use of two separate categories for Asian and Native Hawaiian/Other Pacific Islander. Where possible, I will present separate data for these two categories.

3. It is important to note that rates of overweight and obesity are only a rough proxy for healthy eating. Recent evidence shows that other factors are also implicated, though to a lesser degree than healthy eating (i.e., genes and family history, conditions such as hypothyroidism and Cushing's syndrome; National Heart, Lung, and Blood Institute, 2012).

4. By definition, all heavy alcohol users are also binge alcohol users (drinking five or more drinks on the same occasion on at least 1 day in the past 30 days).

5. Though beyond the scope of this particular essay, it is important to know that residential segregation was not a natural event. Instead, it was created by federal housing policy established by President Roosevelt's New Deal legislation in the 1930s and reinforced by subsequent state and local policies and practices that limited access to residential mortgages for people of color, especially outside of poor neighborhoods (see Ioanide in this volume).

SUGGESTED ADDITIONAL RESOURCES

LaVeist, T. A., Gaskin, D., & Trujillo, A. J. (2011). *Segregated spaces, risky places: The effects of racial segregation on health inequalities.* Washington, DC: Joint Center for Political and Economic Studies.

National Center for Health Statistics. (2016). *Health, United States, 2015: With special feature on racial and ethnic health disparities.* Hyattsville, MD: Author.

Williams, D. R., & Sternthal, M. (2010). Understanding racial/ethnic disparities in health: Sociological contribution. *Journal of Health and Social Behavior, 51*(Suppl.), S15–S27.

QUESTIONS FOR FURTHER DISCUSSION

1. What, if any, of the health issues discussed here are problems for members of your own family? What are some of the reasons why, according to family discussions? (How) are those explanations similar to or different from those discussed by the author?

2. (Why) is it important to think about health outcomes at the individual and group level? How do these differences connect to patterns discussed in other essays in this volume?

REACHING BEYOND THE COLOR LINE

1. With other members of your class, take some time to build a "health map" of your neighborhood or community. Identify the parks, playgrounds, places with sidewalks, gyms, and so forth. What patterns can you see?

2. In 2015, the average Supplemental Nutritional Assistance Program (SNAP, formerly known as "food stamps") benefit per month was $142 for a single person. Using information from the U.S. Department of Agriculture on the five food groups, brainstorm with your classmates about how to use the monthly SNAP benefit allotment to eat (for the full month) according to USDA recommendations. What challenges do you face?

3. Living at, near, or below the poverty line can be stressful. Go to http://playspent .org and explore some of the daily stressors experienced by people living in poverty. How might those experiences affect health?

REFERENCES

Adler, N. E., & Ostrove, J. M. (1999). Socioeconomic status and health: What we know and what we don't. *Annals of the New York Academy of Sciences, 896,* 3–15.

American Stroke Association. (2017). About stroke. Retrieved from http://www.strokeas sociation.org/STROKEORG/AboutStroke/About-Stroke_UCM_308529_SubHome Page.jsp

Bird, C. E., & Rieker, P. P. (2008). *Gender and health: The effects of constrained choices and social policies.* Cambridge, UK: Cambridge University Press.

Blackwell, D. L., Lucas, J. W., & Clarke, T. C. (2014). Summary health statistics for U.S. adults: National health interview survey, 2012. *Vital Health Statistics, 10*(260). Retrieved from https://www.cdc.gov/nchs/data/series/sr_10/sr10_260.pdf

Braveman, P. A., Cubbin, C., Egerter, S., Williams, D. R., & Pamuk, E. (2010). Socioeconomic disparities in health in the United States: What the patterns tell us. *American Journal of Public Health, 100*(Suppl. 1), S186–S196.

Centers for Disease Control and Prevention. (2014). Effects of high blood pressure. Retrieved from https://www.cdc.gov/bloodpressure/effects.htm

Diabetes Research Institute. (2016). What is diabetes? Retrieved from https://www.diabetesre search.org/what-is-diabetes

Farmer, M. M., & Ferraro, K. F. (2005). Are racial disparities in health conditional on socioeconomic status? *Social Science & Medicine, 60*(1), 191–204.

Ferrie, J. E., Shipley, M. J., Smith, G. D., Stansfeld, S. A., & Marmot, M. G. (2002). Change in health inequalities among British civil servants: The Whitehall II study. *Journal of Epidemiology and Community Health, 56*(12), 922–926.

Fesahazion, R. G., Thorpe, R. J., Bell, C. N., & LaVeist, T. A. (2012). Disparities in alcohol use: Does race matter as much as place? *Preventive Medicine, 55*(5), 482–484.

Gee, G. C., Ro, A., Shariff-Marco, S., & Chae, D. (2009). Racial discrimination and health among Asian Americans: Evidence, assessment, and directions for future research. *Epidemiologic Reviews, 31*(1), 130–151.

Geronimus, A. T., Hicken, M., Keene, D., & Bound, J. (2006). "Weathering" and age patterns of allostatic load scores among Blacks and Whites in the United States. *American Journal of Public Health, 96*(5), 826–833.

Gordon-Larsen, P., Nelson, M. C., Page, P., & Popkin, B. M. (2006). Inequality in the built environment underlies key health disparities in physical activity and obesity. *Pediatrics, 117*(2), 417–424.

Kaiser Family Foundation. (2015). *Opioid overdose deaths by race/ethnicity, 2014*. Washington, DC: Author. Retrieved from kff.org/other/state-indicator/opioid-overdose-deaths-by-raceethnicity/

Kawachi, I., Daniels, N., & Robinson, D. E. (2005). Health disparities by race and class: Why both matter. *Health Affairs (Project Hope), 24*(2), 343–352.

Lantz, P. M., House, J. S., Lepkowski, J. M., Williams, D. R., Mero, R. P., & Chen, J. (1998). Socioeconomic factors, health behaviors, and mortality: Results from a nationally representative prospective study of US adults. *Journal of the American Medical Association, 279*(21), 1703–1708.

LaVeist, T. A., Gaskin, D., & Trujillo, A. J. (2011). *Segregated spaces, risky places: The effects of racial segregation on health inequalities*. Washington, DC: Joint Center for Political and Economic Studies.

LaVeist, T., Pollack, K., Thorpe, R., Fesahazion, R., & Gaskin, D. (2011). Place, not race: Disparities dissipate in southwest Baltimore when Blacks and Whites live under similar conditions. *Health Affairs, 30*(10), 1880–1887.

LaVeist, T. A., Thorpe, R. J., Galarraga, J. E., Bower, K. M., & Gary-Webb, T. L. (2009). Environmental and socio-economic factors as contributors to racial disparities in diabetes prevalence. *Journal of General Internal Medicine, 24*(10), 1144. https://doi.org/10.1007/s11606-009-1085-7

Lewis, K., & Burd-Sharps, S. (2015). *American human development report: The Measure of America, 2013-2014*. Brooklyn, NY: Measure of America, Social Science Research Council. Retrieved from http://www.measureofamerica.org/wp-content/uploads/2013/06/MOA-III.pdf

Logan, J. R. (2013). The persistence of segregation in the 21st century metropolis. *City & Community, 12*(2), 160–168.

Macartney, S., Bishaw, A., & Fontenot, K. (2013). *Poverty rates of selected detailed race and Hispanic groups: 2007–2011* (No. ACSBR/11-17). Washington, DC: U.S. Census Bureau.

Marmot, M. G., Shipley, M. J., & Rose, G. (1984). Inequalities in death—specific explanations of a general pattern? *Lancet (London, England), 1*(8384), 1003–1006.

Marmot, M. G., Smith, G. D., Stansfeld, S., Patel, C., North, F., Head, J., White, I., . . . Feeney, A. (1991). Health inequalities among British civil servants: The Whitehall II study. *The Lancet, 337*(8754), 1387–1393.

Mayo Clinic Staff. (2014). Diseases and conditions: Heart disease. Retrieved from http://www.mayoclinic.org/diseases-conditions/heart-disease/basics/definition/con-20034056

McEwen, B. S., & Stellar, E. (1993). Stress and the individual: Mechanisms leading to disease. *Archives of Internal Medicine, 153*(18), 2093–2101.

National Center for Health Statistics. (2015). *Health behaviors of adults: United States, 2011–2014*. Washington, DC: Author. Retrieved from https://ftp.cdc.gov/pub/Health_Statistics/NCHS/NHIS/SHS/2011-2014_AHB_Table_PA-1.pdf

National Center for Health Statistics. (2016). *Health, United States, 2015: With special feature on racial and ethnic health disparities*. Hyattsville, MD: Author.

National Heart, Lung, and Blood Institute. (2012). *What causes overweight and obesity?* Retrieved from http://www.nhlbi.nih.gov/health/health-topics/topics/obe/causes

Ogunwole, S. U., Drewery, M. P., Jr., & Rios-Vargas, M. (2012). *The population with a bachelor's degree or higher by race and Hispanic origin, 2006–2010* (American Community Survey Briefs No. ACSBR/10-19). Washington, DC: U.S. Census Bureau. Retrieved from http://www.census.gov/library/publications/2012/acs/acsbr10-19.html

Pew Research Center. (2011). *Wealth gaps rise to record highs between Whites, Blacks, and Hispanics*. Washington, DC: Pew Research Center.

Schnittker, J., Massoglia, M., & Uggen, C. (2011). Incarceration and the health of the African American community. *Du Bois Review: Social Science Research on Race, 8*(1), 133–141.

Sewell, A. A., Jefferson, K. A., & Lee, H. (2016). Living under surveillance: Gender, psychological distress, and stop-question-and-frisk policing in New York City. *Social Science & Medicine, 159*, 1–13.

Thorpe, R. J., Jr., Brandon, D. T., & LaVeist, T. A. (2008). Social context as an explanation for race disparities in hypertension: Findings from the Exploring Health Disparities in Integrated Communities (EHDIC) study. *Social Science & Medicine, 67*(10), 1604–1611.

U.S. Bureau of Labor Statistics. (2016). *Labor force characteristics by race and ethnicity, 2015* (No. 1062). Washington, DC: Author. Retrieved from http://www.bls.gov/opub/reports/race-and-ethnicity/2015/home.htm

U.S. Department of Health and Human Services. (2012). *Overweight and obesity statistics*. Washington, DC: Author. Retrieved from https://www.niddk.nih.gov/health-information/health-statistics/Pages/overweight-obesity-statistics.aspx

van Rossum, C. T. M., Shipley, M., van de Mheen, H., Grobbee, D., & Marmot, M. (2000). Employment grade differences in cause specific mortality: A 25-year follow-up of civil servants from the first Whitehall study. *Journal of Epidemiology and Community Health, 54*(3), 178–184. https://doi.org/10.1136/jech.54.3.178

Williams, D. R. (2012). Miles to go before we sleep: Racial inequities in health. *Journal of Health and Social Behavior, 53*(3), 279–295.

Williams, D. R., & Sternthal, M. (2010). Understanding racial-ethnic disparities in health sociological contributions. *Journal of Health and Social Behavior, 51*(Suppl.), S15–S27.

Wilson, W. J. (1990). *The truly disadvantaged: The inner city, the underclass, and public policy* (Reprint ed.). Chicago, IL: University of Chicago Press.

Wilson-Frederick, S. M., Thorpe, R. J., Bell, C. N., Bleich, S. N., Ford, J. G., & LaVeist, T. A. (2014). Examination of race disparities in physical inactivity among adults of similar social context. *Ethnicity & Disease, 24*(3), 363–369.

Xu, J., Murphy, S. L., Kochanek, K. D., & Bastian, B. A. (2016). *Deaths: Final data for 2013* (National Vital Statistics Report No. 64). Atlanta, GA: Centers for Disease Control and Prevention. Retrieved from http://www.cdc.gov/nchs/data/nvsr/nvsr64/nvsr64_02.pdf

"Now All the Good Jobs Go to Them!"

Affirmative Action in the Labor Market

Wendy Leo Moore

Texas A&M University

In September of 1965, President Lyndon B. Johnson signed Executive Order 11246, prohibiting discrimination on the basis of race, color, religion, sex, or national origin in federal public contracts. This executive order, in addition to prohibiting discrimination, called for federal contractors to "take affirmative action to ensure that applicants are employed, and that employees are treated during employment, without regard to race, color, sex or national origin." The innocuous command of EO 11246, to act affirmatively to ensure people are treated equally, contrasts sharply with contemporary rhetoric concerning affirmative action. These two words have come to signify conflicting meanings concerning U.S. democracy and racial inequality; the mere mention of the term *affirmative action* can lead to heated and emotional debates including assertions of "unfair race-based privilege" or "reverse discrimination" (see Curry, 1996; Pierce, 2012).

By the 1990s, the discourse surrounding affirmative action had shifted from one about discrimination and equality to one about White innocence and injury resulting from the hiring of unqualified people of color. Pierce (2012) notes that throughout the 1990s, media stories slanted against affirmative action were much more common than stories in support of affirmative action—as many as 3:1 tilted against affirmative action (p. 35). In January of 1994, the topic of affirmative action made the cover story of *Business Week*, where the issue was titled "White, Male and Worried," and the July 1995 *Newsweek* cover read "Race and Rage" (Pierce, 2012, p. 27). The discursive framing of affirmative action had shifted dramatically from the frame constructed by President Johnson in 1965. The sentiment is summed up by a 2011 blogger on world-inconversation.org who responded to a question about opinions of affirmative action by saying, "I don't agree with hiring someone who may or may not be less qualified than someone else just because their race needs to be represented better"[1] (see also Bonilla-Silva, 2009; Moore, 2008). To understand this debate and also the context of President Johnson's command for affirmative action, it is necessary to journey into the history of race and government action.

Where the Story Begins: A Legacy of Affirmative Action for Whites

Most of the informed public is aware of the history of racialized slavery in the United States, the institution through which Blackness became a justification for the enslavement of people of African descent (see Harris, 1993). During the centuries of slavery in this country, race and class converged as people of color were prohibited from access to resources such as education, property, and political rights. As Cheryl Harris (1993) suggests, the economic interests of Whites were so integral to the law and politics of the United States that Whiteness itself was valued by the government like a form of property. Initially, this occurred through explicit legal and political policies concerning who had the right to own property (Whites), who did not (American Indians), and who became the object of property (Blacks). However, for at least 100 years after the end of slavery, U.S. law and social policy continued to overtly and explicitly privilege the economic interests of Whites, perpetuating the material value of Whiteness.

The end of racialized slavery did not mean the end of systematic racial oppression. After the Civil War, Southern states immediately enacted laws, such as those making vagrancy or joblessness a crime, which forced Blacks back into exploitative economic relations (Du Bois, 2001; Woodward, 2002). A new economic system, based on tenant farming, sharecropping, and a convict-lease system, combined with legally mandated segregation, supported by the Supreme Court in the 1896 case of *Plessy v. Ferguson,* resulted in a racial order that was not meaningfully different from slavery (Woodward, 2002). Within this social and historical context begins the real story of a legacy of affirmative action *for Whites*—that is, affirmative government action taken to protect and stabilize the economic conditions of White people during times of economic disruption.

At the end of the 1920s, the world experienced a severe economic depression. Millions of Americans were thrown into joblessness and poverty. The widespread suffering caused by the Great Depression led to support for massive government intervention. In the 1930s, President Franklin D. Roosevelt proposed and signed into law a series of legislative initiatives designed to ease economic suffering. Roosevelt's New Deal legislation created federally funded unemployment insurance, public assistance for the poor, old age pensions, and work relief for the unemployed, and injected federal funds into severely depressed local economies (Takaki, 2008). These programs were the most extensive government economic aid interventions in the history of the United States, and they helped end the severe economic depression. Yet, to secure the Southern votes necessary to enact the New Deal legislation, Southern states required that terms be implemented to ensure that these policies would not disrupt the racial status quo of Jim Crow (Katznelson, 2005).

Three mechanisms allowed Whites to benefit from government economic assistance while Blacks were excluded (Katznelson, 2005, pp. 22–23). First, work-related policies such as unemployment and social security were constructed to leave out as many Blacks as possible through racially coded definitions of work. New Deal employment-related policies excluded individuals employed in farm-related or domestic-labor jobs. Nationwide, in the 1930s, 60% of Blacks were employed in these sectors; in the South, that figure was 75%. Thus, the vast majority of Black workers were excluded from all the federal employment assistance programs. The second mechanism that functioned to exclude Blacks from federal benefits was the placement of the administration of federal funds in the hands of local officials. In the South, this resulted in widespread racial discrimination in the implementation of these programs and the enactment of explicitly racist policies at the local level; the level of poverty required to qualify for financial aid was set much lower for Blacks than for Whites (see Katznelson, 2005, p. 37). And finally, Southern House and Senate members resoundingly rejected the attachment of antidiscrimination provisions to the legislation. The lack of antidiscrimination measures in the New Deal bills facilitated Southern states' segregation and racist policies with regard to the administration of federal aid programs, leaving no recourse for Blacks denied federal assistance by local administrators.

The New Deal "combined unprecedented [levels of government] assistantship with racist policies," the result of which was a program of affirmative government action created to end economic suffering largely for Whites only (Katznelson, 2005, p. 29). But the New Deal policies were not the end of affirmative action for Whites. During and after World War II, economic shifts led to more government actions to stabilize the economy. When the United States entered World War II, there was an immediate need for military to fight in the war effort. Many White men left their jobs to join the military (or were drafted), which resulted in a shortage of workers in Northern industrial jobs. Blacks faced widespread discrimination in the military, either through complete exclusion from service or, when they were allowed to serve, exclusion from advanced military training programs necessary for skilled positions (Katznelson, 2005; Takaki, 2008). By contrast, employers with labor shortages engaged in a campaign to recruit Black workers to take positions from which Blacks had previously been excluded. These new job opportunities, on the one hand, and the desire to escape the racist violence of the South on the other, facilitated an unprecedented migration of Blacks from the rural South to the urban North (Massey & Denton, 1993). Unfortunately, however, these jobs were not permanent. At the end of World War II, when White men returned from military service, many Blacks lost the jobs they had been recruited for.

At the same time, a widespread housing shortage and desire to ensure postwar economic stability led the federal government, at the end of World War II, to enact the Selective Service Readjustment Act, widely known as the GI Bill. The GI Bill assisted veterans with buying homes, attending college, getting loans to start up small businesses, and finding skill-appropriate jobs. Many young veterans, most of them White, used these government services and as a result were able to move into the middle class (Katznelson, 2005; Massey & Denton, 1993). As well, the GI Bill, in combination with the construction of the Federal Housing Authority, which provided government subsidies enabling Americans to secure loans to purchase homes without huge down payments, facilitated a boom in homeownership, the result of which was the largest swelling of the middle class in U.S. history (Massey & Denton, 1993). However, repeating a history of White economic advantage, the boom in the middle class occurred disproportionately for Whites. The majority of Blacks were shut out through explicit discrimination in the implementation of the GI Bill, which like the New Deal programs took place at the local level, as well as through policies of discriminatory lending and racial segregation.

Black veterans wishing to access the education assistance of the GI Bill found that there were not enough spaces for them in Black educational institutions, but they were excluded from White institutions in the South completely and Northern schools allowed only a small number of non-White applicants each year. In 1947, 20,000 Black veterans eligible for GI Bill education assistance could not find schools to attend because Black colleges and vocational schools were filled (Katznelson, 2005, p. 133). Blacks, veterans, and nonveterans wishing to purchase homes were excluded in two ways. First, many Blacks faced explicit discrimination from local administrators of the GI Bill, as well as from banks, so they were not able to secure loans to purchase homes. Second, residential segregation and lending policies often meant that even those who could qualify for loans could not find neighborhoods where they could purchase homes. White neighborhoods were off limits to Blacks through legal instruments such as racially restrictive covenants and government policies that favored segregation, so they could not secure loans for houses in these White neighborhoods (Massey & Denton, 1993). Black neighborhoods were in a state of economic crisis—resulting mainly from the massive loss of employment that occurred as Blacks were displaced from jobs they had been recruited for when White men returned from military service. The result of the poverty and economic instability in these neighborhoods meant that banks could "redline" Black neighborhoods, which literally meant that these neighborhoods had red lines across them on maps, signifying they were ineligible for federally secured housing loans (Massey & Denton, 1993).

Katznelson (2005) notes, "There was no greater instrument for widening an already huge racial gap than the G.I. Bill" (p. 121). The reason for the widening economic gap was not just racial discrimination against Blacks, which was nothing new, but instead was a result of the widespread *upward mobility* of huge numbers of Whites resulting from affirmative government actions to facilitate their economic security and growth. Thus, affirmative government actions resulted in the racially unjust enrichment of Whites and corresponding unjust impoverishment of Blacks (see Feagin, 2010, p. 10).

It was within this context on June 4, 1965, only months before President Johnson issued Executive Order 11246, that he called for affirmative government action to create equality in his speech "To Fulfill These Rights" at Howard University. Acknowledging the connection between racial inequality and government action, Johnson said

You do not take a person who, for years, has been hobbled by chains and liberate him, bring him up to the starting line of a race and then say, "you are free to compete with all the others," and still justly believe that you have been completely fair . . . [E]qual opportunity is essential, but not enough, not enough. Men and women of all races are born with the same range of abilities. But ability is not just the product of birth. Ability is stretched or stunted by the family that you live with, and the neighborhood you live in—by the school you go to and the poverty or the richness of your surroundings.

The U.S. government, which had for centuries acted affirmatively to create economic stability and prosperity for Whites, would now have to act not merely passively by no longer permitting racial discrimination but affirmatively again to correct the structural racial inequalities resulting from centuries of racial discrimination.

Affirmative Inaction: The Policy That Wasn't

Although President Johnson articulated a government obligation to take affirmative steps beyond just ending discrimination to create economic security for Blacks, Johnson's view of affirmative action never came to pass. There occurred a political backlash against affirmative action, one that has been virulent and pervasive throughout the decades since Johnson's speech. Rhetorical assertions of the supposed unfairness of unqualified minorities' gaining access to jobs that should go to Whites as a result of quotas, as illustrated in the introduction to this chapter, have guided that backlash into a frenzied attack on the idea of affirmative action (Pierce, 2012). What is particularly confounding about this anti-affirmative action sentiment is that U.S. law does not permit quotas as part of affirmative action programs. In fact, the language of Title VII of the 1964 Civil Rights Act that prohibited racial discrimination in employment also explicitly prohibits quota-type systems. Section 703(j), titled "Preferential treatment not to be granted on account of existing number or percentage imbalance," specifies that

> nothing contained in [this subchapter on nondiscrimination in employment] shall be interpreted to require any employer . . . to grant preferential treatment to any individual or to any group because of the race, color, religion, sex, or national origin of such individual or group on account of an imbalance which may exist with respect to the total number or percentage . . . employed by any employer.

Moreover, in 1978, the U.S. Supreme Court ruled definitively on the issue of quotas in the case of *The Regents of the University of California v. Bakke*, outlawing quota systems, even as a remedy for historical discrimination, in higher education admissions (Greene, 1989).

Rigid quotas were never legal, and there was never an intention to create a system of affirmative action employing such a method. What affirmative action was, then, was a system of laws and policies designed to allow educational institutions and businesses to take into consideration the social consequences of racial inequality when making decisions about *equally* qualified candidates in school admissions and employment. Affirmative action occurred in two ways in employment. First, private (nongovernment) employers were legally able to enact *voluntary* affirmative action programs as part of a program to increase their numbers of underrepresented groups, including racial minorities (see Greene, 1989; Pierce, 2012; Reskin, 1998). The types of voluntary affirmative action programs employers could enact ranged from advertising in news outlets catering to people of color to recruiting from schools that are predominantly of color to giving preference to an *equally qualified* candidate for hire or promotion because the person was a member of a group underrepresented in the institution (Greene, 1989). Note, however, that when private businesses choose to implement voluntary affirmative action plans that include giving preference to underrepresented groups in hiring and promotion decisions, they must take on the heavy burden of documenting that their business does in fact have an underrepresentation (this must include statistical demonstration) and that their race-conscious employment decisions are based only on otherwise equally qualified candidates and will remain only until the underrepresentation is remedied (Greene, 1989). The burden of this requirement is one reason many businesses do not implement this form of affirmative action (as opposed to purely recruiting programs).

The second labor market arena in which affirmative action–based programs take place is in federal contract compliance. Federal agencies and employers who hold federal contracts in excess of $50,000 must demonstrate that they are "affirmative action compliant," which means that they are taking positive steps to increase racial equality in their organizations (Greene, 1989; Pierce, 2012). To be compliant with this regulation, businesses must illustrate that they are making a "good faith" effort to recruit underrepresented minorities (they need not actually recruit underrepresented minorities, only show a good faith effort). Although President Johnson conceived of an affirmative action program that would set aside a percentage of government contracts (10% to be exact) for qualified minority-owned businesses (businesses whose ownership was at least 50% racial minorities), the U.S. Supreme Court rejected that program as unconstitutional, first prohibiting state government set-asides in the 1989 *City of Richmond v. J. A. Croson Co.* case, then federal contract set-asides in the 1995 *Adarand Constructors, Inc. v. Peña* case. Thus, even this limited attempt at redistribution of government resources to remedy racial inequalities was declared unconstitutional.

There is one other area of government policy that has sometimes mistakenly been considered affirmative action; it is not actually affirmative action at all but antidiscrimination enforcement. The enactment of the civil rights legislation of the 1960s, which prohibited discrimination on the basis of race in U.S. institutions and organizations such as education and employment, was met with resistance, particularly in the South. For example, in 1972 the Alabama Department of Public Safety was held to have engaged in "egregious discrimination" by systematically excluding Blacks from employment and promotion among state troopers. After the initial finding of discrimination, the department failed to enact remedies to correct the discrimination, particularly in the promotion of Black employees. As a result, in 1981 the court ordered that the department promote one Black trooper for every White trooper promoted until the systematic discrimination was remedied (see *United States v. Paradise*, 1987). Court orders such as this one may be a source for the myth that affirmative action means quotas and "reverse discrimination"; yet these remedies were not affirmative action but punitive court-ordered sanctions for failing to comply with antidiscrimination laws.

Racial inequality continues to organize U.S. society today, as it did before the civil rights movement. The inequalities in wealth resulting from the housing boom experienced by Whites post–World War II, which largely excluded people of color, has left us with extreme and pervasive racial inequalities in wealth (Massey & Denton, 1993; Oliver & Shapiro, 2006). In 2011, the census reports that the median net worth (total assets minus total debt) of White, non-Hispanic families was $110,500, whereas the median wealth of non-White and Hispanic families was $41,408.[2] These figures, because they compare Whites to all non-Whites, obscure the disparities between White and Black families; the Pew Research Center reported that in 2014, White family wealth had declined (possibly due to the housing crisis) to a median of $144,200, but median family wealth for Blacks in 2014 was only $11,200.[3] This difference in wealth, as Melvin Oliver and Thomas Shapiro (2006) explain, means differential access to equity, which may be used for such things as collateral for education or small-business loans and a cushion during times of economic recession. Blacks and other people of color do not have the same access to these resources as Whites, and this is largely the structural result of wealth disparities solidified post–World War II.

Wealth inequality is distinct from inequality in income and employment. In 2009, 11.3% of Black families made less than $10,000 per year, compared with 4.2% of White families. On the opposite end of the spectrum, among families that made between $100,000 and $149,999 per year, 15.7% of White families were represented and only 8.1% of Black families (U.S. Bureau of Labor Statistics, 2011).

This can be partially explained by the fact that Blacks remain overrepresented in unskilled labor. As Bonilla-Silva (2013) notes, in managerial and professional occupations, we find "35.43 percent of white males and 40.64 percent of white females, compared to 21.65 percent of black males and 31 percent of black females" (p. 55), whereas in service-related occupations, we find "20.23 percent of black males and 26.39 percent of black females compared to 10.85 percent of white males and 17.03 percent of white females" (pp. 55–56). Although much of this inequality can be linked to inequalities in education, researchers also continue to find persistent patterns of racial discrimination in employment (see, e.g., Bendick, Jackson, Reinoso, & Hodges, 1991; Pager, 2003).

Thus, affirmative action—as a policy originated to remedy the unjust enrichment of Whites and unjust impoverishment of people of color resulting from years of government-sponsored racial discrimination—has widely failed. Although exceptional individual Blacks and other Americans of color have probably benefited from affirmative action programs (and it is hard to know what portion of the benefit is a result of nondiscrimination, as opposed to true affirmative action programs), these programs have failed to change the inequalities in the racial social structure. Moreover, a 1995 study conducted by the U.S. Department of Labor revealed that of the 300 cases filed by Whites against employers for so-called "reverse discrimination," only *six* cases were found to have been unlawfully based on race. The rest of the cases involved erroneous assumptions, on the part of Whites who did not receive jobs or promotions, that affirmative action was used to give less-qualified minorities the position (Pierce, 2012, p. 39). Thus, much of the vehement criticism and debate concerning "reverse discrimination" and preferences for undeserving or unqualified minorities is simply factually inaccurate.

White Racial Framing: Turning the Myth of Reverse Discrimination on Its Head

Given that quotas, as well as all allocation programs that consider racial demographics in any meaningful way, have been declared illegal, it is curious that the rhetoric of quotas and reverse racism persists. Even more curious is the continued persistence of heated and emotional debates concerning affirmative action in the face of its clear failure to affect structural racial inequality. Sociologist Jennifer L. Pierce (2012) notes that the notion of reverse discrimination against victimized Whites became part of a dominant narrative in the post–civil rights era and thus became a "broader cultural memory" (p. 3). The cultural memory of the victimization of Whites by affirmative action supplanted our memory of a legacy of affirmative government action *for* Whites and President Johnson's comment that equal opportunity was not enough to remedy the resulting racial inequality. Because of that shift in cultural memory, Whites massively rejected and resisted affirmative action (as well as antidiscrimination laws), and the result is that affirmative action has been a bust as a policy.

This process is an example of what Joe R. Feagin (2006) has called "White racial framing." The *White racial frame* can be defined as "an organized set of racialized ideas, emotions, and inclinations, as well as recurring or habitual discriminatory actions, that are consciously or unconsciously expressed in, and constitutive of the routine operation and racist institutions of US society" (p. 23). This frame facilitates the development of a cultural memory of (false) White victimization and the collective forgetting of a legacy of (true) racial advantage for Whites and oppression of people of color. If we were to reject the White racial frame and reframe the debate about affirmative action in the context of the structural reality that President Johnson emphasized in his Howard speech, we could create a new and more accurate argument concerning affirmative action: Racially conscious affirmative action is *necessary* for democracy and the assessment of individuals based solely on their merit. Historical and current racial conditions provide Whites with unfair advantages in the form of access to resources that have been denied to people of color. To prevent Whites from feeling inferior because their successes are not based on merit alone, but instead stem from unearned privilege, we must institute affirmative action programs that correct for structural racial differences and racial oppression. This will result in a better system of evaluation of the talents and contributions of all individuals based on their relative access to resources.

Wendy Leo Moore is an associate professor of sociology at Texas A&M University and the author of the award-winning 2007 book *Reproducing Racism: White Space, Elite Law Schools, and Racial Inequality,* published by Rowman & Littlefield. Her research focuses on the intersections of race and law.

NOTES

1. What is your opinion of affirmative action, and has the lecture had an effect on you? 119 Blog. (2011, February 23). World Conversation Project. Retrieved June 9, 2012, from http://www.worldinconversation.org/2011/02/23/what-is-your-opinion-of-affirmative-action-and-has-thelecture-had-an-effect-on-you-119-blog/.

2. See https://www.census.gov/topics/income-poverty/wealth.html.

3. See http://www.pewsocialtrends.org/2016/06/27/1-demographic-trends-and-economic-well-being/.

SUGGESTED ADDITIONAL RESOURCES

Feagin, J. R. (2006). *The White racial frame.* New York, NY: Routledge.

McIntosh, P. (2003). White privilege: Unpacking the invisible knapsack. In S. Plous (Ed.), *Understanding prejudice and discrimination* (pp. 191–196). New York, NY: McGraw-Hill.

Pierce, J. (2012). *Racing for innocence: Whiteness, gender, and the backlash against affirmative action.* Stanford, CA: Stanford University Press.

Reskin, B. (1998). *The realities of affirmative action in employment.* Washington, DC: American Sociological Association.

Wise, T. (2005). *Affirmative action: Racial preference in Black and White.* New York, NY: Routledge.

Websites

African American Policy Forum: http://www.aapf.org

American Association for Access, Equity, and Diversity: https://www.aaaed.org

American Civil Liberties Union: http://www.aclu.org/racial-justice/affirmative-action

Americans for a Fair Chance: http://www.civilrights.org/equal-opportunity/fact-sheets/fact_sheet_packet.pdf

U.S. Department of Labor: https://www.dol.gov/ofccp/regs/compliance/ca_11246.htm

QUESTIONS FOR FURTHER DISCUSSION

1. Watch the YouTube video titled "Unequal Opportunity Race," created by the African American Policy Forum (http://www.youtube.com/watch?v=eBb5 TgOXgNY). Talk about the elements of structural racism visually presented in the video and the discussions about material inequality presented in this chapter. What role, if any, should government play in the dismantling of racial inequality? Does it matter that government policies facilitated the creation of racial inequality?

2. What do you think of the counterframe presented at the end of this chapter? Would merit be more accurately evaluated if we considered people's accomplishments in relation to their access to differential resources?

3. Given that quotas and the hiring of less-qualified people of color over more-qualified Whites is not legal affirmative action, why do you think the myth of quotas has had such staying power?

4. How do you think the current myths about affirmative action affect the experiences of people of color who are presumed to be in institutions (employment and education) as a result of affirmative action and not their qualifications?

5. In a democracy, what is the relevance of racial inequality, or conversely, does a democracy require a commitment to some level of racial equality?

REACHING BEYOND THE COLOR LINE

1. Imagine that you are the chief human resources officer for a major company in a diverse city and your board has asked you to develop a diversity plan to ensure that the company is truly providing equal opportunities to the community in which it is located. Using the materials you've learned from this reading, develop a diversity plan for the company that considers the following:

   • Recruiting (i.e., where will you advertise for your hires or go to locate your workforce?)
   • Hiring (i.e., how will individual applicants be evaluated in the hiring process?)
   • Retention (i.e., what kinds of steps will you take to ensure that people from different backgrounds feel welcome in your company?)
   • Promotion (i.e., what kinds of trainings or opportunities for promotion will you implement so people from diverse backgrounds will rise to positions of experience and power?)

REFERENCES

Adarand Constructors, Inc. v. Pena, 515 U.S. 200 (1995).

Bendick, M., Jackson, C. W., Reinoso, V. A., & Hodges, L. E. (1991). Discrimination against Latino job applicants: A controlled experiment. *Human Resource Management, 30*(4), 469–484.

Bonilla-Silva, E. (2009). *Racism without racists* (3rd ed.). Lanham, MD: Rowman & Littlefield.

Bonilla-Silva, E. (2013). *Racism without racists* (4th ed.). Lanham, MD: Rowman & Littlefield.

City of Richmond v. J. A. Croson Co., 488 U.S. 469 (1989).

Curry, G. (Ed.). (1996). *The affirmative action debate.* Reading, MA: Addison-Wesley.

Du Bois, W. E. B. (2001). The spawn of slavery: The convict lease system in the South. In S. Gabbidon, H. Greene, & V. Young (Eds.), *African American classics criminology and criminal justice* (pp. 83–88). Thousand Oaks, CA: Sage.

Feagin, J. R. (2006). *The White racial frame.* New York, NY: Routledge.

Feagin, J. R. (2010). *Racist America* (2nd ed.). New York, NY: Routledge.

Greene, K. (1989). *Affirmative action and principles of justice.* New York, NY: Greenwood Press.

Harris, C. (1993). Whiteness as property. *Harvard Law Review, 106*(8), 1709–1795.

Johnson, L. B. (1965, June 4). "To fulfill these rights." Commencement address at Howard University, Washington, DC. Retrieved from http://www.presidency.ucsb.edu/ws/?pid=27021

Katznelson, I. (2005). *When affirmative action was White: An untold history of racial inequality in twentieth-century America.* New York, NY: W. W. Norton.

Massey, D., & Denton, N. (1993). *American apartheid: Segregation and the making of the underclass.* Cambridge, MA: Harvard University Press.

Moore, W. L. (2008). *Reproducing racism: White space, elite law schools and racial inequality.* Lanham, MD: Rowman & Littlefield.

Oliver, M., & Shapiro, T. (2006). *Black wealth/White wealth: A new perspective on racial inequality.* New York, NY: Routledge.

Pager, D. (2003). The mark of a criminal record. *American Journal of Sociology, 108,* 937–975.

Pierce, J. L. (2012). *Racing for innocence: Whiteness, gender, and the backlash against affirmative action.* Stanford, CA: Stanford University Press.

Plessy v. Ferguson, 163 U.S. 537 (1896).

Reskin, B. (1998). *The realities of affirmative action in employment.* Washington, DC: American Sociological Association.

Takaki, R. (2008). *A different mirror* (Rev. ed.). New York, NY: Bay Back Books.

The Regents of the University of California v. Bakke, 438 U.S. 265 (1978).

United States v. Paradise, 480 U.S. 149 (1987).

U.S. Bureau of Labor Statistics. (2011, August). *Labor force characteristics by race and ethnicity, 2010.* Washington, DC: U.S. Department of Labor, Bureau of Labor Statistics. Retrieved from https://www.bls.gov/opub/reports/race-and-ethnicity/archive/race_ethnicity_2010.pdf

Woodward, C. V. (2002). *The strange career of Jim Crow.* New York, NY: Oxford University Press.

"Why Do They Get to Use the N-Word but I Can't?"

Privilege, Power, and the Politics of Language

Geoff Harkness

Rhode Island College

Nigger may be the most controversial word in the history of the English language, capable of provoking everything from outrage to violence when uttered by the "wrong" person or in the wrong context. In 2010, conservative talk-radio host Dr. Laura Schlessinger shocked listeners by using the term repeatedly during an on-air rant. "Black guys use it all the time," Schlessinger declared during the tirade. "Turn on HBO and listen to a Black comic, and all you hear is nigger, nigger, nigger. I don't get it. If anybody without enough melanin says it, it's a horrible thing. But when Black people say it, it's affectionate. It's very confusing." Schlessinger issued a public apology the following day but announced her retirement from nationally syndicated radio a week later. (She eventually moved to a satellite channel.)

The outcry over Schlessinger's liberal use of the N-word was partially attributable to the word's history as a racist term: It dates to at least the 17th century, when it was applied to slaves as an insult (Asim, 2007). Schlessinger's initial defense, however, echoed the same question raised by many White students today: Isn't it unfair that Whites are prohibited from saying a word that Blacks are allowed to use without prohibition? After all, Black comedian Chris Rock went from bit player to superstar after declaring during a 1996 comedy routine that he "hated niggas" and hoped to join the Ku Klux Klan. A decade later, actor Michael Richards instantly torpedoed his career after screaming the N-word at a group of Black hecklers during a stand-up comedy appearance. Is there a double standard here, based on race? And what do we make of Paula Deen, the White southern restaurateur and celebrity chef who lost numerous endorsement deals after she testified during a 2013 court case that "of course" she had used the N-word? In defending herself during a *Today Show* interview, Deen swore that her use of the term did not mean that she was racist, arguing: "It's very distressing to me to go into my kitchens and I hear what these young people are calling each other. . . . These young people are gonna have to take control and start showing respect for each other and not throwing that word at each other."

Deen's and Schlessinger's "analyses" are shortsighted at best and represent a denial of the word's rooting in our troubled racial history. For many Blacks and non-Blacks alike, the word is a powerful symbol of the history of anti-Black oppression in the United States. On its own, the word has come to represent the virulent and violent institutions of slavery, Jim Crow, and a post–Jim Crow era marked by varied forms of institutional racism. In June 2015, President Barack Obama made international headlines for mentioning the word in a discussion about the ongoing problem of racism toward Blacks in the United States. In an interview for the podcast *WTF with Marc Maron*, Obama said,

> Racism, we are not cured of it. And it's not just a matter of it not being polite to say "nigger" in public. That's not the measure of whether racism still exists or not. It's not just a matter of overt discrimination. Societies don't, overnight, completely erase everything that happened 200 to 300 years prior.

Certainly, the term has been applied to enslaved Africans and to men and women lynched during legalized segregation, and it is *still* applied toward Blacks in a negative fashion. For example, in August 2013, a famed statue of Black baseball legend Jackie Robinson was vandalized in Brooklyn, New York, including the words "Die nigger" scrawled in black marker. In October 2013, self-proclaimed White supremacist Kynan Dutton disrupted a town council meeting in Leith, North Dakota, ranting about what he perceived to be a lack of civil rights for White people: "You treat me worse than a freakin' black man in the [19]60s. . . . I'm not a nigger; I shouldn't be treated liked one." In May 2013, police arrested five White males for beating a Black man on the streets of Seattle. Because witnesses overheard the accused calling the victim "nigger" during the beating, the five were charged with a hate crime. Yet a good deal of the controversy and confusion over the term arises from its frequent use in rap music.

A Bad Rap?

Frequent and varied use of the N-word in present-day rap music remains a common—albeit controversial—claim to authenticity. Some believe that the use of the word in rap music has stripped it of its original racist meaning; others assert that any use of the term should be forbidden. This debate is further complicated by overlapping and intertwined matters of race, social class, and gender, all of which impact one's "right" to say America's most controversial word.

Nigga, a derivation of the pejorative *nigger,* has become somewhat commonplace, particularly in rap music, where it has been deployed with growing frequency. Even so-called "conscious" rappers say it often (Asim, 2007). Among the primary justifications for the widespread use of the N-word in rap music is that it has undergone what linguist Geneva Smitherman (1997) calls *semantic inversion,* or a process whereby people "take words and concepts from the [English] lexicon and either reverse their meanings or impose entirely different meanings" (p. 17). In this context, the N-word is no longer a racist term but one whose original meaning is reversed to symbolize camaraderie or affection. When Kanye West raps that he's got his "niggas in Paris," in a 2012 song of the same title, this is how it is intended and interpreted. In June 2012, however, White actress Gwyneth Paltrow caused a minor stir in Paris, France, when she attended a concert by West and Jay-Z and tweeted "Ni**as in paris for real." The Twitterverse instantly lit up with accusations of racism, while Paltrow defended herself by tweeting, "Hold up. It's the title of a song!" Thus, even in contexts where White use of the word is intended to signify the inverted use of the term, it can be interpreted as symbolizing its original racist meaning, which is important for Whites to understand when using the term. As historian Jeffrey O. G. Ogbar (2007), author of *Hip-Hop Revolution: The Culture and Politics of Rap,* explains, "Black people have refused Whites' opportunity to partake in the term, whether they hope to use it affectionately or not. . . . The Black intolerance for White use of the N-word clearly reflects the sensitivity of the word to Black people and the resilience of its power" (p. 67). Nevertheless, the N-word is routinely employed in rap music and other entertainment outlets, where its use is further complicated by matters of gender and class.

Gender, Class, and the N-Word

Musicologist Emmett Price (2006) points out that having exclusive right to the term in rap music places Blacks in a "subtle position of power" over other ethnoracial groups, especially Whites (p. 57). In this context, the N-word upends (however symbolically and temporarily) longstanding hierarchies of race by giving Blacks power and authority over Whites. This may help explain the appeal of rap music for Blacks, particularly young Black men, a historically marginalized group. Rap music is a space where this group is afforded a command and respect not found as easily in other realms of social life. Moreover, its use by Black men is not only an effort to upend racial hierarchies but also an attempt to reinforce masculinity and stake a claim to patriarchal power. Rap music often entails a hypermasculine performance, where the frequent usage of the N-word appears to play a key role in that performance. Even Black female MCs such as Eve, Foxy Brown, and Lil' Kim have employed the N-word frequently in their rhymes, typically as a means by which to accentuate both Blackness and masculinity. For example, on the posse track "The Illest," Jean Grae boasted that she would "fuck your girl like a nigga." In doing so, Grae made a claim to authenticity, equated here (as elsewhere in hip-hop culture) with both Blackness and maleness. Performance studies scholar Shanté Paradigm Smalls (2011) notes that Grae's lyrics are a declaration that she is "quite capable, because of her tremendous skill, of inserting herself into the position held for men" (p. 87).

White female rappers have also attempted to use the term, with a very different response. In 2011, Kreayshawn, a White female MC from Oakland, tweeted, "WTF YOU WANT FROM A NIGGA?! *DMX VOICE*." The tweet caused an immediate media and online stir, and received a swift denunciation from Black male rapper Game, who blasted Kreayshawn on a track titled "Uncle Otis": "Lil' White bitch, better stay in your place/You call me a nigga, I'ma put the K in your face." Game told a reporter, "You can't be playing with that word, some people will take it serious. Especially coming from someone that's [not Black]. There's a lot of tragic history behind it" (Rodriguez, 2011). Taken at face value, Game problematized the term due to its racist history, rather than its use by a woman. "Uncle Otis," however, implies that White "bitches" have a position subordinate to men and that women who challenge male authority by using the N-word can be subjected to violence.

When asked about the kerfuffle, Kreayshawn responded that she never used the N-word in her recorded music but occasionally did so when freestyling. In Oakland, she claimed, all racial groups routinely used the term and members of the lower classes should be allowed to do so. "That word is used in the low income community more than anything," she said. "I can see if I was some rich crazy trick and I was just saying this because it's hip-hop. No, I was raised around this. Me and my sisters were all raised around this. People call me that" (Gipson, 2011).

Communications scholar Kembrew McLeod links rap's emphasis on Black masculinity to "authenticity," or the socially constructed belief that something or someone is genuine, original, true, or pure. McLeod (1999) asserts that, "to its core community members, hip-hop remains strongly tied to Black cultural expression" and male dominance (p. 140). Thus, in rap music, Black masculinity denotes "keeping it real," while Whiteness and femininity are equated with artifice. According to McLeod, Black male rappers create verbal "rules" related to authenticity to preserve its "pure" core from co-option by outsiders, including Whites and women. Extending McLeod's theory to the N-word, the prohibition against White and female use of the term is a means by which Black men can protect rap music from White and/or female co-option by upholding the belief that authentic rap music is the exclusive domain of Black men. This strategy is complicated by the fact that rap music is also created and consumed by plenty of folks who do not fit the Black–White racial binary.

Beyond Black and White

Scholars of the N-word (Asim, 2007; Kennedy, 2003) tend to frame debates over its use as matters of Black versus White, but lots of rappers and rap-music fans who don't fit either ethnoracial category use the word. Concurrent with rap's rise in popularity, by the turn of the century, "numerous non-Black communities began using the term, and it became prominent in the lyrics of top-selling artists. Asian American, Latino, and numerous other non-Black practitioners and fans began to call one another by the term" (Price, 2006, p. 57). For example, Puerto Rican rapper Big Pun's posthumous 2000 CD, *Yeeeah Baby,* included a track called "Nigga Shit" that detailed his love for smoking pot, dealing drugs, getting drunk, going to jail, beating his children, "talkin' loud at flicks," and a host of additional Black "ghetto" stereotypes. Pun's appropriation of the N-word in the song could be viewed as a signifier of Black authenticity in a Black-dominated field: He portrayed himself as a "real nigga" with the pedigree to prove it. Backlash over the track was nonexistent and *Yeeeah Baby* sold more than half a million copies within months of its release. This raises an important question: If Black use of the term is considered acceptable and White use is forbidden, where do Latinos and other ethnoracial groups fit into the debate?

Ogbar (2007) points out that Latino rap acts such as Cypress Hill, Fat Joe, and Cuban Link have employed the N-word in their songs without censure, while artists such as Kid Frost have avoided it. Ogbar believes that part of the reason for this is that Latinos who said the term generally had Caribbean lineage that afforded them a degree of leeway not enjoyed by rappers with Chicano roots. He argues that the division between Latinos of Caribbean and Chicano origin reveals

> (1) the historical, cultural, and social relationships between different Latino nationalities and African Americans and (2) African diasporic connections between people in the Caribbean and North America. Since the early twentieth century, Puerto Ricans and African Americans in New York City have had relatively close social relations in various cultural and political institutions from sports teams (professional and recreational), to residential areas, to musical groups, and to politics. (p. 48)

While it may be true that Puerto Ricans claim a unique relationship to Blacks that renders rappers from this group less scrutinized than Latino MCs of other ethnic backgrounds, studies of rap music (Harkness, 2008) find a conviction among Latino MCs of all ethnic backgrounds that these groups share historical, social, and cultural characteristics with Blacks in the United States, an opinion often echoed by Black rappers as well.

Still, even Puerto Rican artists find themselves under scrutiny when employing the N-word. For example, in Jennifer Lopez's 2001 remix of her song "I'm Real," featuring rapper Ja Rule, she sang this lyric: "Now people screamin' what the deal with you and so-and-so/I tell them niggas, mind their biz, but they don't hear me though." Lopez was lambasted across media outlets by Blacks (and others) who thought her use of the word was inappropriate. In some part, the critique was due to the fact that she isn't considered Black despite her Puerto Rican roots and diasporic connections and despite the fact that she dated prominent rap mogul Diddy (a.k.a. Sean "Puffy" Combs). The outcry might also have been due to her status as a woman; where Big Pun and other Puerto Rican rappers have been given a "pass," she was not and her claim to power through use of the word was firmly denied. The differences in these cases reiterate the complexities of the N-word's use among other groups of color.

Use of the term among Asian rappers provides further illustration of the controversies surrounding the N-word. Race and ethnicity scholar Nitasha Tamar Sharma's (2010) study of South Asian American (or "desi") rappers finds that male desis frequently use the N-word in referring to themselves and their friends, "particularly when there [are] no Black people around" (p. 241). While Sharma's desi MCs decry White use of the term as racist, in their own use of the word, they "emphasize their knowledge of context, respect for the music, and their position as non-White 'outsider' contributors" to rap music and hip-hop culture (p. 242). In February 2016, celebrity singer-actress Tila Tequila raised eyebrows with a series of Twitter posts that questioned Black ownership of the word. "You can't expect people of all races 2 listen to popular music and not have the N-word embedded into their heads," she wrote. Tequila, a first-generation American immigrant who was born in Singapore to a French Vietnamese mother and a Vietnamese father, received pushback for the tweet but insisted in another post, "If u want change then stop saying it in songs," before adding that rapper Nicki Minaj "has a song where she says 'Nigga' over 100 times. . . . What outcome did u expect?" Despite these and other arguments, some Blacks might find Asian use of the word offensive, particularly in light of the ways (some) Asian American groups are positioned as "model minorities" and thus enjoy a social prestige often not accorded to Blacks (for further discussion, see Zhou in this volume). Yet the question remains: Should Asians and any other non-Blacks be "allowed" to use the term?

In hip-hop culture—where Blackness is associated with authenticity and Whiteness with inauthenticity, and those who do not fit the Black–White racial binary fall somewhere in between—use of the N-word serves as a signifier of Blackness in a culture where Blackness is at the center of the status system. It also functions as a verbal means of distancing oneself from alleged White fakeness. Having the "right" to say the N-word is a claim to authenticity in a culture where "keeping it real" is paramount. Yet the fact remains that non-Black use of the word is questionable at best, offensive at worst. Essentially, artistic license aside, language is a powerful conveyor of inequality, where the N-word remains historically and presently loaded with connotations of racism and inequality. Nevertheless, it is sometimes the "artistic license" aspect of the term that leads to its use among non-Blacks, especially those in the rap industry. But race is not the only factor in whether or not an artist, group, or individual employs the term; among Blacks, class also factors into the word's use.

Class Matters

As alluded to above in the Kreayshawn example, class clearly plays a role in use of the N-word. Studies that frame its use as a simple matter of ethnoracial status overlook the crucial role of social class. While race is important, "more common, however, is the use of 'nigga' to describe a condition rather than skin color or culture. Above all, 'nigga' speaks to a collective identity shaped by class consciousness" (Kelley, 1996, p. 137).

Despite popular perceptions to the contrary, in terms of sheer numbers, most poor people in the United States are White, and most Blacks are members of the middle or working classes. In part, this is due to the ongoing expansion of the Black middle class, a group that is increasing numerically and as a percentage of the Black population (Marsh, Darity, Cohen, Casper, & Salters, 2007, p. 20; Pattillo-McCoy, 1999). These structural changes have impacted culture within the Black community: There is a growing cultural divide between middle-class Blacks and those from lower and working classes. Cherise Harris and Nikki Khanna (2010) point out that, "because of the conflation of race and class in America, middle-class culture is often understood as Whiteness and Blackness is understood as the behavior and experiences associated with the urban ghetto" (p. 644).

Within the Black middle class there is an emphasis on "academic excellence, conservative styles of hair and dress, proficiency in Standard English, and the values of sacrifice and delayed gratification" (Harris & Khanna, 2010, p. 653). Adopting such behaviors, however, does not come without penalty. Black people who do not dress, speak, act, and consume culture that symbolizes alleged Black low-income and working-class membership sometimes face accusations of selling out or being deemed inauthentically Black. As Harris and Khanna (2010) note, "Black middle-class respondents frequently describe rejection by other Blacks, often because of their lack of familiarity with Black lower-class culture that has in large part become the standard by which authentic Blackness is measured" (p. 652). From this perspective, Blacks who signal association with the upper and middle classes by refusing to say the N-word may be labeled inauthentic by low-income and working-class Blacks. Conversely, Blacks who signal association with the Black lower and working classes by saying the N-word may do so as a claim to authentic "hood" membership.

The perception that there are two "types" of Blacks, symbolized by linguistic differences associated with upper- and lower-class status, illustrates the increasing cultural, social, and economic disparities described by scholars of the Black middle class. Michael Eric Dyson (2005) writes of an *Afristocracy,* which he defines as "upper-middle-class Blacks and the Black elite who rain down fire and brimstone upon poor Blacks for their deviance and pathology, and for their lack of couth and culture" (pp. xiii–xiv). He contrasts this with what he calls the *Ghettocracy,* which consists of the Black underclass and working poor. Dyson's Ghettocracy construct also includes celebrity rappers "whose values and habits are alleged to be negatively influenced by their poor origins" (p. xiv) and who romanticize a fabled (and fictional) Black ghetto in their music and lifestyles.

These issues are not limited to the Black population. Similar class-based differences have been found in studies of the growing Latino middle class. For example, Rodriguez (1996) finds that Latinos are often stereotyped in the mainstream media as gangbangers or irate political activists. As occurs in the Black population, middle-class Latinos are accused by their working-class and low-income counterparts of being sellouts, White wannabes, and cultural traitors: "Apparently, retaining one's 'authentic' Latino ethnicity requires remaining in place both socioeconomically and geographically. Even the accomplished have often felt a need to feign 'street-wise' mannerisms and humble roots" (p. 2).

These class-based divisions, disparities, and tensions are reflected in rap music, mirrored, for example, in the perceived split between the so-called "conscious" rap subgenre and gangsta rap, where the N-word is found more frequently. According to historian Robin Kelley (1996), the style and sound of gangsta rap, including its use of the N-word, is partially a Black underclass response to the Black middle class. Gangsta rappers "remind listeners that they are still second-class citizens—'Niggaz'—whose collective lived experiences suggest that nothing has changed *for them* as opposed to the Black middle class. In fact, 'Nigga' is frequently employed to distinguish urban Black working-class males from the Black bourgeoisie" (p. 137).

Thus, in addition to its use as a linguistic divider between ethnoracial groups, the N-word is also deployed within ethnoracial groups to make class-based distinctions. From this point of view, the N-word is a discursive means of creating a space where, for example, working-class and low-income Blacks and Latinos have more power than their middle-class counterparts, thereby reversing social-class hierarchies found within ethnoracial categories. While scholars of rap music have spent considerable energy on matters of race and ethnicity, less attention has been afforded to social class, particularly within ethnoracial groups. Focusing on the intersection of ethnoracial status and social class offers a more complete understanding of present-day rap-music culture, including its varied use or non-use of the N-word.

Some scholars believe that rap music serves as a sort of racial melting pot that dis-integrates existing race-based tensions and allows for greater understanding between ethnoracial groups. For example, Pancho McFarland (2008) describes rap music as an "interethnic contact zone," a location where "young people of various ethnicities come together and exchange ideas, experiences, understandings, and analyses, resulting in profound changes in individuals and in the cultures of each group" (p. 173). Hip-hop scholar and author Bakari Kitwana (2005) asserts that White assimilation into hip-hop culture marks "the dawning of a new reality of race in America" (p. xii).

The politics of language surrounding the N-word, however, serve as a potent reminder that ethnoracial and social class divisions have hardly disappeared. Debates over who has the "right" to say the N-word or how using the term reflects on those who choose to say it or not say it illustrate how race, social class, and gender continue to be key means by which people remain divided. Nevertheless, what cannot be forgot-ten is the loaded history of the terms *nigger* and *nigga*, which is why they remain controversial in the first place.

Privilege, Power, and the N-Word

While most of this essay focuses on the N-word and the varied ways some justify its use, it is important to consider arguments for why it shouldn't be used. As noted above, the N-word is, to say the least, racially loaded and embedded in a long, trou-bled, and violent history of anti-Black oppression. As such, while it is commonly used in the rap industry, some White rappers don't believe they have the right to use the term. Eminem, easily the world's most prominent and respected White MC, has never used the term publically or on a commercial recording, saying to a *Rolling Stone* reporter in 2000, "That word is not even in my vocabulary" (DeCurtis, 2000, p. 18). When an early homemade recording of a teenage Eminem using the term in a derogatory manner surfaced a few years later, he immediately issued a public apology. What did Eminem understand that Paula Deen, Laura Schlessinger, and Kreayshawn didn't? Perhaps he understood that even as a prominent player in the Black-dominated rap industry, he was still a White man, and given his White privilege, it was inappropriate for him to use even a derivation of a word that has been used to oppress Black people in systematic fashion. In a 2011 interview for the Southern Poverty Law Center's magazine, *Teaching Tolerance*, Neal A. Lester (2011), dean of humanities and former chair of the English department at Arizona State University, argued:

> We know that as early as the 17th century, "negro" evolved to "nigger" as intentionally derogatory, and it has never been able to shed that baggage since then— even when black people talk about appropriating and reappropriating it. The poison is still there. The word is inextricably linked with violence and brutality on black psyches and derogatory aspersions cast on black bodies. No degree of appropriating can rid it of that bloodsoaked history.

Lester, who in 2008 taught the first ever college-level course designed to explore the word *nigger*, went on to discuss how students in his classes admit to using the term:

> In their circles of white friends, some are so comfortable with the N-word because they've grown up on and been nourished by hip-hop. Much of the commercial hip-hop culture by black males uses the N-word as a staple. White youths, statistically the largest consumers of hip-hop, then feel that they can use the word among themselves with black and white peers. . . . But then I hear in that same discussion that many of the black youths are indeed offended by [whites using the N-word]. And if blacks and whites are together and a white person uses the word, many blacks are ready to fight. So this word comes laden with these complicated and contradictory emotional responses to it. It's very confusing to folks on the "outside," particularly when nobody has really talked about the history of the word in terms of American history, language, performance and identity.

While this discussion from Lester further illustrates the complexity of the term's use, it also illustrates this unmistakable, simple truth: At its core, the word is freighted with a history of anti-Black racism and oppression that still resonates today. For these reasons, it cannot be casually used without consequence by Whites and other non-Blacks whose ancestors haven't been victimized by anti-Black oppression and who don't currently experience this kind of oppression. Moreover, as Lester (2011) indicates, Black use of the word as a method of reappropriation and reclamation may also be ineffective, as "the poison is still there." In this manner and in other ways, the power reclaimed by Blacks' reappropriation of the term may be temporary and fleeting in a society still characterized by institutional racism and the continued systematic subjugation of Black Americans.

Geoff Harkness is an assistant professor of sociology at Rhode Island College. His scholarship focuses on the interactive practices of youth cultures and the role of stratification in shaping the content and character of youth culture and identity. His research on hip-hop has been published in *Poetics, Cultural Sociology, American Behavioral Scientist, Journal of Popular Music Studies, Journal of Workplace Rights,* and *Contexts.* His book *Chicago Hustle and Flow* is an ethnography that examines street gangs and rap music through the lens of social class.

SUGGESTED ADDITIONAL RESOURCES

Asim, J. (2007). *The N word: Who can say it, who shouldn't and why.* New York, NY: Houghton Mifflin.

Forman, M., & Neal, M. A. (Eds.). (2012). *That's the joint! The hip-hop studies reader* (2nd ed.). New York, NY: Routledge.

Harkness, G. (2008). Hip hop culture and America's most taboo word. *Contexts, 7*(3), 38–42.

Harrison, A. K. (2009). *Hip hop underground: The integrity and ethics of racial identification.* Philadelphia, PA: Temple University Press.

Jeffries, M. (2011). *Thug life: Race, gender, and the meaning of hip-hop.* Chicago, IL: University of Chicago Press.

Kennedy, R. L. (1999–2000). Who can say "nigger"? And other considerations. *Journal of Blacks in Higher Education, 26,* 86–96.

Lacy, K. (2007). *Blue-chip Black: Race, class, and status in the new Black middle class.* Berkeley: University of California Press.

Oware, M. (2014). (Un)conscious (popular) underground: Restricted cultural production and underground rap music. *Poetics, 42,* 60–81.

Sharma, N. T. (2010). *Hip hop desis: South Asian Americans, Blackness, and a global race consciousness.* Durham, NC: Duke University Press.

Audio/Visual

Barack Obama discusses racism and other issues on the podcast *WTF with Marc Maron*: http://www.wtfpod.com/podcast/episodes/episode_613_-_president_barack_obama

A conversation about the N-word between rapper KRS-ONE and comedian Paul Mooney, titled "When the 'N' Word Is Part of a Routine": http://www.npr.org/templates/story/story.php?storyId=6560171

Radio Capicu discusses and debates Latino use of the N-word in a show titled "Should Latinos Use the 'N' Word?": http://www.blogtalkradio.com/radiocapicu/2008/02/28/radio-capicu-should-latinos-use-the-N-word

QUESTIONS FOR FURTHER DISCUSSION

1. Is the N-word more or less acceptable when stated by certain people? If so, for whom is it more or less acceptable? What role do race, social class, and gender play in this?

2. Do people make too big of a deal over the N-word? Do you believe that it has lost its original racist meaning?

3. Is the "-er" form of the N-word more offensive than the "-ga" form? Why or why not? Is the N-word acceptable in the context of rap music and hip-hop culture? Why or why not?

4. Would you feel comfortable saying the N-word in any context? If not, under which contexts would you feel comfortable or uncomfortable saying it? What are your reasons for this?

5. How is the N-word different from or similar to other forms of "injurious speech," such as *redneck*, *spic*, *chink*, *bitch*, *ho*, *gay*, *queer*, and *fag*?

REACHING BEYOND THE COLOR LINE

1. If you are a White student who says the N-word, think about when and how you use it. Do you say it publically and privately? Do you say it around people of color? Do you believe that there is a double standard for Whites when it comes to White use of the N-word? If yes, why do you think this double standard exists?

2. If you are a Black student who uses the N-word or doesn't use the N-word, what are your reasons for this decision? What standards or rules should apply to Whites when it comes to the term? Should all Whites be "allowed" to say the word or just certain Whites? If only certain Whites should be allowed to say it, which ones and why? What about those who do not fit the Black–White racial binary?

3. If you are a non-White and non-Black student who uses or does not use the N-word, what is your justification for this? Do you believe that there are different standards applied to different ethnoracial groups, such as Latinos, Asians, Arabs, Native Americans, and others, when it comes to the N-word? What are these standards, and why do you think they exist?

REFERENCES

Asim, J. (2007). *The N word: Who can say it, who shouldn't and why*. New York, NY: Houghton Mifflin.

DeCurtis A. (2000). Eminem responds: The rapper addresses his critics. *Rolling Stone, 846*, 18.

Dyson, M. E. (2005). *Is Bill Cosby right? Or has the Black middle class lost its mind?* New York, NY: Basic Civitas Books.

Gipson, B. (2011, June 8). Kreayshawn on that million dollar (?) deal with Columbia/Sony, being a femcee and working with Lil B and Snoop Dogg. *OC Weekly.* Retrieved from http://www.ocweekly.com/music/kreayshawn-on-that-million-dollar-deal-with-columbia-sony-being-a-femcee-and-working-with-lil-b-and-snoop-dogg-6598871

Harkness, G. (2008). Hip hop culture and America's most taboo word. *Contexts, 7*(3), 38–42.

Harris, C. A., & Khanna, N. (2010). Black is, Black ain't: Biracials, middle-class Blacks, and the social construction of Blackness. *Sociological Spectrum, 30*(6), 639–670.

Kelley, R. D. G. (1996). Kickin' reality, kickin' ballistics: Gangsta rap and postindustrial Los Angeles. In W. E. Perkins (Ed.), *Droppin' science: Critical essays on rap music and hip hop culture* (pp. 117–158). Philadelphia, PA: Temple University Press.

Kennedy, R. L. (2003). *Nigger: The strange career of a troublesome word.* New York, NY: Vintage.

Kitwana, B. (2005). *Why White kids love hip hop: Wankstas, wiggers, wannabes, and the new reality of race in America.* New York, NY: Basic Books.

Lester, N. (2011, Fall). Straight talk about the N-word. *Teaching Tolerance, 40.* Retrieved from http://www.tolerance.org/magazine/number-40-fall-2011/feature/straight-talk-about-N-word

Marsh, K., Darity, W. A., Cohen, P., Casper, L., & Salters, D. (2007). The emerging Black middle class: Single and living alone. *Social Forces, 86*(2), 1–28.

McFarland, P. (2008). Chicano hip-hop as interethnic contact zone. *Aztlán: A Journal of Chicano Studies, 33*(1), 173–183.

McLeod, K. (1999). Authenticity within hip-hop and other cultures threatened with assimilation. *Journal of Communication, 49*(4), 134–150.

Ogbar, J. O. G. (2007). *Hip-hop revolution: The culture and politics of rap.* Lawrence: University Press of Kansas.

Pattillo-McCoy, M. (1999). *Black picket fences: Privilege and peril among the Black middle class.* Chicago, IL: University of Chicago Press.

Price, E. (2006). *Hip hop culture.* Santa Barbara, CA: ABC-CLIO.

Rodriguez, G. (1996, October). *The emerging Latino middle class.* Malibu, CA: Pepperdine University Institute for Public Policy. Retrieved from http://publicpolicy.pepperdine.edu/davenport-institute/content/reports/latino.pdf

Rodriguez, J. (2011, July 22). Game says "Uncle Otis" is "just fun," not a Jay-Z Dis. *XXL.* Retrieved from http://www.xxlmag.com/xxl-magazine/2011/07/game-says-"uncle-otis"-is-just-fun-not-a-jay-z-dis/

Sharma, N. T. (2010). *Hip hop desis: South Asian Americans, Blackness, and a global race consciousness.* Durham, NC: Duke University Press.

Smalls, S. P. (2011). "The rain comes down": Jean Grae and hip hop heteronormativity. *American Behavioral Scientist, 55*(1), 86–95.

Smitherman, G. (1997). "The chain remain the same": Communicative practices in the hip hop nation. *Journal of Black Studies, 28*(1), 3–25.

"It's Appreciation, Not Appropriation! I Don't Know Why You're Offended!"

Understanding Exploitation and Cultural Appropriation

Brittney Dennis

Florida State University

In 2015, activist and actress Amandla Stenberg posted a video on social media about Black cultural appropriation, the process of taking another's culture and adopting it as one's own (Young, 2010). Stenberg, an African American teenage actress, posted the video with a fellow classmate as an assignment for a history class. Because of her status and platform as an actress, the video gained many views and received media attention. The video discussed aspects of Black culture in America such as music, the hip-hop industry, and hair, and showcased how the historical appropriation of these things by White artists has been used for their own benefit. Later that same year, Stenberg received critical attention again when she responded on social media to teen socialite Kylie Jenner after Jenner posted a picture of herself wearing a cornrow wig. Cornrows and other natural styles that are commonly associated with individuals of African descent have long been criticized as unprofessional or unacceptable for business settings (Byrd & Tharps, 2001; Thompson, 2008). Stenberg posted a reply to the picture, stating that what Jenner was doing was cultural appropriation, as she was profiting from wearing a Black hairstyle.

Many replies to Stenberg's response chastised her for starting an argument about race, as many were convinced that the original post by Jenner was merely meant to be a fun fashion statement. She eventually posted a reply reiterating that appropriation occurs when members of dominant-status groups are praised for exhibiting features or engaging in mannerisms of a subordinate group that is frequently discriminated against for engaging in the same behavior and practices. Cornrows (and other types of protective hairstyles, such as braids, for Black women with natural hair) have a meaning and history that disappears when appropriated. Cornrows serve as a protective style for many women with natural hair and are used to help hair maintain its length and fullness while also preventing breakage. Cornrows also serve as a symbol for fashion and creativity within the Black community in terms of the various designs possible. However, in White-dominated spaces, styles such as cornrows and braids are considered unprofessional and have even led to Black women being fired from their jobs and Black girls being punished in schools (Byrd & Tharps, 2014). By contrast, when Whites wear the same hairstyle, they are praised as "edgy" or "trendy." Moreover, hair is a part of one's presentation of self and is reflective of one's identity (Synnott, 1987; see also Goffman, 1959). It is also symbolic of beauty, economic power, status, and individual beliefs (Bellinger, 2007). Within African culture specifically, it reflects status, gender, ethnic origin, leadership role, personal taste, or place in the life cycle (Sieber & Herreman, 2000, p. 56; see also Bellinger, 2007). For all these reasons, Jenner's cornrow wigs are a form of cultural appropriation ultimately designed to capitalize on elements of Black and African culture while Blacks who wear cornrows are deemed unprofessional and undesirable.

Perhaps a good example of how Blacks are punished for natural hairstyles is the reaction to Zendaya Coleman's locs at the 2015 Academy Awards. Along with her locs, Zendaya wore a formal white gown, pulling off what many deemed a regal and elegant look. But Giuliana Rancic, host of *The Fashion Police*, criticized her locs and suggested that she probably smelled of patchouli oil and marijuana, likely because both are associated with Rastafarian and even "hippie" culture. A major media backlash ensued, and Coleman condemned Rancic's harsh statement on social media. In reference to the Coleman–Rancic controversy, Jeffrey C. Stewart, chair of the Department of Black Studies at the University of California–Santa Barbara, commented, "There's a long history of racist comments about black people in terms of how they smell" (*People* Staff, 2015; see also Feagin, 2013). Typically, celebrities serve as trendsetting figures who are idolized by the general public. Yet in this instance, Coleman's cultural expression and Rancic's mocking of it are perceived to indicate how a majority of people truly feel about Blackness. Later that same year, actress and singer Miley Cyrus wore locs to the MTV Video Music Awards, and the commentary from fashion gurus applauding her choice as stylish and trendy was a stark difference to the way Coleman's locs were received. When Miley Cyrus (and more recently, Justin Bieber) wears locs, it is a trend; when Zendaya Coleman does it, it must mean she is a marijuana user.

Not only does cultural appropriation occur when a member of the dominant-status group is praised for doing something for which a subordinate group member would be othered, it also applies when members of the dominant group are given credit for something they did not create. For example, Cyrus is given credit for popularizing a dance move called twerking. However, twerking has origins in African culture and has been a mainstay of Black American culture. The dance showcases the hips and is generally an expression of one's sexuality. Music videos featuring this dance have not been included in mainstream media but have instead kept within Black culture. It is also a dance requiring great skill, as it involves the isolation of the hips and buttocks. When Black women engage in this dance, they are perceived as "ghetto," hypersexual, and vulgar—long-standing stereotypes of Black women (McMillan Cottom, 2013). However, when Cyrus performed a watered-down version of twerking at the MTV Video Music Awards, the media praised her for popularizing it, some even going so far as to say she *invented* the dance move. The Oxford English Dictionary subsequently added *twerking,* and many news sources gave Cyrus the credit. She was also praised for her boldness and assertiveness and for using the performance to establish her departure from her former status as a Disney teen pop sensation.

Indeed, cultural appropriation is a fairly common phenomenon, affecting a variety of different cultures. For example, for a time, Gwen Stefani appropriated Japanese culture and aspects of broader Asian culture. She included the Harajuku Girls in her lineup for a number of years, exploiting a sect of real women from the Harajuku district in Japan known for their unique style and independence. While some may argue that Stefani was merely appreciating and showcasing their style, the fact that she used the Harajuku Girls as human accessories when she appeared in public suggested objectification of these women and profiting from that objectification.

In another example of Asian cultural appropriation, some have taken to wearing a bindi as a fashion accessory. The bindi comes from Hinduism and is a dot of red color placed in the center of a woman's forehead. It represents the Nasadiya Sukta, which is considered the point at which creation begins. It further symbolizes wisdom, concentration, and energy, and represents the "third eye" (which is a concept in many religions that represents perception and foresight). Some celebrities (e.g., Beyoncé, Selena Gomez, Iggy Azalea) have chosen to wear a bindi as a fashion statement, despite its deep religious and cultural intent. Furthermore, it is common to see it worn at music festivals, where in fact many aspects of Indian, Native American, and Asian cultures are appropriated. This is problematic in part because the activities at these concerts usually include alcohol and drug use and the symbolism behind wearing a bindi (or kimono or Native American headdress) is defiled through its juxtaposition with such activities.

Wide-scale instances of cultural appropriation occur each year at Halloween. When individuals "dress up" as cultures not their own, they are exaggerating the features of another's culture, which can be very offensive to the origin culture and when done frequently, contributes to ideal type depictions that become the societal expectations of the origin culture. For example, many Native American "costumes" available in retail stores have no symbolic meaning. By contrast, every bead and every feather on a tribal outfit has a specific meaning to that specific tribe ("Indian Pow Wow Attire," n.d.). Mass-produced Halloween costumes do not provide this meaning, and often such costumes are sexualized, which in the case of religious robes is particularly offensive to Native American communities (Keene, 2013). Also, there is a qualitative difference between dressing up as a supernatural character such as a zombie and dressing up as a Native American, Asian, or Black person. Unlike zombies, these are real people who throughout history have been exploited and oppressed. When an individual appropriates a culture, it is a covert form of discrimination that does not take into consideration the social significance of another group's experience.

Perhaps the most common example of cultural appropriation occurs in sports, through the use of Native American mascots. Many of these mascots are caricatures with exaggerated features and practices (see also Williams in this volume). The misrepresentation of Native Americans has a long history in the United States—from the exploitation and genocide of Native Americans under colonialism to the stereotypical portrayal of Native Americans in film (Churchill, 1998). This history is what has led to the decimation of the Native American population, thus spawning portrayals of Native peoples as people of the past and therefore exploitable through mascots and company logos. At times, cultural appropriation occurs that is considered religiously and morally offensive to origin cultures. This has been the case for Native Americans where, for example, sacred symbols and figures have been used to sell products such as liquor and tobacco (Alaniz & Wilkes, 1998; Merskin, 2001). Because they are perceived as people of the past and objectified by mascots and logos, we often overlook or ignore the social problems that affect Native American communities, such as extreme poverty, disease, and unemployment. As seen in the above examples, cultural appropriation is problematic because it threatens the identity of a culture and/or its members and leaves its members vulnerable to discrimination, stereotypes, and diminished resources and opportunities (Young & Brunk, 2009).

Some companies are beginning to recognize the damage caused by cultural appropriation. For example, in 2015, Adidas agreed to provide financial support and creative design to any high school willing to drop its Native American mascot (Wagner, 2015). Some schools and universities have received approval to use mascots associated with particular tribes, while others have embraced a mascot change (Remillard, 2005; Strauss, 2014; Ulmer, 2014). However, many college and professional sports teams are unwilling to change their mascots due to fan appeal, unwillingness to work with the tribe, or financial greed (Brady, 2014). Some argue that fans might initially object to the changing of a mascot but, ultimately, fans would likely still attend games because of the appeal of the broader sports culture (Ryan, 2016). To understand why cultural appropriation exists despite widespread objection to it, we need to understand the social issues and questions behind it.

A Closer Look at Cultural Appropriation

To provide some background on the impact of cultural appropriation, one needs to understand the concept of assimilation, as it contributes a great deal to racial, ethnic, and cultural dynamics in the United States. Ostensibly, the United States is a proverbial melting pot made up of numerous cultures, races, ethnicities, and nationalities. Of course, invoking the melting pot metaphor means one might envision a process whereby all cultures eventually blend into one broader culture: the "American" culture.

However, when you think of different cultures within the United States, do you envision just one culture or do you envision various subcultures? If we envision the latter, then a more appropriate metaphor for America would probably be something like a salad bowl. The salad metaphor recognizes the different components of the salad individually, but collectively, the contents are labeled "salad."

The problem with the melting pot metaphor is that it assumes each culture does blend smoothly into the dominant or White American culture. The term *dominant culture* refers to the culture of the group with the most social, political, and economic power in any given social category that by extension becomes the referent group in public discourse. As the referent group, it becomes the standard or "norm" and thus invisible while the social characteristics of groups without power become highlighted. For example, when we speak of "race," we think of Blacks, Latinos, or Asians. Whites are often not included in the immediate thought because public discourse deems Whites "normative." Another such referent group is cisgender men. When one speaks of "gender," usually people think of cisgender women. However, gender also applies to men and transgender people. The dominant group controls and has access to the distribution of various resources, capital, and power. Thus, it influences ideologies and which beliefs ultimately become the status quo. This process is known as "hegemony" (Gramsci, 1971). In a social world where White upper-class (and even middle-class) cisgender men compose the hegemonic group, they define and control cultural values and norms—values and norms that have historically devalued and presently devalue the cultural attributes of people of color.

Cultural hegemony allows for control of cultural production, where Whites as the hegemonic group can ultimately use media and public discourse to maintain hegemony, or power and privilege. One way that happens is through the use of controlling images. According to Collins (2004), the 20th century brought the influx of such images through White-dominated and White-controlled media outlets such as newspapers, magazines, movies, television, and the Internet. It is through these media outlets that people of color become "othered." Othering is the social process of a dominant group designating the parameters of a subordinate group (Schwalbe et al., 2000). Schwalbe et al. (2000) use the term *oppressive othering* to describe how one group seeking domination over another frames the subordinate group as morally or intellectually inferior. This is a form of boundary maintenance where dominant groups maintain boundaries between subordinate-status groups to protect their access to resources and maintain their social, economic, and political advantage. The White-dominated media participate in oppressive othering and boundary maintenance by, for example, framing Blacks as unintelligent, Latinos as hypersexual, Asian Americans as perpetual foreigners, and Native Americans as people of the past. Collins (2004) argues that these kinds of images are then used by social institutions to unequally distribute goods and resources such as education, employment, and housing, to name a few.

Indeed, cultural appropriation is another way Whites maintain cultural hegemony. When cultural appropriation occurs, the culture of an oppressed group is taken on by a dominant group. Cultural significance is often left out during the adaptation process, and what remains are features or elements of the oppressed culture as adapted by members of the dominant group. The intentional borrowing of culture from a histori-cally subordinate status group is problematic, as the values and reasoning behind the original groups' rituals or practices are undermined or erased completely. When we allow this to happen, the cultures of people of color are exaggerated and denigrated, which by extension elevates White culture. As such, the cultures of people of color remain othered, White culture remains the norm, and the cultural hegemony that Whites enjoy remains intact.

Often, cultural appropriation goes unnoticed, particularly by Whites who may be guilty of it. In large part, this is due to Whites' racial privilege, meaning the access to resources, opportunity, power, or prestige that they enjoy simply by having White skin (Acker, 2006). It is important to note that while not all Whites have the power and means to establish and carry out this dominance (e.g., poor Whites), all Whites benefit from being a part of this dominant-status group. This is particularly true of cultural appropriation, where even poor Whites benefit from having the status of Whiteness elevated—a natural consequence of appropriation. Because of White privilege, Whites who are accused of appropriation may argue that they are simply appreciating a group of color's culture—not co-opting it—and have a right to show their appreciation. However, when there is widespread backlash from people of color, it is not necessarily the right of a member of the dominant group (who has been afforded social privileges, whether he or she is aware of it or not) to question people of color's claims of appropriation. Instead, it is perhaps an opportunity for Whites to reflect on how their behavior could be exploiting or offensive. When Whites dismiss these concerns, they run the risk of further perpetuating the long history of exploitation, racism, and institutional discrimination that has long characterized the experiences of people of color in the United States. For these reasons, when cultural appropriation occurs, it needs to be called into question.

How Do I Know If I Might Be Appropriating?

When one is a member of a privileged group, it is always important to remain aware of privilege and instances where you might be using your privilege to oppress another group. In the case of cultural appropriation, you can do the following:

1. *Assess.* Simply ask yourself if you would be offending a culture by your actions. Most individuals are aware of their own culture, race, or ethnicity. If you are trying a new style and are considering wearing a bindi, locs, or a Native American headdress, think about why members of those origin cultures do so. Many of these cultural markers have come to be associated with fashion statements, but that is not how they are perceived in the origin cultures.

2. *Consider your social location.* Becoming more aware of your own privilege will help you be more socially responsible. We are individuals with the right to express ourselves, but we are also morally and ethically aware that there are

things that should not be said or done. This is because all actions occur in context, and we should require ourselves to be aware of how such actions have historically contributed to the disadvantaged circumstances of subordinate groups.

3. *Recognize and acknowledge.* If the culture is not yours, it is not your place to make a claim that you are appreciating the culture or that members of the culture should be proud their culture is being displayed. Bonilla-Silva (2010) discusses such flawed arguments in his book *Racism Without Racists,* where he showcases how Whites use coded language or actions that ultimately contribute to the boundary maintenance of dominant-status groups.

Remember that the ability of subordinate groups to question or challenge a system that has historically kept them under disadvantaged circumstances and restricted them in certain sectors of the housing and labor markets and education is a sign of progress. Challenging an oppressor who has systematically kept various status groups at political, economic, and social disadvantage is a step toward parity.

Brittney Dennis is a doctoral student in sociology at Florida State University, with research interests in race, health, and urban sociology. She recently completed her master's thesis, which sought to examine whether the inverse association of collective efficacy and externalizing behaviors in children varied by race and ethnicity within neighborhoods. She is looking forward to completing a dissertation regarding neighborhoods, race, and health. She also occasionally writes for *Sociology Lens,* an academic blog.

SUGGESTED ADDITIONAL RESOURCES

Brown, T., & Kopano, B. (2014). *Soul thieves: The appropriation and misrepresentation of African American popular culture (contemporary Black history).* New York, NY: Palgrave MacMillan.

Brown Givens, S. M., & Monahan, J. L. (2005). Priming mammies, jezebels, and other controlling images: An examination of the influence of mediated stereotypes on perceptions of an African American woman. *Media Psychology, 7*(1), 87–106.

Collins, P. H. (2000). *Black feminist thought: Knowledge, consciousness, and the politics of empowerment.* New York, NY: Routledge.

McIntosh, P. (2011). White privilege and male privilege: A personal account of coming to see correspondences through work in women's studies. In E. F. Provenzo Jr. (Ed.), *The teacher in American society: A critical anthology* (pp. 121–134). Thousand Oaks, CA: Sage.

McMillan Cottom, T. (2013, August 29). Brown body, White wonderland: To celebrate herself, Miley Cyrus used other women's bodies as a joke—women who look like me. *Slate.* Retrieved from http://www.slate.com/articles/double_x/doublex/2013/08/miley_cyrus_vma_performance_white_appropriation_of_black_bodies.html

Omi, M., & Winant, H. (1994). *Racial formation in the United States: From the 1960s to the 1990s.* New York, NY: Routledge

Rogers, R. A. (2006). From cultural exchange to transculturation: A review and reconceptualization of cultural appropriation. *Communication Theory, 16*(4), 474–503.

Ziff, B. H., & Rao, P. V. (1997). *Borrowed power: Essays on cultural appropriation.* New Brunswick, NJ: Rutgers University Press.

QUESTIONS FOR FURTHER DISCUSSION

1. Prior to reading this essay, how would you have defined cultural appropriation? After reading it, has your definition changed? If so, why or how?

2. How does the salad bowl metaphor help us understand the impact and harm that cultural appropriation causes to subordinate-status groups?

REACHING BEYOND THE COLOR LINE

1. Spend some time discussing popular occurrences of cultural appropriation, perhaps by a sports team or celebrity, with the people sitting near you. Is the impact of these occurrences as harmful as occurrences of cultural appropriation within your own peer group or your school?

2. Now that you have had the chance to read and reflect, have you ever participated in cultural appropriation? Be honest and reflective. This exercise is meant to help you recognize your privilege and instances of injustice. With your new knowledge, discuss in a group what you could have done differently not to appropriate a culture or what you will do in your own peer group to bring awareness to a situation where cultural appropriation might be occurring.

3. Consider the collection of images featured in the following article:

   Rice, Z. C. (2015, May 12). Stunning images show how Native American fashion looks without cultural appropriation. *Mic.* Retrieved from https://mic.com/articles/118150/ stunning-images-show-how-american-indian-fashion-looks-without-cultural-appropriation# .BCqJ5HhIn

   In what ways does this collection address the issues of cultural appropriation discussed in this essay?

REFERENCES

Acker, J. (2006). Inequality regimes: Gender, class, and race in organizations. *Gender & Society, 20,* 441–464.

Alaniz, M. L., & Wilkes, C. (1998). Pro-drinking messages and message environments for young adults: The case of alcohol industry advertising in African American, Latino, and Native American communities. *Journal of Public Health Policy, 19*(4), 447–472.

Bellinger, W. (2007, Fall). Why African American women try to obtain "good hair." *Sociological Viewpoints, 23,* 63–72.

Bonilla-Silva, E. (2010). *Racism without racists: Color-blind racism and the persistence of racial inequality in the United States.* Lanham, MD: Rowman & Littlefield.

Brady, E. (2014, September 16). Critics of Redskins name attack NFL on profits, abuse. *USA Today.* Retrieved from https://www.usatoday.com/story/sports/nfl/redskins/2014/09/16/congress-letters-nfl-owners-washington-redskins-mascot/15734981/

Byrd, A., & Tharps, L. (2001). *Hair story: Untangling the roots of Black hair in America.* New York, NY: St. Maria's Press.

Byrd, A., & Tharps, L. (2014, April 30). When Black hair is against the rules. *New York Times.* Retrieved from https://www.nytimes.com/2014/05/01/opinion/when-black-hair-is-against-the-rules.html?_r=0

Churchill, W. (1998). *Fantasies of the master race.* San Francisco, CA: City Lights Books.

Collins, P. H. (2004). *Black sexual politics: African Americans, gender, and the new racism.* New York, NY: Routledge.

Feagin, J. R. (2013). *The White racial frame.* New York, NY: Routledge.

Goffman, E. (1959). *The presentation of self in everyday life.* New York, NY: Anchor Books.

Gramsci, A. (1971). *Selections from the prison notebooks of Antonio Gramsci* (Q. Hoare & G. Smith, Eds. & Trans.). New York, NY: International.

Indian pow wow attire. (n.d.). *See California.* Retrieved September 16, 2016, from http://www.seecalifornia.com/culture/indian-powwow-clothing.html

Keene, A. (2013, October). The one stop for all your "Indian costumes are racist" needs! [Blog post]. *Native Appropriations.* Retrieved from http://nativeappropriations.com/2013/10/the-one-stop-for-all-your-indian-costumes-are-racist-needs.html

McMillan Cottom, T. (2013, August). When your (brown) body is a (white) wonderland [Blog post]. Retrieved from https://tressiemc.com/uncategorized/when-your-brown-body-is-a-white-wonderland/

Merskin, D. (2001). Winnebagos, Cherokees, Apaches, and Dakotas: The persistence of stereotyping of American Indians in American advertising brands. *Howard Journal of Communications, 12,* 159–169.

People Staff. (2015, March 4). Part of Giuliana Rancic's Zendaya joke was edited out, says source. Retrieved from http://people.com/celebrity/giuliana-rancic-zendaya-controversy-part-of-joke-was-edited-out-source-says/

Remillard, A. J. (2005). Holy war on the football field: Religion and the Florida State University Indian mascot controversy. In J. A. Vlasich (Ed.), *Horsehide, pigskin, oval tracks and apple pie: Essays on sport and American culture* (pp. 104–118). Jefferson, NC: McFarland.

Ryan, S. (2016, May 3). Illinois to select new mascot; Chief Illiniwek backer's "not going to stop." *Chicago Tribune.* Retrieved from http://www.chicagotribune.com/sports/college/ct-university-of-illinois-mascot-chief-illiniwek-20160502-story.html

Schwalbe, M., Godwin, S., Holden, D., Schrock, D., Thompson, S., & Wolkomir, M. (2000). Generic processes in the reproduction of inequality: An interactionist analysis. *Social Forces, 79,* 419–452.

Sieber, R., & Herreman, F. (2000). Hair in African art and culture. *African Arts, 33*(3), 55–69.

Strauss, V. (2014, June 19). From Redskins to Redhawks: Why one Washington high school changed team name after 88 years. *Washington Post.* Retrieved from https://www.washingtonpost.com/news/answer-sheet/wp/2014/06/19/from-redskins-to-redhawks-why-one-washington-high-school-changed-team-name-after-88-years/?utm_term=.03cb72300a6d

Synnott, A. (1987). Shame and glory: A sociology of hair. *British Journal of Sociology, 38*(3), 381–413.

Thompson, C. (2008). Black women and identity: What's hair got to do with it? *Politics and Performativity, 22*(1), 78–90.

Ulmer, J. (2014, August 30). The Dalles becomes latest Oregon school to drop Native American mascot. *Oregonian*. Retrieved from http://highschoolsports.oregonlive.com/news/article/-3668039736778055308/the-dalles-becomes-latest-oregon-school-to-drop-native-american-mascot/

Wagner, L. (2015, November 5). Adidas offers to help U.S. high schools phase out Native American mascots. *NPR*. Retrieved from http://www.npr.org/sections/thetwo-way/2015/11/05/454902114/adidas-offers-to-help-u-s-high-schools-phase-out-native-american-mascots

Young, J. O. (2010). *Cultural appropriation and the arts*. West Sussex, UK: John Wiley.

Young, J. O., & Brunk, C. G. (2009). Introduction. In J. O. Young & C. G. Brunk (Eds.), *The ethics of cultural appropriation* (pp. 1–10). West Sussex, UK: Wiley-Blackwell.

"#BlackLivesMatter Is Racist; It Should Be #AllLivesMatter!"

#AllLivesMatter as Post-Racial Rhetoric

Mark Orbe

Western Michigan University

In the first verse of the Academy Award–winning song "Glory," rapper Common asserts: "Justice is juxtapositionin' us / Justice for all just ain't specific enough." These powerful lyrics—featured in the 2015 film *Selma*—capture the essence of a rhetorical struggle between those that advocate for the existence of a post-racial U.S. society and those that vehemently deny its existence.[1] In 2012, #BlackLivesMatter was created following the acquittal of the man who killed Trayvon Martin; the movement's call to action is against the "virulent anti-Black racism that permeates our society."[2] Shortly after #BlackLivesMatter became a nationally recognized symbol, it was re-configured, co-opted, and/or replaced by some with the more inclusive and racially neutral alternative, #AllLivesMatter.[3]

This analysis utilizes the core elements associated with a critical race theoretical frame to highlight how post-racial fantasies render the legitimacy of race-specific assertions as null and void.[4] In particular, I argue that #AllLivesMatter is akin to larger rhetorical devices—like the notion of a color-blind society—that are used to promote post-racism, something that was not possible with other political slogans during earlier civil rights struggles.[5] In order to frame this argument, I first offer a brief description

---

Essay reprinted from Orbe, M. (2015). #AllLivesMatter as post-racial rhetorical strategy. *Journal of Contemporary Rhetoric, 5*(3–4), 90–98. Mark Orbe can be reached for comment on this essay at orbe@wmich.edu.

305

of the Black Lives Matter movement (see also Taylor in this volume). Then, I articulate how critical race theory serves as a key foundation for my rhetorical critique of #AllLivesMatter.

#BlackLivesMatter

Following the 2013 George Zimmerman's acquittal of the death of Trayvon Martin, #BlackLivesMatter emerged as a social media call to action for people of all racial and cultural backgrounds interested in protesting "the obvious truth that the criminalization of Blackness is entertained as just and acceptable."[6] The movement associated with the hashtag continued to gain momentum in 2014 and 2015 as it was used to create a collective consciousness of a number of issues facing African Americans, including racial profiling, police brutality, the militarization of policing in black communities, as well as mass incarceration.[7] The organization's website includes an abundance of information, including the following objective statement:

> #BlackLivesMatter is working for a world where Black lives are no longer systematically and intentionally targeted for demise. We affirm our contributions to this society, our humanity, and our resilience in the face of deadly oppression. We have put our sweat equity and love for Black people into creating a political project—taking the hashtag off of social media and into the streets. The call for Black lives to matter is a rallying cry for ALL Black lives striving for liberation.[8]

The movement has been criticized through national media outlets that characterize it as rebellious, irrational, leaderless, and unfocused—and, consequently fleeting.[9] While some objectives of #BlackLivesMatter are quite broad ("ending mass incarceration, de-militarizing the police, and securing full employment"), others are more specific ("specific legislative efforts, congressional hearings, and indictments of police officers that have shot and killed unarmed black men").[10] According to Kang, "The movement does shy away from specific policy prescriptions. Instead, the work seems to be aimed at an abrupt, wide-scale change in consciousness, channeling the grief and anger that these police killings engender around the country."[11]

Dozens of Black Lives Matter chapters exist across the U.S. and abroad; these grass-roots organizations have been instrumental in staging over a thousand demonstrations worldwide.[12] These protests take a variety of forms including assemblies, rallies, vigils, marches, and die-ins. The central theme here is that individuals united behind the purpose of #BlackLivesMatter are making political declarations, most often publically to mourn the loss of African American lives—a form of human existence that historically has been situated as less significant than that of other races. Such demonstrations are crucially important. As Yancy and Butler articulate, when the collective grieve the loss of individuals whose lives are considered ungrievable they are making political statement that these lost lives are not acceptable losses.[13]

Described by some as "the most formidable American protest movement of the 21st century to date," the effectiveness of #BlackLivesMatter has relied on the strengths of social media: "the swift morally blunt consensus that can be created by hashtags; the personal connection that a charismatic online persona can make with followers; the broad networks that allow for easy distribution of documentary photos and videos—with an effort to quickly mobilize protests in each new city where a police shooting occurs."[14] In this regard, #BlackLivesMatter represents the new form of online activism; something that has allowed names such as Trayvon Martin, Michael Brown, Eric Garner, Tamir Rice, Tony Robinson, Walter Scott, and Freddie Gray to become recognized within one collective stream of consciousness despite that their lives ended thousands of miles and weeks/months/years apart. As such, the movement demonstrates how Twitter has become a site of a revolution and a conduit for the protest rhetoric of activists.[15] In 2014, #BlackLivesMatter was recognized by The American Dialect Society as the word of the year.[16]

From its inception, #BlackLivesMatter was rooted in the lived experiences of people of African descent in the U.S., especially those who actively resist their own dehumanization. In addition, the movement sought to advance the lives of all African Americans while simultaneously singling out those whose lives have been traditionally marginalized with Black liberation movements. According to the information provided on the website, Black Lives Matter "affirms the lives of Black queer and trans folk, disabled folks, Black-undocumented folks, folks with records, women and all Black lives along the gender spectrum."[17] This is an important rhetorical distinction, as it demonstrates how the movement negotiates the dialectical tension of how black lives matter exists alongside a continuum of similarity←—→difference and privilege←—→advantage.[18] On a larger scale, it is this very issue that is at the core of the fierce debates regarding the use of #AllLivesMatter as a more inclusive form of #BlackLivesMatter. In order to contextualize the arguments in this essay, I turn to critical race theory as a salient theoretical frame.

Critical Race Theory

The origins of critical race theory can be traced back to the late 1970s and early 1980s.[19] During this time, civil rights activists were seeing many of the gains achieved during the 1960s disappearing.[20] Initially, scholars in critical legal studies questioned the impact of the dominant values of equal opportunity and justice for all in a context of racial inequalities. Over the past two decades, communication scholars have drawn on this established theoretical framework to inform their research on race, ethnicity, and communication.[21] Critical race theory, given #BlackLivesMatter as contemporary form of civil rights activism, provides an invaluable foundation for this rhetorical analysis.

At the core of critical race theory are six key elements.[22] First, it begins with recognition that racism is an integral part of the United States. Critical race theorists do not debate whether racism can ever be totally eliminated; instead they focus on challenging existing structures that reinforce racial oppression. Second, critical race theory "rejects dominant legal and social claims of neutrality, objectivity, and color blindness."[23] Laws, policies, slogans, and other rhetorical devices promoted as "race-neutral" are criticized. Critical race theoretical work embraces the subjectivity that comes with the lived experiences of people of color; as such their work is seen as explicitly political. The third core element rejects analyses of contemporary racial relations void of any historical context that frames current realities. Accordingly, they believe that any attempts to understand race in the 21st century are only possible through an awareness of the history of race in the United States.

The fourth key element of critical race theory focuses on the experiential knowledge that is generated from various cultural standpoints. In other words, the theory values perspectives grounded through the racialized collective experiences of those groups that have historically been marginalized in the U.S. The fifth key element speaks to the interdisciplinary and synergistic nature of critical race theory. The ideas of this theory are borrowed from several traditions, including feminism, Marxism, critical/cultural studies, and postmodernism.[24] The sixth and final key element highlights the social activism associated with the theory: In no uncertain terms, the objective of critical race theory is the elimination of racial oppression. A focus on race, however, does not prohibit seeking an understanding of how racism is closely tied to other oppressions based on gender and gender identity, socioeconomic status, abilities, spirituality, and sexual orientation. Within this context, #BlackLivesMatter is best understood as critical race theory in action.

Critical race scholars have argued that the rhetoric of race has paid too much attention to elite courtrooms while ignoring how social justice issues are interpreted by lay persons. As such, this form of theorizing is regarded as both pragmatic and idealized in its attempt to address the immediate needs of those individuals whose lives exist on the margins of society. New foci of critical race scholarship have emerged over the years, including the use of narratives, personal stories, poems, and fiction.[25] The debate between the effectiveness of #AllLivesMatter versus #BlackLivesMatter fosters another area of growth for critical race theorists. It represents an extension of the work of communication scholars who have utilized the ideals of critical race theory to advance rhetorical theory. Specifically, Hasian and Delgado have advocated for "racialized critical rhetorical theorizing" which promotes assessment of "the ways in which public and legal notions of race influence the ways in which we create histories, cultural memories, narratives, myths, and other discursive units."[26] Political rhetoric, like #AllLivesMatter, is a form of public discourse that contains a number of subnarrative and texts.[27] While the hashtag appears neutrally affirming—on face value and within its implications—it must be situated within a larger frame that includes historical, social, cultural, and contextual understandings.[28] Consequently, this analysis draws from the key components of critical race theory generally, and racialized critical rhetorical theorizing specifically, to "gain an appreciation of the ways that purportedly neutral discussions of race often mask racial categories, experiences, and values."[29]

#AllLivesMatter, Post-Racism, and White Privilege

This section represents the heart of the essay; the objective is two-fold. First, I will explicate the rhetorical power of post-racism and describe colorblindness as a post-racial strategy. Second, I will situate #AllLivesMatter as a strategic form of post-racial rhetoric and illustrate the ways in which rhetors who use the hashtag do so through a prism steeped in white privilege. I conclude the rhetorical analysis by arguing for the necessity of #BlackLivesMatter as a form of counter post-racial discourse.

Post-Racial Rhetoric

The election of Barack Obama as the 44th U.S. President is the single most important accomplishment associated with the emergence of post-racial rhetoric in the United States.[30] Although it's absurd to think that one event could "automatically and instantaneously end racism,"[31] Obama's election appeared to some as the culmination of decades of progress for people of color and the mark of a post-racial state. Consequently, from the perspective of some whites—including young people who do not have the collective memory of racial injustice[32]—contemporary lives in the U.S. are being played on a level playing field in terms of race.[33] According to some critical race scholars,[34] post-racial rhetoric can be understood as a form of "historical amnesia"[35] whereby the intergenerational effects of centuries of racism are forgotten.

Race-neutral discourses—such as self-descriptions of being color-blind—are rhetorical strategies of post-racism.[36] "I don't see color" is a common form of race-neutral discourse. Another example is the often heard "It doesn't matter if a person is black, white, red, yellow, green, purple, or polka-dot." This rhetoric defines racial identities through the color of one's skin, which for many is the defining marker of race. The logic associated with this rhetoric is straightforward and seemingly irrefutable: If a person doesn't see race, then they cannot be racist. For many Whites, advocating for a race-neutral, color-blind world is a practical strategy toward an admirable goal: the elimination of racism.[37] While the end goal is laudable, what oftentimes remains unspoken (and unchallenged) are the ways in which color-blind rhetoric fails to recognize and address continued forms of racial discrimination and institutionalized racism. Thus, perceptions of the U.S. as a post-racial society are best understood as a reflection of a lived experience steeped in white privilege.[38]

On face value, colorblind approaches appear to be politically neutral, yet according to Husband, they actually work to exacerbate racial oppression.[39] This and similar approaches represent a liberal assumption of neutrality which fosters a "lack of understanding of the historical, systemic influences that race has on contemporary lived experience."[40] When white privilege is not acknowledged, individuals develop what Freire calls a "magical" or false consciousness of race and racism.[41] When individuals do not work to understand diverse lived experiences beyond that which is generated by their own cultural location, the logical conclusion is that no social action is warranted because since race is not an issue for people who identify as white then the same must be the same for all members of society.[42] Consequently, racial neutral rhetoric—while seemingly positive, affirming, and forward-thinking—implicitly reinforces the unearned benefits that come with white privilege.

One of the most troubling consequences of post-racial discourse is the way in which it works to silence individuals who seek to challenge racism.[43] For instance, when a person of color requests that Whites consider the saliency of race in any given context, they are criticized for "playing the race card"—bringing up race in a contemporary time frame where racism no longer exists. The power of the rhetorical discourse of color-blindness, in the context of post-racism, manifests when the person of color themselves are accused of being racists as they to confront racism.[44] Recognizing the underpinnings of post-racial discourse is crucial to understanding the resistance to #AllLivesMatter, yet it is a rhetorical frame that has largely gone unarticulated.

#AllLivesMatter as Post-Racial Rhetoric

In most instances, #AllLivesMatter emerges as a response to Twitter posts that include the hashtag, #BlackLivesMatter. Some Whites describe the more universally inclusive alternative as a form of solidarity and a declaration against police brutality of people of all races.[45] Within social media exchanges, these individuals argue that by singling out African Americans specifically, rhetors are creating racial separation and promoting divisiveness. Moreover, advocating for #AllLivesMatter as a universal affirmation, void of race, is situated within racial neutrality that is consistent with post-racism.

As established earlier, having a race-neutral approach to questions such as "which lives matter?" negates the historical and current-day realities whereby African American lives are not deemed as equally valuable. The fact that all lives matter should be a given, but to truly embrace the essence of this mantra we must "foreground those lives that are not mattering now, to mark that exclusion, and militate against it."[46] According to Landrum,

> The fact that "All Lives Matter" is being used to *argue against* the idea that Black lives matter is proof that (1) People spreading that slogan don't really believe Black lives matter, at least not equally, and (2) It's therefore not true that all lives do matter equally in their eyes. The statement's use belies itself. If all lives matter, then black lives matter, so why the argument? Why the comeback? The comeback proves that statement false, and proves it for what it is—a response born of fear and racism. Consistent with critical race theory, a historical context is crucial here.[47]

#AllLivesMatter negates the well-documented reality that the United States constitution defined people of African descent as property. As evidenced by an intense political contestation and compromise—something that reflected dominant social and cultural ideologies—Black lives were valued as only a portion (factually, three-fifths) of white lives.[48] In this context, "some lives mattered more, were more human, more worthy, more deserving of life and freedom."[49] This is the historical context from which the present-day reality is framed. How do we know that black lives still do not matter as much as white lives? We can look to the disproportionate number of U.S. Americans of color who are detained, in prison, and on death row. We can critique subsequent institutional efforts, and unbalanced media attention, when African American and European American women and children are reported missing. We can observe increasingly apparent health disparities (see Mouzon in this volume) based on race and the lack of critical research, internal reform, and public advocacy.[50] These are just a few contexts that represent a social norm that effectively communicates that black lives do not matter. In no uncertain terms, the idea that African American lives are viewed as less valuable than their white counterparts has "built up over time, through daily practices, modes of address, through the organization of schools, work, prison, law and media."[51]

Situating #AllLivesMatter as a postracial strategy facilitates a recognition of how it represents an extension of colorblindness that refutes the core purpose of #BlackLivesMatter.[52] From a critical racialized rhetorical theorizing frame, it can be seen as a hollow attempt to neutralize the fact that certain forms of injustices and brutality target people of color almost exclusively. #AllLivesMatter, in this regard, can be understood as a means to reshape a narrative so that one's colorblindness can remain intact. As Yancy and Butler explain, "When some people rejoin with 'All Lives Matter' they misunderstand the problem, but not because their message is untrue. It is true that all lives matter, but it is equally true that not all lives are understood to matter which is precisely why it is important to name the lives that have not mattered, and are struggling to matter in the way they deserve."[53] This is a crucially important point, one that appears throughout the website dedicated to Black Lives Matter. According to the website, founders of the movement clearly state: "Telling us that all lives matter is redundant. We know that already. But, just know, police violence and brutality disproportionately affects my people. Justice is not applied equally, laws are not applied equally and neither is our outrage."

Concluding Thoughts: #BlackLivesMatter as Rhetorical Necessity

This rhetorical analysis utilizes critical race theory to critique #AllLivesMatter as a problematic response to #BlackLivesMatter. In short, I identify #AllLivesMatter as a rhetorical technique consistent with colorblind discourse—all of which exists within a society falsely proclaiming its post-racial existence. Clearly, all lives matter is laudable as an ideological principle; however, in practice, all lives seemingly are not valued to the same extent. This is the issue at the core of #BlackLivesMatter, a rhetorical strategy that is explicitly racialized. Within this essay, I argue that #AllLivesMatter is also racialized, albeit more implicitly because of the cloak of white privilege. In the end, the insights generated through a critical analysis of this contemporary form of racialized discourse demonstrates the problematic nature of post-racism, and the consequences that come with rhetoric that reinforces a privileged dominant discourse.

Historically, rhetoric highlighting the importance of recognizing the humanity and value of African American lives has always existed against the backdrop of anti-Black racism. The most common examples took the form of language, naming, and labels which over time continued to promote self-definition, agency, and empowerment.[54] During the civil rights movement, Black men carried signs asserting "I am a man." African Americans of all ages claimed "Black Power" and proclaimed that "Black is Beautiful." This discourse was important as a form of social activism in a time when anti-Black racism was acknowledged (to some extent) by most U.S. Americans. Did we see many responses that stated that "White is Beautiful" or European American men holding signs that boldly stated the obvious? Some isolated examples might have existed, however, they were not offered in the spirit of universal commonality but within white supremacist ideologies (e.g., White Power, White is Beautiful). At the time, most U.S. citizens recognized the stark racial realities that necessitated pro-Black statements as counter protests to the status quo. However, in post-racial U.S. society, #AllLivesMatter exists as a preferred replacement to #BlackLivesMatter because the specificity of race is overpowered by the saliency of perceived human universality.

The necessity of #BlackLivesMatter as a form of protest discourse continues to be highlighted by social justice activists within social media. In fact, the emergence of #AllLivesMatter appears as evidence for the necessity of the movement itself. According to some critics, the more race-neutral alternative is "an affront to Black heritage, people, and culture and does nothing but take away from the potent truth that the Black existence deserves ample recognition.[55] According to Yancy and Butler,

> One reason . . . 'Black Lives Matter' is so important is that it states the obvious but the obvious has not yet been historically realized. So it is a statement of outrage and a demand for equality, for the right to live free of constraint, but also a chant that links the history of slavery, of debt peonage, segregation, and a prison system geared toward the containment, neutralization and degradation of Black lives, but also a police system that more and more easily and often can take away a Black life in a flash because some officer perceives a threat.[56]

Yancy and Butler highlight an important issue within this controversy: What is the meta-message implied by #BlackLivesMatter? According to Yancy, it is "a statement that should be obviously true but apparently is not . . . [W]hat we see is that some lives matter more than others, that some lives matter so much that they need to be protected at all costs, and that other lives matter less, or not at all."[57] Within this contextual frame, #AllLivesMatter, according to Nick Montgomery, "is used to dismiss and distract from the struggles of black people."[58] This post-racial form of rhetoric implicitly erases the specific forms of oppression that are bound up in anti-Black racism. He goes on to assert, "'All lives matter' is being chanted and tweeted in a context where the people being murdered are Black, and they're being murdered because of anti-Black racism."[59]

#BlackLivesMatter founder Alicia Garza has criticized various mainstream adaptations of the hashtag in light of what she describes as a repudiation of the very spirit behind the movement. She has made her criticism of #AllLivesMatter crystal clear. According to Garza, "changing Black Lives Matter to All Lives Matter is a demonstration of how we don't actually understand structural racism in this county."[60] Landrum connects this issue with post-racial articulations that minimize the current inequalities that exist and instead make proclamations of social equality that do not exist. She goes on to assert, "If one truly believes that all lives matter, then what's important right now is to proclaim loudly that Black lives matter."[61] In a subsequent Twitter post, Garza concisely concludes: "If you really believe that all lives matter, you will fight like hell for Black lives."[62] This is a sentiment that is reflected in the core elements of critical race theory: Race-neutral discourse, like #AllLivesMatter, presumably reflects a mantra highlighting objectivity, equality, and color-blindness. Yet, such discourse when articulated in contexts where anti-Black racism continues to exist reinforces racial inequalities. That's why on the surface, #AllLivesMatter can easily be embraced as a worthy universal mantra. However, in the racialized reality of contemporary U.S. society, #BlackLivesMatter as a rhetorical device is necessary to highlight existing disparities based on race. In this context, it isn't used as a strategy for separation and division but as a crucial educational tool toward greater social justice. Ultimately, the lesson is quite simple for a country attempting to eliminate racial oppression: "Justice for all just ain't specific enough."

Mark Orbe is professor of communication and diversity in the School of Communication at Western Michigan University, where he also holds a joint appointment in the Department of Gender & Women's Studies. His award-winning teaching and research activities focus on exploring the inextricable relationship between culture, power, and communication. Widely published, he is also CEO of Dumela Communications, an international consulting company that specializes in providing cultural competency professional development workshops to a variety of clients.

NOTES

1. Mark Orbe, *Communication Realties in a "Post-racial" Society: What the U.S. Public Really Thinks about Barack Obama* (Lanham, MD: Lexington Books, 2011), 216–217.

2. "About the Black Lives Matter Network," Black Lives Matter, http://blacklivesmatter.com/about/.

3. George Yancy and Judith Butler, "What's Wrong With 'All Lives Matter?'" *New York Times*, January 12, 2015, http://opinionator.blogs.nytimes.com/2015/01/12/whats-wrong-with-all-lives-matter/?_r=0.

4. See Mari J. Matsuda, Charles R. Lawrence III, Richard Delgado, and Kimberlè Williams Crenshaw, eds., *Words that Wound: Critical Race Theory, Assaultive Speech, and the First Amendment* (San Francisco, CA: Westview Press, 1993).

5. Eduardo Bonilla-Silva, *Racism Without Racists: Color-Blind Racism and Racial Inequality in Contemporary America,* 3rd ed. (Lanham, MD: Rowman & Littlefield, 2010), 55; Kent Ono, "Postracism: A Theory of the 'Post' – as Political Strategy," *Journal of Communication Inquiry,* 34 (2010): 228–229.

6. Black Millennials, "What You Mean by #AllLivesMatter," Black Millennials, December 1, 2014, http://blackmillennials.com/2014/12/01/what-you-mean-by-alllivesmatter/comment-page-1/.

7. Michael Segalov, "We Spoke to the Activist Behind #BlackLivesMatter about Racism in Britain and America," *Vice,* February 2, 2015, http://www.vice.com/read/patrisse-cullors-interview-michael-segalov-188.

8. "About the Black Lives Matter Network."

9. Leah Hunt-Hendrix, "The Media vs. The Movement: 3 Ways The 'New York Times' Completely Misunderstands #BlackLivesMatter and Movements in General." *Huffington Post,* January 22, 2015, http://www.huffingtonpost.com/leah-hunthendrix/three-ways-the-nytimes-co_b_6510530.html.

10. Hunt-Hendrix, "The Media vs. The Movement."

11. Jay Caspian Kang, "Our Demand is Simple: Stop Killing Us." *MSN News,* May 4, 2015, http://www.msn.com/en-us/news/us/%E2%80%98our-demand-is-simple-stop-killing-us%E2%80%99/ar-BBj9Yxb

12. "At Least 1134 Black Lives Matter Demonstrations Have Been Held in the Last 513 Days," *Elephrame,* December 7, 2015, https://elephrame.com/textbook/protests.

13. Yancy and Butler, "What's Wrong With 'All Lives Matter?'"

14. Kang, "Our Demand is Simple."

15. Kang, "Our Demand is Simple."

16. R.L.G., "Johnson: Words of The Year: #BlackLivesMatter," *The Economist.* January 15, 2015, http://www.economist.com/blogs/prospero/2015/01/johnson-words-year-0.

17. "About the Black Lives Matter Network."

18. Judith Martin and Thomas Nakayama, "Thinking Dialectically About Culture and Communication," *Communication Theory,* 9 (1999): 1–25.

19. Kimberlè Crenshaw, Neil Gotanda, Gary Peller, and Kendall Thomas, eds., *Critical Race Theory: The Key Writings That Formed That Movement* (New York: Free Press, 1995).

20. Matsuda, Lawrence, Delgado and Crenshaw, *Words that Wound.*

21. Rachel A. Griffin, "Critical Race Theory as a Means to Deconstruct, Recover, and Evolve in Communication Studies," *Communication Law Review,* 10 (2000): 1–9.

22. Matsuda, Lawrence, Delgado and Crenshaw, *Words that Wound.*

23. Mark Orbe and Tina Harris, *Interracial Communication: Theory Into Practice* (Thousand Oaks, CA: Sage, 2015), 154.

24. Orbe and Harris, *Interracial Communication.*

25. Matsuda, Lawrence, Delgado and Crenshaw, *Words that Wound.*

26. Marouf Hasian and Fernando Delgado, "The Trials and Tribulations of Racialized Critical Rhetorical Theory: Understanding the Rhetorical Ambiguities of Proposition 187," *Communication Theory*, 8 (1998): 247.

27. Hasian and Delgado, "The Trials and Tribulations," 257.

28. Hasian and Delgado, "The Trials and Tribulations," 258.

29. Hasian and Delgado, "The Trials and Tribulations," 264.

30. Ono, "Postracism"; Orbe, *Communication Realties in a "Post-racial" Society*, 91.

31. Ono, "Postracism," 228.

32. Orbe, *Communication Realties in a "Post-racial" Society*, 91–108.

33. Mary D. Vavrus, "Unhitching From the 'Post' (of Postfeminism)." *Journal of Communication Inquiry* 34 (2010): 225.

34. Ono, "Postracism," 231.

35. Hasian and Delgado, "The Trials and Tribulations," 257.

36. Ono, "Postracism," 230.

37. Orbe, *Communication Realties in a "Post-racial" Society*, 146.

38. Orbe, *Communication Realties in a "Post-racial" Society*, 147.

39. Terry Husband, Jr., "'I Don't See Color': Challenging Assumptions About Discussing Race with Young Children," *Early Childhood Education Journal*, 39 (2011): 365.

40. Hasian and Delgado, "The Trials and Tribulations," 250.

41. Paulo Freire, *Pedagogy of the Oppressed* (New York: Continuum, 1972).

42. Husband, "'I Don't See Color,'" 365.

43. Catherine Squires, "Running Through the Trenches: Or, an Introduction to the Undead Culture Wars and Dead Serious Identity Politics," *Journal of Communication Inquiry*, 31 (2010): 212.

44. Bonilla-Silva, *Racism Without Racists*, 55.

45. Black Millennials, "What You Mean by #AllLivesMatter."

46. Yancy and Butler, "What's Wrong With 'All Lives Matter?'"

47. Cynthia Landrum, "Deconstructing the 'All Lives Matter' Response," *thelivelytradition*, November 25, 2014, http://www.tomschade.com/2014/11/deconstructing-all-lives-matter-response.html.

48. Orbe and Harris, *Interracial Communication*, 44.

49. Yancy and Butler, "What's Wrong With 'All Lives Matter?'"

50. Mary Bassett, "#BlackLivesMatter – A Challenge to the Medical and Public Health Communities," *The New England Journal of Medicine*, 52 (2015): 1–3; Black Millennials, "What You Mean by #AllLivesMatter."

51. Yancy and Butler, "What's Wrong With 'All Lives Matter?'"

52. Black Millennials, "What You Mean by #AllLivesMatter."

53. Yancy and Butler, "What's Wrong With 'All Lives Matter?'"

54. Orbe and Harris, *Interracial Communication*, 115.

55. Black Millennials, "What You Mean by #AllLivesMatter."

56. Yancy and Butler, "What's Wrong With 'All Lives Matter?'"

57. Yancy and Butler, "What's Wrong With 'All Lives Matter?'"

58. Black Millennials, "What You Mean by #AllLivesMatter."

59. Black Millennials, "What You Mean by #AllLivesMatter."

60. Alicia Garza, "A Herstory of the #BlackLivesMatter Movement by Alicia Garza," *The Feminist Wire*, October 7, 2014, http://thefeministwire.com/2014/10/blacklivesmatter-2/.

61. Landrum, "Deconstructing the 'All Lives Matter' Response."

62. Black Lives Matter, Twitter post, December 6, 2014, 3:17 a.m. https://twitter.com/blklivesmatter/status/541159362610212866.

SUGGESTED ADDITIONAL RESOURCES

Bry, D. (2015, November 23). "All lives matter" is and always was racist—and this weekend's Trump rally proved it. *Guardian*. Retrieved from https://www.theguardian.com/commentisfree/2015/nov/23/all-lives-matter-racist-trump-weekend-campaign-rally-proved-it

Stubblefield, R. E. (2016, July 13). "All Lives Matter" and "Blue Lives Matter" supporters miss the point. *The Hill*. Retrieved from http://thehill.com/blogs/pundits-blog/civil-rights/287442-all-lives-matter-and-blue-lives-matter-supporters-are-missing

Taylor, K. (2016). *From #BlackLivesMatter to Black liberation*. Chicago, IL: Haymarket Books.

Yancy, G., & Butler, J. (2015, January 12). What's wrong with 'all lives matter'? *New York Times*. Retrieved from https://opinionator.blogs.nytimes.com/2015/01/12/whats-wrong-with-all-lives-matter/?smid=tw-share&_r=0

Websites

For information and policy recommendations on ending police violence in the United States, see Campaign Zero: https://www.joincampaignzero.org/#vision

For more on the Black Lives Matter organization and to locate local chapters, see blacklivesmatter.com

QUESTIONS FOR FURTHER DISCUSSION

1. How do language and public discourse shape our ideas of racial and ethnic groups?

2. Consider the author's discussion on the importance of hashtags. What are your thoughts on hashtag activism? In what ways is #blacklivesmatter similar to or different from other movements started or enhanced by hashtags?

3. Regarding Orbe's discussion of post-racial rhetoric as a form of historical amnesia, how does historical amnesia play a role in the present-day treatment of other racial and ethnic groups?

4. According to its website (blacklivesmatter.com), Black Lives Matter is an intersectional movement that values Black lives regardless of gender identity, sexual identity, economic status, disability, religious beliefs, and other categories of difference. Do you think most Americans are aware of this? How does this knowledge inform your opinion of the movement?

REACHING BEYOND THE COLOR LINE

1. Supporters of the Black Lives Matter movement were present at the women's marches held around the country after the election of Donald Trump. Some of the reactions to their signs were documented in Vanessa Willoughby's article for *Teen Vogue*: http://www.teenvogue.com/story/signs-at-the-womens-march-on-washington-called-out-white-feminism. With a classmate, analyze the reactions to these signs and what they tell us about claims of post-racialism and the assertion that "all lives matter."

2. Look up the origin and purpose of the Blue Lives Matter movement. Debate your classmates on (1) whether or not this movement is necessary and (2) its relationship to the Black Lives Matter movement.

3. Research the Zachary Hammond case featured in Nick Wing's article "A Cop Killed a White Teen and the #AllLivesMatter Crowd Said Nothing" (http://www.huffing tonpost.com/entry/zachary-hammond-police-killing_us_55c0e240e4b0c9fdc 75dfda3). What can that case tell us about #alllivesmatter supporters?

4. With a classmate, research U.S. support for President Trump's executive order banning entry of individuals from predominantly Muslim countries. What does this tell us about #alllivesmatter? What does support for this executive order and social discourse around "all lives matter" suggest about whose lives matter in the United States? What does the order tell us about the social construction of race/ethnicity?

5. Take some time to explore www.nodapl.life, the website created by the Standing Rock Sioux Tribe to protest the Dakota Access Pipeline through native lands. Consider how effective #NoDAPL has been in creating awareness and attracting support for this cause. Given past treatment of Native Americans/Indigenous People, how important do you think social media has been in social movements? Draft a pro/con argument to the following statement: "Social media platforms have dramatically changed social movements in the U.S. and across the globe." Provide examples to support your argument.

"I'm Not Racist; Some of My Best Friends Are . . . "

Debunking the Friends Defense and Revisiting Allyship in the Post-Obama Era

Cherise A. Harris

Connecticut College

Of all the names White Americans could be called in American society, *racist* ranks as one of the worst. As psychology professor Beverly Daniel Tatum says, "The word *racist* holds a lot of emotional power. For many White people, to be called racist is the ultimate insult" (Tatum, 1997). One of the reasons why the term is considered anathema by most Whites is because of the images it conjures in the public imagination. For example, in Joe Feagin and Hernán Vera's (2000) book *White Racism*, one of their White respondents referred to Blacks a number of times as "apes" and admitted that her parents "always instilled in me that blacks aren't equal," but she nevertheless maintained: "I don't consider myself racist . . . when I think of the word racist, I think of KKK [Ku Klux Klan], people in white robes burning black people on crosses and stuff, or I think of the Skinheads or some exaggerated form of racism" (pp. 215–216; see also Ashmore, 2009; Culp, 1993). Essentially, many Whites are reluctant to admit their racial prejudices and instead believe that "racism does not exist among the people of goodwill in America, who include most Americans. Racism and white supremacy are relegated in our time to the David Dukes and the few white supremacists" (Culp, 1993, pp. 211–212; see also Feagin, 2013).

Yet the widespread support for former Republican presidential candidate and now president Donald Trump and his overtly racist and ethnocentric rhetoric indicates that much has changed in the post-Obama era. There is now a greater willingness among many in the United States to tolerate or accept the most blatant forms of racism while also continuing to ignore subtler and often more insidious forms like employment discrimination, funding inequity in schools, voter disenfranchisement, and sentencing disparity. In the contemporary United States, it is important to understand that racism is frequently practiced by people of "good will" and in the contexts of both individual and institutional racism. Being a "mean" person or a "bad" or "evil" person isn't necessarily a requirement for participating in racist behavior. Racists are often people who go to church, do charity work, love their families, and generally experience themselves and are experienced by others as "nice people" or "good people" (see Feagin, 2013). However, under particular circumstances, they are willing to participate in racist, discriminatory behavior.

Writer Ta-Nehisi Coates (2013) gives an example of this in his *New York Times* op-ed piece "The Good, Racist People":

> In modern America we believe racism to be the property of the uniquely villainous and morally deformed, the ideology of trolls, gorgons and orcs. We believe this even when we are actually being racist. In 1957, neighbors in Levittown, Pa., uniting under the flag of segregation, wrote: "As moral, religious and law-abiding citizens, we feel that we are unprejudiced and undiscriminating in our wish to keep our community a closed community." A half-century later, little [has] changed.

As Coates suggests in his recounting of the skirmishes over integrating Levittown, Pennsylvania (one of the now iconic post–World War II planned suburban communities), racism isn't limited to people many consider "evil" or "bad," like White supremacists, but is also the practice of everyday Whites who consider themselves "good" people, who don't see themselves as racist at heart or who believe their words or actions aren't intended to be racist. However, focusing on what's in a person's "heart" rather than the impact of that person's racist behaviors actually further perpetuates racism. It privileges White Americans' feelings and alleged intent over and above the harm to people of color caused by their behavior—behavior that frequently results in individual and institutional racism.

In large part, the distinction between intent and impact was at the center of the contentious 2016 presidential race. Trump and his supporters were often accused of racism but frequently countered that advocating for a candidate who declared Mexicans rapists and criminals, who encouraged supporters to physically assault Black attendees at his rallies, or who suggested Muslim Americans should be made to register didn't mean that Trump or his supporters were practicing racism or were racist at heart. Meanwhile, nonsupporters continued to stress the impact such attitudes and behaviors would have on these groups, particularly if they were coming from the president of the United States. Indeed, within 10 days of taking office, Trump signed an executive order immediately banning entry to the United States for citizens from seven predominantly Muslim countries, which also led to the initial detainment and deportation of thousands of people and families, including those with green cards who had already been living and working in the United States, visa holders, translators for the U.S. military, and refugees fleeing persecution (*Globe* Staff, 2017; Singhvi & Parlapiano, 2017).

When Whites are accused of racism, a common refrain is, "I'm not racist!" which is frequently followed by another popular refrain: "Some of my best friends are [insert targeted group here, e.g., Black, Latino, Asian, Native American]!" Whatever the content of a particular individual's friendship group, this is clearly an effort to avoid the stigma that accompanies the term *racist*. Indeed, when public figures face accusations of racism, "friendship" with people of color or familiarity with their culture is one of the first defenses offered. For example, when accused of prejudice toward Latinos, Trump tweeted photos of himself eating tacos, with the accompanying text: "#HappyCincodeMayo! The best taco bowls are made in Trump Tower Grill. I love Hispanics!" (Parker, 2016). When skewered for proposing a ban on Muslims entering the United States during his campaign, he said in a December 2015 CNN interview: "I'm doing good for the Muslims. . . . Many Muslim friends of mine are in agreement with me" (Krieg, 2015). In yet another instance, right before his inauguration, Trump took meetings with prominent Black celebrities like Kanye West and Steve Harvey—meetings that many believed were photo ops designed to combat the notion that he was prejudiced against Blacks. Despite his "friendship" (McDermott, 2016) with West, when asked why West wasn't performing during the inaugural festivities when the Trump team was struggling to find willing performers, the chair of Trump's inaugural committee said, "We haven't asked him. . . . [Kanye] considers himself a friend of the President-elect, but it's not the venue. The venue we have for entertainment is . . . going to be typically and traditionally American, and Kanye is a great guy but we just haven't asked him to perform" (Diaz, 2017). The snub and subsequent comments from the Trump team suggested that perhaps Trump and West weren't really friends after all and that rap music, even from an alleged Trump friend, wouldn't be "American enough" for an inauguration.

Trump's use of the friends defense follows the pattern of many public figures accused of racism. For instance, when radio personality Don Imus was accused of being a racist after calling the Rutgers University women's basketball team "nappy-headed hoes," his defense was, "I'm not a white man who doesn't know any African-Americans" (MSNBC, 2007). He went on to discuss his work with ill children and how he attends funerals for many of the children, not just the White ones. The friends defense was also used in the George Zimmerman case. After the White Hispanic man killed 17-year-old Trayvon Martin in his father's neighborhood because he looked suspicious, Zimmerman "family friend" Joe Oliver gave interviews vouching for Zimmerman, saying: "I'm a black male and all I know is that George has never given me any reason whatsoever to believe he has anything against people of color" (Trotta, 2012; see also MSNBC, 2012). Yet, when pushed, Oliver seemed to know few other details about Zimmerman's life (Agyeman-Fisher, 2012; Valbrun, 2012), thus ultimately casting doubt on their "friendship" and the extent to which he could vouch for Zimmerman's racial proclivities.

In a noteworthy application of the friends defense, in 2010, singer John Mayer caused an uproar when, during an interview with *Playboy* magazine, he boasted about his Black friends (e.g., "Black people love me") and wondered aloud whether those relationships made him eligible for a "hood pass" or "nigger pass." He went on to make several additional racist and sexist statements, including describing his penis as having White-supremacist tendencies, because he doesn't seek out sexual relationships with Black women (Tannenbaum, 2012). Mayer was trounced in the media and subsequently lamented his arrogance while vowing never to say the N-word again (see Harkness in this volume for further discussion of the N-word).

The friends defense is also used by college students to excuse racist behavior. Leslie Houts Picca and Joe Feagin (2007) analyzed journals from 626 White students at more than two dozen colleges and universities in several regions over a course of 6 to 9 weeks. The diarists were asked to record their observations of everyday events in their lives that "exhibited racial issues, images, and understandings" (Feagin, 2013, p. 123). Hannah, one of their diarists, discussed being out with three other White friends when her friend Dylan started telling racist jokes, including referring to Black people as "porch monkeys" and joking that the most confusing day of the year in Harlem is Father's Day. Despite noting her own discomfort about his "jokes," Hannah firmly maintained, "My friend Dylan is not a racist person. He has more black friends than I do, that's why I was surprised he so freely said something like that. Dylan would never have said something like that around anyone who is a minority" (Picca & Feagin, 2007, pp. 17–18, cited in Feagin, 2013). As Picca and Feagin's research suggests, in the minds of many Whites, social interactions with people of color frequently serve as proxy for racial tolerance and understanding. Yet Hannah's account reflects three important points: (1) how easy it is for Whites, like Dylan, to have friends of color and still make racist statements; (2) that for many Whites, like Hannah, such statements are not enough for them to label a person like Dylan a racist; and (3) that a good deal of racist commentary from people who allegedly have friends of color happens in the social "backstage," or areas where only Whites are present, and not on the "frontstage," where strangers or people from diverse racial backgrounds are present and might express disapproval (Feagin, 2013, p. 123; Picca & Feagin, 2007; see also Goffman, 1959). Moreover, that Dylan would make such racist comments about a group with whom he purportedly has friendships means that we must also look at how Whites often overestimate or in other ways mischaracterize their friendships and relationships with people of color and the subsequent way they conflate these relationships with being an ally.

The Friends Defense Debunked

When we take a closer look at the friends defense and examine its merits, several issues arise. First, there is considerable doubt over whether these friendships even exist. A recent study from the Public Religion Research Institute (PRRI) found that "fully three-quarters of white Americans report that the network of people with whom they discuss important matters is entirely white, with no minority presence" (Cox, Navarro-Rivera, & Jones, 2016). This finding suggests that many Whites don't have close relationships with people of color—a finding we might expect given extensive neighborhood and school segregation.

Research also shows that Whites tend to exaggerate the depth of their friendships with people of color. In his book *Racism Without Racists*, sociologist Eduardo Bonilla-Silva (2010) used survey data from the Detroit Area Study to investigate the nature of White friendships. The data set included 323 Whites, 66 of whom were randomly selected for in-depth interviews. Of the 66, a little more than a third ($n = 24$) claimed that they had Black friends whom they characterized as "good friends," "best friends," or friends with whom they "hung out." However, after probing a bit further, Bonilla-Silva (2010) found that the strength of these friendship ties was more tenuous than his respondents originally indicated. For example, White respondents tended to "otherize" their Black friends, using distancing terms like "these people" or "them," and often didn't (or couldn't) identify them by their first names. Additionally, the contact with these friends proved very superficial and typically took place in the context of sports, music, or the occasional friendly talk with a fellow student or coworker; all of these were characterized as "friendships." Yet, as Bonilla-Silva indicates, "missing from these reports of friendship with blacks is evidence of trust, of the capacity of confiding, and of interactions with these friends beyond the place or situation of formal contact (classroom, assigned roommates, or job)" (p. 111). Finally, these "friendships" tended to evaporate after the class, rooming experience, band season, or job ended (p. 111). Thus, the friendships proved to be rather shallow and incomplete, which casts doubts on whether or not having "friends" of color can really be used to prove one doesn't have racial prejudices.

Moreover, even if one did have friendships or repeated interactions with people of color, research shows that when the stakes of social interaction are even higher, deeper racial prejudices emerge. *Social distance* is the level of intimacy a person is willing to accept in his or her relations with people of other social groups. The creator of the social distance scale, Emory Bogardus (1933), specified seven dimensions of social distance: (1) close kinship by marriage, (2) members of one's club or personal friends, (3) neighbors on one's street, (4) employed in one's occupation, (5) citizens in one's country, (6) visitors to one's country, and (7) would exclude from one's country (cited in Healey, 2012, p. 27). Frequently, racial prejudices surface the further one travels on the social distance scale. For example, while people might be accepting of a Latino person in their workplace (Dimension 4) or living in their neighborhood (Dimension 3), they may not be as accepting of a Latino person marrying into the family (Dimension 1). In these ways, those who might present or view themselves as racially tolerant frequently show signs of prejudice as the contact in question becomes more intimate. In *Why Are All the Black Kids Sitting Together in the Cafeteria*, Beverly Daniel Tatum (1997) illustrates how this phenomenon is evident in the changing racial composition of children's birthday parties as children get older, termed the "birthday party effect" (pp. 56–57). Tatum observes that in elementary school, birthday parties in multiracial communities reflect the area's diversity, but as children get older, parents' anxiety about puberty raises fears about interracial dating and causes birthday parties to become more racially homogeneous.

Indeed, attitudes toward interracial dating often expose hidden prejudices even among those who appear racially tolerant and open-minded. Erica Chito Childs (2005) suggests that attitudes toward interracial dating and marriage serve as "a miner's canary, revealing problems of race that otherwise can remain hidden, especially to whites" (p. 6; see also Bonilla-Silva, 2003, and Khanna in this volume). Childs witnessed this firsthand in her own family. She married a Black man and noted that her sister and her family never expressed any opposition to her relationship and, in fact, appeared supportive. However, when her sister's daughter wanted to attend the prom with a Black schoolmate she was dating, the sister and her husband refused to let him in the house, claiming he was "not right" for their daughter (Childs, 2005, p. 4). Childs maintains, "It was clear to everyone, however, that skin color was the problem. To this day, my niece will tell you that her parents would never have accepted her with a black man" (p. 4). From this story, it seems that Childs's sister and brother-in-law were accepting of interracial dating in theory, but when it came to *their daughter* potentially becoming involved with a Black person, the stakes were much higher and hidden prejudices suddenly emerged. In these ways, Whites who are seemingly tolerant can hold racist views that become evident when put to the test.

Perhaps most detrimental is when this type of discrimination occurs within the context of more formal spaces like the workplace. Here, discrimination can be more than psychologically painful; it can lead to differential outcomes in hiring and promotion. For instance, legal scholar Jerome McCristal Culp Jr. (1993) offers several examples of how his family members have battled this type of discrimination. In one instance, he tells the story of a relative who worked in a state agency and finished first on the approved tests for a particular position but was still denied the position by her supervisors and was instead offered another position with equal pay but less flexibility. In another instance, he tells the story of how his uncle who served on a police force was at the top of the promotion list but was forced to take an additional test beyond those previously required of White candidates before he could become the first Black lieutenant on the force. As Culp explains about these examples, "In none of these situations were white people always evil or impolite to black people. Many of the supervisors thought they were true friends of my relatives, but they were willing to manipulate the situation to ignore the concerns of black people" (p. 241). While these instances may appear anecdotal, the presence of this kind of discrimination in the workplace has been well-documented (Bertrand & Mullainathan, 2004; Cose, 1993; Feagin & Sikes, 1994; Pager & Shepherd, 2008). In these ways, White Americans who are experienced as otherwise "nice" and "friendly" people may discriminate if it is to their advantage. The failure to acknowledge these more covert forms of racism results in a worldview where many may believe that racism no longer exists and that America is a meritocracy where the playing field is level and anyone who works hard can be successful (Bonilla-Silva, 2010; Gallagher, 2004; McIntosh, 2007; see also Ioanide in this volume). In these ways, the subtler forms of racism that are more prevalent and more destructive go undetected and remain unchallenged.

To be sure, avoidance of racial topics and issues fits well within the recent discourse on "post-racialism," where some have argued that race doesn't matter or carries much less importance than in previous moments in American history.

(For a debate on the term *post-racial*, see National Public Radio, 2010; see also Bonilla-Silva, 2010, and Wise, 2009, 2010, for critical responses to the term.) Use of this term became more frequent after the election of America's first Black president, Barack Obama. Social critics, political pundits, and academics alike asserted that his election wouldn't have been possible had the nation not been taking a gradual turn toward post-racialism.

Nevertheless, voter data show that it is entirely possible to hold racist views and still vote for a Black president (Pettigrew, 2009). For example, in his article "Racial Views Steer Some Away from Obama," Ron Fournier (2008) of the Associated Press (also cited in Pettigrew, 2009) found that a third of White Democrats ascribed one or more negative adjectives (e.g., *violent, complaining, lazy, irresponsible*) to Blacks, yet 58% of them still supported Obama in the 2008 election. Moreover, as Thomas F. Pettigrew (2009) pointed out, "while Nebraska voters gave one of its electoral votes to Obama, they also passed by 58% to 42% a ban on race- and gender-based affirmative action. Previously, voters in California, Michigan and Washington State had passed similar referenda, yet all three provided Obama wide winning margins in 2008" (p. 283). The ability of Whites to hold (or at least tolerate) prejudiced views and still vote for a Black candidate is also evident in the fact that some who voted for Obama in 2008 and/or 2012 also voted for Trump in 2016. *Washington Post* data (Uhrmacher, Schaul, & Keating, 2016) found that of the 700 counties that carried Obama in both 2008 and 2012, a staggering one third of them broke for Trump in 2016. *Slate* chief political correspondent Jamelle Bouie (2016) explains the seeming paradox like this: "In the same way it has always been possible for white Americans to love black individuals and vote for the subjugation of black people, it is also possible to like Barack Obama and also yearn for a return to [an] idealized past," one where "whites—and white men in particular—were the uncontested masters of the country." Clearly, the above evidence suggests that it is possible to support and vote for a Black president and still harbor and act upon racial biases.

To some degree, Obama's victories were based on a sense of "enlightened exceptionalism" (Wise, 2009), or a type of racism in which Whites show an affinity for "special" Black people whom they perceive as different from most Blacks. Citing journalism and academic research on Obama's triumph, Bobo and Dawson (2009) provide evidence of this:

> One *New York Times* story reported on racial prejudice as a possible influence even among young voters. It quoted a White student from the University of Kentucky as saying: "I don't have any problem with a black president. I think it would be fine, because a lot of things people stereotype black people with, I don't think Obama has any of them" (Dewan, 2008). In short, Obama had "escaped" or transcended the stereotype. (p. 7)

Enlightened exceptionalism also often occurs with friendships, where one accommodates specific individuals of color without modifying a wider set of attitudes about people of color as a whole. In these ways, it is possible to have friends of color and still be prejudiced toward that same group.

Likewise, it is also possible to express interest in or appreciation for aspects of a group of color's culture (e.g., music, food, language) without having a true awareness or understanding of the sociopolitical struggle that group faces. For example, feminist and race bloggers have been calling attention recently to cultural appropriation (see Dennis in this volume), often dubbed "hipster racism." Some define hipster racism as instances where college-educated Whites (many of whom live in gentrifying areas and claim to have friends of color) co-opt elements of various cultures that belong to people of color, like Native American articles of clothing or symbols or Asian cuisine, for the purposes of entertainment (West, 2012). Critical race theorist Patricia Hill Collins (2009) refers to such behavior as "voyeurism," where the lives of people of color "are interesting for entertainment value" and the "privileged become voyeurs, passive onlookers who do not relate to the less powerful, but who are interested in seeing how the 'different' live" (p. 104). Similarly, Black feminist scholar bell hooks (1992) refers to this phenomenon as "eating the Other," where some Whites believe that exposure to different peoples and cultures "will provide a greater, more intense pleasure than any that exists in the ordinary world of one's familiar racial group" (p. 24; see also Ott & Mack, 2010, p. 145). Many would point to the mass consumption of hip-hop music and culture by middle-class Whites as an example of these phenomena. Passing familiarity with people of color or mass consumption of their cultures rarely serves as proxy for racial understanding and, in fact, frequently reflects a covert form of "othering." For all these reasons, it is important to begin to shift our discourse away from appreciating diverse cultures and having diverse friends as evidence of support for groups of color and instead move toward a definition of what it really means to be an *ally*.

From "Friends" to Allies

Understanding Allyship

The aforementioned racial rationalizations in this essay are often the result of well-meaning Whites attempting to express support for and identification with people of color, albeit in a superficial way (Feagin, 2001). Typically, it's an attempt to present one's self as an ally to people of color. However, as White anti-bias educator Emily Chiariello (2016) says,

> Over-familiarizing with people of color—[i.e.] "I hang out with people of color so I'm not racist"—reduces race to a lifestyle choice and can offer an easy way out of difficult anti-racism work. Appreciating a diverse group of friends or colleagues does not take the place of confronting white privilege, addressing internalized white guilt or responding to the biases of other white people. (p. 33)

The action-oriented nature of allyship is clear in various researchers' and thinkers' definition of an ally:

- According to Andrea Ayvazian (2009): "An ally is a member of a dominant group in our society who works to dismantle any form of oppression from which she or he receives the benefit" (p. 612). She goes on to say that being an ally means taking personal responsibility for the changes necessary in society and not ignoring or leaving others to deal with it: "Allied behavior is intentional, overt, consistent activity that challenges prevailing patterns of oppression, makes privileges that are so often invisible visible, and facilitates the empowerment of persons targeted by oppression" (p. 612).
- Sociologist Kristie A. Ford and co-author Josephine Orlandella (2015) define a White ally as "a person who consciously commits, attitudinally and behaviorally, to an ongoing, purposeful engagement with and active challenging of White privilege, overt and subtle racism, and systemic inequalities for the purposes of becoming an agent of change in collaboration with, not for people of color" (p. 288).
- Paul Kivel (2012) adds that there is no one way to be an ally, as each of us has different relationships to social organizations, political process, and economic structures. Nevertheless, being a racial ally is "an ongoing strategic process in which we look at our personal and social resources, evaluate the environment we have helped to create and decide what needs to be done" (p. 157).

Also important to note is that allies act on the basis of ethical commitments to a sense of justice and fairness, regardless of friendship.

Feagin and Vera's (2012) research on antiracist Whites lends further insight into the behavior of allies. Antiracist Whites, in particular, actively seek out interactions with people in other racial/ethnic groups and have cultivated *close* (emphasis added) friendships across the color line (Feagin & Vera, 2012)—friendships that often open their eyes to the realities people of color experience while also making them aware of their own White privilege (Cabrera, 2012). To be sure, awareness of White privilege alone is not enough; Whites must also be ready to explore their own complicity in racial oppression (Cabrera, 2012) to become allies. As Feagin and Vera (2012) find, antiracist Whites tend to be most aware of their own racism and the racism of others, and while they aren't certain they can really understand the experiences of people of color, they make an honest attempt.

Many Whites come to recognize their own racism after a critical event or experience. One compelling example comes from Feagin and Vera's (2012) "Confronting One's Own Racism," where they talk about a graduate student's project in which she interviewed Whites trying to overcome their racism. One respondent was a White teacher who noticed that she gave support and attention to Latino toddlers but not to Black toddlers where she once worked. She said:

> And it was like I got hit with a bucket of cold water. . . . And I cried and I cried, because I realized that *I had a prejudice.* And I thought I was without it. . . . So

I went back and I picked him up, and I played with him. . . . I sat him on my lap, and we did these little cutey games, patty-cake or whatever. And I had to work myself into it, because it was hard to do. . . . I had to *make myself* do it. . . . It wasn't easy to do, [but] once I knew that I was acting in a way that was prejudiced, I had to work very hard to overcome that. (p. 153; emphasis added)

The authors find that this is a common quality among antiracist Whites, where they go beyond empathy and understanding for what people of color have experienced to taking "proactive stances to confront their own internalized racism and the racist views and actions of other whites" (p. 154).

The above example also suggests that White allyship requires reaching beyond any guilt one may have regarding one's racial privilege and one's own racism to do necessary social justice work. Tatum (1997) discusses the "guilty White liberal persona" (p. 106), where Whites in the beginning stages of developing a racial consciousness might become mired in guilt. This sometimes allows them to divert conversations on race toward how to deal with their own guilt (Apple, 1998; see also Cabrera, 2012). Fixating on guilt over racial privilege typically isn't enough to move one toward action (Cabrera, 2012; Gaffney, 2016; Smith & Redington, 2010). And since it is impossible for Whites to merely give up their racial privilege, "[they] have a responsibility to use it in the service of greater racial justice" (Owen, 2009, p. 203). In the next section, I discuss how Whites have done and are continuing to do this.

White Allies Then and Now

In order for today's White Americans to become allies, they must have role models who can demonstrate what real allied behavior looks like so they can enact similar behaviors and strategies. Essentially, the adage holds true: You cannot be what you cannot see. Ayvazian (2009) discusses how White allies have long played an integral role in social justice movements—allies like Laura Haviland, who was a conductor on the Underground Railroad and helped enslaved Africans flee to Canada; Sarah and Angelina Grimké, who were abolitionists who faced ridicule and abuse for their anti-slavery stance; and John Brown, who was hanged after leading a rebellion against slavery in Harper's Ferry, West Virginia. The civil rights movement includes more examples of White allies, including Virginia Foster Durr, who drove Black workers during the Montgomery bus boycott and, along with her husband, attorney Clifford Durr, and Rev. E. D. Nixon, bailed Rosa Parks out of jail; Rev. James Reeb, a Boston minister who was killed by segregationists during the voting rights march in Selma, Alabama; and Anne and Carl Braden, who fought for desegregated schools and open housing and even bought a house for a Black couple in an all-White neighborhood in Kentucky, for which they had their windows shot out, their house bombed, and a cross burned in their yard.

More recent examples of White allies include Morris Dees, who started the Southern Poverty Law Center and brings lawsuits designed to cripple White-supremacist hate groups; Dr. Laurie Olsen, who has spent decades working on projects designed to improve the treatment of immigrant students and protect the rights of Americans for whom English is a second language; and Dr. Peggy McIntosh, who wrote the ground-breaking piece "White Privilege and Male Privilege: A Personal Account of Coming to See Correspondences Through Work in Women's Studies" (1988) and consults with colleges and universities on creating multicultural and gender-fair curricula. The *actions* of these people are indicative of what it really means to be an ally and support people of color: to be willing to use one's own privilege in the pursuit of social justice and to do so in the face of significant opposition.

White Americans are increasingly taking on the challenge of becoming allies. Social psychologist Kim A. Case's (2012) interviews and observations of 21 White women antiracists has been particularly instructive in this regard. Case researched an organization called White Women Against Racism (WWAR), composed of White women from two universities in the Midwest. Among other things, the group endeavors to "bring White women together to do self-work around racism, privilege, and responsibility for helping effect change" while cultivating their anti-oppression skills in their personal and professional lives through "facing, examining, and decreasing [their] own racism" (Case, 2012, p. 82). Most of these women willfully identified themselves as "racists" or as people who had at least done racist things. While some said this was a difficult identification because of the idea that "you have to be in the Klan to be racist," others embraced the identity, like Pauline, a respondent who said, "We are all so scared that someone is going to call us racist. I find one of the ways to get over that is to do it yourself first" (p. 84; see also Fair, 2015). Some in the group even found that admitting their racism made it easier to talk with other Whites about racism and call them out on their racism.

In her interviews, Case (2012) discussed how WWAR members attempted to be hypervigilant about their privilege, like noting when they were pulled over by police and let go without a ticket or when they were receiving preferential treatment from a landlord. WWAR members also felt that racial activism wasn't limited to marching and legislation but included confronting family members or coworkers about their racism or intervening when a store clerk ignores a Black customer. In addition, a few members also found ways to support and advocate for people of color. For example, one respondent, Madison, who intentionally hired a diverse staff of student workers, searched for scholarships for students of color, and was planning to become a counselor for disadvantaged populations. Another respondent, Kitty, decided to use her business degree for a career in diversity consulting. As Case says, "these daily actions illustrate that these White women wove anti-racism into various settings in their lives" (p. 87).

Case's research is also instructive because it suggests that being a White person with a disenfranchised status (in this case, a cisgender woman) doesn't automatically translate into a greater understanding of racism. Some of her respondents even discussed how their focus on sexism and their identities as feminists kept them from critically examining their Whiteness because "there is an assumption that feminists 'get it'" (Case, 2012, p. 86). Similarly, in his research on White men working through their Whiteness, Nolan L. Cabrera (2012), an assistant professor of higher education, found that White men who were also gay or Jewish were able to express greater empathy toward people of color but that those statuses did not guarantee an understanding of how racism operates. Having that understanding is key to allyship (Smith & Redington, 2010; see also Cabrera, 2012).

The examples in this section suggest that White allies have maintained a constant presence in the United States, despite the lack of attention they have received. Key to all of their stories is a sense of action and an unwillingness to abide by racist practices and behaviors even if their group ultimately benefits from them. In the final section of this essay, I discuss concrete ways Whites can begin to practice allyship, while keeping in mind that allyship is more of "a personal striving rather than a goal with a definitive ending" (Case, 2012, p. 91; see also Ford & Orlandella, 2015).

Ways You Can Be an Ally

As the actions of White Women Against Racism suggest, there are *many* ways to be an ally. In "Ten Things You Can Do to Improve Race Relations," racial inequality scholar Charles A. Gallagher (2012) offers that while ongoing and pervasive institutional racism may lead us to believe that there is nothing that can be done to improve race relations, "at the individual, interpersonal, and community level you can engage in activities to promote equal opportunity while building bridges between people from different racial backgrounds" (p. 401). Below is a list of ways to fight racism, from leading scholars, thinkers, and activists (Cabrera, 2012; Case, 2012; Fair, 2015; Gaffney, 2016; Gallagher, 2012; Smith & Redington, 2010).

- Respectfully engage friends and family in what you learn in your race classes, including politely and nonjudgmentally asking them about the origins of their racial prejudices.
- Correct outdated language like *colored* or *Oriental*.
- Stop others from telling racist jokes.
- Challenge commonly held stereotypes of groups of color so folks of color don't have to continuously educate their oppressors.
- Be introspective and honest enough to examine why you act or behave in a certain way toward someone of a different ethnic or racial group.
- Step out of your comfort zone and involve yourself in situations where you will be exposed to people of different racial and ethnic backgrounds.
- Be a positive role model to younger people in your life who look up to you, and explain what it really means to live in a multiracial, multiethnic society.

Also of great importance is remembering that as an ally, "your voice should never be louder than that of the people you are supporting" (Fair, 2015, p. 85). As Deen Fair says in her piece "An Open Letter to 'White Allies' From a White Friend," "think of it this way: You are a backup singer to the movement. Your voice should merely serve as a part of the chorus, supporting the leading roles in the play" (p. 85). In addition, Whites should not expect credit for being an ally and should be ready to thoughtfully accept any criticism for how they may be practicing allyship (Gaffney, 2016, p. 36).

To be sure, allyship can be challenging. People who practice it admit that sometimes they remain silent because they are avoiding disapproval and conflict, because of power differences between them and the person participating in racist behavior, because they fear that they won't be able to effectively confront the behavior, or because they are simply exhausted (Case, 2012; see also Smith & Redington, 2010). White women in Case's study also talked about the gendered pressures of the "good girl" persona, where girls and women are often taught to "be nice, good, don't start trouble, [and] be tactful" (p. 88). Yet Case rightfully notes that none of these women acknowledged the tension and unpleasantness that was already present for them as soon as the racist remarks or behaviors occurred. Essentially, we have been socialized to accept racism as the norm, and openly rejecting it is perceived as deviant behavior.

Indeed, being an ally is risky, as it may result in losing friends or relatives who aren't like-minded. As a result, it may be difficult to enact or practice with a great deal of consistency (Ayvazian, 2009; Case, 2012). The level of discomfort involved in understanding privilege can itself be enough to put off Whites who are considering becoming allies. As psychologists Laura Smith and Rebecca M. Redington (2010) claim, "newcomers to multicultural and social justice training often find the path challenging as they are called upon to examine previously unquestioned assumptions" (p. 547). For example, for many White students who first begin to engage with a definition of racism that moves beyond the individual to the systemic, understanding dynamics of power and privilege can be quite difficult. They may feel a sense of embarrassment, guilt, compassion, or even obligation (see Hardiman, 2001; Tatum, 1997) toward people of color and may want to act out of empathy. When students of color are on the receiving end of this behavior, they may react with frustration toward yet another well-meaning White person who "doesn't *really* get it" (see Tatum, 1997) or in other ways exhibit what White students might perceive as a lack of proper appreciation. While this may cause White students to become angry at not being seen as individuals (Tatum, 1997) or as "one of the good ones," coming to terms with the challenges of social justice is part of the racial identity development process for Whites in a racialized society (Hardiman, 1994; Helms, 1990; Tatum, 1992). Furthermore, Paul Kivel (2012) notes in "How White People Can Serve as Allies to People of Color in the Struggle to End Racism" that the point of being an ally isn't necessarily to curry favor with people of color: "We are not fighting racism so that people of color will trust us. Trust builds over time through our visible efforts to be allies and fight racism. Rather than trying to be safe and trustworthy, we need to be more active, less defensive, and put issues of trust aside" (p. 160). Thus, being a true ally requires some "unglamorous" work and often the help and support of like-minded others (Ayvazian, 2009; Case, 2012; Ford & Orlandella, 2015; Kivel, 2012; Owen, 2009; Smith & Redington, 2010; Tatum, 1997; Welp, 2009). And while all this may be hard work, it is important to realize that on the other side of the struggle to become an ally is "a joyful feeling of connection to humanity and a sense of integrity that comes with translating one's beliefs into action" (Smith & Redington, 2010, p. 547).

Cherise A. Harris is an associate professor of sociology at Connecticut College. She specializes in race, class, and gender, and teaches courses on the sociology of ethnic and race relations; the sociology of inequality; race, gender, and the mass media; and middle-class minorities. Her book, *The Cosby Cohort: Blessing and Burdens of Growing Up Black Middle Class*, was published in 2013. She is also on the editorial board of *Teaching Sociology* and has been published in other journals, such as *Sociological Spectrum* and *Journal of African American Studies*.

SUGGESTED ADDITIONAL RESOURCES

Bonilla-Silva, E. (2010). *Racism without racists: Colorblind racism and the persistence of inequality in America.* Lanham, MD: Rowman & Littlefield.

Cabrera, N. L. (2012). Working through Whiteness: White male college students challenging racism. *Review of Higher Education, 35*(3), 375–401.

Chiariello, E. (2016). Why talk about Whiteness? *Teaching Tolerance, 53,* 31–33. Retrieved from http://www.tolerance.org/magazine/number-53-summer-2016/feature/why-talk-about-whiteness

Coates, T. (2015). *Between the world and me.* New York, NY: Spiegel & Grau.

DiAngelo, R. (2016). *What does it mean to be White? Developing White racial literacy.* New York, NY: Peter Lang.

Doane, A. W., & Bonilla-Silva, E. (2003). *White out: The continuing significance of racism.* New York, NY: Routledge.

Feagin, J. R. (2013). *The White racial frame: Centuries of racial framing and counter-framing* (2nd ed.). New York, NY: Routledge.

Moore, E., Jr., Penick-Parks, M. W., & Michael, A. (2015). *Everyday White people confront racial and social injustice: 15 stories.* Sterling, VA: Stylus.

Tatum, B. D. (1997). *Why are all the Black kids sitting together in the cafeteria? And other conversations about race.* New York, NY: HarperCollins.

Trainor, J. S. (2005). "My ancestors didn't own slaves": Understanding White talk about race. *Research in the Teaching of English, 40*(2), 140–167.

Wise, T. (2009). *Between Barack and a hard place: Racism and White denial in the age of Obama.* San Francisco, CA: City Lights Books.

Wise, T. (2010). *Colorblind: The rise of post-racial politics and the retreat from racial equity.* San Francisco, CA: City Lights Books.

Websites

Alliance of White Anti-Racists Everywhere—Los Angeles (AWARE-LA): http://www.awarela.org

The group's mission is "to work toward the abolition of the white supremacist system and all systems of supremacy through building communities of Radical White people in solidarity with people of color in the larger movement for racial, social, economic, and environmental justice."

Safehouse Progressive Alliance for Nonviolence: http://www.safehousealliance.org/index.cfm

The website also offers extensive information on racism and antiracism in the organization's manual, *Tools for Liberation: Building a Multi-Ethnic, Inclusive & Antiracist Organization.*

Training for Change: http://www.trainingforchange.org

Provides activist training for groups standing up for justice, peace, and the environment through strategic nonviolence

White Anti-Racism: Living the Legacy: http://www.tolerance.org/supplement/white-anti-racism-living-legacy

From *Teaching Tolerance,* published by the Southern Poverty Law Center

White Men as Full Diversity Partners: http://www.wmfdp.com

Audio/Visual

Mulholland, L. (Director & Writer). (2013). *An ordinary hero.* United States: Taylor Street Films. (Film documents the story of Joan Trumpauer Mulholland, a White antiracist who spent months in prison during the Freedom Rides and fought alongside leaders in the civil rights movement.)

Wah, L. M. (1994). *The color of fear.* United States: Stir Fry Productions. (Film features a multiracial cast of men discussing the state of race relations and the challenges of allyship.)

QUESTIONS FOR FURTHER DISCUSSION

1. Do you think it is possible to have friends of another race and still hold racist attitudes? Why or why not?

2. Do you think it is possible to oppose interracial dating and not have racist attitudes? Why or why not?

3. What aspects of other cultures have you embraced? Do you feel equally as comfortable with the group of people who consider that culture their own?

4. Often in popular media, celebrities and artists co-opt parts of a racial or ethnic group's culture (e.g., Madonna, Gwen Stefani, Miley Cyrus). What do you think about the way some celebrities co-opt Asian or Black culture, for example? Is this racist? Is it similar to or different from the use of Native American culture in the naming of sports teams (e.g., Washington Redskins, Atlanta Braves, Cleveland Indians, Florida State Seminoles, etc.), as Williams discusses in his essay in this volume? Debate your classmates.

5. Consider Bogardus's scale. List the major racial and ethnic groups in America and apply them to each dimension on the scale. As you travel up the scale, how do you feel about increased contact with a particular racial group? What do you make of your findings? Now think about yourself as a parent and do the scale again. Would your level of comfort toward particular racial or ethnic groups change if they lived in your neighborhood and could play with your child or date your child when he or she became a teenager?

6. If you're still struggling with issues of race and racism, with what do you struggle? What are your hang-ups around this issue?

REACHING BEYOND THE COLOR LINE

1. If you are a White student, think about the people of color whom you consider friends and examine the depth of your friendship. Do you know their last names? Do you know how many brothers or sisters they have? Do you know where they grew up? What is their experience of being students of color on campus? Consider finding out the answers to these questions if you don't already know them.

2. If you are a student of color, think about the White people whom you consider friends and examine the depth of your friendship. How much do you know about them? How much do they know about you? Do you ever hold back on telling them things about your life? Why or why not? Do you feel that White people will ever be able to "get it"?

3. Given the information above on being an ally, what are you committed to do to promote greater social justice? And what else do you need to move forward (e.g., greater education or knowledge, the support of like-minded others)?

REFERENCES

Agyeman-Fisher, A. (2012, March 28). Zimmerman's "Black friend" exposed as fraud. *NewsOne.* Retrieved from http://newsone.com/1963015/joe-oliver-lawrence-o-donnell-last-call-interview

Apple, M. (1998). Foreword. In J. Kincheloe, S. Steinberg, N. Rodriguez, & R. Chenault (Eds.), *White reign: Deploying Whiteness in America* (pp. ix–xiii). New York, NY: St. Martin's Griffin.

Ashmore, K. (2009). Is your world too White? A primer for Whites trying to deal with a racist society. In A. Ferber, C. M. Jimenez, A. O. Herrera, & D. R. Samuels (Eds.), *The matrix reader: Examining the dynamics of oppression and privilege* (pp. 638–642). New York, NY: McGraw-Hill.

Ayvazian, A. (2009). Interrupting the cycle of oppression: The role of allies as agents of change. In A. Ferber, C. M. Jimenez, A. O. Herrera, & D. R. Samuels (Eds.), *The matrix reader: Examining the dynamics of oppression and privilege* (pp. 612–616). New York, NY: McGraw-Hill.

Bertrand, M., & Mullainathan, S. (2004). Are Emily and Greg more employable than Lakisha and Jamal? A field experiment on labor market discrimination. *American Economic Review, 94*(4), 991–1013.

Bobo, L. D., & Dawson, M. C. (2009). A change has come: Race, politics, and the path to the Obama presidency. *DuBois Review, 6*(1), 1–14.

Bogardus, E. (1933). A social distance scale. *Sociology and Social Research, 17,* 265–271.

Bonilla-Silva, E. (2003). *Racism without racists: Colorblind racism and the persistence of inequality in America.* Lanham, MD: Rowman & Littlefield.

Bonilla-Silva, E. (2010). *Racism without racists: Colorblind racism and the persistence of inequality in America.* Lanham, MD: Rowman & Littlefield.

Bouie, J. (2016, November 11). Why did some white Obama voters go for Trump? *Slate.* Retrieved from http://www.slate.com/articles/news_and_politics/politics/2016/11/why_did_some_white_obama_voters_for_trump.html

Cabrera, N. L. (2012). Working through Whiteness: White, male college students challenging racism. *Review of Higher Education, 35*(3), 375–401.

Case, K. A. (2012). Discovering the privilege of Whiteness: White women's reflections on anti-racist identity and ally behavior. *Journal of Social Issues, 68*(1), 78–96.

Chiariello, E. (2016). Why talk about Whiteness? *Teaching Tolerance, 53,* 31–33. Retrieved from http://www.tolerance.org/magazine/number-53-summer-2016/feature/why-talk-about-whiteness

Childs, E. C. (2005). *Navigating interracial borders: Black-White couples and their social worlds.* Piscataway, NJ: Rutgers University Press.

Coates, T. (2013, March 6). The good, racist people. *New York Times.* Retrieved from http://mobile.nytimes.com/2013/03/07/opinion/coates-the-good-racist-people.html

Collins, P. H. (2009). Toward a new vision: Race, class, and gender as categories of analysis and connection. In A. Ferber, C. M. Jimenez, A. O. Herrera, & D. R. Samuels (Eds.), *The matrix reader: Examining the dynamics of oppression and privilege* (pp. 97–108). New York, NY: McGraw-Hill.

Cose, E. (1993). *The rage of a privileged class: Why are middle-class blacks angry? Why should America care?* New York, NY: HarperCollins.

Cox, D., Navarro-Rivera, J., & Jones, R. P. (2016). Race, religion, and political affiliation of Americans' core social networks. PRRI. Retrieved from http://www.prri.org/research/poll-race-religion-politics-americans-social-networks/

Culp, J. M., Jr. (1993, Fall). Water buffalo and diversity: Naming names and reclaiming the racial discourse. *Connecticut Law Review, 26,* 209–263.

Dewan, S. (2008, October 15). The youth vote: In generation seen as colorblind, Black is yet a factor. *New York Times.* Retrieved from http://www.nytimes.com/2008/10/15/us/politics/15youth.html?_r=0

Diaz, D. (2017, January 17). Despite "famous" friendship, Trump team hasn't asked Kanye to perform. CNN. Retrieved from http://www.cnn.com/2017/01/16/politics/donald-trump-kanye-west-tom-barrack-inauguration/

Fair, D. (2015). An open letter to White "allies" from a White friend. *Understanding & Dismantling Privilege: The Official Journal of the White Privilege Conference and the Matrix Center for the Advancement of Social Equity and Inclusion, 5*(2), 82–86.

Feagin, J. R. (2001). *Racist America: Roots, current realities, and future reparations.* New York, NY: Routledge.

Feagin, J. R. (2013). *The White racial frame: Centuries of racial framing and counter-framing* (2nd ed.). New York, NY: Routledge.

Feagin, J. R., & Sikes, M. P. (1994). *Living with racism: The Black middle-class experience.* Boston, MA: Beacon.

Feagin, J. R., & Vera, H. (2000). *White racism: The basics.* New York, NY: Routledge.

Feagin, J. R., & Vera, H. (2012). Confronting one's own racism. In P. S. Rothenberg (Ed.), *White privilege: Essential readings on the other side of racism* (pp. 151–155). New York, NY: Worth.

Ford, K. A., & Orlandella, J. (2015). The "not-so-final remark": The journey to becoming White allies. *Sociology of Race and Ethnicity, 1*(2), 287–301.

Fournier, R. (2008, September 20). Racial views steer some away from Obama. *Politico.* Retrieved from http://www.politico.com/news/stories/0908/13658.html

Gaffney, C. (2016). Anatomy of an ally. *Teaching Tolerance, 53,* 34–37.

Gallagher, C. A. (2004). Color-blind privilege: The social and political functions of erasing the color line in post-race America. In C. A. Gallagher (Ed.), *Rethinking the color line: Readings in race and ethnicity* (pp. 575–588). New York, NY: McGraw-Hill.

Gallagher, C. A. (2012). Ten things you can do to improve race relations. In C. A. Gallagher (Ed.), *Rethinking the color line: Readings in race and ethnicity* (pp. 400–402). New York,

NY: McGraw-Hill.

Globe Staff. (2017, January 8). After helping US military, Iraqi refugee is detained at JFK. *Boston Globe*. Retrieved from https://www.bostonglobe.com/news/nation/2017/01/28/even-after-detention-iraqi-says-america-land-freedom/iPeD4juVSxssdIhmDg4zNN/story.html

Goffman, E. (1959). *The presentation of self in everyday life*. New York, NY: Doubleday.

Hardiman, R. (1994). White racial identity development in the United States. In E. P. Salett & D. R. Koslow (Eds.), *Race, ethnicity and self: Identity in multicultural perspective* (Chap. 6). Washington, DC: National Multicultural Institute.

Hardiman, R. (2001). Reflections on White identity development theory. In C. L. Wijeyesinghe & B. W. Jackson III (Eds.), *New perspectives on racial identity development: A theoretical and practical anthology* (pp. 108–128). New York: New York University Press.

Healey, J. F. (2012). *Diversity and society: Race, ethnicity, and gender*. Thousand Oaks, CA: Pine Forge.

Helms, J. E. (1990). Toward a model of White racial identity development. In J. E. Helms (Ed.), *Black and White racial identity: Theory, research and practice* (pp. 49–66). Westport, CT: Greenwood.

hooks, b. (1992). *Black looks: Race and representation*. Boston, MA: South End.

Kivel, P. (2012). How white people can serve as allies to people of color in the struggle to end racism. In P. S. Rothenberg (Ed.), *White privilege: Essential readings on the other side of racism* (pp. 157–165). New York, NY: Worth.

Krieg, G. (2015). Trump: "I'm doing good for the Muslims." CNN. Retrieved from http://edition.cnn.com/2015/12/09/politics/donald-trump-don-lemon-cnn-interview/

McDermott, M. (2016, December 14). "You are a great friend": Trump gifted Kanye an autographed "TIME" magazine. *USA Today*. Retrieved from https://www.usatoday.com/story/life/people/2016/12/14/donald-trump-gifted-kanye-west-autographed-copy-time-magazine/95422670/

McIntosh, P. (2007). White privilege: Unpacking the invisible knapsack. In M. L. Andersen & P. H. Collins (Eds.), *Race, class, and gender: An anthology* (pp. 99–104). Belmont, CA: Wadsworth.

MSNBC. (2007, April 9). Transcript: Imus puts remarks into context. MSNBC. Retrieved from http://www.msnbc.msn.com/id/18022596/ns/msnbc_tv-imus_on_msnbc

MSNBC. (2012, March 27). Joe Oliver: 'My role in this just doesn't make sense' [Interview]. *The Last Word with Lawrence O'Donnell*. Retrieved from http://www.msnbc.com/the-last-word/watch/joe-oliver-my-role-in-this-just-doesnt-make-sense-44141635668

National Public Radio. (2010, January 18). The 'post-racial' conversation, one year in [Radio series episode]. *Talk of the Nation*. Washington, DC: Author. Retrieved from http://www.npr.org/templates/story/story.php?storyId=122701272

Ott, B. L., & Mack, R. L. (2010). *Critical media studies: An introduction*. Malden, MA: Wiley-Blackwell.

Owen, D. S. (2009). Privileged social identities and diversity leadership in higher education. *Review of Higher Education, 32*(2), 185–207.

Pager, D., & Shepherd, H. (2008). The sociology of discrimination: Racial discrimination in employment, housing, credit, and consumer markets. *Annual Review of Sociology, 34*, 181–209.

Parker, S. (2016, May 5). Donald Trump's 'taco bowl' message: 'I love Hispanics.' *New York Times*. Retrieved from https://www.nytimes.com/politics/first-draft/2016/05/05/donald-trump-taco-bowl/

Pettigrew, T. F. (2009). Post-racism? Putting President Obama's victory into perspective. *Du Bois Review, 6*(2), 279–292.

Picca, L. H., & Feagin, J. R. (2007). *Two faced racism: Whites in the backstage and frontstage.* New York, NY: Routledge.

Singhvi, A., & Parlapiano, A. (2017, February 3). Trump's immigration ban: Who is barred and who is not. *New York Times.* Retrieved from https://www.nytimes.com/interactive/2017/01/31/us/politics/trump-immigration-ban-groups.html

Smith, L., & Redington, R. M. (2010). Lessons from the experiences of White antiracist activists. *Professional Psychology: Research and Practice, 41*(6), 541–549.

Tannenbaum, R. (2012, December 1). Playboy interview: John Mayer. *Playboy.* Retrieved from http://www.playboy.com/playground/view/playboy-interview-john-mayer?page=2

Tatum, B. D. (1992). Talking about race, learning about racism: The application of racial identity development theory in the classroom. *Harvard Educational Review, 62*(1), 1–24.

Tatum, B. D. (1997). *Why are all the Black kids sitting together in the cafeteria? And other conversations about race.* New York, NY: Basic Books.

Trotta, D. (2012, March 25). Joe Oliver, George Zimmerman's friend, defends shooter in Trayvon Martin case. *HuffPost.* Retrieved from http://www.huffingtonpost.com/2012/03/25/joe-oliver-george-zimmerman-trayvon-martin_n_1378390.html

Uhrmacher, K., Schaul, K., & Keating, D. (2016, November 9). These former Obama strongholds sealed the election for Trump. *Washington Post.* Retrieved from https://www.washingtonpost.com/graphics/politics/2016-election/obama-trump-counties/

Valbrun, M. (2012, April 2). Rewriting the script won't change the facts in the Trayvon Martin case. *Slate.* Retrieved from http://www.slate.com/blogs/xx_factor/2012/04/02/trayvon_martin_zimmerman_s_black_friend_and_hispanic_defenses_won_t_work_.html

Welp, M. (2009). Vanilla voices: Researching White men's diversity learning journeys. In A. Ferber, C. M. Jimenez, A. O. Herrera, & D. R. Samuels (Eds.), *The matrix reader: Examining the dynamics of oppression and privilege* (pp. 622–628). New York, NY: McGraw-Hill.

West, L. (2012, April 26). A complete guide to 'hipster racism.' *Jezebel.* Retrieved from http://jezebel.com/5905291/a-complete-guide-to-hipster-racism

Wise, T. (2009). *Between Barack and a hard place: Racism and White denial in the age of Obama.* San Francisco, CA: City Lights Books.

Wise, T. (2010). *Colorblind: The rise of post-racial politics and the retreat from racial equity.* San Francisco, CA: City Lights Books.

About the Editors

Stephanie M. McClure is a professor of sociology at Georgia College. She teaches classes on racial stratification, social theory, and the sociology of education. Her research interests are in the area of higher education, with a focus on college student persistence and retention across race, class, and gender, and a special emphasis on post-college student experiences that increase student social and academic integration. She has published in the *Journal of Higher Education, Symbolic Interaction,* and the *Journal of African American Studies.*

Cherise A. Harris is an associate professor of sociology at Connecticut College. She specializes in race, class, and gender, and teaches courses on the sociology of ethnic and race relations; the sociology of inequality; race, gender, and the mass media; and middle-class minorities. Her book, *The Cosby Cohort: Blessing and Burdens of Growing Up Black Middle Class,* was published in 2013. She is also on the editorial board of *Teaching Sociology* and has been published in other journals, such as *Sociological Spectrum* and *Journal of African American Studies.*

intersectionality

Best captures the
lived experiences of
human by embracing
the complexities of
social systems upon
which construction of
race, class, gender one built